주한미군지위협정(SOFA)

재무 · 상무 · 교통 분과위원회 1

주한미군지위협정(SOFA)

재무 · 상무 · 교통 분과위원회 1

한국학술정보

| 머리말

미국은 오래전부터 우리나라 외교에 있어서 가장 긴밀하고 실질적인 우호 · 협력관계를 맺어 온 나라다. 6 · 25전쟁 정전 협정이 체결된 후 북한의 재침을 막기 위한 대책으로서 1953년 11월 한미 상호방위조약이 체결되었다. 이는 미군이 한국에 주둔하는 법적 근거였고, 그렇게 주둔하게 된 미군의 시설, 구역, 사업, 용역, 출입국, 통관과 관세, 재판권 등 포괄적인 법적 지위를 규정하는 것이 바로 주한미군지위협정(SOFA)이다. 그러나 이와 관련한 협상은 계속된 난항을 겪으며 한미 상호방위조약이 체결로부터 10년이 훌쩍 넘은 1967년이 돼서야 정식 발효에 이를 수 있었다. 그럼에도 당시 미군 범죄에 대한 한국의 재판권은 심한 제약을 받았으며, 1980년대 후반 민주화 운동과 함께 미군 범죄 문제가 사회적 이슈로 떠오르자 협정을 개정해야 한다는 목소리가 커지게 되었다. 이에 1991년 2월 주한미군지위협정 1차 개정이 진행되었고, 이후에도 여러 사건이 발생하며 2001년 4월 2차 개정이 진행되어 현재에 이르고 있다.

본 총서는 외교부에서 작성하여 최근 공개한 주한미군지위협정(SOFA) 관련 자료를 담고 있다. 1953년 한미 상호방위조약 체결 이후부터 1967년 발효가 이뤄지기까지의 자료와 더불어, 이후 한미 합동위원회을 비롯해 민 · 형사재판권, 시설, 노무, 교통 등 각 분과위원회의 회의록과 운영 자료, 한국인 고용인 문제와 관련한 자료, 기타 관련 분쟁 자료 등을 포함해 총 42권으로 구성되었다. 전체 분량은 약 2만 2천여 쪽에 이른다.

2024년 3월

한국학술정보(주)

| 일러두기

· 본 총서에 실린 자료는 2022년 4월과 2023년 4월에 각각 공개한 외교문서 4,827권, 76만 여 쪽 가운데 일부를 발췌한 것이다.

· 각 권의 제목과 순서는 공개된 원본을 최대한 반영하였으나, 주제에 따라 일부는 적절히 변경하였다.

· 원본 자료는 A4 판형에 맞게 축소하거나 원본 비율을 유지한 채 A4 페이지 안에 삽입하였다. 또한 현재 시점에선 공개되지 않아 '공란'이란 표기만 있는 페이지 역시 그대로 실었다.

· 외교부가 공개한 문서 각 권의 첫 페이지에는 '정리 보존 문서 목록'이란 이름으로 기록물 종류, 일자, 명칭, 간단한 내용 등의 정보가 수록되어 있으며, 이를 기준으로 0001번부터 번호가 매겨져 있다. 이는 삭제하지 않고 총서에 그대로 수록하였다.

· 보고서 내용에 관한 더 자세한 정보가 필요하다면, 외교부가 온라인상에 제공하는 『대한민국 외교사료요약집』 1991년과 1992년 자료를 참조할 수 있다.

| 차례

정 리 보 존 문 서 목 록					
기록물종류	일반공문서철	등록번호	532	등록일자	
분류번호	729.415	국가코드		보존기간	영구
명 칭	SOFA 한.미국 합동위원회 재무분과위원회, 1972-73				
생 산 과	안보담당관실	생산년도	1972-1973	담당그룹	북미국
권 차 명					
내용목차	* 내용 : 비세출자금기관(P.X.) 이용 문제, 양담배 부정유출 방지, 미군화물 수송용 유류에 대한 면세조치 요청, 주한미군 근무 한국인 종업원에 대한 주민세 특별 징수				

결번

넘버링 오류

〈의제 2〉 국제연합군용 수입신고서 양식 개정

1. 관계규정

제5차 합동위원회 제정 SOFA 제9조 2항의 운용을 위한 절차 : 합중국 군대가 수입하는 각종화물의 적절한 증명서의 양식및 제출 방법.

2. 경위

가. 세관 행정의 EDPS 화에 따라 일반수출입 신고서 양식이 1972年 초부터 개정되었으며 이에 따라 SOFA 제9조 2항에 의한 국제연합군용 수입신고서의 양식을 개정토록 조치해줄 것을 관세청으로 부터 건의하여 왔음.

나. 협력 1245-60호 (1972. 1. 22)로 외무부에 이를 건의함.

다 제7차 SOFA 한미 합동위원회에서 재무분과 위원회에 과제부여됨 (첨부 1 참조)

라. 미측에 한국측 의견을 송부함 (첨부 2 참조)

기 재무부 관세국

3

마, 미측의 대안을 제시받음 (첨부 3 참조)

3. 대책

가. 주한미군 지위협정의 적용을 받은 개인이 한국에 반입하는 물품의 수입신고에 대해 지금까지 SOFA 제9조 2항의 군사화물에 대한 증명 양식을 사용하여 왔으나 SOFA 및 동 관계 규정에 의하면 개인용품에 대해서는 한국 정부가 정하는 어떠한 수입신고 양식도 사용할수 있게 되어있음.

나. 따라서 협정 제9조 2항의 군사화물 증명 양식을 개정 이를 협정 제9조 3항의 개인용품 수입신고에 대해서도 겸용하도록 하는 최초의 방침 대신에, 협정 제9조 2항의 군사화물 증명 양식은 개정하지 않고 협정 제9조 3항의 개인용품에 대해서는 한국 정부가 정하는 양식을 사용토록하고 이를 미측에 통보하여 그 협조를 구하도록 함.
(첨부 4 참조)

재무부 관세국

4

다. 그 이유는 미측의 대안에 의하면 개인용품의 면세 여부를 미군 통관 장교가 확인 하도록 되어있고 차후 개인용품에 대한 수입 신고서 양식을 개정할 필요가 생길때 마다 일일이 미측과의 합의를 얻어야 하도록 되어있음.

재무부 관세국

5

공　　　　란

1. 입 항 Date of Entry
2. 선하증권번호 B/L No
3. 적재선 (기) 명 Vessel (Aircraft)
4. 적재선 (기) 국적 Flag
5. 적출국 (지) Place of Shipment
6. 입항지 Place of Entry
7. 생산지, 원산국 (지) Place of Production
8. 장치장소 Place of Storage

부 호 Code No

대 한 민 국 세 관
Korea Customs Service

국제연합군수입신고서 Land
Import Declaration [redacted] USFK
certification

9. 세관부호 Customs Code No	10. 수입종별 Sort of Import	11. 신고번호 Declaration No

12. 신 고 서 Date of Declaration 19 . . .
~~13. 검 사 Date of Examination 19 . . .~~
~~14. 조 정 Date of Levy 19 . . .~~
~~15. 면 허 Date of Permit 19 . . .~~

결재	계	주 무	과 장

16. 품명 및 규격 Description of Articles & Grade	17. 중량 Weight / 18. 수량 Quantity	19. 단위 Unit	20. 신고가격 Declared Value / ~~21. 감정가격 Appraised Value~~	22. 세번 Heading / 23. 부호 Code No	~~24. 세율 Rate~~	~~25. 관세액 Amount of Customs Duty~~	26. 관세면세근거 및 부호 Duty Exemption Code No
(1)		Kg	CIF$ / ₩		%	₩	
(2)		Kg	CIF$ / ₩		%	₩	

27. 비 고 Remark
계 Total CIF$ ₩
환 율 Exchange Rate
₩

28. 기호, 번호, 포장종류와 개수 ~~Mark, Number, Type of Package~~
Markings:

~~30. 내 국 세~~

1. 과세가격	2. 세 별	3. 세 종	4. 세율	5. 세 액
(1)			%	₩
(2)			%	₩

~~원천과세표준~~

29. 신고서 매 란 Declared Paper Sheet Column

31. 비 고 Remarks

32. 첨 부 서 류 Attached herewith if any
송 품 장 ( ) Invoice
포장명세서 ( ) Packing List
원산지증명 ( ) Certificate of Origin
운임명세서 ( ) Freight Sheet
보험영수증 ( ) Receipt of Insurance
선하증권사본 ( ) Copy of B/L
Others ( )

~~상기 각항에는 허위가 없을뿐아니라 당해물품은 개인용품, 업무용품으로서 결코 판매 또는 교환등의 방법에 의하여 타용도에는 사용하지 않겠기 자이 서약함.~~

~~The above statement is true and correct to the best of my knowledge and I hereby affirm that the above articles are not for resale, exchange or other such purpose and will be used as personal or official items only:~~

33. 면 허 인 Signature of Permit

상가 물품에 대하여 수입통관면허를 신청함.
국제연합군 통관관리장교 certify
I hereby make application for permission to import the above goods for the use of [redacted] USFK

신고자성명 Name and Signature of Declarer

통관장교 서명 Signature of Customs clearance Officer

신고자주소 Address of Declarer 7

부 대 명 Department of ~~the Army~~ / Air Force

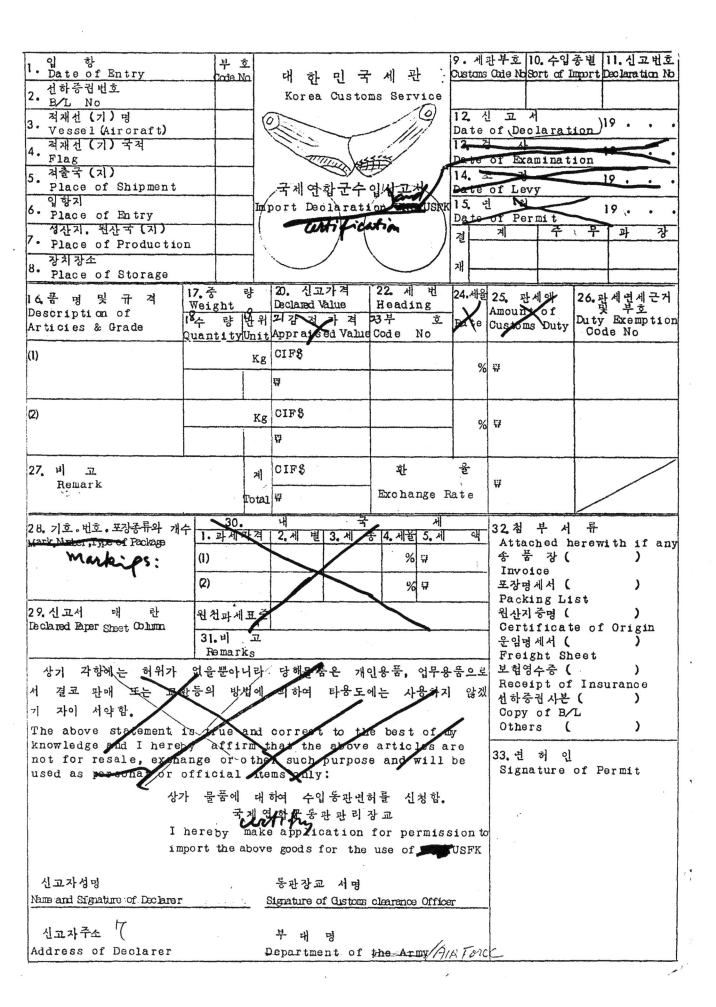

REPUBLIC OF KOREA - UNITED STATES
FINANCE (PERSONNEL AFFAIRS) SUBCOMMITTEE

22 June 1972.

MEMORANDUM FOR: The Joint Committee

1. Subcommittee Members:

United States	Republic of Korea
COL Dana F. McFall, Jr, Chairman	Mr. Park Dong Hee, Chairman
COL Wilbur R. Pugh, USAF	Mr. Lee Jae Sup
COL David J. Helterbran, USA	Mr. Kim Kee Joe
COL Robert J. Kriwanek, USA	Mr. Kim Ik Taik
COL Edwin D. Beers, USA	Mr. Shin Yung Su
COL Willard A. Barnes, USAF	Mr. Shin Myoung Ho
LTC Sherry E. Awtrey, USA	Mr. Lee Jin Moo
LTC Robert H. Hulley, USA	Mr. Kang Yung Joo
LCDR Robert E. Spydell, USN	
CAPT Larry L. Laab, USA	
Mr. Samuel Pollack	
Mr. Francis K. Cook	

2. Subject to Recommendation: Review of import declaration forms contained in inclosure (5) to the minutes of fifth Joint Committee meeting on 11 April 1967.

3. Recommendation:

a. It is recommended that the forms of import declaration contained in inclosure (5) to the minutes of the fifth meeting of the ROK-US Joint Committee on 11 April 1967, be abolished and the forms attached to this memorandum be approved.

b. It is further recommended that the effective date of this recommendation be the 1st day of the second month from the month in which it is approved by the Joint Committee.

4. Security Classification: Unclassified.

Mr. Park Dong Hee Chairman, ROK Component Finance Subcommittee	COL Dana F. McFall, Jr, USAF Chairman, US Component Finance (Personnel Affairs) Subcommittee

8

DRAFT

PROCEDURES FOR CERTIFICATION OF USFK IMPORTS UNDER PARAGRAPHS 2 AND 3 OF ARTICLE IX OF THE US-ROK SOFA, SAID PROCEDURES RELATING SPECIFICALLY TO THE FORMS AND METHODS OF PRESENTATION OF THE APPROPRIATE CERTIFICATION TO BE MADE ON VARIOUS USFK IMPORTS.

The purpose of the proposed procedures and forms contained herein is to insure that USFK certification is presented to ROK officials on imports entering the ROK under paragraphs 2 and 3 of Article IX of the US-ROK SOFA. It is expressly understood that USFK imports which enter the ROK on Military Sealift Command, Military Airlift Command or US Government Bill of Lading will require no additional certification since these shipments are, by nature of their shipment, expressly for the use of the USFK. Certification for USFK imports which arrive in the ROK by means other than those stated above will be made through the use of forms and procedures delineated below.

PROCEDURES FOR CERTIFICATION AND PRESENTATION OF FORMS FOR USFK IMPORTS:

1. Certification. The consignee of a USFK import will present the appropriate shipping documents (bill of lading, waybill, purchase

DRAFT

9

DRAFT

order, invoice, etc.) to a duly appointed USFK customs clearance officer. This officer will direct the preparation of the Import Declaration UNC/USFK ~~is prepared~~ in six copies (five copies for use by ROK customs authorities and one copy for the USFK customs clearance officer's files) and reproduction of the shipping document so that one copy of these documents are appended to each copy of the Import Declaration UNC/USFK. The USFK customs clearance officer shall insure that shipments are authorized ~~duty~~-free entry and that blocks 1 through 8, 12, 16 through 20, 26 and 32 are properly filled in. Note: ROK authorities shall provide USFK customs clearance officers with the appropriate information for block 26 ten days prior to the effective date of this procedure and upon occurence of changes in the Duty Exemption Code Numbers. The USFK customs clearance officer will make certification on the Import Declaration UNC/USFK and appropriate shipping documents with his stamp and signature (samples of USFK customs clearance officer signature will be provided to ROK customs officials).

2. Presentation: The consignee will present five copies of the Import Declaration UNC/USFK with appropriate shipping documents to the ROK Customs House. ROK customs officials will verify the USFK customs clearance officer signature, process the documents as quickly as possible and release the cargo to the consignee. Maximum effort shall be made by ROK customs officials to expedite delivery.

2 DRAFT

16

2. Subject to Recommendation: Review of Declaration and Certification on Imports consigned to persons subject to the ROK-US SOFA as contained in inclosure (5) to the minutes of the Fifth Joint Committee Meeting on 11 April 1967.

3. Recommendation: a. It is recommended that the procedures for certification of various USFK imports as contained in inclosure (5) to the Fifth Joint Committee Meeting be abolished and replaced by those in the attachment to this memorandum.

b. It is further recommended that the effective date of this recommendation be the first day of the second month from the month in which it is approved by the Joint Committee.

4. Security Classification: Unclassified.

PARK DONG HEE
Chairman, ROK Component
Finance Subcommittee

JOSEPH T. FORDHAM
COL, USAF
Chairman, US Component
Finance (Personnel Affairs)
Subcommittee

DRAFT

REPUBLIC OF KOREA - UNITED STATES
FINANCE(PERSONNEL AFFAIRS) SUBCOMMITTEE

12 August 1972.

MEMORANDUM FOR : The Joint Committee

1. Subcommittee Members :

United States	Republic of Korea
COL Joseph T. Fordham, USAF	Mr. Park Dong Hee, Chairman
LCDR Robert E. Spydell, USN	Mr. Lee Jae Sup
COL Theodore D. Cameron, USAF	Mr. Kim Kee Joe
COL Robert A. Little, USA	Mr. Kim Ik Taik
COL George F. Proudfoot, USA	Mr. Shin Yung Su
COL Harlan R. Schmidt, USA	Mr. Shin Myoung Ho
COL Willard A. Barnes, USAF	Mr. Lee Jin Moo
LT David K.Marten, USA	Mr. Kang Yung Joo
MR Samuel Pollack	
MR Francis K. Cook	
LTC William P. Sewell, USA	

2. Subject of Recommendation : Introduction of the new form of declaration on imports consigned to persons subject to the ROK - US SOFA.

3. Redommendation :

a. The declaration form as contained in inclosure 5 to the minutes of the Fifth Joint Committee Meeting on 11 April 1967 has to date been applied not only to imports by the agencies specified in paragraph 2 of SOFA Article IX, but also to imports consigned to individuals who are subject to the ROK - US SOFA.

b. According to the ROK - US SOFA and related regulations, the Republic of Korea Customs Administration can apply any declaration forms to imports consigned to individuals subject to the ROK - US SOFA.

c. The customs authorities of the Republic of Korea are planning to use the new declaration form as attached to this memorandum on imports consigned to persons who are subject to the ROK - US SOFA, from the date of 1 November 1972.

12

REPUBLIC OF KOREA - UNITED STATES
FINANCE (PERSONNEL AFFAIRS) SUBCOMMITTEE

d. It is recommended that the mutual cooperation between the Republic of Korea and the US Forces will be made for the introduction of the above mentioned import declaration forms.

4. Security Classification : Unclassified.

Mr. Park Dong Hee Chairman, ROK Component Finance Subcommittee	COL Joseph T. Fordham, USAF Chairman, US Component Finance (Personnel Affairs) Subcommittee

13

(의제 3)　　통제품목의 추가

1. 관계규정

가. 협정 제9조에 대한 합의 의사록 1항 :

합중국 군대의 비세출자금 기관이 ....수입하는 물품의 양은 이러한 사용을 위하여 합리적으로 소요되는 한도에 한정되어야 한다.

나. 제65차 합동위원회 제정 비세출 자금기관에 탁송되는 화물에 관한 정보제공 :

35개 통제품목에 대한 17개 지역별 매상보고를 매월 미측으로부터 송부받고 있으며 주류에 대해서는 월별 수입량 보고를 받고 있다.

2. 경위

가. 군민관계 임시 분과 위원회는 PX 및 COMMISSARY 의 통제품목을 추가하고 개인의 합리적 소요량을 초과한 물품이 판매 부정 유출되는 것을 방지 하기위한 절차를 검토 하기로 합의 하였고, 이것이 합동위원회에서 채택되어 재무분과위원회에서 이 문제를 검토 하도록 제72차 합동위원회에서 과제 부여된 바 있다.(첨부 1 참조)

나. 한국측은 이에따라

(1) 주류, 연초, 커피를 통제품목으로 추가하고

(2) 한미 합동 수사반에게 PX외 판매상황에 대한 조사및 감시권을 부여토록 할 것을 제의 하였다.

다. 한국측 제안에 대하여 미측은

14

(1) 한미 합동수사반에게 PX 의 판매 상황에 대한 조사및 감시권을 부여하는 문제는 합동위원회가 과제 부여한 사항이 아니므로 재무분과 위원회의 토의대상이 될 수 없으며

(2) 주류, 연초, 커피를 통제품목으로 추가하는 문제에 대해서는 검토하겠다고 했다

3. 대책

(1) 주류, 연초, 커피를 통제품목으로 추가한다.

(2) 상기 추가 품목의 판매 수량에 대한 미측의 자율규제 강화를 요구한다.

(3) 현재의 35개 통제품목을 승인 (LOA = Letter of Authorization) 품목으로 전환 요구 한다.

(주) 현재는 7개 품목만이 승인품목임.

15

공 란

(외제 4) 면세물품 양도 양수 절차 검토

1. 관계규정

가. 협정 제9조 6항 (면세물품의 처분)

나. 제10차 합동위원회 제정 면세물품 양도조건 절차

2. 경위

외제차량의 인수창구를 관광공사로 일원화 함에 따라 제10차 합동위원회에서 제정된 면세물품의 양도 양수 절차를 재검토 하도록 재무분과 위원회에 과제 부여 되었음.

3. 대책

아래의 두 가지 방안중 하나를 선택 한다.

(제 1 안)

합동위원회에서 제정된 면세물품의 양도 절차를 개정하여 차량의 경우 양수자를 관광공사로 한정토록 한다.

(제 2 안)

상기 면세물품의 양도 양수절차에 의하면 세관장은 대한민국 법규에 의하여 관계서류를 심사하고 양도 승인을 한다고 되어 있으므로 차량의 양수인을 관광공사에 한 하도록 국내 규정으로 이를 정한다.

17

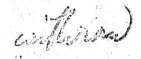

공 란

재무분과위원회에 부여된 과제는 아니지만 검토가 요구되고 있는 사항

(1) 초청 계약자 업무용 장비의 면세통관 여부

2. APO 우편소포 검사 절차 개정

(가) 등기 우편소포를 검사 대상으로 추가

나. 마약류등에 대한 세관검사의 강화

3. 세관직원에게 PX 등 비세출 자금기관에 대한 출입및 감시권 부여

4. 기타:

미측은 차량등 면세물품 양도에 관하여 수입면장이 불필요하다고 주장하고 이를 논의의 대상으로 제기할 가능성이 있음.

19

공　　란

공 란

SOFA 재무분과위원회 회의자료

의 제	관 계 규 정	배 경	대 책
1. APO 의 이동에 따른 군사우편소도 검사 절차 개정	제6차 합동위원회에서 체결되고 제61차 및 제66차 합동위원회에서 수정된 APO 를 통한 군사우편소도 검사 절차	가. 현재 규정상의 APO 우편소도 검사장 : 선박편 (인천), 항공편 (김포, 오산) 다. 인천기지 APO ⟶ 부산으로 이동 : 선박편으로 반입되는 군사우편소도 검사장의 신규 지정이 요구됨	1) APO 우편소포 검사장 : 부산, 김포, 오산 2) 시설문제는 한미양측 관계자의 현지조사에 의해 요조 시 시설 결정
2. 주한 미군용 수입신고서 양식 개정	제5차 합동위원회 지정 SOFA 제9조 2항의 수용을 위한 절차 : 한국에 주둔하는 수입되는 각종 화물의 적절한 증명서의 양식 및 제출방법	가. 전관업무의 EDIS 화에 따라 SOFA 제9조 2항에 의한 주한미군 군사화물 증명 양식의 변경이 필요하게 됨 나. 미측은 협정 제9조 2항의 증명양식을 제9조 2항의 간이용 수입신고서도 사용된 것을 주장하고 있음.	1) 협정 제9조 2항에 의한 미군사 화물 증명 양식은 한미간의 상의에 의해 개정 2) 협정 제9조 3항의 간이용 수입신고서는 한국측이 일방적으로 제정 실시
3. 세출자금 품목의 추가	가. 협정 제9조에 따라 합의 의사록 1항 : 합중국 군대와 비세출 자금 기관이 수입하는 물품의 양은 이러한 사용을 위하여 합리적으로 소요되는 한도에 한정되어야 한다. 나. 제55차 합동위 지정 : 비세출자금 기관이 탁송되는 화물에 관한 정보 제공	미 및 COMMISSARY 의 통제품목은 주가되고 개인의 합리적소요량을 초과한 물품이 한미 부정유출되는 것을 방지 하기위한 절차를 검토 미기로한 군관관계 임시 분과위원회의 합의에 따라 재무분과위원회에 과제 부여된 사안임.	1) 주류, 연초, 커피등 통제품목으로 추가 한다. 2) 상기 추가 품목의 관리 수량이 더 한 기준의 적용 규정 강화를 요구 한다. 3) 현재의 35개 통제품목을 승인 (10A) 품목으로 전환 요구 한다.

재 무 부 관 세 국

의 제	관 계 규 정	배 경	대 책
4. 면세물품 양도 양수 절차 검토	가. 협정 제9조 6항 (면세물품의 처분) 나. 제10차 합동위 결정: 면세물품 양도조건 절차	외제 차량의 인수 창구를 관광공사로 일원화 함에 따라 제10차 합동위원회에서 결정된 면세물품의 양도 양수 절차는 재검토코자 한다.	외제차량 인수 창구 일원화 문제의 미확정으로 인하여 당 의제는 보류함

재 무 부 관 세 국

증산 수출 건설

재 무 부

협력 1243- 722 1972. 8. 25

수신 수신처참조

제목 P. X 및 COmmissary의 월판매 금액및 수량통제

미군측 SOFA 재무분과 위원회가 보낸 P. X및 Commissary 의 1인당 및 1가구당 월판매 수량및 금액통제표를 송부하오니 업무에 참고하시기 바랍니다.

첨부 : SOFA 자료 1부 (영문) 끝.

0538

재 무 부 장

수신처 : 외무부 장관, 관세청 장

내집살림 나라살림 저축으로 부강하자

발송 No. 1972 8. 25 재무부

24

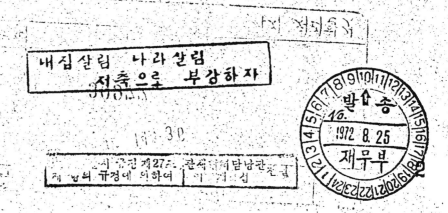

외

접일 25 AUG '72 14:36

30977

담당자

까지 처리할것

23-1.E

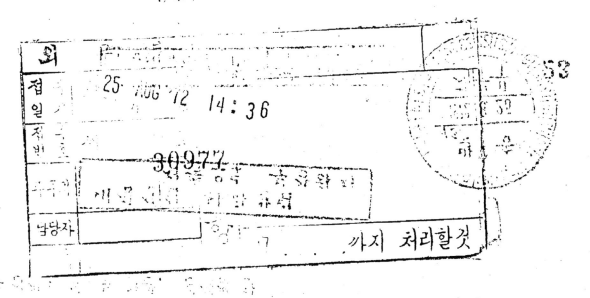

[redacted]Reg 60-1
th AD Reg 147-3
CNFKINST-4066.1B

EXCHANGE RATIONING LIMITATIONS

1. MONTHLY DOLLAR LIMITATIONS. Primary control on purchases shall be exercised through a fixed monthly dollar amount which may be spent in the exchange. This dollar amount is determined by the size of the household in Korea.

a. The monthly dollar limitations are computed on the following basis:

Status	Monthly Dollar Limitation
Sponsor or unaccompanied individual	$75.00
Spouse	$50.00
Dependent (over 18 years of age)	$50.00
Dependent (under 18 years of age)	$25.00
Sponsor or spouse with limited privilege (no controlled items)	$50.00

b. Purchases totaling $0.99 or less will not be counted toward the monthly dollar limitation.

c. Purchases which have a unit value of $25.00 or more will not be counted toward the monthly dollar limitation.

d. Purchases of military uniforms and accessories by military personnel will not be counted toward the monthly dollar limitation.

e. Purchases of books and periodicals will not be counted toward the monthly dollar limitation.

f. The aggregate household limitation can be determined by adding the applicable monthly dollar limitations for each status of person in the household.

2. CONTROLLED ITEMS. These items, listed below, may be purchased once during a tour in Korea. Those items indicated by an asterisk (*) require a Letter of Authorization (LOA) for initial purchase. Subsequent purchase of any item listed will require an LOA.

Appendix 1 to ANNEX F

25

EA Reg 60-1
314th AD Reg 147-3
CNFKINST-4066.1B

CONTROLLED ITEMS

23 - Still Camera over $40
24 - Still Camera under $40

*31 - Television
32 - Radio over $25
34 - Stereo Music System
35 - Tuner/Amplifier/Receiver
36 - 2 Speakers over $25
38 - Turntable
39 - Phonograph over $25

41 - Tape Deck
42 - Tape Recorder over $25

52 - Typewriter
*53 - Firearm
*54 - Diamond Ring
55 - Watch over $50 (excluding costume jewelry watches)

61 - Electric Blender
62 - Electric Rice Cooker
63 - Electric Toaster
64 - Electric Coffee Pot
65 - Electric Skillet
66 - Electric Fan
67 - Electric Steam and/or Dry Iron

*71 - Washing Machine
*72 - Clothes Dryer
*73 - Range
*74 - Vacuum Cleaner
*75 - Floor Polisher
*76 - Refrigerator
*77 - Freezer
*78 - Water Heater
*79 - Air Conditioner
*95 - Special Purchases for clubs or organizations

3. LIMITED ITEMS. Those items in temporary short supply or unusual demand on a local basis. The purchase quantity limitations will be determined by local exchange management and will be posted at the stockage/display point and enforced at the checkout counters.

Appendix 1 to ANNEX F

EA Reg 60-1
314th AD Reg 147-3
CNFKINST-4066.1B

COMMISSARY RATIONING LIMITATIONS

1. MONTHLY DOLLAR LIMITATION.

a. Primary rationing control will be accomplished by limiting the amount of money which may be spent in the commissary during each month. The amount which may be spent is determined by the number of authorized patrons supported within a household in Korea. The monthly dollar limitations are:

Number of Patrons Supported	*Monthly Dollar Limitation
1 (Unaccompanied Personnel on subsistence/separate rations/LQA)	$ 70.00
2	140.00
3	170.00
4	205.00
5	230.00
6	255.00
7	265.00
8 or more	280.00

* Includes surcharge

b. Unaccompanied personnel not on subsistence/separate rations/LQA will be limited to fifty percent of the unaccompanied personnel on subsistence/separate rations/LQA monthly dollar limitation.

2. CONTROLLED ITEMS. Items which are limited in purchase quantity on a monthly basis. Procedure to receive authorization for excess purchases of controlled items is contained in Annex G. The quantity limitations on controlled items are scaled by the number of patrons supported and are as follows:

Appendix 2 to ANNEX F

27

EA Reg 60-1
314th AD Reg 147-3
CNFKINST-4066.1B

CONTROLLED ITEMS LIST

ITEM	UNIT	1	2-3	4-5	6-7	8+
		Number of Patrons Supported / QUANTITY AUTHORIZED PER MONTH				
*Baby Formula, Liquid	cn	0	8	8	8	8
Chocolate/Cocoa	16 oz cn	2	3	4	5	6
Ground Coffee	lb	6	8	8	8	8
or						
Instant Coffee	oz	30	40	40	40	40
Mayonnaise	32 oz qt	1	2	3	4	5
Olive Oil	16 oz	1	2	2	3	3
Pepper	4 oz cn	1	2	2	2	3
Salad Oil	32 oz qt	1	4	8	8	8
Soluble Cream	16 oz jar	1	2	2	2	4
Tang	26 oz jar	2	3	4	5	6
Salt	26 oz	1	1	2	2	2

*One (1) baby will receive eight (8) units of baby formula per month. One unit is equal to:

4 cns of 13 oz concentrated liquid
3 cns of 32 oz ready to use liquid
12 bottles of 8 oz ready to use liquid
24 bottles of 4 oz ready to use liquid
1 cn of 16 oz powder

This items list was based on an average factor of 720 oz that a baby (1-4 months) will consume a month.

Appendix 2 to ANNEX F

3. <u>LIMITED ITEMS</u>. Those items in temporary short supply or unusual demand on a local basis. Determination of items to be so designated will be made by local management. Purchase quantity limitations will be posted at stockage/display points and enforced at checkout counters.

EA R[illegible]0-1
314th AD Reg 147-3
CNFKINST-4066.1B

ALCOHOLIC BEVERAGE RATIONING LIMITATIONS-PURCHASE CONTROL

1. ALCOHOLIC BEVERAGES. Primary control on purchases shall be exercised through monthly limitations on the amount of alcoholic beverages which may be purchased. These limitations are:

a. Active duty military personnel in the grade of 06 and above and U.S. civilian employees, grades GS-15 and above (or equivalent): No purchase limitations.

b. Active duty military personnel in the grade of 05 and below, U.S. civilian employees, grades GS-14 and below (or equivalent) and all others authorized Class VI store privileges:

(1) Accompanied: Ten (10) quarts/fifths of alcoholic beverages per month.

(2) Unaccompanied: Five (5) quarts/fifths of alcoholic beverages per month.

2. BEER/MALT LIQUOR. Twenty-four (24) bottles/cans per day. Malt liquor may only be purchased by personnel twenty (20) years of age or older.

Appendix 3 to ANNEX F

30

증산 수출 건설

재 무 부

협력 1243-741 1972. 9. 4.

수신 외무부장관

제목 SOFA재무분과 위원회 회의 및 대책회의 개최 통보

1. 1972. 9. 8 14:00 재무부 회의실에서 SOFA 재무분과 위원회 회의를 개최하오니 각위원들은 필히 참석하여 주시기 바라며

2. 이에 관련하여 1972. 9. 7일 16:00시 재무부 관세협력담당관실에서 대책회의를 개최하오니 각위원들은 필히 참석하여 주시기 바랍니다. 끝.

발송 1972. 9. 4 재무부

재 무 부 장

재무부장관

내집살림 나라살림 저축으로 부강하자

문서 규정 제27조 규정에 의하여 관세국장 박동희 전결

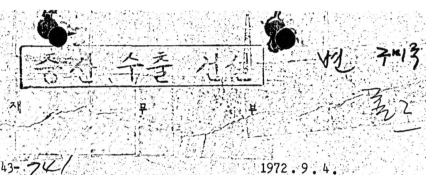

30

외 무 부			
접수 일시	1972. 9. 5.	14:39	
	제 32527 호		
처리	1972.		

0726

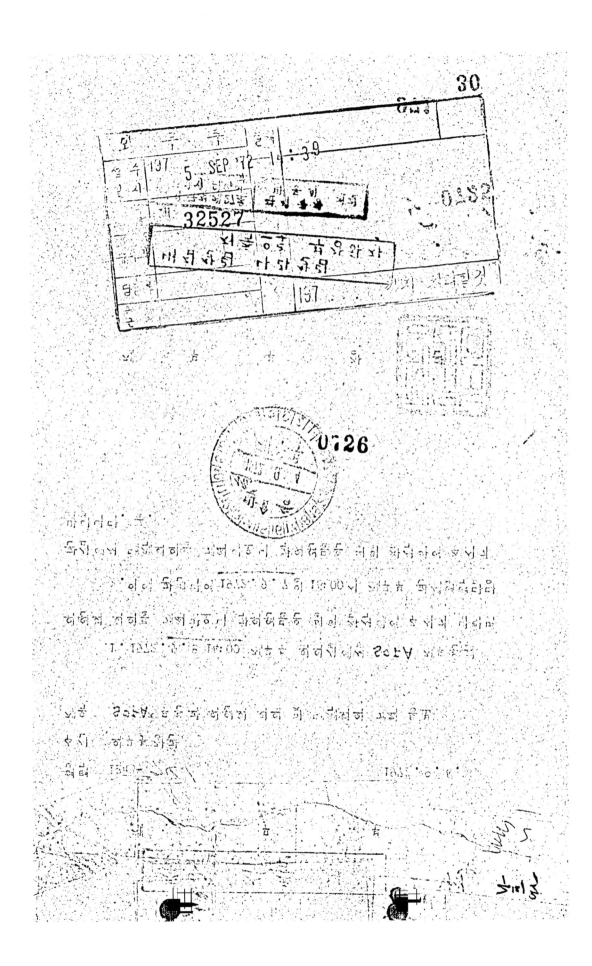

SOFA 재무분과 위원회 대책회의 결과 보고

1. 참석자: 외무부 북미 2과장 김 기조
   " 북미2과 변 승국
   재무부 관세협력과장 이 재섭
   " 관세협력과 강 영주
   관세청 세무과 윤 필수
   " " 정 기성
   " 심리과 김 재흡

2. 회의일시: 72. 8. 16. 14:00-16:40

3. 회의장소: 재무부 관세협력과 사무실

4. 토의및 합의내용

(의제 1): APO 의 이동에 따른 군사우편 소포검사 절차 개정

가. 문제점:

APO 를 통하여 반입되는 소포에 대한 한국세관 검사는 항공편으로 반입되는것은 김포 및 오산에서, 선박편으로 반입되는것은 인천에서 검사를 행하도록 지정되어 있으나, 72년 3월 인천기지 APO 가 김포로 이동되었으므로 해상을 통해 반입되는 우편 소포에 대한 검사장소의 변경 지정이 요구됨.

북미2과	공람	72년 8월 일	담당	과장	국장	차관보	차관	장관
						출장중		

32

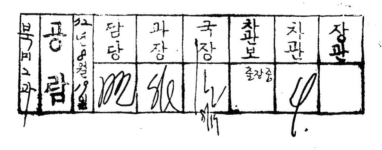

나. 합의 대책

제 1안: 부산항에 입항하는 모든 우편 소포에 대하여 반입 직후 세관 검사를 실시함.

* 71년 9월 인천 미군 수송대가 부산항으로 이동한 후에는 종전 인천항을 통해 반입되던 군사 우편 소포가 부산항을 통해 반입되고 있음.

제 2안: 부산항 입항시 우편 소포를 적재한 Container 에 대한 점검만 실시한 후 육로로 수송, 김포 및 오산에서 세관검사를 실시함. 단 부산 인근지역에 배부될 우편소포에 대하여는 부산에서 세관검사 실시

(의제 2): 주한 미군군용 수입 신고서 양식 개정

가. 문제점:

세관 행정의 EDPS 화에 따라 일반 수출입 신고서 양식이 72년초부터 개정되었으며 이에따라 주한 미군 군용수입(군용 선편 제외) 신고서 양식을 개정하여야 할것임.

나. 합의 대책:

(1) SOFA 제 9조 2항의 군사화물에 대한 수입(일반상용 선편에 의한) 신고 양식은 별첨 양식과 같이 개정함.

33

(2) 지금까지 SOFA 제9조 2항의 군사화물 수입신고 양식을 준용해 오던 개인용품 수입(군용선편 또는 상용선편에 의한) 신고에 대해서는 한국정부가 새로히 정하는 양식을 사용토록하고 미측에 통보하여 그 협조를 구하도록 함.

(의제 3): 통제 품목의 추가

가. 문제점:

PX 및 Commissary 의 통제품목을 추가하고 물품의 부정 유출을 방지하기 위한 절차를 검토하기로 재무분과위원회에 과제 부여된바가 있음.

나. 합의 대책:

(1) 주류, 연초, 커피를 통제품목으로 추가한다.

(2) 상기 추가 품목의 판매 수량에 대한 미측의 자율규제 강화를 요구한다.

(3) 현재의 35개 통제 품목을 승인 (LOA: Letter of Authorization) 품목으로 전환 요구한다.

(의제 4): 면세 물품 양도 양수절차 검토

가. 문제점:

의제 차량의 인수 청구를 관광공사로 일원화함에 따라 제 10차 합동위원회에서 제정된 면세물품의 양도 절차를 재 검토하도록 재무분과 위원회에 과제 부여된바 있음.

34

나. 합의 대책

관광회사에서 일괄 매수 준비가 완성되지 않았음으로 대미측 교섭을 보류하기로 함.

(기타 의제)

1. 초청 계약자 업무용 장비의 면세 통관 여부

미측은 SOFA 제 9조 2항 및 제 15조 5항의 규정을 원용하여 건설 장비등의 면세 통관을 주장하고 있으나 이러한 건설장비등을 제 9조 2항의 "물품, 시설등에 합체될 자재"등으로 보기는 어렵고 제 15조 5항의 "조세"는 내국세를 의미하는 것이므로 (영문 표기로는 Taxes 로 되어 있음) 관세의 부과가 면제될 수는 없음. 이 문제 검토를 위한 과제 위촉을 하기로함.

2. APO 우편 소포검사 절차 개정

등기 우편 소포를 검사 대상으로 추가하는 문제와 마약류등에 대한 세관 검사를 강화하는 문제에 대하여는 불법 내용물이 내재한다고 의심되는 때에 한하여 검사를 실시하되 시행과정에서 양측의 견해에 차이가 발생할 때에는 그때에 다시 문제를 제기하기로 함.

3. 세관 직원에게 PX 등 비세출 자금기관에 대한 출입 및 감사권을 부여하는 문제는 미측에 자율적인 통제를 강화하도록 요청하는 선으로 우리측 주장을 완화함.

4. 미측은 차량등 면세물품 양도에 관하여 수입면장이 불필요하다고 주장하고 있으나 모든 수입물품은 면세 또는 과세 여부에 불구하고 수입면장을 필요로 하는것이므로 일선 세관에서 필히 수입신고를 받아 면장을 발부게 하도록 제도를 개선한다.

35

1. 입항 Date of Entry	부호 Code No	**대한민국세관** Korea Customs Service
2. 선하증권번호 B/L No		
3. 적재선(기)명 Vessel (Aircraft)		
4. 적재선(기)국적 Flag		
5. 적출국(지) Place of Shipment		**국제연합군수입신고서**
6. 입항지 Place of Entry		Import Declaration ~~UNC~~/USFK or certification
7. 성산지, 원산국(지) Place of Production		
8. 장치장소 Place of Storage		

9. 세관부호 Customs Code No	10. 수입종별 Sort of Import	11. 신고번호 Declaration No

12. 신고서 Date of Declaration	19 . . .
13. 검사 Date of Examination	19 . . .
14. 조정 Date of Levy	19 . . .
15. 면허 Date of Permit	19 . . .

결재	계	주무	과장

16. 품명 및 규격 Description of Articles & Grade	17. 중량 Weight / 18. 수량 Quantity	19. 단위 Unit	20. 신고가격 Declared Value / 21. 감정가격 Appraised Value	22. 세번 Heading / 23. 부호 Code No	24. 세율 Rate	25. 관세액 Amount of Customs Duty	26. 관세면세근거 및 부호 Duty Exemption Code No
(1)		Kg	CIF$		%	₩	
			₩				
(2)		Kg	CIF$		%	₩	
			₩				
27. 비고 Remark		계 Total	CIF$	환율 Exchange Rate		₩	
			₩				

28. 기호, 번호, 포장종류와 개수 Mark, Number, Type of Package	30. 내국세				
	1. 과세가격	2. 세별	3. 세종	4. 세율	5. 세액
	(1)			%	₩
	(2)			%	₩
29. 신고서 매란 Declared Paper Sheet Column	원천과세표준				
	31. 비고 Remarks				

32. 첨부서류 Attached herewith if any
송품장 (　　) Invoice
포장명세서 (　　) Packing List
원산지증명 (　　) Certificate of Origin
운임명세서 (　　) Freight Sheet
보험영수증 (　　) Receipt of Insurance
선하증권사본 (　　) Copy of B/L
Others (　　)

상기 각항에는 허위가 없을뿐아니라 당해물품은 개인용품, 업무용품으로서 결코 판매 또는 교환등의 방법에 의하여 타용도에는 사용하지 않겠기 자이 서약함.

The above statement is true and correct to the best of my knowledge and I hereby affirm that the above articles are not for resale, exchange or other such purpose and will be used as personal or official items only.

상기 물품에 대하여 수입통관면허를 신청함.
국제연합군통관관리장교
I hereby make application for permission to import the above goods for the use of UNC/USFK SOFA

33. 면허인 Signature of Permit

신고자성명 Name and Signature of Declarer

통관장교 서명 Signature of Customs clearance Officer

신고자주소 Address of Declarer

부대명 Department of the Army

증산 수출 건설

별

재 무 부

협력 1243-7841 1972. 9. 21.

수신 외무부장관

제목 미군 군사화물 증명 양식 개정

1. 미이 720-7962(1972. 3. 14) 에 대한 것입니다.

2. SOFA제71차 합동 위원회에서 재무분과 위원회에 과제 부여된 미군사화물증명 양식 개정의 건에 대하여 재무분과 위원회에서 미측과 합의한 내용을 별첨과 같이 작성 송부하오니 합동위원회에서 승인 되도록 필요한 조치를 취하여 주시기 바랍니다.

첨부 : 미군사화물 증명양식 개정에 관한 재무분과 위원회 합의 각서1부. 끝.

0193

북미2과	공람	72년 9월 21일	담당	과장	국장	차관보	차관	장관
					전결			

재무부장관

1972. 9. 21 재무부

공문서 규정 제27조 ... 규정에 의하여 관기 박승희 전결

새집살림 나라살림 저축으로 부강하자

317

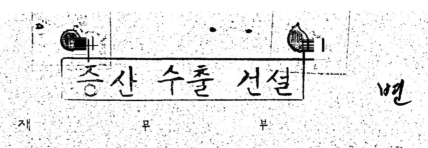

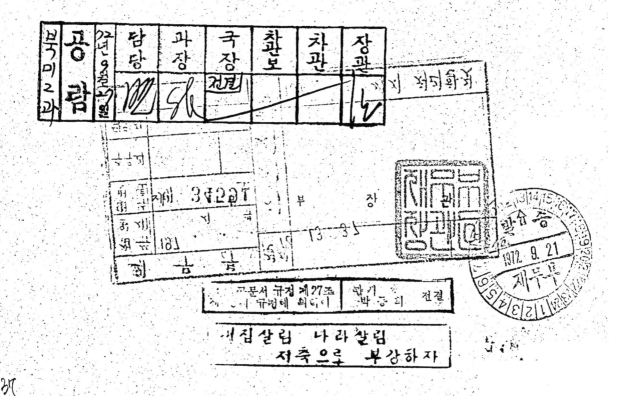

외 무 부		결재	
접수일시	197 . . . 시 분		13:37
접수번호	제 34591호	지시사항	
주무과			
담당자			
결재			197 . . 까지 처리할것

36-1.E

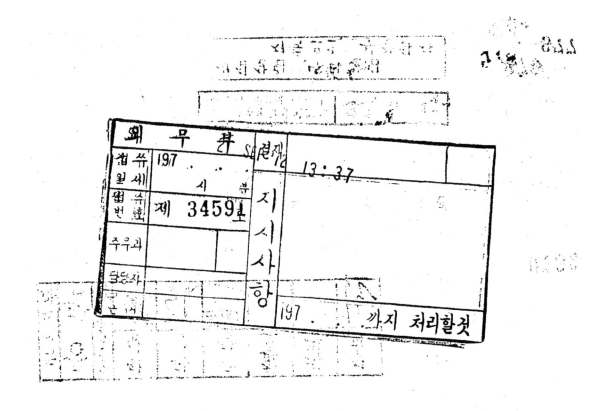

REPUBLIC OF KOREA - UNITED STATES
FINANCE (PERSONNEL AFFAIRS) SUBCOMMITTEE.

MEMORANDUM FOR: THE JOINT COMMITTEE

8 September 1972

SUBJECT: Import Declaration Forms

1. Subcommittee Members:

UNITED STATES	REPUBLIC OF KOREA
COL J. T. Fordham, USAF, Chairman	Mr. Park Dong Hee, Chairman
LCDR Robert E. Spydell, USN	Mr. Lee Jae Sup
COL Theodore D. Cameron, USAF	Mr. Kim Kee Joe
COL Robert A. Little, USA	Mr. Kim Ik Taik
COL George F. Proudfoot, USA	Mr. Shin Yung Su
COL Harlan R. Schmidt, USA	Mr. Shin Myoung Ho
COL Benjamin H. Rosker, USAF	Mr. Lee Jin Moo
LTC William P. Sewell, USA	Mr. Kang Yung Joo
LT David K. Marten, USA	
Mr. Samuel Pollack	
Mr. Francis K. Cook	

2. Subject to Recommendation: Review of procedures relating to forms and methods of presentation of certification on various USFK imports established by the Joint Committee at its fifth meeting on 11 April 1967, contained at Inclosure 5 to the minutes of the fifth Joint Committee meeting.

3. Recommendation: a. It is recommended that the form for certification of USFK imports contained in inclosure 5 to the minutes of the fifth meeting of the ROK-US Joint Committee be rescinded and replaced by the form attached to this memorandum.

b. It is further recommended that the effective date for implementation of this recommendation be the first day of the second month from the month in which it is approved by the Joint Committee.

38

SUBJECT: Import Declaration Forms 8 September 1972

4. Security Classification: Unclassified

Mr. Park Dong Hee
Chairman, ROK Component
Finance Subcommittee

COL Joseph T. Fordham, USAF
Chairman, US Component
Finance (Personnel Affairs)
Subcommittee

39

Monthly Average Sales for 1 Person

Years / Items	1970	1971. 8	Authorized quantity per month requested by Korea Government	Quantity authorized per month under the present control system
Cigarettes	108 packs	100 packs	50 packs	
Liqour	4.1 bottles	3.7 bottles	3 bottles	5 bottles per month for unaccompanied (Club)
Coffee	6.6 lbs. (3.3 bottes) PX authorized persons -55,000-	7.6 lbs. (3.8 bottles) PX authorized persons -40,000-	3 lbs.	6 lbs. of ground coffee per month for a unaccompanied (Commissary)

40

Cigarettes

Unit : 1,000 packs

Year		1970	1971
Domestic products sold in Korea		2,012,719	2,285,483
Cigarettes imported by Korean importers		2,476 ($ 303,000)	2,769 ($ 237,000)
Non - Appropriated - Fund - Cargo (PX)	Sales of Cigarettes	(A) 71,350	(C) 48,003 *
	Estimated Consumption of cigarettes by USFK persons	(B) 39,600 (= 60 packs per month × 55,000 persons × 12 months)	(D) 28,800 (= 60packs per month × 40,000 persons × 12 months)
0037	Estimated outflow to black market	(A) - (B) 31,750	(C) - (D) 19,203
Quantities of Confiscated cigarettes in black market		87	131

* Estimated by informations furnished by USFK pertaining to NAF cargoes

41

PX 판매 실적표

Cigarette unit : Carton

품 명	70 년 도		71 년 도 (8月末現在)		72년도 (6월말 현재)	
	금 액	수 량	금 액	수 량	금 액	수 량
양 주		2,707,487 병		1,797,458병		959,432 병
권 연 초	$10,555,010	6,485,965	$5,397,860	3,126,912		
엽 연 초	$ 315,432	481,059	$ 146,631	378,466		
계 미	$ 2,571,898	2,174,042	$ 680,332	953,926		

經緯
① 1967. 5. 25 第8次JC에서 課題賦与됨
② 韓美間의 見解差異로 継続未決状態
1969. 5月 以後에는 美側에서도 [illegible] 하지 않고 있음.

移徙貨物 및 別送貨物 稅関検査 節次

美側意見	韓國側意見	関係規定
検査与否 및 時間 場所		SOFA 第9條 1項 (協定에서 規定된 경우를 除外하고는 大韓民國 稅関 当局이 집행하고 있는 法令에 따라야한다)
a. 移徙貨物 (Household Goods)		
① 韓國政府가 원한다면 到着後 開装하는 동안에 検査할수 있다	i) 物品을 輸出入하고자할 때에는 稅関長에게 輸出入 申告를 하고 그 免許를 받아야 한다.	関稅法 第137條 (輸出入의 免許)
	ii) 前項의 規定은 当該物品이 関稅法에 規定한 藏置場所에 있는 경우에 限하여 이를 할수있다	関稅法 第138條 (申告의 要件)
	iii) 申告人은 申告한 物品에 対하여 稅関 公務員의 検査를 받아야 한다 다만 稅関公務員이 必要없다고 認定하는 경우에는 検査를 省略할수 있다	関稅法 第140條 (物品의 検査)
② 検査는 貨主 또는 貨主指名人 立会下에 貨主가 정한 時間과 場所에서 実施한다 +	i) 관세법 規定의 藏置場所에서 하여야한다	관세법 第138條 (申告의 要件)
	ii) 原則的으로 稅関開庁 時間内에 検査하여야 한다	관세법 第236條 (稅関의 開庁時間)

43

	iii) 物品의 檢査를 받는 者는 檢査에 參與하고 物品의 開裝 및 再包裝을 하여야 한다	關稅法 施行令 第124條 (申告物品에 대한 檢査)
b 別送貨物 (Unaccompanied Baggage)		
① 個人의 別送貨物은 韓美關係當局이 그 檢査가 兩國의 最上의 利益이 된다고 相互 合意하는 경우를 除外하고는 檢査하지 않는다	i) 物品을 輸出入하고자 할 때에는 輸出入 申告를 하고 그 免許를 받아야 한다	關稅法 第137條 (輸出入의 免許)
	ii) 前項의 申告는 當該 物品이 關稅法에 規定한 藏置場所에 있는 경우에 限하여 이를 할 수 있다	關稅法 第138條 (申告의 要件)
	iii) 申告人은 申告物品에 對하여 稅關公務員의 檢査를 받아야 한다	關稅法 第140條 (物品의 檢査)
② 檢査는 韓國 및 美國 關係官 立會下에 實施한다	i) 物品의 檢査를 받는 者는 檢査에 參與하고 物品의 開裝 및 再包裝을 하여야 한다	關稅法 施行令 第124條 (申告物品에 대한 檢査)

재무부 관세국

44

2. 韓國稅關에 開裝時間通報	上記 條件下에서 貨主가 원하는 時間에 檢査 可能함	
① 稅關은 開裝 1日 以前에 時間과 場所를 通報 받는다.	(要 削 除)	
② 通報는 口頭 또는 文書로써 指定된 稅關 官吏에게 通知 되었을때 成立한다.	(要 削 除)	
③ 韓國 당국은 開裝時間을 稅關官吏에게 通報 하는데 必要한 정보를 美軍司令官에게 提供한다	(要 削 除)	
④ 稅關檢査 官吏가 指定時間에 出頭치 않아도 開裝을 延期하지 않는다.	(要 削 除)	
3. 檢査費用 負担 기타		
① 稅關 檢査로 因해 直接 発生하는 費用은 韓國이 負担한다.	세관 檢査로 인해 直接発生하는 費用은 檢査를 받는 者가 負担한다	

재 무 부 관 세 국

45

② 稅関 当局은 美軍司令官의 同意 없이는 美軍 構成員 등의 家事用品 또는 別送 貨物로 부터 여하한 品目도 押收하지 않는다	輸入 禁止品은 押留한다.	関稅法 才 146條 (輸出入의 禁止) SOFA 才 9條 9項 (b): (합중국 군대는 한국세관에 의하여 압류될 물품을 인도하도록 확보하기 위하여 그의 权限内의 모든 援助를 提供하여야 한다)

재무부 관세국

46

공 란

REPUBLIC OF KOREA-UNITED STATES
FINANCE/PERSONNEL AFFAIRS SUBCOMMITTEE

MEMORANDUM FOR: Republic of Korea-United States Joint Committee

1. Subcommittee Members:

United States	Republic of Korea
COL Raymond Kosmatka, Chairman	Mr. IM Young Duc, Chairman
LCDR Lee Q. McMillan, Secretary	Mr. NAM Sang Chin, Alternate Chairman
COL Charles C. Jeffries	Mr. YANG Bo Sung, Secretary
COL Nicholas Jabbour	Mr. KWAK Byung Ki
COL John J. McAleer	Mr. PARK Joon Kyu
COL James L. Melloh	Mr. CHONG In Yung
COL Charles A. Rigler	Mr. KIM Nam Chin
LTC William D. Newbern	Mr. KIM Ho Kil
MAJ Philip B. Turner	Mr. SHIN Yung Soo
1LT Luis A. Calderon	Mr. LEE Taek Nyung
Mr. Francis F. Cook	Mr. PARK Sam Bong
	Mr. KIM Yong Hae
	Mr. LEE Won Ho
	Mr. HAN Byung Il

2. Subject of recommendation: The issue relating to customs examination of unaccompanied baggage and household goods of USFK personnel under Article IX of the United States-Republic of Korea Status of Forces Agreement.

3. Recommendation: That the procedures set forth in the attachment to this memorandum be approved.

4. Security Classification: UNCLASSIFIED.

COLONEL RAYMOND KOSMATKA Chairman, United States Component Finance/Personnel Affairs Subcommittee	IM YOUNG DUC Chairman, Republic of Korea Component Finance/Personnel Affairs Subcommittee

48

AGREED PROCEDURES FOR CUSTOMS CLEARANCE OF HOUSEHOLD GOODS AND UNACCOMPANIED BAGGAGE OF MEMBERS OF THE UNITED STATES ARMED FORCES, CIVILIAN COMPONENT, US INVITED CONTRACTOR PERSONNEL AND DEPENDENTS OF THE FOREGOING WHEN SUCH PERSONNEL ARRIVE OR DEPART THE REPUBLIC OF KOREA IN ACCORDANCE WITH ARTICLE IX, REPUBLIC OF KOREA-UNITED STATES STATUS OF FORCES AGREEMENT

1. The soverign right of the Republic of Korea to inspect the household goods and unaccompanied baggage of members of the United States armed forces, civilian component, US-invited contractor personnel and dependents is acknowledged. In order to assist in the accomplishment of the United States mission in defense of the Republic of Korea, with a minimum administrative burden and expense, it is mutually agreed that any inspection of household goods and unaccompanied baggage will be conducted as follows:

a. Household goods may be inspected if such inspection is desired by the Government of the ROK, only during unpacking, after arrival in Korea, or while being packed in preparation for shipment from Korea. The inspections will be conducted in the presence of the owners or their designated representatives at the time and place designated by the owner.

b. Unaccompanied baggage will not be inspected except when it is

49

mutually agreed by appropriate authorities of the Republic of Korea and the United States Forces, Korea that the inspection of unaccompanied baggage of an individual is in the best interests of the Republic of Korea and the United States. Inspection of unaccompanied baggage will be made in the presence of officials from both the United States and Republic of Korea. A report containing all circumstances associated with any inspection of unaccompanied baggage will be made by the United States official witnessing the inspection to Commander, US Forces, Korea.

2. ROK customs authorities of the Republic of Korea will be advised of the time and location that household goods are to be packed or unpacked no later than the day preceding the date that packing or unpacking is to commence. Notification will be considered to have been accomplished when a designated Republic of Korea customs official has been notified, either verbally or in writing. The Republic of Korea officials will provide Commander, US Forces, Korea with the necessary information to notify the appropriate customs officials, either in English or Hangul, of the time that packing or unpacking of the household goods will occur. To avoid

import permitted Date and

50

additional expense and delay of household goods shipments, it [illegible] mutually agreed that packing and unpacking will not be delayed if customs inspectors are not present at the designated time that packing or unpacking is scheduled to commence.

3. Costs that accrue directly from the customs inspections pursuant to the US-ROK SOFA and Joint Committee procedures will be borne by the Republic of Korea. Customs authorities will not confiscate any item from the household goods or unaccompanied baggage of any member of the US armed forces, civilian component, US-invited contractor personnel, and dependents without the concurrence of Commander, US Forces, Korea.

51

대 한 민 국 세 관
KOREAN CUSTOMS SERVICE
수 입 신 고 서 (반입) (갑지)
IMPORT DECLARATION

1 처리기간 197 . . .(일간)		
2 ※입항 Date of Entry 197 . . .	부호	
3 ※선화증권번호 B/L No		
4 ※선(기)명 적재선(기) Name of Vessel (Aircraft)		
국적 Nationality of Vessel (Aircraft)		
5 ※적출국 Country of Shipment		
6 ※입항지 Place of Entry		
7 ※원산국 Country of Production		
8 ※장치장소 Place of Storage		

11※세관부호	12※수입재원별	13 신고번호

※ 14 수입허가	기관
	번호
	년월일 197 . . .
15 신고	197 . . .
16 검사	197 . . .
17 조정	197 . . .
18 면허	197 . . .

9※ 수입자		10※ 수 입 형 태 별		19※ 신고자	
주소 Importer address		① 면 허 전 반 출	⑤ 면허전반출완결분	주소 Declarant Address	
주민등록번호		② 보 세 공 장 반 입	⑥ 보세공장 수입 면허분	주민등록 번호	
상호 및 무역등록No.		③ 보 세 건 설 장 반 입	⑦ 보세건설장수입면허분	상호	
성명인 Name and Signature		④ 보 세 전 시 장 반 입	⑧ 보세전시장수입면허분	성명인 Name and Signature	

20 ※ 품명 및 규격 DESCRIPTION OF ARTICLES & GRADE	21※ 중량 WEIGHT / 22※ 수량 QUANTITY	23※ 단위 UNIT	24※ 신고가격 DECLARED VALUE / 25 감정가격 APPRAISED VALUE	26 세번 / 27 특관세종	부호	28 세율 / 29 세율	30 관세액 / 31 특관세액	32 통관근거부호 / 33 관세면제근거부호
(1)	kg		CIF, $			%	₩	
			₩	( )				
			특		종	%	₩	
(2)	kg		CIF, $			%	₩	
				( )				
			특		종	%	₩	
34 비고	합계		CIF, $	35 환율			₩	
			₩					
			특				₩	

36 내국세					37 증지증연	38 세별계	(가) 고지번호	(나) 세액
① 과세가격	②세별	③ 세종	④세율	⑤ 세액				
₩			%	₩	매 개	①관세		
₩			%	₩	매 개	②특관세		
⑥ 원천과세 표준 ₩				합계	매 개	③물품세		
42 비고						④ 세		
						⑤영업세		
						⑥소득세 법인세		

39 신고서 비란

40 허가서 분할 □원본은 신고번호 (. .) 첨부

41 검사: 생략□ 검사장□ 장치장소□ 검정서□ — 수입인지 첨부란

43 ※ 기호, 번호, 포장 종류와 개수 Markings, Numbering, Type and Number of Packages	44 ※ 보세운송	45 면허인	46 ※ 첨부서류 Attached herewith, if any
	목적지:	permit stamp and signature	수입허가서 ( ) □ Import License
	경유지:		송품장 ( ) □ Invoice
	수송: ①육로□ ②해로□ ③공로□		포장명세서 ( ) □ Packing List
	기간: . . 부터 . . 까지		원산지증명 ( ) □ Certificate of Origin
	도착일: . .		운임명세서 ( ) □ Freight Sheet
			보험영수증 ( ) □ Receipt of Insurance
			선화증권사본 ( ) □ copy of B/L
			( ) □ others

입회	검사	주무	과장	주무	과장	장
52						

3502-2-1A-1 1971. 11. 승인 ※ 표시는 신고자 기입 210㎜×300㎜(백상지40g/㎡ 3매 백상지60g/㎡)

미측기록지

2. 입항 Date of Entry 19 . .	부호 Code No.	대한민국 세관 Korean Customs Service	11. 세관부호 Customs Code No.	
3. 선하증권번호 B/L No.			12. 수입종별 Sort of Import	
4. 적재선(기)명 Name of Vessel(Aircraft)			13. 신고번호 Declaration No.	
적재선(기)국적 Nationality of Vessel(Aircraft)			15. 신고 Date of Declaration 19 . .	
5. 적출국(지) Country of Shipment		주한미군용 수입신고서 Import Declaration /Certification USFK, ROK-US SOFA and permit for use of	결재: 계 / 주부 / 과장	
6. 입항지 Place of Entry				
7. 생산지,원산국(지) Country of Production				
8. 장치장소 Place of Storage				

21. 품명및 규격 Description of Articles & Grade	22. 중량 Weight	23. 수량 Quantity	24. 단위 Unit	25. 신고가격 Declared Value	27. 세번 Heading	28. 부호 Code No.
(1)				CIF $		
(2)				CIF $		
(3)				CIF $		
35. 비고 Remarks	계 Total			CIF $		

45. 기호, 번호, 포장종류와 개수
Markings, Numbering, Type and Number of Packages

상기 물품은 SOFA 제9조 제2항에 의거 주한 미군용으로 수입되는 것임을 증명함.

I hereby certify the import of the above goods for use of USFK in accordance with the ROK-US SOFA, Article IX, Paragraph 2.

신고자 성명
Name and Signature of Declarant

통관장교 서명
Signature of Customs Clearance Officer

신고자 주소
Address of Declarant

부대명
Department

46. 첨부서류
Attached herewith if any
송품장
Invoice
포장명세서
Packing List
원산지 증명
Certificate of Origin
운임명세서
Freight Sheet
보험영수증
Receipt of Insurance
선화증권사본
Copy of B/L
기타
Others

47. 면허일및 면허인자
Entry under ROK-US SOFA Article IX, Paragraph 2 Certified, Signature and Date

~~Seal~~ Permit ~~Stamp~~ ~~Date~~ and signature import ~~imported~~ permit date and stamp sign

53

재무부

외 무 부

정세보고처리전 1972. 11. 11.
( )

담 당	과 장	국 장	차 관	장 관	공 람

발 신 인 SOURCE

요약및비고 주한미군 개인용품에 대한 수입신고서

1. 72. 11. 1. 부터 주한미군의 개인용품 반입에 대하여 일반수입신고서 양식을 사용한다는 관세청의 대 미군측 통보에 대하여,

2. 미군측에서는 수입신고서 양식의 개정에 앞서 세관검사 절차의 검토가 선행되어야 할 것이라는 회한을 재무부에 발송한바 있음.

3. 이에 대하여 재무부는 다시 다음과 같은 내용의 대 미군측 공한을 발송함.

(1) 개인용품에 대한 수입신고서 양식은 SOFA 내 문제가 아니므로 한국 관세청이 제정한 일반 수입신고서 양식에 따라야 할 것이며,

(2) 동 수입신고서 용지는 민간기관인 관세협회에서 팔고있으나 관세청은 관세협회와 협의하여 미군에 무료로 배부할 수 있는 방안을 강구할 것임.

(3) 세관검사 절차는 현행 SOFA 규정에 따라 실시될 것이며, 새로운 절차를 검토할 필요는 없을것임.

64

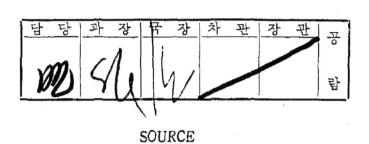

분류번호 보존기간

수 선 전 설

북미 2 2

재 무 부

협력 1245-870 1972. 11. 2.

수신 외무부장관

제목 주한 미군 개인용품에 대한 수입신고서

72. 11. 1 부터 주한 미군의 개인 용품에 대하여 일반 수입 신고서 양식을 사용한다는 관세청의 대 미군측 통보에 의거 미군측에서 제기한 의견 (72. 10. 27) 에 대한 한국측 입장을 별첨 공한 사본과 같이 미측에 통보하였으니 참고 하기 바랍니다.

첨부 : 대 미측 재무분과 위원장 공한 사본 1부.

접수 1972. 11. 2 재무부

재 무 부 장 관

공문서 규정 제27조 그 규정에 의하여 관세국장 박동희 전결

3%의 알뜰살림 나라살림 저축으로 부강하자

55

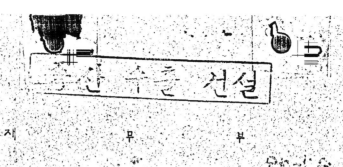

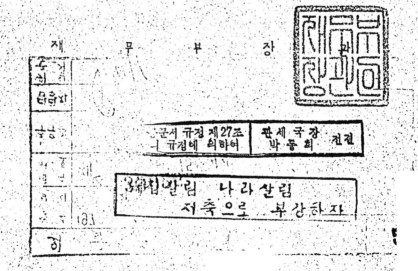

외 무 부	
접수일시	197
접수번호	제 39626 15 : 44
주무과	
담당자	
위임	4/6

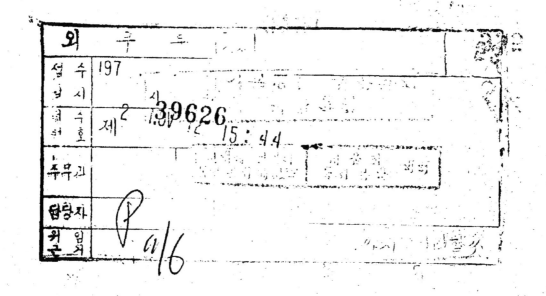

MINISTRY OF FINANCE
THE REPUBLIC OF KOREA
SEOUL, KOREA

1 November, 1972

JOSEPH T. FORDHAM
Colonel, USAF
Chairman, US Component
Finance (Personnel Affairs) Subcommittee

Dear Col. FORDHAM:

In response to your letter, dated 27 October 1972, I would like to make clear our position regarding some problem areas with the form for declaration and certification of Paragraph 3, Article IX, "Imports".

1. No declaration form for personal effects has been stipulated in the SOFA and related regulations. This should be construed to use the generalized forms designed by the Office of Customs Administration. The Office of Customs Administration is scheduled to adopt the newly designed import declaration forms for personal effects beginning on 1 November 1972. Accordingly, it is, I believe, warranted to apply the above forms for your personal effects.

2. Import declaration forms are provided and sold by the Korean Tariff Association, a civil organization apart from the Government. This does not fall within the category of exemption of charges described in Paragraph 3, Article IX, SOFA. However, the Office of Customs Administration has negotiated with the above association to furnish the forms free to USFK.

3. Block 19 (Declarant) may be used as USFK customs clearance officer certification of entitlement for duty free entry.

4. As for current customs clearance procedures which have been suspended since the task assignment on 25 May 1967 by the Joint Committee, customs clearances for personal effects have been performed without trouble as described in the present SOFA, except the exemption from customs examination described in Paragraph 5, Article IX, SOFA. Accordingly, I don't believe it is necessary

56

1 November, 1972

to establish any special customs examination procedures for personal effects.

Your kind understanding in this matter will be appreciated.

Sincerely yours,

Park Dong Hee
Chairman, ROK Component
Finance Subcommittee

517

재 무 부

협력 1243-890 1972. 11. 10.

수신 외무부장관

제목 SOFA 비 적용 대상자에 대한 협정상의 특권 부여

1. 관세청으로 부터 별첨 보고에 의하면 주한 미군 지위 협정 (SOFA) 적용 대상자가 아닌 ① 주월미군 가족 ② 미군 제대군인 ③ 고용계약이 끝난 초청계약자와 그 가족에 대하여도 미군 당국은 비세출 기관 및 미군사 우체국의 이용권과 SOFA 상의 차량 등록 번호 발급등의 조치를 취하고 있다고 하는바

2. 상기인에 의한 물품 부정유출의 우려가 특히 크다는 점에서 미군 당국에 이를 시정 조치토록 강구하여 주시기 바라며,

3. 특히 SOFA 제 28차 합동위원회 회의록에 의하면 미국측 대표는 "미군 제대군인 및 주월 미군 (가족)"을 SOFA 제 12조에 대한 합의의사록 (가) 항의 "통상적으로 이와 같은 특권이 부여되는 합중국 정부의 기타 공무원및 직원"으로 간주하여 비세출 자[illegible] 여 하고 있다고 설명하고 있는바, 이와 같은 해석이 현 차원에서도 타당한지 여부를 회시하여 주시기 바랍니다.

첨부 : 관세청건의 공한 사본 1부. 끝.

재 무 부 장 관

세 규정 제27조 이 정에 의하여 | 관세국장 박동희 전결

내 집 살림 나라 살림 저축으로 부강하자

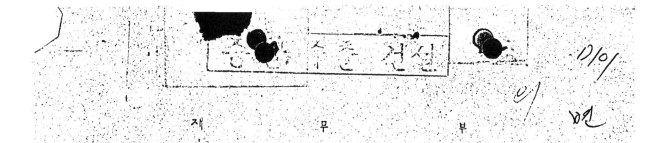

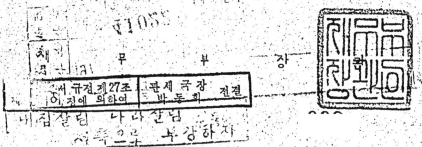

외 무 부

접수 일시	197
접수 번호	제 41022 13 NOV '72 14 : 51
주무과	
담당자	
처리 기간	. . 까지 처리할것

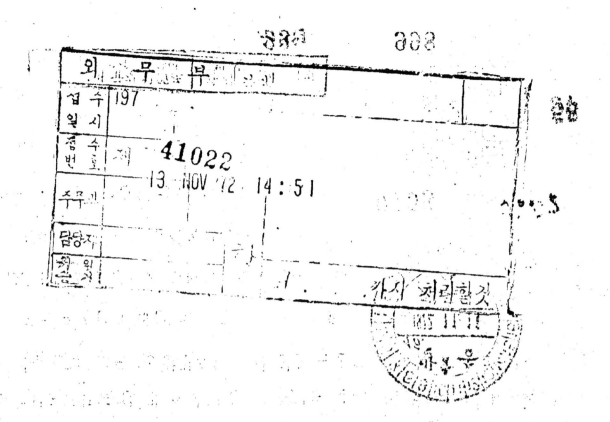

증산 수출 건설

관 세 청

심리 1245-1225 1972. 10. 31.

수신 재무부장관

참조 관세국장

제목 SOFA 대상자에 대한 합동위원회 건의

SOFA 제1조에 의거 대한민국 영역안에 주둔한 현역에 복무하는 합중국 군대의 구성원, 군속 및 그들의 가족과 제15조에 의한 초청계약자에 한하여 제4조 및 제13조에 명시된 미군사우체국과 비세출자금 기관의 이용권을 부여하게 되어 있는바,

1. 미8군 당국은 다음에 열거한 비 SOFA 대상자에게 SOFA에 의한 "신분증과 레숀플레이트"를 교부하여 주고 SOFA대상자로 취급하고 비세출 자금기관과 미군사우체국의 이용권 및 SOFA에 의한 차량등록 등 면세특권을 부여 함으로서 면세특권을 악용하고 있고 SOFA 협정에 위배되는 처사이오니 이를 조속히 시정조치 하도록 한미 합동 위원회에 건의하여 주시기 바랍니다.

발송 No. 1972 10 31 관세청

다 음

(1) 상당수에 달하는 주월 미군 가족
(주로 국제결혼한 한국출신 부인)

(2) 상당수에 달하는 미군제대 군인

(3) 상당수에 달하는 고용 계약이 끝난 초청계약자와 그 가족
(미8군 초청계약회사인 A.A.E.O 회사에서 회사원 로저 아이, 에디 및 미러 박, 큐미고가 1971. 6. 30 퇴직하였음에도 불구하고 현재까지 계속 동사 직원으로 가장 APO 및 PX 이용권은 물론 면세차량

58

59

심리 1245- 1972. 10. 31.

도 계속 사용케 하고 있음을 적발 72. 9. 30 미8군 헌병부에 번호판을 이첩한 사례가 있음)

첨부 : 1. SOFA 차량 번호판 송부 공문 사본 1매.
2. A.A.E.O 회사장 진술서 사본 1매. 끝.

관 세 청

서축의 날마다 서축하자

민수산업

60

공산 ─ 출 선 설

관 세 청

심이 1245-1774 1972. 10. 31.

수신 주한 미8군 헌병부장

제목 SOFA 차량 번호판 송부

귀하의 당청 관세 행정업무에 협조하여 주신데 대하여 사의를 표하는 바입니다.

1. 주한 미8군 조정계약회사인 A.A.E.O 회사에서는 1971. 6. 30 까지 동사에 근무하다 퇴직한바 있는 다음과 같은 사람에게 그후 계속하여 SOFA대상자로 취급하여 차량을 등록 사용케하고 있음을 적발하였음으로,

2. 앞으로는 비 SOFA 대상자에게 SOFA 에 의한 차량번호판의 교부 조치가 없도록 시정하여 주시기 바랍니다.

다 음

소 속 : A.A.E.O 회사

가. 성 명 : 로저 아이. 에디 (RODGER I. EDDY)

등록차량번호 : 2-2090

나. 성 명 : 피터 피. 큐피크 (PETER P. KUPIEC)

등록차량번호 : 2-1206 (본인이 72. 10. 27 헌병대에 반납 하였다고 함)

첨부 : 1. 번호판 (2-2090) 1조

2. 검사증 (2-1206) 1매. 끝.

관 세 청

60

61

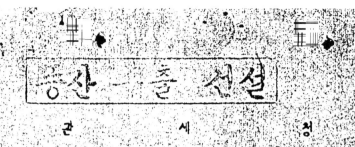

APO SAN FRANCISCO 96301

ENGINEERING - DESIGN A[illegible] OF CONSTRUCTION - INSPECTION - TECHNICA[illegible]ANCE - CONSULTATION

SEOUL, KOREA | TEL. 52-7803
Y8 3727

S T A T E M E N T

25 October 1972

Mr. Peter P. Kupiec and Mr. Rodger I. Eddy was dropped from the employ of AAE, according to the SOFA report, on 30 June 1971 and was again employed by me in May and June of 1972, also indicated on the SOFA report, terminating on 30 June 1972. According to records, Mr. Eddy was issued an ID Card on 17 March 1972 which appears to be in advance of his actual employment of record, resulting in a procedures violation. The reason for termination on 30 June 1972 was not receiving the award of contract expected to start on 1 July 1972, for which planning and preparatory work was in progress since March of 1972. Mr. Eddy was engaged in this phase of management duties, especially with regard to fact-finding research. Special care will be taken in the future to avoid any technical violations with regard to issuing ID Cards in advance of reported employment dates.

I wish to apologize on behalf of my company for the technical violation and will do my best to prevent this from happening again.

Sincerely,

Wayne G. Mayotte

WAYNE G. MAYOTTE
President
Associated American Engineers

CABLE ADDRESS: "ASAMEN, TOKYO" "ASSOCAMEN, SEOUL" "ASAMEN, OKINAWA" "ASAMEN, SAIGON"

62

증산 수출 건설

재 무 부

협력 1243- 891 1972. 11. 10.

수신 외무부장관

제목 주한미군의 개인용품 수입신고 및 세관 검사 절차

1. 주한 미군 지위 협정 (SOFA) 제9조 3항의 개인용품에 대한 수입신고 및 세관 검사 절차에 관한 미측의 초안을 송부하오니 참고 하시기 바라며,

2. 이에 대한 우리나라의 입장 수립을 위하여 SOFA 재무분과위 한국측 대책회의를 가까운 시일내에 가질 예정이니 준비 하시기 바랍니다.

첨부 : 미측 초안 1부. 끝.

외 무 부	결재	
접수일시	197	
접수번호	제 41023	
주무과		
담당자		
위임근거		

발송 1972 11.11 재무부

재 무 부 장 관

정부공문서 규정 제27조 제2항의 규정에 의하여 관세국장 전결

내 집 살림 나라 살림

北美2課

63

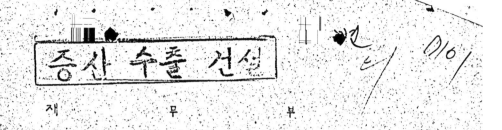

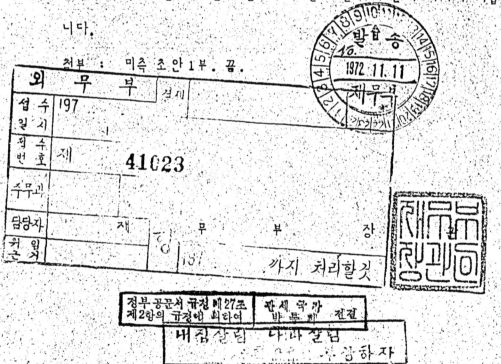

DRAFT

AGREED PROCEDURES FOR DOCUMENTING DUTY/CUSTOMS FREE ENTRY OF PROPERTY CONSIGNED TO AND FOR THE USE OF MEMBERS OF THE UNITED STATES ARMED FORCES, THE CIVILIAN COMPONENT AND THEIR DEPENDENTS UNDER PARAGRAPH 3, ARTICLE IX, ROK-US SOFA

The United States military authorities in the Republic of Korea agree to furnish to the Government of the Republic of Korea in accordance herewith documentation for the exemption from customs duties and other such charges for property consigned to and for the personal use of members of the US Armed Forces, civilian component, and their dependents as provided for under paragraph 3 of/ and paragraph 2 of the agreed Minute to Article IX of the ROK-US SOFA.

PROCEDURES FOR DOCUMENTING USFK DUTY/CUSTOMS FREE PERSONAL PROPERTY

1. FURNITURE, HOUSEHOLD GOODS, AND PERSONAL EFFECTS:

a. Containers in which shipments of furniture, household goods and/or personal effects are shipped under US Government bill of lading shall be cleared through ROK customs at their point of entry into the ROK. The containers will be cleared by the transportation officer at

DRAFT

64

DRAFT

the port of entry where at least seven copies of the bill of lading and/or cargo manifests will be provided to the local USFK Customs Clearance Officer for preparation of the import document (Inclosure 1). The USFK Customs Clearance Officer shall prepare seven copies of the import document and verify the entitlement to duty/customs free entry. In preparing the import document blocks______, ________, ______ and ______ shall be filled in and the verification to duty/customs free entry entitlement accomplished in block 19. The transportation officer shall cause six copies of the import document, bill of lading, and cargo manifest to be delivered to local ROK customs officials for processing to clear the containers for onward routing to the consignee. Two complete copies of the import document with bill of lading will be returned to the transportation officer, one copy for local records and one copy for delivery to the consignee at the time ultimate delivery of the shipment occurs. It is expressly agreed that under no circumstances does the clearance of the container authorize inspection/examination of the container's contents. Such inspection/examination will follow procedures mutually agreed upon for implementation of customs examination of unaccompanied baggage and household goods of USFK personnel in accordance with Article IX of the SOFA. It is further mutually agreed that in order to keep the

2

DRAFT

65

DRAFT

administrative burden to a minimum, the containers will remain in US military channels from the point of entry into the ROK until delivery to the consignee.

b. Furniture, household goods and personal effects which are not shipped under a US Government bill of lading and which enter the ROK through commercial channels into ROK customs holding areas will be cleared by the consignee obtaining the bill of lading and cargo manifest for delivery to the nearest USFK Customs Clearance Officer who will prepare the import document, verifying the entitlement of the consignee to customs/duty free entry of the shipment. The USFK Customs Clearance Officer shall provide the consignee with six copies of each of the aforementioned documents for presentation to the ROK customs officials to clear the goods for duty/customs free entry into Korea. Based upon the documentation presented, ROK customs officials shall permit entry free from duty/customs charges. This category of goods shipped into Korea at the consignee's expense via commercial transportation may be subjected to a ROKG customs examination at the customs holding facility at the port of entry prior to release. This category of goods is not subject to customs duties or other related charges.

2. PRIVATELY OWNED VEHICLES

a. Privately owned vehicles shipped under US Government bill of lading shall be cleared through ROK customs at the port of delivery /.

DRAFT

66

DRAFT

of the vehicle to the consignee. After the consignee has receipted for the vehicle, he will obtain seven copies of the bill of lading and/or cargo manifest and deliver these documents to the nearest USFK Customs Clearance Officer. The USFK Customs Clearance Officer shall prepare seven copies of the import document and verify the entitlement of the consignee to duty/customs free entry of the vehicle. In preparing the import document blocks _____, _____, _____, and _____, shall be filled in and the verification of duty/customs free entry entitlement accomplished in block 19. The consignee shall take the vehicle, six copies of the import document, bill of lading and/or cargo manifest to the ROK customs house at the port of delivery of the vehicle for clearance of the vehicle to enter the ROK. ROK customs officials shall expeditiously process the documentation so as not to delay the consignee in returning to his duty station. Examination of the vehicle is authorized as a part of the clearance procedure. Upon completion of the processing, the ROK customs officials shall provide the consignee with two copies of the import document.

b. Privately owned vehicles which are not shipped under a US Government bill of lading and which enter the ROK through commercial channels into ROK customs holding areas will be cleared by the consignee obtaining the bill of lading and cargo manifests for delivery to the nearest

DRAFT

67

DRAFT

USFK Customs Clearance Officer who will prepare the import document, verifying the customs/duty free entry entitlement of the consignee. The USFK Customs Clearance Officer shall provide the consignee with six copies of the aforementioned documents for presentation to the ROK customs officials. The consignee shall deliver the documents to the ROK Customs officials at the port of entry of the vehicle for clearance for duty/customs free entry into the ROK. ROK customs officials shall expeditiously process the documentation so as not to delay the consignee from returning to his duty station. Examination of the vehicle is authorized as a part of the clearance procedure. Upon completion of the processing, the ROK customs officials will release the vehicle to the consignee and provide the consignee with two copies of the import document. This category of vehicle is not subject to customs duties or other related charges.

3. REASONABLE QUANTITIES OF PERSONAL EFFECTS AND HOUSEHOLD GOODS DELIVERED THROUGH UNITED STATES MILITARY POST OFFICES.

a. Reasonable quantities of personal effects and household goods delivered through US military post offices in the ROK will not require ROK customs documentation for entry into the ROK.

DRAFT

68

DRAFT

b. Personal effects and household goods delivered through US military post offices in the ROK, which during authorized customs examination by ROK-US personnel are considered unreasonable in quantity under currently effective jointly agreed procedures for examination of parcel post packages delivered through US military post office channels, shall be handled in the following manner:

(1) The addressee will be permitted to re-export the goods from the Republic of Korea, or

(2) The addressee may complete an import document for the goods determined to be unreasonable in quantity and pay standard applicable customs duties. Presentation of the addressee's copy of the import document which indicates the customs duties have been paid to ROK customs officials will be required to secure release of the goods which are unreasonable in quantity to the addressee. Since unreasonable quantities of goods delivered through US military post offices remain under US control, they will not be required for examination at the ROK customs house during processing of the import document as such an examination was the basis for the determination of unreasonable quantity. ROK customs examiners at the APO mail examination point shall state in writing the quantity, type and grade of the unreasonable quantities of goods for ROK customs house use in determining the appropriate standard customs duties.

6

DRAFT

69

4. IMPORT DOCUMENT

The Republic of Korea Government shall provide, free of charge, required quantities of the import document (Inclosure 1) to USFK Customs Clearance Officers for use in clearing paragraph 3, Article IX imports.

70

대 한 민 국 세 관
KOREAN CUSTOMS SERVICE
수 입 신 고 서 (반입)
IMPORT DECLARATION
(갑지)

1 ※ 접수일자 197 . . . (접수) 번호
2 ※ 입항 Date of Entry 197 . . . 부 호
3 ※ 선하증권번호 B/L No
4 ※ 선(기)명 Name of Vessel (Aircraft)
5 ※ 선(기)적 Nationality of Vessel (Aircraft)
6 ※ 적출국 Country of Shipment
6 ※ 입항지 Place of Entry
7 ※ 원산국 Country of Production
8 ※ 장치장소 Place of Storage

11 ※ 세관부호 | 12 ※ 수입재원별 | 13 신고번호

14 ※ 수입허가 기관 / 번호 / 년월일 197 . .
15 신 고 197 . .
16 검 사 197 . .
17 조 정 197 . .
18 면 허 197 . .

9 ※ 수입자 주소 Importer address
주민등록번호
상호 및 무역등록No.
성명인 Name and Signature

10 ※ 수 입 형 태 별
① 면허전반출 ⑤ 면허전반출완결분
② 보세공장반입 ⑥ 보세공장수입면허분
③ 보세건설장반입 ⑦ 보세건설장수입면허분
④ 보세전시장반입 ⑧ 보세전시장수입면허분

19 ※ 신고자 주소 Declarant Address
주민등록번호
상호
성명인 Name and Signature

20 ※ 품명 및 규격 DESCRIPTION OF ARTICLES & GRADE	21 ※ 중량 WEIGHT / 22 ※ 수량 QUANTITY	23 ※ 단위 UNIT	24 ※ 신고가격 DECLARED VALUE / 25 감정가격 APPRAISED VALUE	26 세번 / 27 특관세종	부호	28 세율 / 29 세율	30 관세액 / 31 특관세액	32 통관근거부호 / 33 관세면제근거부호
(1)	kg		CIF, $ / ₩ / 특	( ) 종		% / %	₩ / ₩	
(2)	kg		CIF, $ / ₩ / 특	( ) 종		% / %	₩ / ₩	
34 비고	합계		CIF, $ / ₩ / 특	35 환율			₩ / ₩	

36 내국세

① 과세가격	② 세번	③ 세종	④ 세율	⑤ 세액	37 증지증연
₩			%	₩	매 개
₩			%	₩	매 계
⑥ 원천과세표준 ₩				합계	매 계

42 비고

38 세별계	(가) 고지번호	(나) 세액
①관세		
②특관세		
③물품세		
④ 세		
⑤영업세		
⑥소득세 법인세		

39 신고서 매 린
40 허가서 분할 □원본은
신고번호______(. . .) 첨부

41 검사
생략□
검사장□
장치장소□
검정시□

수입인지 첨부란

43 ※ 기호, 번호, 포장종류와 개수 Markings, Numbering, Type and Number of Packages

44 ※ 보세운송
목적지:
경유지:
수송: ①육로□ ②해로□ ③공로□
기간: . . 부터
도착일: . . 까지

45 면허인

46 ※ 첨부서류 Attached herewith, if any
수입허가서 ( ) □ Import License
송품장 ( ) □ Invoice
포장명세서 ( ) □ Packing List
원산지증명 ( ) □ Certificate of Origin
운임명세서 ( ) □ Freight Sheet
보험영수증 ( ) □ Receipt of Insurance
선하증권사본 ( ) □ copy of B/L

접수	검사	주무	과장	주무	과장	장
71						

70

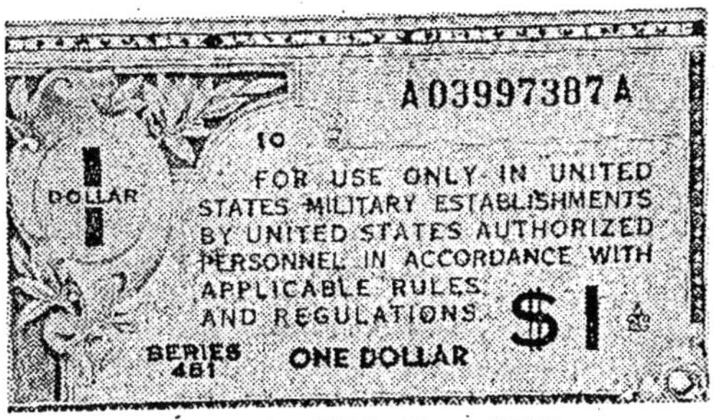

Series 461 (Sept. 1946 to March 1947)
The first MPC

Series 481 (June 1951 to May 1954)
This MPC was used during the Korean War.

'72. 11. 12. <K.T.> 2면

U.S. Forces Pay

MPC Use Curbs Black Market

By Don C. Terrill

Although the U.S. greenback dollar is famous as a standard of international payment, foreigners in Korea may also encounter another type of U.S. paper money known as Military Payment certificates or MPC.

These notes are used as payment to U.S. forces personnel, and these personnel are forbidden by regulation to possess greenbacks. MPC is good only in certain overseas areas and worthless in the United States itself.

Before MPC was used, troops were paid in local currencies and were allowed to exchange that currency for greenbacks upon their departure. It became clear that some persons were redeeming far more money than they could have reasonably saved from their pay. As a result the first MPC's were issued on Sept. 16, 1946.

Authority to possess MPCs is officially restricted to persons having a current Eighth Army "Ration Control Plate."

Access to the PXs and commissaries is tightly restricted, and the transfer of funds to the United States is complicated and carefully controlled. Nevertheless, the black-marketing of PX goods and MPC currency flourishes in the camp villages, and after army paydays there may very well be more MPCs in the hands of unauthorized persons than in the hands of authorized ones.

This situation has existed for as long as the U.S. forces have been in Korea despite "tight" control of MPCs combined with a fantastic succession of rationing schemes. Still, the military authorities regard MPCs as a valuable weapon against blackmarketing, and one can only suppose how much worse the situation would be if MPCs did not exist.

The current MPC series in Korea (Series 651) consists of $1, $5, and $10 notes, and until early 1967 MPCs here also included small notes of values 50, 25, 10, and 5 cents. Today, these small notes have been replaced by U.S. coins.

The current notes are initially printed on sheets of paper measuring 32 by 54 inches, so that a sheet will fit 70 one-dollar or 50 five- or ten-dollar notes. On the face of each MPC there is a small number, much smaller than the serial number, which indicates at what position that MPC was on the sheet at the time of printing.

There have been nine different MPC series used in Korea and four separate series used in Vietnam, and these notes follow an identifiable pattern.

First, each series number indicates the date of the design and whether it was the first or second design during that year. For example, U.S. Forces in Korea now use Series 651, indicating that it was designed in 1965 and was the first design of that year. U.S. Forces in Vietnam presently use Series 692, which was designed in 1969 and was the second design of that year.

Further, the serial numbers of MPCs begin and end with a letter, and every series has used a higher letter. For example, the first MPCs (in 1946) were "A", the next series was "B", and so on (with letter "I" omitted) until the letter "J" was used. Following "J", "A" was again reused (Korea now) followed by "B", "C," and "E" in Vietnam. The entire pattern of MPCs looks like this:

Series 461 "A"
Sep 16, 1946 to Mar 10, 1947
Series 471 "B"
Mar 10, 1947 to Mar 22, 1948
Series 472 "C"
Mar 22, 1948 to Jun 20, 1951
Series 481 "D"
Jun 20, 1951 to May 25, 1954
Series 521 "E"
May 25, 1954 to May 27, 1958
Series 541 "F"
May 27, 1958 to May 26, 1961
Series 591 "G"
May 26, 1961 to Jan 6, 1964
Series 611 "H"
Jan 6, 1964 to Apr 28, 1969
Series 641 "J" (Vietnam)
Aug 31, 1965 to Oct 21, 1968
Series 651 "A" (Korea now)
Apr 28, 1969 to now
Series 661 "B" (Vietnam)
Oct 21, 1968 to Aug 11, 1969
Series 681 "C" (Vietnam)
Aug 11, 1969 to Oct 7, 1970
Series 692 "E" (Vietnam now)
Oct 7, 1970 to now

As we can see from the pattern, Series 691 "D" is missing, and it is speculated by American and Korean collectors that 691 is destined to be used next in Korea. The date of the next MPC change is, of course, unknown, but the recent trend is to change MPC in Korea every three or four years.

MPCs are usually designed with an illustration of a woman's face. These women are imaginary and do not represent any real or famous person (except for certain designs showing the Statue of Liberty). An exception to this pattern was Series 681 which was used in Vietnam between August 1969 and October 1970. Series 681 featured well-designed pictures of soldiers and sailors and their equipment.

Although old MPCs are worthless after the series is changed, collectors (especially myself) have great difficulty locating old MPCs. This seems quite strange since it would be assumed that illegal money changers and other persons would be stuck with large quantities of MPCs during MPC changes. It is known, for example, that during the last MPC change in 1969 that more than one million dollars was not turned in to be redeemed.

Where did it all go? The idea staggers the imagination since it represents a quantity of money which (with $1 notes) if layed end-to-end would stretch from Osan Air Base all the way to Taejon City. The missing MPC could provide every American souvenir hunter in Korea with a lunchbox full of notes. Readers who enjoy solving mysteries might enjoy trying to solve that modern-day mystery which is right at their own doorsteps.

In summary, it is reasonable to suppose that the foreign and Korean readers of this newspaper who have a little patience will have the opportunity to see a new series of this colorful and peculiar currency issued in the near future.

* *

The writer resides in Taegu.

SOFA 재무분과위원회 회의 합의내용

(1972. 9. 8.)

1. APO 의 이동에 따른 군사우편소포검사 절차 개정문제

미측 주장 :

김포 및 오산으로 반입되는 우편소포는 개인 용품이 대부분이나, 부산으로 반입되는 우편소포는 대부분이 군사화물이며 부산을 새로운 검사장으로 지정하기 위하여는 검사시설을 새로히 갖추어야 하는 문제가 있으므로 부산항에 입항하는 우편소포 (군사화물)에 대하여는 Container 에 한.미 공동으로 jointly sealing 을 한다음 김포, 오산으로 보세 운송하여 이곳에서 개장 검사하도록 한다.

한국측 주장 :

1) 군사화물의 반입이 주로 되더라도
2) 부산을 검사장으로 부터 제외할수는 없고
3) 장래의 필요한 경우에 대비되어야 한다.

합의 결과 :

부산항을 possible designated location 으로 지정한다.

73

2. 주한미군용 수입신고서 양식 개정

가. 군사화물 ~~증명~~(수입신고서) 양식 개정 (협정 9조 2항)

양식중 ㊽번의 수입면허난은 "import permitted, date and signature"의 문구를 삽입하기로 합의.

나. 개인용품 수입신고서 양식 제정

미측 주장 :

(제8차 회의) 6?. 5. 27. 과제부여된 household goods and unaccompanied baggage 에 대한 검사절차에 대한 토의가 선행되어야 할것임.

한국측 주장 :

이 문제는 다시 양측 간사의 실무적인 검토에 맡기는 것이 좋을것임. 한국측 주장에 미측도 동의.

3. PX 통제품목의 추가

주류, 연초, 커피를 통제품목으로 할것을 주장하고 주류는 월간 1인당 현행 5 bottles 에서 3 bottles 로 하고 연초는 100 packs 에서 50 packs 으로, 커피는 6 lbs 에서 3 lbs 로 각각 판매수량을 줄일것을 주장. 이에 대하여 미측은 예산상의 이유등으로 난색을 표명하고 한국측은 다시 연초, 커피를 판매량 보고 품목으로 할것으로 주장을 완화하였으나, 이에 대하여서도 미측은 합동위원회로부터의 과제부여가 필요하다는 이유로 결정을 보류, 합의를 보지 못함.

74

SOFA 재무분과위원회 안의 자료

의 제	관 계 규 정	미 측 의 견	한 국 측 의 견	비 고
1. APO 와 이도이 따른 군사 우편소포 검사 절차 개정	제9차 합동위원회에서 지성되고 제64차 및 제66차 합동 위원회에서 부분 개정된 APO 를 통한 군사우편 소포 검사 절차	1) 우편소포 검사장: 김포, 오산 2) 시설문제의 미결에 따라 "부산"도 검사장으로 추가 가능 possible 군사화물만 반입	1) 우편소포 검사장: 부산, 김포, 오산 2) 입항지 세관장의 승인을 얻은 경우 Container 로서 운송 가능(특히 부산이 port of entry로 되는 경우) ~~3) 시설문제:~~ 한미 양측 관계자 현시 조사후 조속한 조치.	
2. 주한미군용 수입신고서 양식 개정	제5차 합동 위원회 지정 SOFA 제9조 2항의 운용은 위한 절차: 합중국 군대가 수입하는 각종 화물의 적절한 증명서와 양식및 제출 방법	1) 협정 제9조 2항에 의한 미군사 화물 증명 양식 개정 찬성 2) 협정 제9조 3항의 개인용품 수입신고 가) 수입신고서 양식: 검토중 나) 세관검사절차: 미측의 편의가 확보 되어야 함 (별첨 참조)	1) 협정 제9조 2항에 의한 미군사화물 증명 양식 개정: 합의안 작성 2) 개인용품 수입신고 가) 신고서 양식: 일반 수입신고서 양식 사용 나) 세관절차: ① 1967. 5. 25 제8차 합동 위원회에서 과제 부여된 시안으로 당 의제와는 분리하여 다루어야 함. ② 개인용품의 세관검사 절차는 한국관세법의 규정을 준수 하여야 함.	import permit, date and signature 검사일자

재 무 부 관 세 국

75

의제	관계규정	미측의견	한국측의견	
3. PX 통제품목의 추가	가. 협정 제9조에 대한 합의 의사록1항: 합중국 군대의 비세출 자금 기관이 ...... 수입하는 물품의 양은 이러한 사용을 위하여 합리적으로 소요되는 한도에 한정되어야 한다. 나. 제65차 합동위 제정: 비세출 자금 기관에 탁송되는 화물에 관한 정보 제공	1) 현재PX 등의 판매제도에 의해 충분한 통제가 가능하며 통제 제도의 개편은 예산상의 이유등 제요인에 의해 곤란함.	1) 주류, 연초, 커피를 통제품목으로 추가 2) 상기 추가품목의 판매수량에 대한 미측의 자율규제 강화 요구 3) 현재의 통제품목을 승인 (LOA) 품목으로 전환 요구	1. Larceny and Black Marketing Subcommittee [illegible] (한국측 통제 [illegible]) 2. [illegible] [illegible] [illegible] ㅇ PX [illegible]

재무부 관세국

126

REPUBLIC OF KOREA - UNITED STATES
FINANCE(PERSONNEL AFFAIRS) SUBCOMMITTEE

8 September 1972

MEMORANDUM FOR : The Joint Committee

1. Subcommittee Members :

United States	Republic of Korea
COL Joseph T. Fordham, USAF	Mr. Park Dong Hee, Chairman
LCDR Robert E. Spydell, USN	Mr. Lee Jae Sup
COL Theodore D. Cameron, USAF	Mr. Kim Kee Joe
COL Robert A. Little, USA	Mr. Kim Ik Taik
COL George F. Proudfoot, USA	Mr. Shin Yung Su
COL Harlan R. Schmidt, USA	Mr. Shin Myoung Ho
COL Willard A. Barnes, USAF	Mr. Lee Jin Moo
LTC William P. Sewell, USA	Mr. Kang Yung Joo
LT David K. Marten, USA	
MR Samuel Pollack	
MR Francis K. Cook	

2. Subject of Recommendation : Review of procedures established by the Joint Committee at its ninth meeting on 5 June 1967, sixty-fourth meeting on 29 July 1971 and sixty-sixth meeting on 23 September 1971, relating to the examination by Republic of Korea Customs Inspectors of parcel post packages delivered through United States military post office channels, contained as Inclosure (6) to the minutes of the ninth Joint Committee meeting, Inclosure (27) to the minutes of the sixty-fourth Joint Committee meeting and Inclosure (25) to the minutes of the sixty-sixth Joint Committee meeting.

3. Recommendation :

a. That paragraphs 2, 3a and 3c(2) of Inclosure (25) to the minutes of the sixty-sixth meeting of the Joint Committee be revised to read :

"2. Notification of Mail Arrival.

a. Customs examination by Republic of Korea officials will be made at the designated ports. The listing of said ports is attached hereto as Inclosure 1.

b. The Commanding Officer in charge of postal affairs at the designated ports will furnish the Republic of Korea customs officials with advance information of bulk mail arrival, approximate volume, and the expected time mail will be available for customs inspection.

0017

c. The containers which contain parcel post packages subject to customs examination by the Republic of Korea customs inspectors can be transported in bond between the designated ports in case the transportation in bond is permitted by the Collector of Customs, Republic of Korea, or his designated representative.

3. Detailed Procedures for Examination :

a. It is mutually agreed that the "sample check" inspection of incoming parcels which are subject to customs examination by the Republic of Korea customs inspectors will take place in facilities as the authorities of the United States Armed Forces shall provide at the designated ports.

c. (2) At the designated ports inspections will be completed sufficiently before the scheduled loading time to permit onward transportation to depart on schedule. When custom officials are not present to designate mail for examination, it will be forwarded to its final destination without delay."

b. It is recommended that Inclosure 1 as follows be added to the abovementioned porcedures relating to the examination of parcel post packages delivered through United States Military post office channels :

"Inclosure 1

1. The following are the currently designated ports where the customs examination by Republic of Korea officials of parcel post packages delivered through United States Military post office channels takes place : Pusan, Kimpo, Osan

2. If a change of designation of ports is needed, it will be informed in advance and coordinated through mutual agreement between the appropriate Republic of Korea and United States authorities."

c. It is further recommended that the effective date of this recommendation be the 1st day of the first month from the month in which it is approved by the Joint Committee.

d. The facilities needed for the conduct of customs examination will be established after an on-the-spot survey by both Secretaries of the Finance/Personnel Affairs Subcommittee.

4. Security Classification : Unclassified.

Mr. Park Dong Hee Chairman, ROK Component Finance Subcommittee	COL Joseph T. Fordham, USAF Chairman, US Component Finance (Personnel Affairs) Subcommittee

76

.08

DRAFT

3. RECOMMENDATION:

a. That paragraphs 2, 3a and 3c(2) of Inclosure (25) to the minutes of the sixty-sixth meeting of the joint committee be revised to read:

"2. Notification of Mail Arrival.

a. Customs examination of parcel post packages by Republic of Korea customs officials will be made at mutually agreed upon designated locations. The listing of the designated locations is attached as Inclosure 3. possible designated

b. The Commanding Officer in charge of postal affairs at the designated locations will furnish the Republic of Korea customs officials with advance information of bulk mail arrival, approximate volume, and the expected time such parcel post packages will be available for customs examination.

c. Containers in which parcel post packages subject to customs examination by Republic of Korea customs officials are located will be transported in bond between the port of entry and designated location for examination. The collector of customs, or his designated representative, at the port of entry shall permit transportation in bond and shall not delay movement of US parcel post in conjunction with issuing such permit.

DRAFT

29

DRAFT

"3. Detailed Procedures for Examination:

a. It is mutually agreed that the "sample check" inspection of incoming parcels which are subject to customs examination by the Republic of Korea customs officials will take place in facilities as the authorities of the United States Armed Forces shall provide at the designated locations.

c. (2) At the designated locations inspections will be completed sufficiently before the scheduled loading time to permit onward transportation to depart on schedule. When customs officials are not present to designate mail for examination, it will be forwarded to its final destination without delay."

b. It is further recommended that the effective date of this recommendation be the first day of the first month from the month in which it is approved by the Joint Committee.

2

DRAFT

80

DRAFT

DESIGNATED LOCATION FOR CONDUCT OF REPUBLIC OF KOREA INSPECTION AND EXAMINATION OF PARCEL POST PACKAGES.

Kimpo

Osan

~~Pusan~~ possible ~~alternate~~

Inclosure 3

DRAFT

81

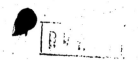

REPUBLIC OF KOREA - UNITED STATES
FINANCE(PERSONNEL AFFAIRS) SUBCOMMITTEE

8 September 1972

MEMORANDUM FOR : The Joint Committee

1. Subcommittee Members :

United States	Republic of Korea
COL Joseph T. Fordham, USAF	Mr. Park Dong Hee, Chairman
LCDR Robert E. Spydell, USN	Mr. Lee Jae Sup
COL Theodore D. Cameron, USAF	Mr. Kim Kee Joe
COL Robert A. Little, USA	Mr. Kim Ik Taik
COL George F. Proudfoot, USA	Mr. Shin Yung Su
COL Harlan R. Schmidt, USA	Mr. Shin Myoung Ho
COL Willard A. Barnes, USAF	Mr. Lee Jin Moo
LTC William P. Sewell, USA	Mr. Kang Yung Joo
LT David K. Marten, USA	
MR Samuel Pollack	
MR Francis K. Cook	

2. Subject to Recommendation: Review of import declaration forms contained in inclosure (5) to the minutes of fifth Joint Committee meeting on 11 April 1967.

3. Recommendation:

a. It is recommended that the forms of import declaration contained in inclosure (5) to the minutes of the fifth meeting of the ROK-US Joint Committee on 11 April 1967, be abolished and the forms attached to this memorandum be approved.

b. It is further recommended that the effective date of this recommendation be the 1st day of the second month from the month in which it is approved by the Joint Committee.

4. Security Classification: Unclassified.

Mr. Park Dong Hee
Chairman, ROK Component
Finance Subcommittee

COL Joseph T. Fordham, USAF
Chairman, US Component
Finance (Personnel Affairs)
Subcommittee

82

REPUBLIC OF KOREA - UNITED STATES
FINANCE(PERSONNEL AFFAIRS) SUBCOMMITTEE

8 September 1972

MEMORANDUM FOR : The Joint Committee

1. Subcommittee Members :

United States	Republic of Korea
COL Joseph T. Fordham, USAF	Mr. Park Dong Hee, Chairman
LCDR Robert E. Spydell, USN	Mr. Lee Jae Sup
COL Theodore D. Cameron, USAF	Mr. Kim Kee Joe
COL Robert A. Little, USA	Mr. Kim Ik Taik
COL George F. Proudfoot, USA	Mr. Shin Yung Su
COL Harlan R. Schmidt, USA	Mr. Shin Myoung Ho
COL Willard A. Barnes, USAF	Mr. Lee Jin Moo
LT David K. Marten, USA	Mr. Kang Yung Joo
MR Samuel Pollack	
MR Francis K. Cook	
LTC William F. Sewell, USA	

2. Subject of Recommendation : Review of import declaration forms contained in inclosure (5) to the minutes of the fifth Joint Committee Meeting on 11 April 1967 and introduction of the new form of declaration on imports consigned to persons subject to the ROK-US SOFA.

3. Recommendation :

a. It is recommended that the forms of import declaration contained in inclosure (5) to the minutes of the fifth meeting of ROK-US Joint Committee on 11 April 1967, be abolished and the forms attached to this memorandum be approved and that the effective date of this revision be the 1st day of the second month from the month in which it is approved by the Joint Committee.

b. According to the ROK-US SOFA and related regulations, the Republic of Korea Customs Administration can apply any declaration forms on imports consigned to individuals subject to the ROK-US SOFA.

c. The customs authorities of the Republic of Korea are planning to use the new declaration form on imports consigned to persons who are subject to the ROK-US SOFA.

83

d. It is further recommended that the mutual cooperation between the Republic of Korea and the US Forces will be made for the introduction of the above mentioned import declaration forms.

4. Security Classification : Unclassified

Mr. Park Dong Hee Chairman, ROK Component Finance Subcommittee	COL Joseph T. Fordham, USAF Chairman, US Component Finance (Personnel Affairs) Subcommittee

84

증산 수출 건설

재 무 부

협력 1243-846 1972. 10. 25.

수신 외무부장관

제목 SOFA제9조 3항에 의한 수입신고서

관세청은 SOFA제9조 3항의 개인용품에 대하여 1972. 11. 1일부터 일괄수입신고서로써 수입신고 하도록 별첨과 같이 조치 하였기 이를 통보 하오니 참고 하시기 바랍니다.

첨부 : SOFA 제9조 3항의 수입신고서에 관한 관세청 공한 사본 1부. 끝.

북미2과	공람	72년 10월 28일	담당	과장	국장	참관보	차관	장관

재 무 부 장

정부공문서 규정 제27조 제2항의 규정에 의하여 관세협력담당관 이재섭 전결

1972.10.25 재무부

외 무 부

접수 일시	197
접수 번호	제 38499 25 OCT 72 14:02
주무과	
담당자	
결재	

83

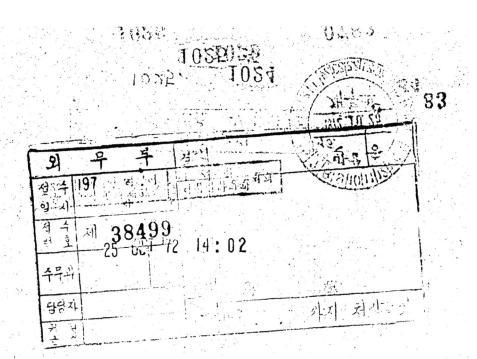

증산 가운 전결

관 세 청

세무 1242 - 2707 (75-3703) 1972. 10. 18.

수신 재무부장관

제목 SOFA 제9조 3항에 의한 수입신고

SOFA 제9조 3항에 의한 수입신고는 72. 11. 1 부터 일반 수입신고서로서 시행토록 별첨과 같이 각 세관에 시달하고 미8군에 조치토록 통보하였음을 보고 합니다.

첨부: 1. 각세관 시달공문 사본 1부.

2. 미8군 통보 공한사본 1부. 끝.

발송 No. 72 10 18 관세청

재무부

접수일시	1972 10 18
접수번호	제 7083
주무과	관세협력과
담당	신 소관현
위임근거	정부공문서규정시행규칙 제2항의규정에의하여

국장 과장

관세청장인

세무국장 송병순 전결

세 청

보존기간 / 폐기 ... 하자

서울 0123

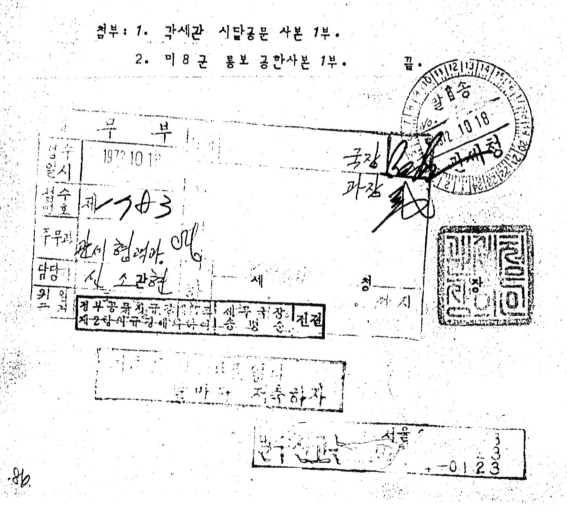

관 세 청

세무 1242 — (75—3703) 1972. 10. 18.

수신 Commanding General
ELGHTH UNIED STATES ARMY
ATTN EAPN APO 96301

제목 sofa 제9조 3항에 의한 수입신고

sofa 제9조 3항에 의한 합중국 군대의 구성원, 군속 및 그들 가족의 가정용품 및 개인물품에 대한 수입신고는 별첨 수입신고서 양식에 의거 72. 11. 1 부터 사용하게 되었으니 관하 각 대에 통보하여 차질이 발생되지 않토록 협조 바랍니다.

첨부: 수입신고서 견본 5 부. 끝.

관 세 청 장

187

Office of Customs Administration

Taxation Section 1242-2702 (75-3703) 18 October 1972

TO: Commanding General
Eighth United States Army
ATTN: EAPM
APO 96301

SUBJECT: Imports Declaration of Paragraph 3, Article 9, SOFA

In accordance with the Paragraph 3, Article 9 of the SOFA, members of the United States Armed Forces, DAC and their dependents customs declaration for household goods and personal effects, should used the attached imports declaration form (sample), effective date 1 November 1972. Inform all of your units, your cooperation is required for prevention of problems.

Director
Customs Administration

88

관 세 청

세무 1242 - (75-3703) 1972. 10. 18.

수신 Commanding General
ELGHTH UNIED STATES ARMY

ATTN EAPN APO 96301

제목 sofa 제 9 조 3 항에 의한 수입신고

sofa 제 9 조 3항에 의한 합중국 군대의 구성원, 군속 및 그들 가족의 가정용품 및 개인물품에 대한 수입신고는 별첨 수입신고서 양식에 의거 72. 11. 1 부터 사용하게 되었으니 관하 각 대에 통보하여 차질이 발생되지 않도록 협조 바랍니다.

첨부: 수입신고서 견본 5 부. 끝.

관 세 청

89

재무

통관 수출 전신

관 세 청

심비 1245-1216 1972. 10. 31.

수신 주한 미군 사령관

참조 참모장

제목 비 SOFA 대상자에 대한조치

귀하와 귀하 관계기관의 당청의 관세행정 업무에 관심을 가지고 협조하여 주신데 대하여 사의를 표하는 바입니다.

1. SOFA 제1조에 의거 대한민국 영역안에 주둔한 현역에 복무하는 합중국 군대의 구성원, 군속 및 그들의 가족과 제15조에 의한 초청계약자에 한하여 제9조 및 제13조에 명시된 미군사 우체국과 비세출자금 기관의 이용권을 부여하게 되어 있는바,

2. 미8군 당국은 다음에 열기한 비 SOFA 대상자에게 SOFA에 의한 신분증과 레손부 레이트를 교부하여 주고 SOFA 대상자로 취급하고 비세출 자금기관과 미군사 우체국의 이용권 및 SOFA에 의한 차량등록 등 면세특권을 부여 함으로서 면세특권을 악용하여 많은 외국물품이 시장에 유출되고 있어 이는 SOFA 협정에 위배됨은 아니라 국가경제 발전에 막대한 지장이 있음으로 이를 조속히 시정 조치하여 주시기 바랍니다.

다 음

1. 상당수에 달하는 주월 미군 가족 1054
(주로 국제결혼한 한국출신 부인)

171 ic
266 dep.

2. 상당수에 달하는 미군제대 군인 400

3. 상당수에 달하는 고용 계약이 끝난 초청 계약자

관 세 청

1030

저축의 날 따로 없다 절약하자 · 저축하자!

발수신 ... 부산 4 = 0123

90

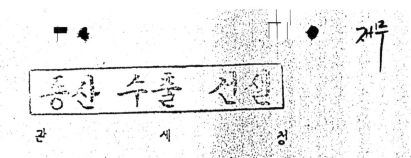

미군 화물수송에 사용되는 유류구입에 대한 면세문제

1. SOFA 제16조 3항에 규정된 "현지조달" (local procurement) 에 따르는 석유류세등의 면세를 위하여는 다음의 요건을 충족하여야 함.

   (가) 합중국 군대 또는 그 공인 조달기관이 대한민국 공급자로 부터 직접 조달하는 품목이어야 하며, (제 16조에 대한 합의의사록 4항)

   (나) 합중국 군대의 최종 소비 사용을 위하여 (for ultimate use)조달되는 품목이어야 한다. 여기서 "최종 소비 사용을 위하여 조달되는 품목" 이라함은 (합중국 군대가 사용하는 물품이나 시설에)"통합될 품목" 이거나 또는 "최종 생산품의 생산을 위하여 필요한 품목" 을 의미한다. (전기 합의의사록 4항)

2. 미군 화물 수송을 위하여 한국 상사등이 소비하는 석유류의 구입은,

   (1) 전기 (가)항의 합중국 군대가 대한민국 공급자로 부터 직접 조달하는 경우로 볼수가 없고,

   (2) 합중국 군대가 사용하는 물품이나 시설에 "통합될 품목" 또는 "최종 생산품의 생산을 위하여 필요한 품목" 에도 해당되지 않음.

3. 따라서 전술한 유류구입은 국내과세 관계법령의 적용을 받게되며, SOFA 규정에 의한 면세는 허용되지 않는것으로 사료됨.

북미2과	공람	72년 11월 17일	담당	과장	국장	참관보	차관	장관
			(서명)	(서명)	(서명)			

국제조세과 3223
~~[illegible]~~ 조윤걸 과장
3

재무부 관세과 89
민종식 씨 4/10.

91

~~동~~산 수출 건설

재 무 부

관세 1235-1068 7?-3??2 1972. 7. 16.

수신 서울특별시 중구 중부로 2가 9

건양기업주식회사 대표이사 손 ? ?

제목 석유류세 면제에 대한 질의

미군용물자수송에 소요되는 유류에 대한 면세 요청.

1. 건기 제 호 (72. 7. 1?)에 대한 회신입니다.

2. 본건의 경우 한미행정협정 제11조 및 제16조의 규정에 의한 석유류세 면세는 공인 조달기관을 포함한 합중국 군대가 대한민국 안에서 공용을 위하여 조달하는 석유류 또는 합중국 군대의 최종소비자를 위하여 조달하는 석유류에 한하는 것이오니 양지하시기 바랍니다. 끝.

재 무 부 장 관

1972. 7. 19
재무부

저축의 날

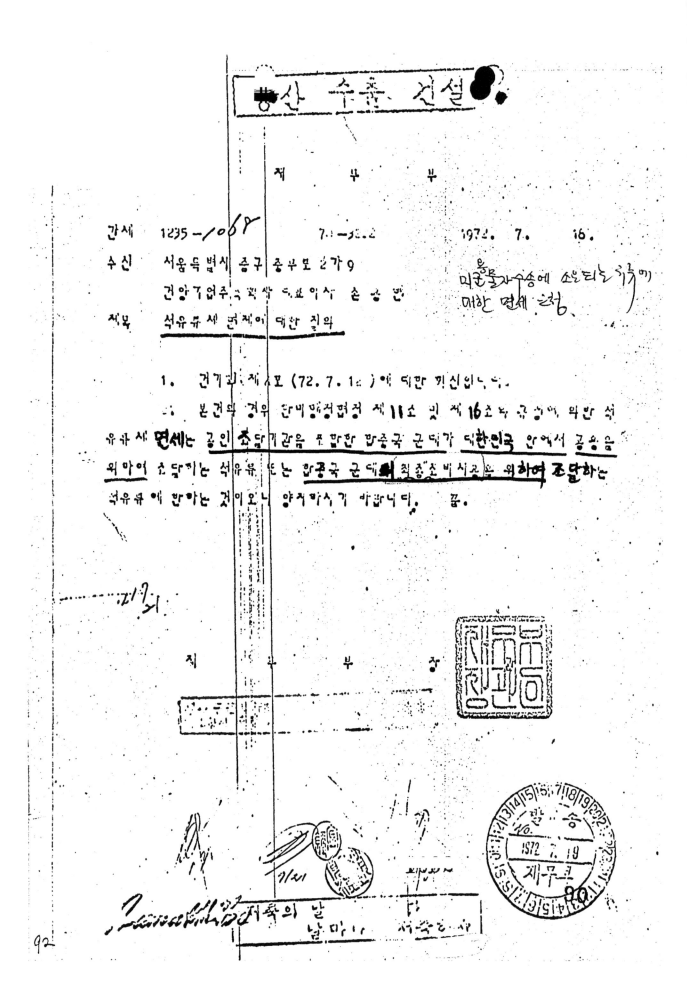

[illegible] 1487 [illegible] 1972.9.[illegible]

[illegible]

제목 미군 화물 수송을 위한 구입 연료의 면세 신청

1. 한전 제 175호 (72.9.9)에 대한 회신 입니다.

2. 현행 법상 미군 화물 수송용 석유류의 면세는 [illegible]

관세국장

93

Joint Committee approve these four new assignments for the Facilities and Areas Subcommittee. The ROK Representative stated that his Government agreed to the assignment of these new tasks to the subcommittee.

10. The ROK Representative presented a request for release of real estate located at #65-4 3-ka Han Kang No, Yongsan-ku, Seoul, (Inclosure 10). He proposed that the Joint Committee request the Facilities and Areas Subcommittee to submit its recommendation on this assignment. The US Representative concurred.

11. The US Representative proposed one additional assignment for the Commerce Subcommittee (Inclosure 11). Paragraph 3 of Article XVI of the SOFA provides that materials, supplies, equipment and services procured for official purposes in the Republic of Korea by the United States Armed Forces, including their authorized procurement agencies, or procured for ultimate use by the United States Armed Forces, shall be exempt from certain taxes upon appropriate certification in advance by the United States Armed Forces. The US Representative proposed that the Commerce Subcommittee present recommendations on the procedures and format under which such certification would be accomplished. The US Representative requested ROK approval for the assignment of this new task to the Commerce Subcommittee and the ROK Representative concurred.

12. The US Representative proposed agreement on the joint press release, which had been developed by the ROK and US Secretaries (Inclosure 12), and requested the ROK Representative's comments. The ROK Representative agreed with the press release, which was mutually approved for release.

13. The US Representative proposed the next Joint Committee meeting be held on Thursday, 11 May, at 1500 hours, at the ROK Capitol Building and the ROK Representative concurred.

14. The ROK Representative stated that before the sixth Joint Committee meeting was adjourned that he wished to express his gratitude on behalf of both his colleagues and himself for the detailed and enlightening briefing presented by the US Representative earlier that afternoon. The ROK Representative said that this was a most effective briefing which would be helpful to the Joint Committee in its future work. Mr. Yoon also stated that he wished to announce that Mr. KIM Ock, who had been the Secretary of the Commerce Subcommittee,

6th JC
28 Apr 67

공 란

공 란

공 란

공 란

공 란

공 란

공　　란

공 란

공 란

공 란

공 란

공 란

공 란

공 란

공 란

공　　란

공 란

공 란

증산 수출 건설

별첨 0/2

관 세 청

세무 1242 - 2920 (75-3703) 1972. 11. 17.

수신 외무부장관

제목 SOFA 제 78 차 한.미 합동위원회 회의록

1. 미이 723 -34916 (72. 11. 6) 호에 관련된 것 입니다.

2. 본건과 관련하여 당청해당 사항을 별첨과 같이 각 세관에 조치 하였음을 통보 합니다.

첨부: 각세관 시달공문 사본 1부. 끝.

발송 No. 11 17 관세청

관 세 청

관세청장인

전부공무서규정제27조 제2항의규정에의하여	세무국장 송병순	전결

0812

1052

저축의 날 따로 없다 날마다 저축하자

113

밀수신고는 110 서울 28-0123 인천 3-0123 부산 4-0123

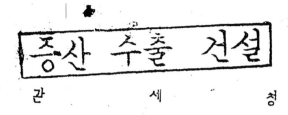

외 무 부		18 NOV 72 11:36	
접수일시	197 . . . 시	결재	
접수번호	제 41809		
주무과			
담당자			
위임근거			

. . .까지 처리할것

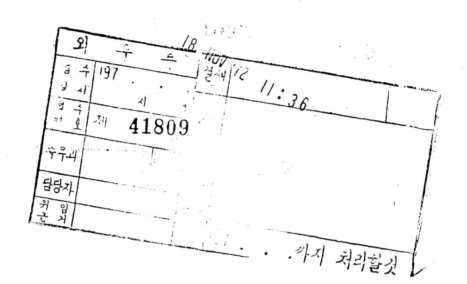

관 세 청

세무 1242 - (75-3703) 1972. 11. 16.

수신 수신처 참조

제목 SOFA 제78차 한.미 합동위원회 회의록

1. SOFA 제78차 한.미 합동위원회가 72. 10. 5 개최 되었는바 동 위원회의 합의 사항중

가. SOFA 제9조 제2항 (주한미군 수입품)에 대한 수입신고서가 별첨과 같이 승인되어 72. 12. 1 부터 시행토록 합의 되고

나. "SOFA 제9조 합의 양해사항 1-4 에서 규정한 APO를 통한 우편소포에 대한 한국세관 검사절차" 가 별첨과 같이 개정 합의 되었음을 통보하니 업무처리에 차질이 없도록 할것. (72. 11. 1 시행)

첨부: 1. 주한미군용 수입신고서 1매

2. 한미군대 지위협정 제9조 합의 양해사항 1-4 에서 규정한 미군사 우체국을 통한 우편소포에 대한 한국세관 검사절차 개정 원문 1부. 끝.

관 세 청 장

114

수신처: ㄴ.

[redacted]

2. 입항 Date of Entry 19	부호 Code No.	대한민국 세관 Korean Customs Service	11. 세관부호 Customs Code No.
3. 선하증권번호 B/L No.			12. 수입종별 Sort of Import
4. 적재선(기)명 Name of Vessel(Aircraft)			13. 신고번호 Declaration No.
적재선(기) 국적 Nationality of Vessel(Aircraft)		주한 미군용 수입 신고서 Import Declaration/Certification USFK, ROK-US SOFA	15. 신고 Date of Declaration 19
5. 적출국(지) Country of Shipment			계 / 주무 / 과장
6. 입항지 Place of Entry			기
7. 생산지.원산국(지) Country of Production			재
8. 장치장소 Place of Storage			

21. 품명 및 규격 Description of Articles & Grade	22. 중량 Weight	23. 수량 Quantity	24. 단위 Unit	25. 신고가격 Declared Value	27. 세번 Heading	28 부호 Code No.
(1)				CIF $		
(2)				CIF $		
(3)				CIF $		
35. 비고 Remarks / 계 Total				CIF $		

45. 기호, 번호, 포장종류와 개수
Markings, Numbering, Type and Number of Packages

상기 물품은 SOFA 제9조 제2항에 의거 주한 미군용으로 수입되는 것임을 증명함.

I hereby certify the import of the above goods for use of USFK in accordance with the ROK-US SOFA, Article IX, Paragraph 2.

신고자 성명
Name and Signature of Declarant

통관장교 서명
Signature of Customs Clearance Officer

신고자 주소
Address of Declarant

부대명
Department

48. 첨부서류
Attached herewith if any
송품장
Invoice
포장명세서
Packing List
원산지 증명
Certificate of Origin
운임명세서
Freight Sheet
보험영수증
Receipt of Insurance
선하증권 사본
Copy of B/L
기타
Others

47. 면허 및 면허 일자
Import Permitted,
Signature and Date

210mm x 300mm

115

PROCEDURES RELATING TO EXAMINATION BY REPUBLIC OF KOREA CUSTOMS INSPECTORS OF PARCEL POST PACKAGES DELIVERED THROUGH UNITED STATES MILITARY POST OFF-ICE CHANNELS WITH REGARD TO ARTICLE IX, AGREED UNDERSTANDING, SUBPARAGRAPH I THROUGH 4 OF THE STATUS OF FORCES AGREEMENT.

개 정 전	개 정 후
I. a. . . . . . the United States Operations Mission (USOM-K) 2. Notification of Mail Arrival The Commander, 1st Base post Office, Inchon, and the Commanding Officer in charge of postal affairs at Kimpo and Osan Air Bases will furnish the Republic of Korea Customs Officials with advance information of bulk mail arrival, and approximate volume, and the expected time mail will be available for customs inspection.	I. a. . . . . . the United States Operations Mission-Korea(USOM-K) 2. Notification of Mail Arrival: a. Customs examination of parcel post packages by Republic of Korea customs officials will be made at mutually agreed upon designated locations. The listing of the designated and possible designated locations is attached as Inclosure I. b. The Commanding Officer in charge of postal affairs at the designated locations will furnish the Republic of Korea customs officials with advance information of bulk mail arrival, approximate volume, and the expected time such parcel post packages will be available for customs examination. c. Containers in which parcel post packages subject to customs eximination by Republic of Korea customs officials are located will be transported in bond between the port of entry and designated locations for eximination. The collector of customs, or his designated representative, at the port of entry shall permit transportation in bond and shall not delay movement of US parcel post in conjunction with issuing such permit.

개 정 전	개 정 후
3. a. . . . by the Republic of Korea customs inspectors will take place in facilities of the 1st Base Post Office at Inchon and in the space as the authorities of the United States Armed Forces shall provide at Kimpo and Osan Bases."	3. a. . . . by the Republic of Korea customs officials will take place in facilities as the authorities of the United States Armed Forces shall provide at the designated locations.
c. (2) At Inchon and at Kimpo and Osan Air Bases	c. (2) At the designated locations . . . . . .
4. . . . . " Form, at inclosure I, by	4. . . . . " Form, at Inclosure 2, by . . . . .
5. c. . . . . as Inclosure 2.	5. c. . . . . as Inclosure 3.

117

DESIGNATED LOCATIONS FOR CONDUCT OF REPUBLIC OF KOREA

INSPECTION AND EXAMINATION OF PARCEL POST PACKAGES

Kim Po

O San

POSSIBLE DESIGNATED LOCATION FOR CONDUCT OF ROK

INSPECTION AND EXAMINATION OF PARCEL POST PACKAGES

Pu San

(Incl 1)

118

DESIGNATED LOCATIONS FOR CONDUCT OF REPUBLIC OF KOREA

INSPECTION AND EXAMINATION OF PARCEL POST PACKAGES

Kim Po

O San

POSSIBLE DESIGNATED LOCATION FOR CONDUCT OF ROK

INSPECTION AND EXAMINATION OF PARCEL POST PACKAGES

Pu San

(Incl 1)

119

개 정 전	개 정 후
Subject : Record on Condition of parcel	Subject : Record on Condition of parcel
(Incl 1)	(Incl 2)
35 개 지정품목	35 개 지정품목
(Incl 2)	(Incl 3)

20

ITT International Electric Corporation
A Subsidiary of ITT

BOX 112 JUSMAG-K (AF SECTION)
APO SANFRANCISCO 96276

November 1972

Honorable Minister,
Ministry of Foreign Affairs
Republic of Korea
Seoul, Korea

Dear Sir:

ITT Far East Pacific, respectively request permission to give a donation of surplus electronic parts which was left over from our Up-Grade/Modification effort for the ROKAF under USAF Contract number F34601-71-C-0134 completed this year. This surplus parts etc. came in Country duty free in support of the above mentioned contract.

We wish to donate these electronic parts to the Korea Advanced Institute of Science and or to the Yonsei University. Please refer to a copy of Mrs. Gertrude Ferrar's letter which is attached for your information. We would like to make this presentation if at all possible sometime this month. These parts will not be used in any way contrary to or in violation of any existing ROK laws, regulations or customs.

Sincerely Yours,

Burton G. Schetzle
ITT/IEC Representative
Box 87
JUSMAG-K, AF Section
APO San Francisco 96483

외 무 부		결재	
접수일시	1972.12.5. 시 분	지시사항	
접수번호	제4546호		
주무과			
담당자			
위 근			. . 까지 처리할 것

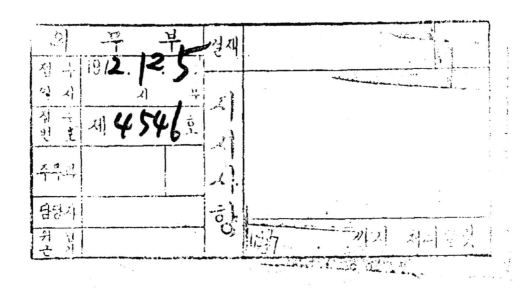

International Electric Corporation
A Subsidiary of ITT

BOX 112 JUSMAG-K (AF SECTION)
APO SANFRANCISCO 96276

November 1972

Honorable Minister,
Ministry of Foreign Affairs
Republic of Korea
Seoul, Korea

Dear Sir:

ITT Far East Pacific, respectively request permission to give a donation of surplus electronic parts which was left over from our Up-Grade/Modification effort for the ROKAF under USAF Contract number F34601-71-C-0134 completed this year. This surplus parts etc. came in Country duty free in support of the above mentioned contract.

We wish to donate these electronic parts to the Korea Advanced Institute of Science and or to the Yonsei University. Please refer to a copy of Mrs. Gertrude Ferrar's letter which is attached for your information. We would like to make this presentation if at all possible sometime this month. These parts will not be used in any way contrary to or in violation of any existing ROK laws, regulations or customs.

Sincerely Yours,

Burton G. Schetzle

Burton G. Schetzle
ITT/IEC Representative
Box 87
JUSMAG-K, AF Section
APO San Francisco 96483

122

JOINT COMMITTEE
UNDER
THE REPUBLIC OF KOREA AND THE UNITED STATES
STATUS OF FORCES AGREEMENT

December 9, 1972

addressed to H.E. the Foreign minister,

Dear Mr. Schetzle:

I wish to acknowledge the receipt of your letter regarding your offer to donate ~~surplus~~ electronic parts etc. to a Korean institute. On his behalf, I wish to thank you for your thoughtfulness.

Since ITT Far East Pacific holds the status of a U.S. invited contractor under the provisions of the ROK-US Status of Forces Agreement, your ~~could make a~~ donation of such goods ~~as imported duty-free into the Republic of Korea, if you make application,~~ and obtain approval, ~~in accordance with~~ the procedures adopted by the ROK-US Joint Committee at its 10th session on June 22, 1967, which ~~are available either at this Ministry, North America Section II, or at the USFK, J5.~~

~~I am appreciative of your thoughtfulness.~~

shall be regulated by

a copy of is attached herewith for your reference. Your applications for the donation and acquisitions of an approval from the Office of Customs Adm is required.

Sincerely yours,

For the Minister

Kim Dong-Whie
Republic of Korea
Representative
ROK-US Joint Committee

~~According to the procedure, your application and~~

1062

Burton G. Schetzle
ITT/IEC Representative
Box 87
JUSMAG-K, AF Section
APO San Francisco 96483

북미2과	고재	72년 12월 일	담당	과장	국장	차관보	차관	장관
			[signature]	[signature]				

In this regard, this Ministry has made explanations to officials of on the goods to MK.

123

JOINT COMMITTEE
UNDER
THE REPUBLIC OF KOREA AND THE UNITED STATES
STATUS OF FORCES AGREEMENT

December 9, 1972

Dear Mr. Schetzle:

I acknowledge receipt of your letter regarding your offer to donate surplus electronic parts etc. to a Korean institute.

Since ITT Far East Pacific holds the status of a U.S. invited contractor under the provisions of the ROK-US Status of Forces Agreement, you could make a donation of such goods as imported duty-free into the Republic of Korea, if you make application, and obtain approval, in accordance with the procedures adopted by the ROK-US Joint Committee at its 10th session on June 22, 1967, which are available either at this Ministry, North America Section II, or at the USFK, J5.

I am appreciative of your thoughtfulness.

Sincerely yours,

For the Minister

Kim Dong-Whie
Republic of Korea
Representative
ROK-US Joint Committee

Burton G. Schetzle
ITT/IEC Representative
Box 87
JUSMAG-K, AF Section
APO San Francisco 96483

124

JOINT COMMITTEE
UNDER
THE REPUBLIC OF KOREA AND THE UNITED STATES
STATUS OF FORCES AGREEMENT

December 14, 1972

Dear Mr. Schetzle:

I wish to acknowledge the receipt of your letter addressed to H.E. the Foreign Minister, regarding your offer to donate electronic parts etc. to a Korean institute. On his behalf, I wish to thank you for your thoughtfulness.

Since ITT Far East Pacific holds the status of a U.S. invited contractor under the provisions of the ROK-US Status of Forces Agreement, your donation of such goods shall be regulated by the procedures adopted by the ROK-US Joint Committee at its 10th session on June 22, 1967, a copy of which is attached herewith for your reference. Your application for the donation and acquisition of an approval from the Office of Customs Administration ~~is~~ are required.

In this regard, officials of this Ministry have made explanations on the goods which have been imported into, or purchased in, the Republic of Korea duty-free may be transferred by sale or donation, as a single item or group of items...to Mr. Moon Young Chul, Vice President of Korea Advanced Institute of Science.

Sincerely yours,

~~For the Minister~~

Kim Dong-Whie
Republic of Korea
Representative
ROK-US Joint Committee

Burton G. Schetzle
ITT/IEC Representative
Box 87
JUSMAG-K, AF Section
APO San Francisco 96483

북미2과	기안	12 14	담당	과장	국장			

125

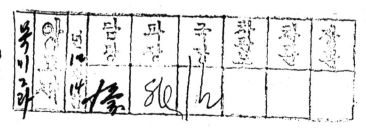

JOINT COMMITTEE
UNDER
THE REPUBLIC OF KOREA AND THE UNITED STATES
STATUS OF FORCES AGREEMENT

December 14, 1972

Dear Mr. Schetzle:

I wish to acknowledge the receipt of your letter addressed to H.E. the Foreign Minister, regarding your offer to donate electronic parts etc. to a Korean institute. On his behalf, I wish to thank you for your thoughtfulness.

Since ITT Far East Pacific holds the status of a U.S. invited contractor under the provisions of the ROK-US Status of Forces Agreement, your donation of such goods shall be regulated by the procedures adopted by the ROK-US Joint Committee at its 10th session on June 22, 1967, a copy of which is attached herewith for your reference. Your application for the donation and acquisition of an approval from the Office of Customs Administration is required.

In this regard, officials of this Ministry has made explanations on the goods which have been imported into, or purchased in, the Republic of Korea duty-free may be transferred by sale or donation, as a single item or group of items...to Mr. Moon Young Chul, Vice President of Korea Advanced Institute of Science.

Sincerely yours,

For the Minister

Kim Dong-Whie
Republic of Korea
Representative
ROK-US Joint Committee

Burton G. Schetzle
ITT/IEC Representative
Box 87
JUSMAG-K, AF Section
APO San Francisco 96483

126

2. 1973년

1217

주한 외국공관원에 대한 미군 비세출자금기관 이용 특전 부여

1. 관계 규정

SOFA 제13조1항 및 제 13조 에 대한 합의의사록

2. 비세출자금기관 이용권자

가. SOFA 제 13조 제 1항에 의한 이용권자

(1) 합중국 군대의 구성원, 군속 및 그 가족

* Technical Representative 도 군속으로 간주됨. (합동위 14차회의에서 합의)

나. SOFA 제 15조 에 의한 초청계약자와 그 가족 (1967. 2. 7. 이후 입국한 제 3국인 제외)

다. SOFA 제 13조 합의의사록 에 의한 이용권자

(1) 통상적으로 이와같은 특권이 부여되는 합중국 정부의 기타 공무원 및 직원 (미대사관, USAID)

* 합동위 28 차회의에서 다음 자들도 이 범주 에 포함되는 것으로 밝혀짐.

북미2과	공람	73년 1월 9일	담당	과장	국장	참관보	차관	장관
			[signature]	[signature]	[signature]	[signature]	✓	1

✓ 사본 의비담당관 관계부처 회의에서 협의 지시

128

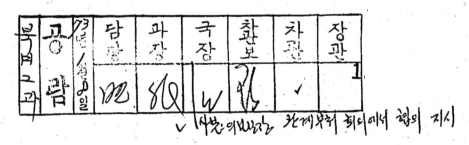

가) 퇴역군인과 그 가족

나) 전몰장병 미망인 (재혼전)과 그 자녀

다) 타지역 주둔 미군인의 가족 (주월 미군중 한국인 부인등이 많음)

라) 한국을 통과하는 기타 PX 특권 보유자의 가족 (90일간 한정)

(2) 합중국 군대로부터 군수 지원을 받는 통합사령부 산하 주한 외국군대 및 그 구성원 (유엔 참전국군)

(3) 대한민국 국민이 아닌자로서 그의 대한민국 에서의 체류목적이 합중국정부 에 의하여 재정적 지원을 받는 계약용역의 이행만을 위한자 (미국 정부 와의 계약자 - 미 대사관 및 USAID 와의 계약자, 미 원조 계획에 의한 계약자)

(4) 미 적십자사, USO 와 같은 주로 합중국 군대의 이익이나 용역을 위하여 대한민국에 체류하는 기관 및 대한민국 국민이 아닌 직원 (미국의 Service Organizations)

(5) 전 각항에 규정된자의 가족

(6) 대한민국 정부의 명시적인 동의를 얻은 기타 개인과 기관.

129

3. 현재 SOFA 제13조 합의의사록 (바)항에 의하여 대한민국 정부의 명시적인 동의를 얻음으로써 예외적으로 이용권이 부여된 기관은 다음과 같음.(합동위 제1차 회의 1967. 2. 9. 에서 동의)

가. 국제연합 한국 통일부흥 위원단 (15명)

나. 국제연합군 묘지관리단 (2명)

다. 중립국 휴전 감시위원단 (18명)

이 유

(1) 국제연합 한국 통일부흥 위원단

가) 한국의 부흥과 통일을 위하여 한국에만 특별히 파견된 유엔의 기관임.

나) 한국의 대유엔외교에 있어서 차지하는 비중이 매우 큼.

다) 주한 유엔군과 밀접한 관계가 있음.

(2) 국제연합군 묘지관리단

가) 유엔군 묘지관리를 위하여 한국에만 특별히 파견된 유엔의 기관임.

나) 주한 유엔군의 일부분으로 간주될수 있을 정도로 유엔군과 밀접한 관계가 있음.

(3) 중립국 휴전 감시위원단

가) 휴전감시를 위하여 한국에만 특별히 주재하는 기관임.

나) 주둔위치가 휴전선지역에 있기 때문에 주한미군에 전적으로 의지하지 않을수 없음.

130

4. 주한 외국 공관원에 대한 이용권 부여 문제

가. 방 안

SOFA 제13조 합의의사록 (바)항을 원용, 주한~~미군당국~~의 요청에 의거, 이들에 대한 명시적 동의를 부여함.

나. 문 제 점

(1) 기타기관 및 개인도 형평의 원칙을 주장하여 상술한 기관의 이용권을 요청하는 사례가 발생하게 될것임. (UNICEF, UNDP 등도 이용권을 요청한 사례가 있음.)

(2) 허용범위의 문제

가) 공관장 및 그 배우자만 허용하는 경우

나) 참사관 이상 및 그 배우자만을 허용하는 경우

다) 외교단 전원 및 그 배우자

다. 관계 관청

외무부, 재무부, 상공부

라. 협의 절차

SOFA 합동위원회 재무분과위원회에 과제 부여

마. 조 건

(1) 출입 PX 를 지정할것

(2) 개인별 구매액수를 매월 보고도록 할것.

131

(3) 단가 $ 10 이상 품목 구입시는 본인의 판매 ticket 에 서명토록 할것. (?)

(4) 텔레비존, 냉장고, 전축, 소제기등 특수상품은 3년 1회에 한하여 구입토록 할것.

(5) 당해 대사관의 본국에 주재하는 아국 공관직원에 대하여도 동일한 특혜를 부여할 것이라는 공문상의 보장을 받은후 관계 대사관의 PX 이용을 허가할것. (상호주의 원칙 적용)

132

협 조 문

응신기일

분류기호 및 문서번호	미이 723	제 목	주한 외국 공관원의 미군 P.X. 이용 요청에 관한 대책 회의
수 신	방교국장, 의전실장	발신일자	1973. 1. 17. (협조제의)

(참조) (조약과장) (의전과장)

양고(시)	담당	과장	국장	차관보	차관	장관

발신명의 구미국장

(제 1 의 견)

표제건에 관한 관계부처간의 대책회의를 다음과 같이 개최하오니 참석 바랍니다.

1. 회의 일시 및 장소 : 73. 1. 23 (화) 14:00시 외무부 회의실

2. 참석범위 :

재무부 (관세협력과장, 국제조세과장, 관세조정과장)

(제 2 의 견)

상공부 (수출 3과장)

관세청 (심리과장, 세무과장)

국세청 (소비세과장, 외국인세과장)

외무부 (북미 2과장, 조약과장, 의전과장)

첨부 : 회의자료 1 부. 끝.

0120-1. -2B
1969. 11. 10승인

190mm×268mm(신문용지)
(조달청) 300,000매인쇄

제 13조 1항

(가) 합중국 군 당국이 공인하고 규제하는 군 판매점, 식당, 사교클럽, 극장, 신문 및 기타 비세출 자금 기관은 합중국 군대의 구성원, 군속 및 그들의 가족의 이용을 위하여, 합중국 군대가 설치할수 있다. 이러한 제 기관은, 본 협정에 달리 규정하는 경우를 제외하고는 대한민국의 규제, 면허 수수료, 조세 또는 이에 유사한 관리를 받지 아니한다.

(나) 합중국 군 당국이 공인하고 규제하는 신문이 일반 대중에 판매되는 때에는 그 배포에 관한한 대한민국의 규제, 면허, 수수료, 조세 또는 이에 유사한 관리를 받는다.

134

(분류번호 미이 723-28)

기 안 용 지

분류기호 문서번호	미이 723 - 28	(전화번호)	전결규정 조 항 국장 전결사항
처리기간			
시행일자	1973. 1. 17.		
보존년한		국 장	
보조기관	과 장	협	의전실장
기안책임자	변승국	북미 2 과	
경유 수신 참조	수신처 참조	발신 (발송 1973. 1. 17 외무부)	통제 (1973. 1. 18 통제관)
제 목	주한 외국 공관원의 미군 P.X. 이용 요청에 관한 대책회의		

주한 외국 공관원의 미군 P.X. 이용 요청에 관한 관계부처간 회의를 73. 1. 23. (화) 14:00 시 외무부 회의실에서 개최하오니 각부처 관계관을 필히 참석토록 하여주시기 바랍니다. (4층 420회의실)

첨부 : 회의자료 1 부. 끝.

수신처 : 재무부장관 (관세협력과, 국제조세과, 관세조정과)

상공부장관 (수출 3과)

관세청장 (심리과, 세무과)

국세청장 (소비세과, 외국인세과)

법무국 조약과장, 의전실 의전과장

정서 / 관인 / 발송

160

공통서식1-2 (갑) 1967. 4. 4. 승인

190mm ×268mm (1급인쇄용지70g/m²) 조달청 (500,000매 인쇄)

135

AMBASSADE
DE
BELGIQUE

北美2課 : PX 문제

Seoul, January 8, 1973

Dear Dean and Colleague,

I wish to refer to the statement I made at the monthly luncheon of heads of foreign missions, at the Japanese Embassy on January 4th 1973, in connection with the priveledge of obtaining supplies from the PX stores and commissaries which is granted to some of our colleagues and is not to others.

In this connection I would like to emphasize the following points:

1. As I pointed out, I did not raise the problem in its principles, since some of the colleagues were absent. I merely thought it was timely to underline the latest practical developments of the situation; these can be summarized as follows:

   a. As for imports of foodstuffs, drinks and other products, three sources of supplies are available to some colleagues, four to others:

      - direct and duty free import from abroad: All heads of missions.
      - local economy: "
      - Foreign commissaries: "
      - PX stores and commissaries: Heads of missions of country members of UNCURK.

   b. At the present time, local economy is still insufficient to enable most colleagues to cope with the necessities of their usual daily life and to properly fulfill their social and official commitments.

   c. On the other hand it is impossible for many of us, if not all, to import all the products (perishables, particularly) we need, unless the necessary space and means would be available to set up a warehouse in the respective residences!

129

./.

136

d. Lately, supplies in Korean foreign commissaries have drastically and progressively deteriorated to such an extent that basic items such as butter, margarine, cheese, oil, tea, cereals, ham, lemons, etc. etc. are unavailable in any of them.

e. Whereas some colleagues can solve problems b, c. and d. above, by legally purchasing from PX stores and commissaries, others unfortunately are unavoidably compelled to reluctantly resort, in many instances, to a source of supply of which they disapprove as much as all concerned authorities do.

3. You have appreciated the problem and very kindly undertaken to bring it up with the competent authorities. I wish to thank you sincerely for it.

4. In this respect, I would like to express a few personal ideas:

a) It is, in my view, important to ascertain first, if the difference made between UNCURK heads of missions and others, originates in a decision of the US authorities. If the answer is affirmative, it could only be taken up by the Dean, in an unofficial way. Were it to be taken up officially with the US authorities, the necessary steps should then be made bilateraly by each diplomat concerned, if he deems it fit.

b) If the present situation derives from a decision of the Korean government, it is my opinion that the Dean should raise the question officially with them (on behalf and with the previous approval of all the heads of foreign missions residing in Seoul, as usual) and make the appropriate representations to re-establish equality of treatment.

./.

137

- 3 -

This letter is personal, My dear Dean, and intended only for your information and consideration. Should you deem timely however to use all or part of its content with our colleagues and/or the US and/or Korean authorities, I have no objection to it.

Yours sincerely and faithfully,

With warm personal regards,

J.F. Trine
Ambassador

To His Excellency
Benjamin Tria Tirona
Ambassador of the Philippines
Dean of the Diplomatic Corps
Seoul.

138

기 안 용 지

분류기호 문서번호	미이 723 -	(전화번호)	전결규정 조 항 국장 전결사항
처리기간			
시행일자	1973. 2. 1.		
보존년한		국 장	

보조기관	과 장		협 조
기안책임자	변승국	북미 2 과	

경 유 수 신 참 조	수신처 참조	발 신	통 제 1973. 2. 2.

제 목 주한 외국 공관원의 미군 P.X. 등 이용요청에 관한 대책회의

연 : 미이 723 - 28 (73. 1. 17.)

지난 73. 1. 23. (화) 개최 예정이던 주한 외국 공관원의 미군 P.X. 등 이용 요청에 관한 관계부처간 회의가 ~~다음과 같이~~ 연기 개최 ~~되오니, 아래 각 부처~~ 관계관의 빠짐없는 참석을 바랍니다.

1. 변경 일시 : 73. 2. 7. (수) 14:00
2. 장 소 : 외무부 회의실 (4층 420호실)

수신처 : 재무부장관 (관세협력과, 국제조세과, 관세조정과)

상공부장관 (수출 3 과)

관세청장 (심리과, 세무과)

국세청장 (소비세과, 외국인세과)

외무부 (조약과, 의전과)

정서 관인 발송

공통서식1-2(갑) 1967. 4. 4. 승인

190mm×268mm(1급인쇄용지70g/㎡) 조달청 (500,000매인쇄)

139

기 안 용 지

분류기호 문서번호	미이 723 -	(전화번호)	전결규정 조 항 국장 전결사항
처리기간			
시행일자	1973. 2. 5.		국장
보존년한			
보조기관	과 장		협조
기안책임자	변승국	북미 2 과	
경유 수신 참조	총무처장관 총무국장	발신	통제
제목	회의실 사용 협조 의뢰		

주한 외국 공관원의 미군 P.X. 등 이용 요청에 관한 관계 부처간 회의 개최를 위하여 귀부 회의실 (501호실) 사용을 요청하오니 협조 바랍니다.

1. 회의일시 : 73. 2. 7. (수) 14:00
2. 참석인원 : 10 명 끝.

정서

관인

발송

1973. 2. 5
3693
외무부

검열 1973. 2. 5 통제관

공통서식1-2(갑)
1967. 4. 4. 승인

190mm ×268mm (1급인쇄용지70g /m²)
조달청 (500,000매 인쇄)

140

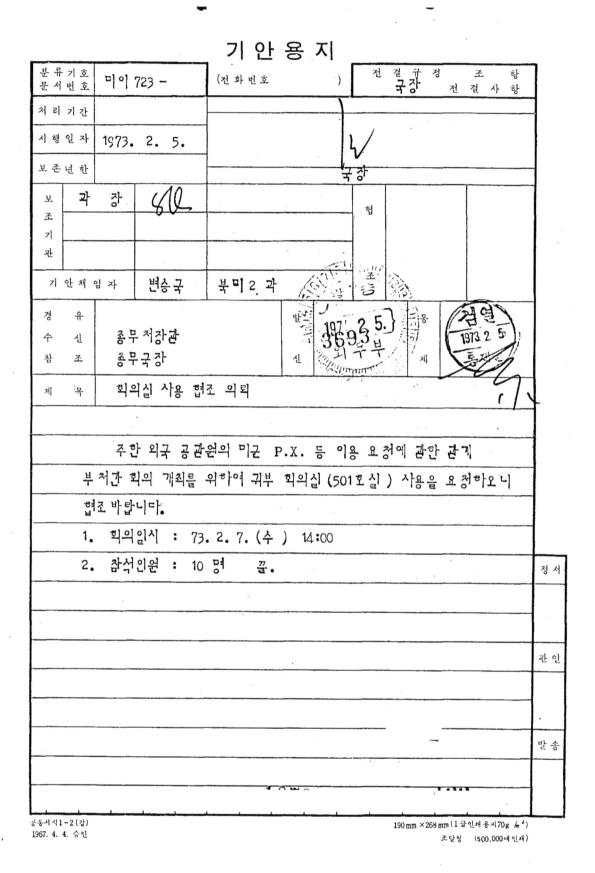

협 조 문	응신기일

분류기호 및 문서번호: 미이 723 - 12

제목: 주한 외국공관원의 미군 P.X 등 이용 요청에 관한 대책회의

수신: 의전실장, 방교국장

발신일자: 1973. 2. 5. (협조제의)

참조: 의전과장, 조약과장

북미 2과	양고재	73년 2월 5일	담당	과장	국장	차관보	차관	장관
			(서명)	(서명)	(서명)			

발신명의 미주국장

(제 1 의 견)

연 : 미이 723 -

지난 73. 1. 23.(화) 개최 예정이던 주한 외국공관원의 미군 P.X 등 이용 요청에 관한 관계부처간 회의가 다음과 같이 연기 개최되오니, 참석을 바랍니다.

1. 변경일시 : 73. 2. 7. (수) 14:00
2. 장 소 : ~~외무부 회의실~~ 총무처 회의실 (501호실)
3. 참석범위 : 재무부 (관세협력과, 국제조세과, 관세조정과) (의 견)
   상공부 (수출 3과)
   관세청 (심리과, 세무과)
   국세청 (소비세과, 외국인세과)
   외무부 (북미 2과, 조약과, 의전과) 끝.

0120-1.-2B
1969.11.10승인

190mm×268mm(신문용지)
(조달청) 300,000매인쇄

141

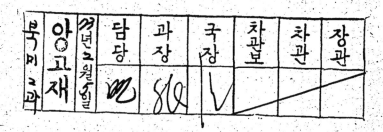

관 세 청

심리 1245-215 (75-3796) 1973. 2. 5.

수신 수신처 참조

제목 밀수방지 종합대책(행정적인 제재) 시행에 따른 제2차 실무자회의 개최

1. 밀수방지 종합대책에 따른 행정적 제재 시행에 관한 제2차 관계부처 실무자회의를 다음과 같이 개최코자 하오니 필히 참석하여 주시기 바랍니다.

(1) 일 시 : 1973. 2. 6. 14:00

(2) 장 소 : 감시국 회의실

(3) 참석범위 : 상공부 상역국 수출기획과장
법무부 출입국관리국 입국심사과장
외무부 북미2과장 끝.

발송 No. 1973. 2. 5. 관세청

관 세 청

수신처 : 상공부, 법무부, 외무부

정부공문서규정 제27조 제2항의 규정에 의하여	감시국장 송대진 전결

밀수신고 : 28-0123 / 3-0123 / 부산 4-0123

주한 외국공관원에 대한 미군 비세출자금기관 이용

특전 부여

1. 관계 규정

SOFA 제 13조 및 제 13조에 대한 합의의사록

2. 비세출 자금 기관 이용권자

가. SOFA 제 13조 제 1항에 의한 이용권자

(1) 합중국 군대의 구성원, 군속 및 그 가족

* Technical Representative 도 군속으로 간주됨. (합동위 14차회의에서 합의)

나. SOFA 제 15조에 의한 초청계약자와 그 가족 (1967. 2. 7. 이후 입국한 제 3국인 제외)

다. SOFA 제 13조 합의의사록에 의한 이용권자

(1) 통상적으로 이와같은 특권이 부여되는 합중국 정부의 기타 공무원 및 직원 (미대사관, USAID)

* 합동위 28차회의에서 다음 자들도 이 범주에 포함되는 것으로 밝혀짐.

143

가) 퇴역군인과 그 가족

나) 전몰장병 미망인(재혼전)과 그 자녀

다) 아직역 주둔 미군인의 가족 (주월 미군중 한국인 부인등이 많음)

라) 한국을 통과하는 기타 PX 특권 보유자의 가족 (90일간 한정)

(2) 합중국 군대로부터 군수지원을 받는 통합사령부 산하 주한 외국군대 및 그 구성원 (유엔 참전국군)

(3) 대한민국 국민이 아닌자로서 그의 대한민국에서의 체류목적이 합중국정부에 의하여 재정적 지원을 받는 계약용역의 이행만을 위한자 (미국정부와의 계약자 - 미 대사관 및 USAID 와의 계약자, 미 원조계획에 의한 계약자)

(4) 미 적십자사, USO 와 같은 주로 합중국 군대의 이익이나 용역을 위하여 대한민국에 체류하는 기관 및 대한민국 국민이 아닌 직원(미국의 Service Organizations)

(5) 전 각항에 규정된자의 가족

(6) 대한민국 정부의 명시적인 동의를 얻은 기타 개인과 기관.

144

3. 현재 SOFA 제13조 합의의사록 (바)항에 의하여 대한민국 정부의 명시적인 동의를 얻음으로써 예외적으로 이용권이 부여된 기관은 다음과 같음. (1967. 2. 9. 합동위 제1차 회의에서 동의)

가. 국제연합 한국 통일부흥 위원단

나. 국제연합군 묘지관리단

다. 중립국 휴전 감시위원단

이 유

(1) 국제연합 한국 통일부흥 위원단

가) 한국의 부흥과 통일을 위하여 한국에만 특별히 파견된 유엔의 기관임.

나) 한국의 대유엔외교에 있어서 차지하는 비중이 매우 큼.

다) 주한 유엔군과 밀접한 관계가 있음.

(2) 국제연합군 묘지관리단

가) 유엔군 묘지관리를 위하여 한국에만 특별히 파견된 유엔의 기관임.

나) 주한 유엔군의 일부분으로 간주될수 있을 정도로 유엔군과 밀접한 관계가 있음.

(3) 중립국 휴전 감시위원단

가) 휴전감시를 위하여 한국에만 특별히 주재하는 기관임.

나) 주둔위치가 휴전선지역에 있기 때문에 주한미군에 전적으로 의지하지 않을수 없음.

145

4. 주한 외국 공관장에 대한 이용권 부여 문제

가. 방 안

SOFA 제 13조 합의의사록 (바)항을 원용, 주한미군당국의 요청에 의거, 이들에 대한 명시적 동의를 부여함.

나. 문 제 점

(1) 기타기관 및 개인도 형평의 원칙을 주장하여 상술한 기관의 이용권을 요청하는 사태가 발생하게 될것임.
(UNICEF, UNDP 등도 이용권을 요청한 사태가 있음.)

(2) 허용범위의 문제

가) 공관장 및 그 배우자만 허용하는 경우
나) 참사관 이상 및 그 배우자만을 허용하는 경우
다) 외교단 전원 및 그 배우자

다. 관계 관청

외무부, 재무부, 상공부

라. 협의 절차

SOFA 합동위원회 재무분과위원회에 과제 부여

마. 조 건

(1) 출입 PX 를 지정할것
(2) 개인별 구매액수를 매월 보고토록 할것.

146

(3) 단가 $ 10 이상 품목 구입시는 본인의 판매 ticket 에 서명토록 할것.

(4) 텔레비죤, 냉장고, 전축, 소제기등 특수상품은 3년 1회에 한하여 구입토록 할것.

(5) 당해 대사관의 본국에 주재하는 아국 공관직원에 대하여도 동일한 특혜를 부여할 것이라는 공문상의 보장을 받은후 관계 대사관의 PX 이용을 허가할것. (상호주의 원칙 적용) ?

147

Inc. 를 指名하였다. 美國代表는 이招請契約者 雇傭員中 美國市民權 所有者에 對한 關係資料는 相互 合意한 節次에 따라 韓美合同委員會를 經由 韓國政府에 提供될 것이라고 말하였다.

韓國代表는 美國招請契約者 Pacific Architects and Engineers, Inc.의 通告를 接受하는바이라고 말하였다.

10. 美國代表는 1967年 9月 20日頃 開通하게 될 것이라고 見聞하고 있는 第一漢江橋로 부터 金浦街道 東南方入口를 連結하는 道路의 通行料 徵收에 따른 駐韓美軍所屬車輛의 地位에 關聯된 覺書를 提出코자 한다고 말하였다(別添 8)

이覺書의 目的은 大韓民國에서 이와 같은 새로운 計劃에 關聯하여 軍隊地位協定 施行을 원활하게 하기爲한 것이며 該當協定 條項에 關하여 두政府의 立場이 다음과 같이 完全 合意하고 있는 것이라고 말하였다.

가. 美軍 車輛은 協定 第10條 第2項에 따라 通行料나 其他 手數料로 부터 免除된다.

나. 駐韓美軍要員과 駐韓美軍 招請契約者들의 個人所有 車輛은 새로운 公路의 標準 通行料를 支拂하여야 한다. 美國代表는 合同委員會가 第14次 會議錄에서 本件에 關한 前記 方針을 確認토록 建議하였다.

11. 韓國代表는 美國의 軍用車輛은 永登浦區에 開設되는 道路의 通行料나 其他 手數料로 부터 免除된다는 美國代表의 主張에 全的으로 同意하는 바이라고 말하였다. 따라서 그는 協定 第10條 第2項의 解釋錯誤로 惹起될지도 모르는 不必要한 混亂 可能性을 除去하기 爲하여 必要한 措置를 取하겠다고 말하였다. 그러나 韓國代表는 道路 保全과 無害通過의 目的으로 有料道路에 課할지도 모르는 諸制限을 駐韓美軍 要員들이 遵守하여야 할 問題等에 關하여 合同委員會에서 諒解되기를 바란다고 말하였다. 프리드만 中將은 自己가 理解하기로는 韓國代表가 말씀하는 것은 重量級추럭이나 其他 大型車輛等의 有料道路 通過等을 指摘하는 것으로 안다고말하고 美國代表는 韓國代表에게 駐韓美軍은 如斯한 制限을 尊重하고 有料道路에 異例的인 重量級 車輛(駐韓美軍의것)의 通過를 制限시키겠음을 保障한다고 말하였다. 韓國代表는 美國代表의 發言이 바로 自己가 생각하고 있던 것이라고 말하고 美國代表의 論評에 感謝한다고 말하였다.

12. 美國代表는 合同委員會 第14次會議錄에 駐韓美軍司에 勤務하는 「技術代表」의 地位를 明白히 하려는 發言要旨를 삽입시켰으면 좋겠다고 말하였다.

그는 說明하기를 美國政府는 複雜한 軍事裝備의 整備를 위하여 特別한 技術이 必要하고 또한 駐韓美軍이나 韓國에서 採用할수 없는 사람으로 美軍이나 韓國要員의 特別講師와 顧問으로 「技術代表」를 雇傭하고 있다고 말하였다. 駐韓美軍의 方針에 關한 訓令에서 「技術代表」는 協定 第15條 履行을 爲한 駐韓美軍의 招請契約者 名單에 包含되어 있지 않기 때문에 軍屬의 一員으로 取扱하고 있다. 美國代表는 따라서 이들「技術代表」를 協定 第1條(나)에서 말하는 駐韓美軍의 軍屬으로 確認해주도록 提議하였다. 韓國代表는 合同委員會 公式會議錄에 「技術代表」는 駐韓美軍의 軍屬이라고 確認하는 美國代表의 提案에 同意하였다.

13. 美國代表는 合同委員會 次期會議를 1967年 9月 28日 木曜日 15.00時 中央廳에서 開催하자고 提議하였으며 韓國代表가 同意하였다.

14. 美國代表는 第14次 會議의 共同發表文을 提示하였고, 韓國代表는 發表文案에 全的으로 同

148

공 란

34. 한국대표는 이 기회를 이용하여 1968년 6월21일자 한국대표의 서한에서 한국은 한미군대지위협정에 규제하고 있는 미군요원들에 대한 형사재판권행사에 있어서 「최대한 억제」하겠다는 성명을 계속 견지하겠다는 점에 미국대표의 주의를 환기하고 싶다고 말하였다.

35. 현재 미결중에 있는 사건에 대한 재판권을 미국당국에 돌려달라는 미국대표의 특별 요청에 관하여, 한국대표는 이요청을 한국정부의 관계당국이 주의깊이 검토할 것이라고 말하였다.

36. 미국대표는 미국측 성명에 대한 한국대표의 회답과 고려에 대하여 사의를 표시하였다.

37. 미국대표는 군대지위협정 제15조하 3명의 신규 초청계약자 지명을 한국정부에 통고하는 각서를 동합위원회에 제출하였다. 주한 미군사령부는 한국측 상무분과위원회 요원들과 협의한 후 Lyon Associates, Incorporated(첨부21) : Daniel, Mann, Johnson & Mendenhall(첨부22) : Trans-Asia Engineering Associates, Incorporated(첨부23)을 미국초청계약자로 지명하였다. 미국대표는 이들 초청계약자의 고용원들에 대한 관계자료는 상호승인된 절차에 따라 한국 정부에 제공될 것이다.

38. 한국대표는 3개 미국업자 즉 Daniel, Mann, Johnson & Mendenhall. Lyon Associates, Inc., 그리고 Trans Asia Engineering Associates, Inc.에 대한 주한미군초청계약자 지명에 관한 미국측 통고를 확인하면서 협의에 대한 합의절차가 이들 지명에 있어서 준수되었음을 확인하게 되어 기쁘다고 말하였다.

39. 한국대표는 상무분과위원회의 건의를 설명하였다. 그는 인천시가 수도 공급시설 확장과 관련하여 주한미군초청계약자인 Trans-Asia Engineering Associates, Inc.의 용역을 이용할 계획을 가지고 있으며, 실제 교섭이 진행중에 있다고 말하였다(첨부24). 이러한 계획은 군대지위협정 제16조 제2항(나)에 포함된 제한문제를 야기케 하는바, 상무분과위원회는, 본건에 있어서, 1967년 8월 14일 합동위원회 제12차 회의에서 Collins Radio Company와 관련하여 확립된 선례와 초청계약자의 지위를 가지고 한국정부와의 다른 업무를 수행할 때의 모순점을 제거하는 조문해석을 Trans-Asia Engineering Associates, Inc.에 그대로 적용토록 건의해 왔다. 한국 대표는 동분과위원회의 건의를 합동위원회가 승인하도록 제의하였다.

40. 미국대표는 상무분과위원회의 건의에 동의하였으며, 한국정부를 위한 계약에 소요되는 추가인원은 군대지위협정하 군수지원이나 특권의 대상이 되지 않는다는 점에 유의하였다.

41. 한국대표는 다음의제는 군대지위협정 제13조 시행에 관한 것으로 정식으로 각서를 제출하는 바이라고 말하였다(첨부25).

42. 한국대표는 협정 제13조 제1항(가)에 의하면 피-엑스 식당, 사교장, 극장, 신문사 기타 미군당국에 의하여 허가되고 규제되는 비세출기관을 미군당국이 군대구성원 군속 및 그들의 가족들에 사용시킬 목적으로 설립할수 있다고 규정한 점에 유의하였다. 그는 또한 제13조에 대한 합의의사록은 주한미군이 제13조 제1항에 참조된 기관의 사용을 다음 사람들에게 부여할 수있다고 규정한 점에 유의하였다.

가. 통상적으로 이와 같은 특권이 부여되는 합중국 정부의 기타 공무원 및 직원,

나. 합중국 정부로부터 군수지원을 받는 통합사령부 산하 주한 외국군대 및 그 구성원,

150

0

다. 대한민국 국민이 아닌 자로서, 그의 대한민국에서의 체류 목적이 합중국 정부에 의하여 재정적 지원을 받는 계약용역의 이행만을 위한 자,

라. 미적십자사, 유·에스·오와 같은 주로 합중국 군대의 이익이나 용역을 위하여 대한민국에 체류하는 기관 및 대한민국 국민이 아닌 직원,

마. 전 각호에 규정된 자의 가족, 및

바. 대한민국 정부의 명시적인 동의를 얻은 기타 개인과 기관.

43. 한국대표는 피·엑스 특권남용을 통제하기 위한 미국당국의 최신의 노력을 상술하고 있는 1968년 2월 22일의 미 제8군 규칙 제60-1(EA Reg. 60-1)에 언급하였다. 동규정의 부록1 「피·엑스 보급증 자격 명단과 배급증 발급기관」에 의하면 다음 범주의 사람들을 포함하고 있다.

√「(11) 퇴역 미군요원」

「(14) 다음요원의 재혼하지 않은 미국시민 미망인과 그들의 가족 육, 해, 공군 요원으로 복무기간 임장중에 사망한자, 훈련중의 예비역요원, 및 군표사용허가를 받은 제대군인요원」

√「(15) 배우자가 한국에 주둔하고 있지 않은 미군요원의 가족 (16, 17, 18항의 제한을 받음」

√「(15차) 제대 미군요원의 가족」

「(15가) 별도로 피·엑스와 군표특권이 부여된 한국동과 가족. 이 특권은 90인을 초과할수 없음.」

44. 한국대표는 상기 범주에 속하는 사람들에 피·엑스 특권을 부여하는데 대한 인간적이고 박애주의적인 고려는 이해하고 있으나 한국정부는 군대지위협정 제13조에는 차범주에 속하는 사람들에게 적용될 해당 규정을 발견하기가 어렵다고 말하면서 미국은 다음과 같은 대안중 택일을 요구하였다.

가. 군대지위협정을 적용할 수 있는 만족할만한 설명을 하거나,

나. 제13조에 대한 합의의사록 제(바)항에 따른 한국정부의 명백한 승인 요청.

45. 미국대표는 제13조에 대한 합의사록에 따라 피·엑스 이용자격자 범주에 관한 한국대표의 견해를 접수하는 바이며, 주한미군은 일반적으로 군대지위협정을 이행하는데 특히 제13조에 대한 합의사록을 이행하는데 있어 한국정부와 긴밀한 협조를 하는데 모든 노력을 해 왔다. 미국측 해석으로는 한국대표의 가서 3항에서 문제시한 피·엑스 특권소지자의 범주는 제13조에 대한 합의의사록 세항(가)에 적용되는 것으로 생각한다. 군대지위협정 미국측 교섭 정대표가 1963년 5월 3일 제21차 교섭회의에서 한국교섭자에게 통보한 바와같이 「통상적으로 이러한 특권이 부여된」이라는 문구가 이 세항에 있어서 구속력 있는 것이다. 그는 이 문구는 미세출 자금시설 이용의 특권을 통상적으로 부여받고 있는 퇴역군인을 포함하고 있다고 특별히 지적하였다. 한국대표가 문제시한 기타 범주도 역시 「통상적으로 이러한 특권을 부여받은」에 속한다.

미국대표는 본 군대지위협정조문 이행은 주한미군에 의하여 모든 관계 요소를 신중하고 주의깊게 고려하면서 완수하고 있다는 신념을 말하였다.

그러나 미국 대표단은 한국정부관리들과 이들에 대하여 검토할 기회를 가지게 되어 기쁘며 원한다면 한미 군대지위협정 간사들이 양국정부에 관계관리들간에 회의를 마련할 수 있으며, 14

151

에 가서 주한미군 관계관이 본건에 관한 미국 입장의 기본을 구체적으로 설명하고 상호 의견을 교환할 수 있을 것이다.

46. 합동위원회 미측대표단은 제13조에 대한 합의의사록 세항(바)에 규정한 비세출자금시설 이용특권 부여에 있어서 예외적 조처로 한국정부의 명시적 승인을 요청하지는 않겠다는 일반적입장을 취하고 있다.

한국정부는 제13조에 대한 합의의사록 세항(바)에 따른 비세출자금기관의 이용특권을 부여받은 개인이 극도로 제한되고 있는 결과로 이 문제에 관하여 대체로 동일한 입장을 취하였다.

47. 한국대표는 미국대표의 설명에 사의를 표하고 동문제는 우호적인 이해를 가지고 타결될수 있을 것이라고 시사하였다. 그는 계속해서 주한미군이 제13조에 대한 합의의사록 세항 (바)에 따라 비세출자금기관에 예외적 출입권에 대한 한국정부의 명시적 승인을 요청한다면 한국정부로서는 아무런 문제가 없을 것이라고 말하였다. 미국대표는 여러 종류의 기관에서 특권요청을 한바 있었으나 번번히 거절되었음을 시사하였다. 그는 의견 차이는 상호협의를 거쳐 해결한수 있으리라는 희망을 표시하였다.

48. 미국대표는 군대지위협정의 규정과 합동위원회 결정에 따라 한국측 군대지위협정 간사에게 다음 자료를 미국측 간사가 제공하였음을 기록하도록 유의하였다.

가. 1968년 5월분 주한미군사건 처리 보고서 5부

나. 1968년 5월분 주한미군 구성원, 군속, 초청계약자 및 그들 가족의 출입국 보고서 20부

다. 국가비상시 긴요하다고 간주하는 미 제8군 및 해군의 한국인 고용원의 개정된 명단 2부

이 명단은 군대지위협정 제17조 5항(나)의 규정에 따라 한국측에 사전에 제공한바 있음. 주한공군과 주한 미초청계약자에서 일하는 주요 한국인 노무자의 개정된 명단은 가까운 장래에 제공하겠음.

49. 한국대표는 군대지위협정 한국측 간사가 미국측 간사로 부터 열거한 제서류를 정히 접수하였음을 확인하는 바이라고 말하였다.

50. 미국대표는 다음 회의를 미국측 군대지위협정 회의실에서 8월 14일(목요일)에 개최하자는 제안에 동의하였다.

그는 또한 다음회의전에 발생한 긴급 조치는 확립된 절차에 따라 양대표의 긴급 조처로서 취급하도록 제안하고 싶다고 말하였다.

본건과 관련하여 그는 1967년 4월 28일 상무분과위원회에 부여한 "제16조, 대한민국내에서의 구매에 대한 면세라는 과제"의 완수를 조속 타결해야 한 것에 유의하였다.

미국대표는 본건에 관한 분과위원회건의를 다음 합동위원회회의 전에는 완수되기를 희망하였으며 또한 가능하다면 건의안을 긴급조치로 양대표가 승인하자는 희망을 표시하였다.

51. 한국대표는 오래동안 미결중에 있는 과제와 더불어 언급된 과제의 조치가 진척되어 합동위원회 절차에 따라 긴급과제로 건의를 취급하는데 동의하였다.

52. 한국대표는 한미 양측 간사가 준비한 공동 발표문의 승인을 제안하였으며, 미국대표는 제안된대로 공동발표문의 채택에 동의하였다.

162

41. The ROK Representative stated that the next agenda item concerned implementation of Article XIII, SOFA, on which subject the ROK Representative presented a formal memorandum (Inclosure 25).

42. The ROK Representative noted that paragraph 1(a), Article XIII provided that military exchanges, messes, social clubs, theaters, newspapers and other nonappropriated fund organizations authorized and regulated by the US military authorities may be established by the US armed forces for the use of members of such forces, the civilian component and their dependents. He also noted that the Agreed Minute to Article XIII provides that the US armed forces may grant the use of the organizations referred to in paragraph 1 of Article XIII to:

a. Other officers or personnel of the US Government ordinarily accorded such privileges;

b. Those other non-Korean armed forces in the ROK under the Unified Command which receive logistical support from the US armed forces, and their members;

c. Those non-Korean persons whose presence in the ROK is solely for the purpose of providing contract services financed by the US Government.

d. Those organizations which are present in the ROK primarily for the benefit and service of the US armed forces, such as the American Red Cross and the United Service Organizations, and their non-Korean personnel;

e. Dependents of the foregoing; and

f. Other persons and organizations with the express consent of the ROK Government.

43. The ROK Representative referred to the Eighth United States Army Regulation Number 60-1 (EA Reg. 60-1) of 22 February 1968, which embodied the best efforts of the US authorities to control abuse of Post Exchange privileges. Inclosure 1 to the regulation, "Post Exchange Ration Card Eligibility List and Issuing Agencies of Ration Cards," included the following categories of persons:

"(11) Retired US military personnel."

"(14) Widows (US citizens) who have not remarried and their dependents of the following: Members of the uniformed services, who die on extended active duty; _

28th JC
995 3 July 68

063

These minutes are considered as official documents pertaining to both Governments and will not be released without mutual agreement.

members of reserve components, inactive duty for training, or inactive duty training; and retired personnel, provided they are authorized the use of MPC."

"(15 d) Dependents of US military personnel whose sponsor is not stationed in Korea. (With limitations, 16, 17, and 18)."

"(15 j) Dependents of retired military personnel."

"(15 k) Dependents otherwise authorized exchange and MPC privileges who are transient in Korea. Privileges will be limited to a period not exceeding 90 days."

44. The ROK Representative stated that, while recognizing human or humanitarian considerations involved in granting PX privileges to these categories of persons the Government of the ROK hardly finds relevant provisions in Article XIII, SOFA, which may be applicable for each of the categories. The ROK Representative requested that the US will take one of the following alternative actions for each of the categories;

a. To give satisfactory explanations for applicability of the SOFA provisions; or

b. To request express consent of the ROK Government in accordance with paragraph (f) of the Agreed Minutes to Article XIII.

45. The US Representative stated he was pleased to receive the views of the ROK Representative regarding the categories of personnel eligible to utilize Post Exchanges, in accordance with the Agreed Minute to Article XIII. The US armed forces in Korea have made every effort to cooperate closely with the ROK Government in the implementation of the SOFA in general, and specifically in this case, in the implementation of the Agreed Minute to Article XIII. It has been the United States' interpretation that the categories of personnel provided PX privileges, which is questioned in paragraph 3 of the ROK Representative's memorandum, in general are covered by subparagraph (a) of the Agreed Minute to Article XIII. As the chief US SOFA negotiator informed the ROK negotiators, at the twenty-first negotiating session on 3 May 1963, the phrase "ordinarily accorded such privileges" was the binding one in this subparagraph. He specifically indicated that this phrase included retired military personnel, who were ordinarily accorded the privilege of utilizing non-appropriated fund facilities. The other categories of personnel questioned by the ROK Representative were also "ordinarily accorded such privileges."

28th JC
3 July 68

996

154

외 무 부

년 2 월 10 일

北美2課長,

1. 本日 儀典室長의 요청 協助要請을 外交團에 ② Milk 와 ④ Butter 만이라도 PX 搬出 制限이 若何 하는 問議임.

2. 外交團의 事項에는 變動이 없음.

3. [illegible] 意見을 [illegible]

4. 外交團의 요청을 [illegible]

155 구 미 국 장 [illegible].

0856

외 무 부

년 월 일

5. 記錄 作成 → 儀典室長에게 송부. [illegible] 不可 [illegible]

6. Miller Butler의 경우도 如此히 갈 것 같으나

但, 當 [illegible]의 위반은의. 추가 기록 [illegible].

(서명)

156

구 미 국 장

북미2과	공람	[redacted] 2월 8일	담당	과장	국장	참관보	차관	장관
			[redacted]			출장중	[redacted]	[redacted]

회 의 록

[illegible] 결론에 동의함

1. 의 제 : 주한 외국 공관원에 대한 미군 비세출자금기관 이용

2. 회의일시 및 장소 : 1973. 2. 7. 1400 - 1500 미주국장실

3. 참석자 : 외무부 미주국장 김동휘
   " 북미 2과장 김기조
   " 의전과 한종희
   " 조약과 이 야
   재무부 관세협력과 원윤묵
   " 국제조세과 장세윤
   국세청 소비세과 김제윤
   " 외국인세과 허성두
   관세청 징수과 송창학
   상공부 수출 3 과 전철순

(기록 : 북미 2과 변승국)

4. 관계부처 의견 종합 :

외 무 부

(현황 설명 및 회의 주재)

1) 최근 주한 외교단의 공식, 비공식 회합에서 이 문제가 빈번히

157

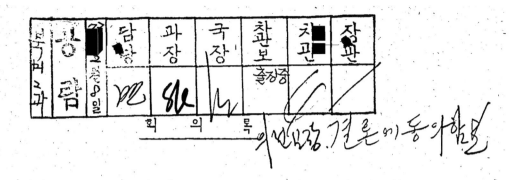

거론된바 있으며, 이에 따라 주한 외교단장인 비율빈 대사의 공식 요청을 받게되었는데, 이들은 현재 예외적으로 이용권이 허용되고 있는 3개 기관 (UNCURK , 국제연합 묘지관리단, 중립국 휴전감시위원단)과의 형평을 요구하여 동일한 특혜를 줄것을 요청하고 있음.

2) 현재 SOFA 협정에 의한 사용권자는,

가) SOFA 제 13조 에 의한 원칙적 이용권자 (군인, 군속 및 그 가족, Technical Representative 도 군속으로 간주됨)

나) SOFA 제 15조 에 의한 초청계약자와 그 가족

다) SOFA 제 13조 합의 의사록에 의한 예외적 이용권자등 3개 범주가 있음.

3) 이 문제에 대한 미측의 견해는 일단 회의적 (개인적 의견임을 명시) 이라고 볼수가 있으나, 미측으로서는 물량적 공급태세를 검토해 보겠으며, 기타 제도적, 법적문제는 한국측에서 검토해 주기를 요청한바 있음.

4) 타국의 예를 볼것같으면 자유중국만이 참사관 이상에 대하여 이용권을 허용하고 있고, 일본이나 불란서의 경우는 전혀 이용권을 주지않고 있음. 독일의 경우도 대체로 이용권을 허용하지 않는것을 원칙으로 하고 있으며, 극히 사소한 특권 (예 : 극장 출입)만이 허용되어 있을뿐임.

158

5) SOFA 제 13조 합의의사록 (바) 항에 의하면 한국정부가 명시적 동의를 함으로써 PX 사용권을 부여할수도 있으나, 이러한 특권부여에 따르는 제반 문제, 예컨대 제도적 또는 법적근거에 관한 문제, 국내시장에 대한 물품 유출과 이를 방지하는 문제, 기타 우리 경제에 미치는 영향이나 세부절차에 이르기까지 각 부처의 기탄없는 의견을 제시해 줄것을 요청함.

(미주국)

1) 이러한 특권 확장에는 현실적으로 여러 곤란한 문제가 있겠으나 국내시장에서 구입할수 없는 물품을 모두 외국으로 부터 직접 수입해서 쓰자면 상당한 시간적, 금전적 부담을 지게 되는것도 사실이므로 각국 대사에 한해서 제한된 범위내의 이용을 허여하는것도 좋을것임.

2) 또한 이들 대사들은 UNCURK 회원국 대사에게만 특혜를 주는것은 차별대우가 아니냐는 불만을 표시하고 형평의 원칙에 입각한 동등한 특권 부여를 요청하고 있음.

(의전과)

재무부

1) 주한 외국 공관원에 대하여 미군 PX 등 비세출자금기관 이용권을 부여하는것은 미군 물품의 부정유출을 방지하려는 SOFA 의 근본취지에 어긋남.

159

2) 상호주의 원칙을 적용한다고 하나, 미군이 주둔하지 않는 지역에서는 이 원칙의 적용은 무의미하게 됨.

3) 현재 예외적으로 이용권을 부여하고있는 3개기관 (UNCURK, 국제연합군 묘지관리단, 중립국 휴전감시위원단)에 대한 특권부여에는 이들 기관이 모두 한국통일등 특수목적을 위하여 한국에만 특별히 파견된 기관이라는 상당한 이유가 있었으나 ~~(별첨 참조)~~, 주한 외국공관원에 대한 특권부여 이유는 납득되지 않음.

4) 주한 외국 공관원에 대하여 이러한 특권을 부여하게 되는 경우, 물품구입의 결제방법은 어떻게 되는가? (예컨대, 이들 공관원에 대하여도 미군표 사용을 허용할 것인지?)

(관세협력과)

1) 현재 주한 외국 공관원 및 그 가족에 대하여는 면세 혜택을 주고있으며, 외국인을 위한 기타 특수물품이라면 현재 Foreigner's Commissary 가 개설, 이용되고 있으며, 외국으로 부터의 직접 수입도 가능하므로 이들에 대하여 또 다시 미군 PX 이용까지 허용할 필요는 없을것임.

(국제조세과)

160

국 세 청

1) 대체로 재무부 의견에 동의하며 상기 3개 기관에 대한 이용권 부여는 상당한 이유가 있다고 보나, 이들 주한 공관원에 대한 이용권 부여는 이해할수 가 없으며, 물품 유출등 여러 곤란한 문제가 있을것으로 봄.

(외국인세과)

1) 미군 PX 물품 판매에 대하여 간접세를 부과해야 하겠으나 실제상 이들에 대한 검사권이 미치지 못하는 문제가 있음. 국세청으로서는 가급적 이들 물품의 국내조달을 희망함.

(소비세과)

관 세 청

1) 사소한 샘플품까지 외국에 주문하는것은 물론 어렵겠지만 현재 미군들에 의한 PX 물품 유출을 단속하는 문제만도 어려운 문제인데 공관원들의 PX 이용까지 허용하게 된다면 이들에 의한 PX 물품 유출을 방지하는것이 매우 어려운 문제가 될것임.

(징수 과)

161

상 공 부

1) 군납부문의 위축 가능성이 없지않으며, 국내 생산업체 및 국내 시장의 유통질서에 대한 혼란도 예상됨.

2) 현재 이용권을 부여하고있는 Invited Contractors 에 대하여도 SOFA 규정을 개정하는 기회가 있으면 이들에 대한 이용권을 제한해주기 바람.

(수출 3 과)

결 론

1. 국내시장에서 구입할수 없는 사소한 생필품까지 모두 외국으로부터 수입하는것은 실제로 매우 곤란한 문제이므로 이들 공관원의 요청은 이해되나, 오늘 제시해준 관계부처의 의견을 종합해보면 현행 SOFA 규정의 테두리내에서는 적당한 제도적 또는 법적 근거를 발견하기 어렵고 기술적으로도 물품구입시의 결제 방법 (예컨대, 군표사용 여부)과 같은 선결되어야할 문제가 있으며, PX 물품의 국내시장 유출과 이에 대한 단속의 어려움, 형평을 이유로한 이용 요청자의 확대등 여러가지 문제로 인하여 대체로 부정적인 견해로 집약되었음.

2. 시내에 Commissary 운영을 더 원활히 하고 기호품이나 일상식료품 종류도 양과 질을 정비시켜야 할 필요성을 교통부에 통고하고 주의를 기우리도록 조치함이 좋을 것임.

(외무부 미주국장)

162

기 안 용 지

분류기호 문서번호	미이 723 - 66	(전화번호)	전결규정 조 항 국장 전결사항
처리기간			
시행일자	1973. 2. 12.		
보존년한		국 장	
보조기관	과 장		협조
기안책임자	변승국	북미 2 과	
경 유			통제
수 신	교통부장관		
참 조	관광국장		
제 목	주한 외교단의 미군 P.X. 등 이용		

발신 1973 2 13 외무부

검토 1973.2.13 통제관

1. 최근 주한 외교단의 미군 P.X. 등 비세출 자금 기관 이용 요청에 대하여 당부는 관계부처 회의 (SOFA 재무분과위원회)를 개최하고 별첨 회의록과 같이 의견을 종합, 이를 통보하오니 업무수행에 참고하시기 바라며,

2. 별첨 회의록에 제시된바와 같이 Foreigner's Commissary 를 통한 생필품 공급이 더욱 원활히 되어야할 필요성을 감안, 상기 Commissary 에 대하여 적절한 조치를 취하여 주시고 그 결과를 당부에 통보해 주시기 바랍니다.

3. 주한 외교단은 상기 관계부처 회의 직후 Milk 와 Butter 만이라도 미군 P.X. 를 통하여 구입할수 있도록 요청하여 왔으나, 이에 대하여도 Foreigner's Commissary 를 통하여 구입하도록 회답할 ~~예정임을 참언합니다.~~ 이오니 그의 수요에 충당할수 있도록 공급조치 하여 주시기 바랍니다.

첨부 : 회의록 1 부. 끝.

정서 / 관인 / 발송

공통서식1-2(갑)
1967. 4. 4. 승인

190mm×268mm (1급인쇄용지70g/㎡)
조달청 (500,000매 인쇄)

163

기 안 용 지

분류기호 문서번호	미이 723 - 65	(전화번호)	전결규정 조 항 국장 전결사항
처리기간			
시행일자	1973. 2. 12.		
보존년한		국 장	
보조기관	과 장		협조
기안책임자	변승국	북미 2 과	
경유 수신 참조	수신처 참조	발신 1973 2 13	통제 검열 1973 2 13 통제관
제목	회의록 송부		

1. 주한 외교단의 미군 P.X. 등 이용 요청에 관한 대책회의록을 별첨과 같이 송부합니다.

2. 주한 외교단은 상기 대책회의 직후 Milk 와 Butter 만이라도 미군 Commissary 등을 통하여 구입할수 있도록 허가해줄것을 요청하여 왔으나, 구입 품목의 제한이 실효를 기할수 없고, 기타 절차상의 난점이 있음을 고려, 동 품목에 대하여도 국내의 Foreigner's Commissary 를 이용하도록 회답할 예정임을 첨언합니다.

첨부 : 회의록 1부. 끝.

수신처 : 재무부장관 (관세협력과, 국제조세과, 관세조정과)

상공부장관 (수출 3과)

관세청장 (심미과, 세무과)

국세청장 (소비세과, 외국인세과) 외무부 (조약과, 의전과)

정서 관인 발송

공통서식1-2(갑)
1967. 4. 4. 승인

190mm ×268mm (인쇄용지 70g/m²)
(조달청 500,000매 인쇄)

164

협 조 문

응신기일

분류기호 및 문서번호	미이 723 - 14	제 목	회의록 송부
수 신	의전실장, 방교국장	발신일자	1973. 2. 13. (협조제의)

북미2과	양고재	73년 2월 일	담당	과장	국장	차관보	차관	장관
			(서명)	(서명)	(서명)			

발신명의 미주국장

(제 1 의 견)

1. 주한 외교사절의 미군 PX 등 이용 요청에 관한 대책회의록을 별첨과 같이 송부합니다.

2. 주한 외교단은 상기 대책회의 직후 Milk 와 Butter 만이라도 미군 PX 또는 Commissary 등을 통하여 구입할수 있도록 허가해줄 것을 요청하여 왔으나, 구입품목의 제한이 실효를 기할수 없고 기타 절차상의 난점이 있음에 감하여, 동 품목에 대하여도 국내의

(제 2 의 견)

Foreigner's Commissary 에서 수요공급을 중심마 마기로 하여 이를 이용하도록 회답할 예정임을 첨언합니다.

첨부 : 회의록 1 부. 끝.

165

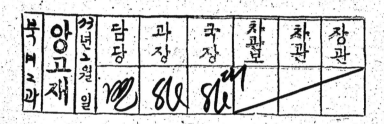

회 의 록

1. 의 제 : 주한 외국 공관원에 대한 미군 비세출자금기관 이용
2. 회의일시 및 장소 : 1973. 2. 7. 1400 – 1500 미주국장실
3. 참 석 자 : 외무부 미주국장 김동휘
   " 북미 2국장 김기조
   " 의전과 한종의
   " 조약과 이 양
   재무부 관세협력과 원윤득
   " 국제조세과 강세윤
   국세청 소비세과 김재윤
   " 외국인세과 이성두
   관세청 징수과 송창악
   상공부 수출 3 과 전범순

(기록 : 북미 2국 변승국)

4. 관계부처 의견종합 :

외무부

(현황 설명 및 회의 주지)

1) 최근 주한 외교단의 공식, 비공식 회합에서 이 문제가 빈번히

156 -1E

166

거론된바 있으며, 이에 따라 주한 외교단장인 비율빈 대사의 공식 요청을 받게되었는데, 이들은 현재 예외적으로 이용권이 허용되고 있는 3개 기관 (UNCURK , 국제연합 묘지관리단, 중립국 휴전감시위원단) 측의 형평을 요구하여 동일한 특혜를 줄것을 요청하고 있음.

2) 현재 SOFA 협정에 의한 사용권자는,

가) SOFA 제13조에 의한 원칙적 이용권자 (군인, 군속 및 그 가족. Technical Representative 도 군속으로 간주됨)

나) SOFA 제15조에 의한 초청계약자와 그 가족

다) SOFA 제13조 합의 의사록에 의한 예외적 이용권자들

3개 범주가 있음.

3) 이 문제에 대한 미측의 견해는 일단 호의적 (개인적 의견임을 명시) 이라고 볼수가 있으나, 미측으로서는 물량적 공급 의사를 검토해 보겠으며, 기타 제도적, 법적문제는 한국측에서 검토해 주기를 요청한바 있음.

4) 타국의 예를 볼것같으면 자유중국만이 참사관 이상에 대하여 이용권을 허용하고 있고, 일본이나 불란서의 경우는 전혀 이용권을 주지않고 있음. 독일의 경우도 대체로 이용권을 허용하지 않는것을 원칙으로 하고 있으며, 극히 사소한 특권 (예: 극장 출입) 만이 허용되어 있을뿐임.

167

5) SOFA 제 13조 합의의사록 (나)항에 의하면 한국정부가 명시적 동의를 받으므로써 PX 사용권을 부여할수도 있으나, 이러한 특권부여에 따르는 제반 문제, 예컨대 제도적 또는 법적근거에 관한 문제, 국내시장에 대한 물품 유출과 이를 방지하는 문제, 기타 우리 경제에 미치는 영향이나 세부 절차에 이르기까지 각 부처의 기탄없는 의견을 제시해 줄것을 요청함.

(미주국)

1) 이러한 특권 확장에는 현실적으로 여러 곤란한 문제가 있겠으나 국내시장에서 구입할수 없는 물품은 모두 외국으로 부터 직접 수입해서 쓰자면 상당한 시간적, 금전적 부담을 지게 되는것도 사실이므로 각국 대사에 한해서 제한된 범위내의 이용을 허여 하는것도 좋을 것임.

2) 또한 이들 대사들은 UNCURK 회원국 대사에게만 특혜를 주는것도 차별대우가 아니냐는 불만을 표시하고 평등의 원칙에 입각한 동등한 특권 부여를 요청하고 있음.

(의전국)

재 무 부

1) 주한 외국 공관원에 대하여 미군 PX 등 비세출자금 기관 이용권을 부여하는것은 미군 물품의 부정유출을 방지하려는 SOFA 의 근본취지에 어긋남.

168

2) 상호주의 원칙을 적용한다고 하나, 미군이 주둔하지 않는 지역에서는 이 원칙의 적용은 무의미하게 됨.

3) 현재 예외적으로 이용권을 부여하고 있는 3개기관 (UNCURK, 국제연합군 묘지관리단, 중립국 휴전감시위원단)에 대한 특권부여는 이들 기관이 모두 한국동란등 특수목적을 위하여 한국에만 특별히 파견된 기관이라는 상당한 이유가 있었으나 주한 외국공관원에 대한 특권부여 이유는 납득되지 않음.

4) 주한 외국 공관원에 대하여 이러한 특권을 부여하게 되는 경우, 물품구입의 결제방법은 어떻게 되는가? (예컨대, 이들 공관원에 대하여도 미군표 사용을 허용할 것인가?)

(관세협력과)

1) 현재 주한 외국 공관원 및 그 가족에 대하여는 면세 혜택을 주고있으며, 외국인을 위한 기타 특수물품이라던 현재 Foreigner's Commissary 가 개설, 이용되고 있으며, 외국으로 부터의 직접 수입도 가능하므로 이들에 대하여 또다시 미군 PX 이용까지 허용할 필요는 없을것임.

(국제조세과)

169

국세청

1) 대체로 재무부 의견에 동의하며 상기 3개 기관에 대한 이용권 부여는 상당한 이유가 있다고 보나, 이들 주한 공관원에 대한 이용권 부여는 이해할수가 없으며, 물품 유출등 여러 곤란한 문제가 있을것으로 봄.

(외국인세과)

1) 미군 PX 물품 판매에 대하여 관세를 부과해야 하겠으나 실제상 이들에 대한 검사권이 미치지 못하는 문제가 있음. 국세청으로서는 가급적 이들 물품의 국내반입을 희망함.

(소비세과)

관세청

1) 사소한 상품등 까지 외국에 주문하는것은 좋은 일 아니겠지만 현재 미군들에 의한 PX 물품 유출을 단속하는 문제만도 어려운 문제인데 공관원들의 PX 이용까지 허용하게 된다면 이들에 의한 PX 물품 유출을 방지하는것이 매우 어려운 문제가 될 것임.

(감 시 과)

170

상 공 부

1) 군납부문의 위축 가능성이 없지않으며, 국내 생산업자 및 국내 시장의 유통질서에 대한 혼란도 예상됨.

2) 면세 이용권을 부여하고 있는 Invited Contractors 에 대하여도 SOFA 규정을 개정하는 기회가 있으면 이들에 대한 이용권을 제한해주기 바람.

(수출 3 과)

검 토

1) 국내시장에서 구입할수 없는 사소한 생필품까지 모두 외국으로 부터 수입하는것은 실제로 매우 곤란한 문제이므로 이들 공급원의 요청은 이해되나, 오늘 제시되온 관계부처의의견을 종합해보면 현행 SOFA 규정의 해두 이내에서는 적당한 제도적 또는 법적 근거를 발견하기 어렵고 기술적으로도 물품구입시의 결제 방법 (외환매, 군표사용 여부)과 같은 선결되어야할 문제가 있으며, PX 물품의 국내시장 유출과 이에 대한 단속의 어려움, 형평을 이유로한 이용 요청자의 확대등 여러가지 문제로 인하여 대체로 부정적인 견해로 집약되었음.

2) 시내의 Commissary 운영을 더 원활히하고 기호품이나 일상 식료품 종류도 양과 질을 정비시키어야 할 필요성을 교통부 에 권고하고 주의를 기우리도록 조치함이 좋을것임.

(외무부 미주국장)

171

주한 미군용 수입신고서 양식개정

1. 군사화물에 대한 수입신고 양식의 개정

가. 관계 규정

SOFA 제9조 2항

나. 문제점

세관행정의 EDPS 화에 따라 일반 수출입 신고서 양식이 72년초부터 개정되었으며, 이에 따라 주한미군용 수입신고서 양식도 개정되어야 할것임.

다. 대 책

SOFA 제78차 합동위원회 정례회의에서 (72.10.5.)한.미 양측이 미리 준비한바에 따라 개정된 양식 (별첨 1) 을 채택할것을 승인함.

※ 여기서 군사화물이라 함은 일반 상용 선편에 의하여 반입되는것을 말하며, 군용 선편에 의한 것은 제외됨.

2. 개인용품에 대한 수입신고서 양식개정

가. 관계규정

SOFA 제9조 3항

172

나. 문제점

지금까지는 편의상 미 군사화물 수입신고서 양식을 준용하여 왔으나, 한국정부 (관세청)는 금번 개정된바 있는 國內用 일반 수입신고서 양식 (별첨 2)을 미측에 통보하였는바 (72.10. 8. 통보, 11. 1. 부터 시행예정), 미측은 동 양식의 내용에 대하여는 대체적으로 찬성하고 있으나 다음의 두 가지점에 관하여 문제를 제기하고 있음.

(1) 관세협회에서 1매당 10원정도의 가격으로 판매되고 있는 동 수입신고서 양식은 미측에 무료로 배부되어야 할 것임.

(2) 동 수입신고서 양식의 개정에 선행하여 제 8차 SOFA 합동위원회 정례회의 (67. 5. 27)에서 과제부여된바 있는 개인용품에 대한 세관검사 절차에 관한 합의가 선행되어야 할 것임. (이 과정에서 미측은 세관검사를 port of entry에서가 아니라 선주의 집에서 하자고 억지쓰고 있음)

다. 한국측 주장

가. 전기 수입신고서 양식은 민간기관인 관세협회에서 만들어 팔고 있는 것이며, 국내 수입업자들도 동 협회로부터 유료로 구매하여 쓰고있음. 따라서 미군측도 이 양식을 유료로 구매해서 쓸수밖에 없는 점은 국내 수입업자들의 경우와 동일하나, 다만 관세청은 전기 관세협회와 협의하여 이를 미군에 무료로 배부할수 있는 방안을 검토중에 있음. (下線部分은 아직 美軍側에 示唆한 바 없음)

173

(2) "수입신고서 양식" 과 "검사절차" 의 문제는 별개 문제로서 검사절차의 확정이 반드시 수입신고서 양식의 개정에 선행되어야 할 논리적 전제가 되는것은 아니고 더욱 수입신고서 양식의 제정, 또는 개정은 한국정부 고유의 사무로서 미군측이 이 문제에 대하여 협의의(協議) 당사자가 될수는 없을것임. (미군측의 협의 요구에 불구하고 관세청은 동 신고서 양식을 예정대로 사용할 예정임.) - 미측은 이 수입신고서 사용을 수락할수 없다는 태도를 취하고 있음. (10. 26. Kinney)

174

(양식 1)

2. 입항 Date of Entry 19 . . .	부호 Code No.	대한민국 세관 Korean Customs Service	11. 세관부호 Customs Code No.	
3. 선화증권번호 B/L No.			12. 수입종별 Sort of Import	
4. 적재선(기) 명 Name of Vessel(Aircraft)			13. 신고번호 Declaration No.	
적재선(기) 국적 Nationality of Vessel(Aircraft)		주한 미군용 수입 신고서 Import Declaration/Certification USFK, ROK-US SOFA	15. 신고 Date of Declaration 19 . . .	
5. 적출국(지) Country of Shipment				
6. 입항지 Place of Entry				
7. 생산지, 원산국(지) Country of Production				
8. 장치장소 Place of Storage				

	계	주무	과장
결재			

21. 품명및 규격 Description of Articles & Grade	22. 중량 Weight	23. 수량 Quantity	24. 단위 Unit	25. 신고가격 Declared Value	27. 세번 Heading	28 부호 Code No.
(1)				CIF $		
(2)				CIF $		
(3)				CIF $		
35. 비고 Remarks / 계 Total				CIF $		

45. 기호, 번호, 포장종류와 개수
Markings, Numbering, Type and Number of Packages

상기 물품은 SOFA 제9조 제2항에 의거 주한 미군용으로 수입되는 것임을 증명함.

I hereby certify the import of the above goods for use of USFK in accordance with the ROK-US SOFA, Article IX, Paragraph 2.

175

신고자 성명
Name and Signature of Declarant

통관장교 서명
Signature of Customs Clearance Officer

신고자 주소
Address of Declarant

부대명
Department

48. 첨부서류
Attached herewith if any
송품장
Invoice
포장명세서
Packing list
원산지 증명
Certificate of Origin
운임명세서
Freight Receipt
보험 영수증
Receipt of Insurance
선화 증권 사본
Copy of B/L
기타
Others

47. 면허 및 면허 일자
Import Permitted,
Signature and Date

165

210mm × 300mm

(양식2)

대 한 민 국 세 관
KOREAN CUSTOMS SERVICE

수입(반입)신고서 (갑지)
IMPORT DECLARATION

1 접수 197 . . . ( )		11 세관부호 / 12 / 13
2 입항일 Date of Entry 197 . . .	부호	14 수입허가 기관 / 번호 / 년월일 197 . . .
3 선하증권번호 B/L No		15 신고 197 . .
4 선(기)명 Name of Vessel (Aircraft)		16 검사 197 . .
5 선(기)국적 Nationality of Vessel (Aircraft)		17 조정 197 . .
6 적출국 Country of Shipment		18 면허 197 . .
7 입항지 Place of Entry		
8 원산국 Country of Production		
9 장치장소 Place of Storage		

9 수입자 주소 Importer address / 주민등록번호 / 상호 / 사업등록번호 / 성명인 Name and Signature	10 수입형태별		19 신고자 주소 Declarant Address / 주민등록번호 / 상호 / 성명인 Name and Signature
	(1) 면허전반출	(5) 면허전반출완전분	
	(2) 보세공장반입	(6) 보세공장수입면허분	
	(3) 보세건설장반입	(7) 보세건설장수입면허분	
	(4) 보세전시장반입	(8) 보세전시장수입면허분	

20 품명 및 규격 DESCRIPTION OF ARTICLES & GRADE	21 중량 WEIGHT / 22 수량 QUANTITY	23 단위 UNIT	24 신고가격 DECLARED VALUE / 25 감정가격 APPRAISED VALUE	26 세번 / 27 목관세종	부호	28 세율 / 29 세율	30 관세액 / 31 목관세액	32 통관중기부호 / 33
(1)	kg		CIF, $ / W / 목	( )	종	% / %	W / W	
(2)	kg		CIF, $ / W / 목	( )	종	% / %	W / W	
(3)	합계		CIF, $ / W / 목	35 환율			W / W	

36 내국세					37 증지증인	38 세별계	(가) 고지번호	(나) 세액	39 신고서
(1) 과세가격	(2) 세번	(3) 세종	(4) 세율	(5) 세액					
			%	W	매계	(1) 관세			40 허가서분실
			%	W	매계	(2) 목관세			신고번호 (. .)
(6) 합계 W				합계	매계	(3) 물품세			41 검사
42 비고						(4) 세			영 리[ ] 검사경[ ] 검사경조[ ] 검정시[ ] / 수입신고서 접수인
						(5) 영업세			
						(6) 소득세 법인세			

43 표시, 번호, 포장 종류와 개수 Marking, Numbering, Type and Number of Packages

44 보세운송
목적지 :
경유지 :
수송 : (1)육로[ ] (2)해로[ ] (3)공로[ ]
기간 : . . . 부터 . . . 까지
도착일 : . . .

45 면허안

접수	계	주무	과장	주무	과장	장
176						

46 첨부서류 Attached herewith, if any
수입허가서 ( ) [ ] Import License
송 품 장 ( ) [ ]
166
포장명세서 ( ) [ ] Packing List
원산지증명 ( ) [ ] Certificate of Origin
운임명세서 ( ) [ ] Freight Sheet
보험료영수증 ( ) [ ] Receipt of Insurance
선하증권사본 ( ) copy of B/L

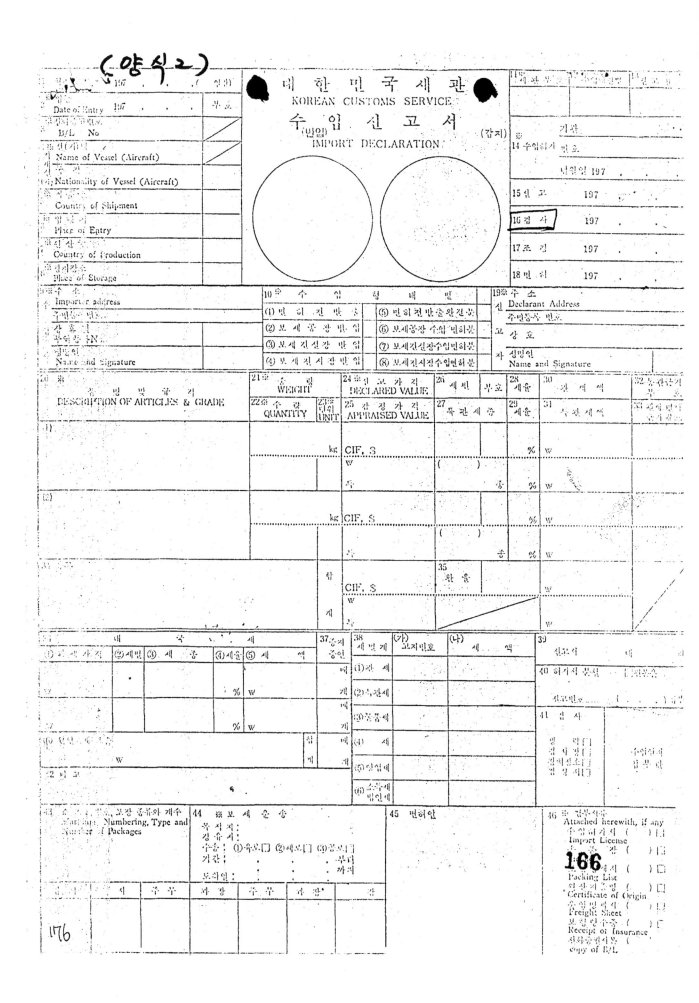

DEPARTMENT OF THE NAVY
COMMANDER NAVAL FORCES KOREA COMPONENT-CHINHAE
FPO SEATTLE 98769

CNFK-CC/C-1:kcy
1746
Ser 98

27 DEC 1972

From: Commanding Officer, Commander Naval Forces, Korea, Component - Chinhae
To: Commander U. S. Forces, Korea (Attn: AJ)

Subj: Alcoholic Beverages Activities - U. S. Navy Messes at Chinhae

Ref: (a) Your ltr USFK-AJ of 2 June 1972

1. In compliance with the provisions of reference (a), a negative report is submitted for the month of December 1972.

P. A. COPE
By direction

Copy to:
COMNAVFORKOREA

1717

제목 : 미군 PX 물품 부정유출에 대한 한.미 합동수사

1. 참고 : 한.미 합동수사반 설치 및 운영지침
67. 12. 21. 제 19차 합동위원회 제정
68. 7. 3. 제 28차 " 개정

2. 미군 PX 물품의 한국 시장에 대한 유출을 방지하기 위하여 한국 관세청, 미군 범죄수사대 및 미 공군 특별수사대는 다음 조치를 취할것을 합의함.

가. 인천 미 8군 보급창에 한국 세관원 2명을 배치하여 PX 물품의 수송상태를 파악함.

나. 미군 PX 본부는 인천 미군 보급창으로 부터 한국 전지역에 수송되는 물품의 적화목록 사본 1부를 한국 관세청에 송부함.

다. 인천 세관은 동 적화 목록을 접수한후 물품의 목적지에 배치되어 있는 각 지구 세관원에게 별첨 1 양식에 의거 동 물품의 자료를 송부함.
각 지구 세관원과 미군 범죄 수사대 또는 미 공군 특별 수사대 요원은 합동으로 도착 물품을 확인함.

라. 도착 물품을 확인한 결과 도난 또는 유출의 혐의가 있는때에는 한국 관세청, 미군 범죄수사대 및 미 공군 특별 수사대는 합동으로 수사를 개시함.

178

마. 미군 PX 당국은 각 지구 PX 관리인들에게 본 계획을 통보함.

바. 미군 범죄수사대 및 미 공군 특별수사대는 본 합의서 사본 1부를 각 지구 파견대에 송부함.

사. 본 합의의 각 당사자는 어느때에나 본 합의의 개정을 요구할 수 있으며, 일방 당사자의 요청에 따라 본 합의는 폐지됨.

아. 본 합의는 한.미 합동위원회에서 승인된날 부터 효력을 발생함.

179

Mr. Byun

증산 수출 건설

재 무 부

협력 1243-240 1973. 3. 29.

수신 외무부장관

제목 미국인 기술자의 미군PX 이용을 위한 협조 요청

풍산 금속 공업 주식회사로부터의 별첨 1과 같은 요청에 대하여 별첨 2와 같이 회신 하였음을 통보하오니 양지 하시기 바랍니다.

첨부 : 1. 풍금(총)73 제139호 (1973. 3. 21) 사본 1부.

2. 당부 회신 공문 사본 1부. 끝.

공람	73년 월 일	담당	과장	국장	차관보	차관	장관

0883

재 무 부 장 관

재무부 문서 규정 제27조 ... 규정에 의하여 세정차관보 남상진 전결

1973. 3. 29 재무부

180

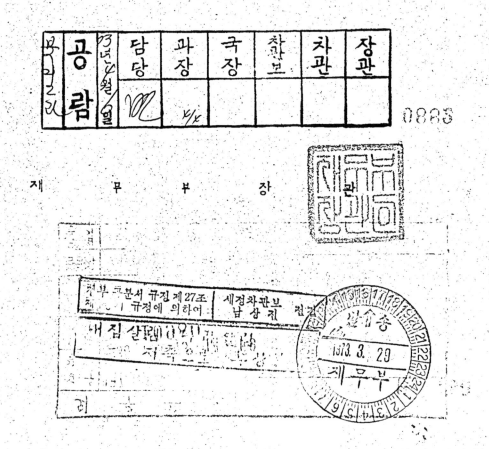

외 무 부		결재	
접수 일시	197 . . . 30 MAR '73 14 : 19		
접수 번호	제 10980		
주무과			
담당자			
처리 근거			

민 [redacted] 서 류

처리기한 : . . . .

풍 산 금 속 공 업 주 식 회 사

풍금(총)73제 139 호 　　　　　　　　　　1973. 3. 21.

수 신 　재무부 장관

참 조 　관세 국장

제 목 　미국인 기술자의 미8군 PX 및 Commissary 이용을 위한 협조 요청.

1. 폐사는 1970. 7. 29일자 제1차 경제공업화 추진위원회(대통령령 제5224호. 1970. 7. 23. 공포)에서 경제공업화 대상업체로 선정받아 현재 경북 월성군 안강읍 산대리에 신동가공공장을 계획된 준공일자(73. 6. 30)에 맞추어 건설중에 있아오며, 이에 따라 미국 Amron 회사와 기술협정을 체결하고 Amron 회사의 부사장인 Mr. Nowlen을 수석으로한 기술진 4명이 72.12.22일부로 입국하여 해당 전문분야에서 종사하고 있읍니다.

2. 이들 기술진은 다음과 같이 직계가족을 동반하고 74.1.31일 77가지 장기 체류하여, 폐사에 종사할 목적으로 현재 남산외국인아파트에 거주하고 있아오나, 의류 및 식료품의 시중구입이 여의치 못할 뿐만아니라, 특히 유아들의 양육을 위해 미국인 전용 Commissary 이용이 불가피한 실정에 있다는 이들의 요청을 받고 이요청이 한미 행정협정제 13조(관세관계규정)에 대한 합의의사록 제6항에 해당할 것으로 사료되어 이들 가족의 미8군 PX 및 Commissary 이용에 필요한 협조를 건의하오니, 선처하여 주시기 앙망하나이다.

181

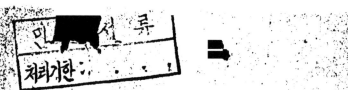

— 다 음 —

가. 동반 가족수

[redacted]	의 가족	7명
	"	4명
	"	4명
	"	4명
총 계		19명

나. 출입요망 기간

1973. 4. 1 — 1974. 1. 31 (10개 월간)

다. 미국인 기술자 4명의 인적사항

성 명	생년월일	직 책	체류기간
[redacted]		General Manager	자: 1973.1.1. 지: 1974.1.31
		Quality Control Manager	"
		Engineering Manager	"
		Plant Manager	"

끝

서울특별시 중구 태평로 2가 70 — 5
풍 산 금 속 공 업 주 식 회 사
대 표 이 사 유

182

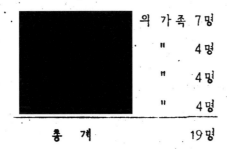

종신 전결

재 무 부

협력 1243- 1973. 3. 29.

수신 서울특별시 중구 태평로 2가 70-5

풍산금속공업주식회사

대표이사 유 찬 우

제목 미국인 기술자의 미군 P.X. 이용을 위한 협조 요청

1. 풍금 (총) 73 제139호 (1973. 3. 21)에 대한 것입니다.

2. 주한 미군 지위협정(SOFA) 제13조에 대한 합의의사록(바) 항에 의하면 미합중국 군대는 대한민국 정부의 명시적 동의를 얻어 미군 PX 등 비세출 자금 기관에 대한 이용권을 부여할수 있도록 되어 있으나 Mr. Nowlen 등에 대하여는 이러한 협의가 이루어 진바 없읍니다.

끝.

재 무 부 장 관

183

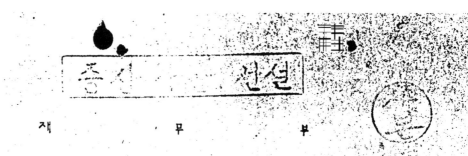

Mr. Byun

10

전 매 청

판매 823.73_ (75_5807) 1973. 4. 3.

수신 외무부장관

참조 미주국장

제목 P.X 및 Commissary의 양담배 통제 요청

1. 주한 미군 P.X 로부터의 양담배 부정 유출은 우리나라 전매세입 수행에 막대한 지장을 초래하고 있으며, 사회적으로도 물의의 대상이 되고 있는바,

2. 당청에서는 강력한 단속과 엄벌을 하고 있음에도 불구하고 그 유출량이 줄지 아니하며,

3. 미국측 당국에서는 판매에 통제를 하고 있다 하나 P.X 에서 한국인 암매상에게 직접 대량을 판매하고 있으니,

4. 한.미 합동위원회에서 다음 사항이 조치되도록 협의하여 주시기 바랍니다.

가. P.X 에서 판매할 양담배는 P.X 이용권자의 실 [illegible] 내 반입토록 할것.

나. 71. 9월 이후 35개 통제 품목에서 제외되었다 하여 [illegible] 아니 [illegible] 양담배 판매량을 통보할것(한.미 군대지위협정 제13조 제4항) [illegible].

발송 1973. 4. 3 전매청

북미2과	공람	년 월 일	담당	과장	국장	차관보	차관	장관

제2회

전 매 청

담배 질 향상 회

184

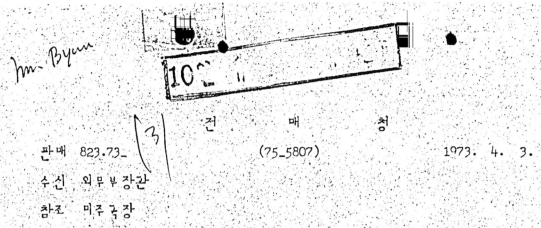

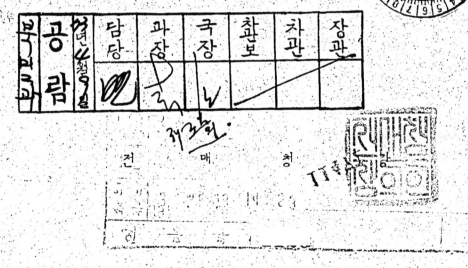

외 무 부	분기		
접수 일시	197 3 APR '73 14 : 53		
접수 번호	제		

11471

협 조 문	응신기일

문서기호 및 문서번호	미이 723 - 35	제 목	SOFA 규정 해석
수 신	방교국장	발신일자	1973. 4. 16. (협조제의)

북미2과	양교재	73년 4월 16일	담당	과장	국장	차관보	차관	장관
			양	(서명)	(서명)			

발신명의 미주국장

(제 1 의견)

주한미군 당국은 SOFA 제 16조 3항 규정에 의거 미군 화물 수송을 위하여 국내 수송업체가 사용하는 유류에 대한 면세조치를 취하여 달라는 요청이 있어 조회하오니 이러한 요청이 동규정에 비추어 타당한지 여부를 검토, 회보하여 주시기 바랍니다.

(제 2 의견)

첨부 : 미측 제안 1통. 끝.

재무부 외국인세과에 비공식 검토의뢰함 4/16

020 1—1—2B
1969.11.10승인

190mm268mm 신문용지 50g/m²
조달청 (200,000매) 인쇄

185

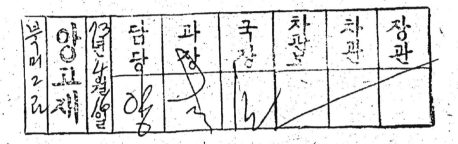

공 란

공　　란

공 란

공 란

공 란

공 란

증 신 신설

재 무 부

협력 1243-318 1973. 4. 30.

수신 외무부장관

제목 비세출 자금기관에 탁송되는 화물에 관한 정보제공품목의 추가 요청

전매청장으로 부터 미군 PX 를 통하여 국내 암거래 시장에 부정유출 되는 양담배의 유출 방지를 위한 조치를 요청하였으므로, 별첨과 같이 문제점을 제기하오니 한미합동회의를 통하여 이 건의가 해결되도록 조치하여 주시기 바랍니다.

첨부 1. 양담배 통제에 관한 문제점 및 건의사항 1부.

2. 전매청 공한 사본 1부. 끝.

No. 1973. 4. 30 재무부

재 무 부 장

T2

정부 공문서 규정 제27조 제 항의 규정에 의하여 세정차관보 남 상 진

1131

192

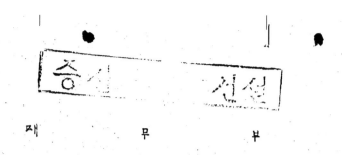

외 무 부		결재	
접수 일시	197		
접수 번호	APR '73 15:02 제 15742		
주무과			
담당자			
처리 기한		197 . . 까지 처리할것	

1973. 4. 30

0896

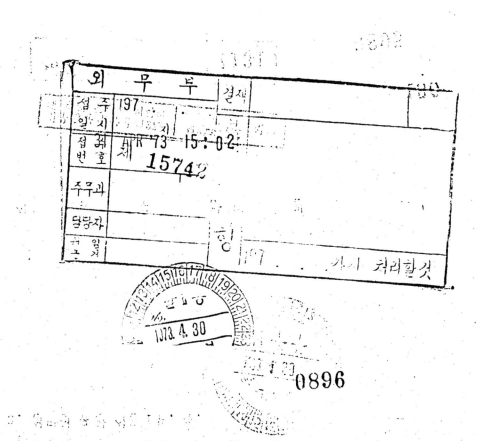

양담배 통제에 관한 문제점 및 건의

의제	현황 (문제점)	건의사항	관계규정
(비세출자금기관에 탁송되는 화물에 관한 정보 제공품목의 담배 추가 요청)	1. 미군 PX 및 Commissary 에서 판매하고 있는 양담배중 많은 수량이 계속 국내 암거래시장에 부정유출되어, 우리나라 전매세입 수행에 막대한 지장을 초래하고 있음.	1. 1971년 8월 26일 제65차 합[illegible] 위원회에서 제정된 비세출[illegible] 기관에 탁송되는 화물에 관[illegible] 정보 제공품목 (35개) 에[illegible] 배를 추가한다.	[illegible]. 제9조에 대한 합의 의사록 3. ─── 비세출 자금기관에 탁송된 화물에 관한 적절한 정보는 정규적으로 대한민국 당국에 제공된다. 적절한 정보의 범위는 합동위원회가 이를 결정한다.
	2. 1971년도 미군의 양담배 추정소모량 및 양담배의 부정유출량 ① PX 담배 판매량: 48,003,000갑 ② 미군의 추정소모량: 28,800,000갑 (40,000 × 60갑 × 12월) ③ 추정부정유출량: 19,203,000갑 (① - ②) ④ 1971년도에 관계기관에 의하여서 압수된 부정양담배량: 131,000갑 ※ 미군측에서 제공한 정보		[illegible]. 제9조 합의 의사록 3에 대한 합의 양해사항 2. 정규적으로 제공되는 정보에 추가하여 기타 관계정보는 합동 위원회를 통한 요구에 따라 제공된다.
	3. 주한 미군 PX 에 반입되는 양담배의 량이 합리적으로 소요되는 량을 초과하고 있음.	2. 주한 미군이 필요로 하는 것보다 많은 수량의 담배를 한국[illegible]에 수입하지 않도록 하여야 한다.	제9조에 대한 합의 의사록 1. 합중국군대의 비세출자금기관이 제13조와 동조의 합의 의사록에 의하여 인정받은 자의 사용을 위하여 제2항에 따라 수입한 물품의 량은 이러한 사용을 위하여 합리적으로 소요되는 한도에 한정되어야 한다.

1132

재무부 관세국

193

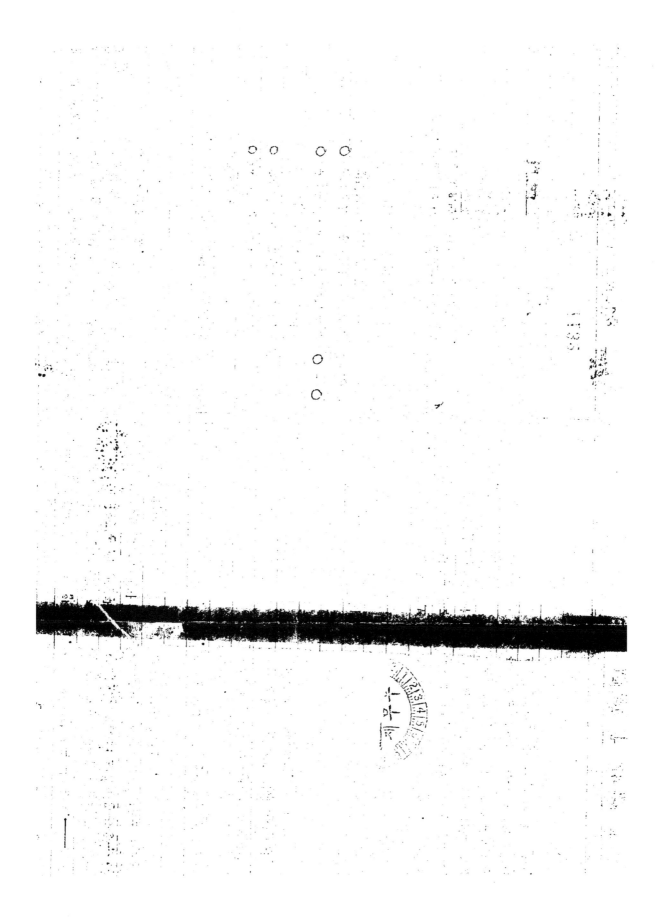

전 매 청

판매 823.73- (75-5807) 1973. 4. 3.

수신 재무부장관

참조 관세국장

제목 P.X 및 Commissary의 양담배 통제 요청

1. 주한 미군 P.X 로 부터의 양담배 부정 유출은 우리나라 전매세입 수행에 막대한 지장을 초래하고 있으며 사회적으로도 물의의 대상이 되고 있는바,

2. 당청에서는 강력한 단속과 엄벌을 하고 있음에도 불구하고 그 유출량이 줄지 아니하며,

3. 미국측 당국에서는 판매에 통제를 하고 있다 하나 P.X 에서 한국인 암매상에게 직접 다량을 판매하고 있으니(한.미 군대지위협정 제9조 제6항 및 제8항 위반이며, 그 증거는 별첨 사진 참조)

4. 한.미 합동위원회에서 다음 사항이 조치되도록 협의하여 주시기 바랍니다.

가. P.X 에서 판매할 양담배는 P.X 이용권자의 실수요량만큼만 국내 반입토록 할것.

나. 72. 9월 이후 15개 통제 품목에서 제외되었다하여 통보치 아니한 양담배 판매량을 통보할것(한.미 군대지위협정 제13조 제4항)

첨부 P.X 에서 직접 유출된 양담배 사진 5매. 끝.

재무부		결재	과장
접수일시	1973 4 3	지시사항	전매청 1133
접수번호	제 5??		
주무과	관세협력과		
담당자	신순현		. . . 까지 처리할 것

194

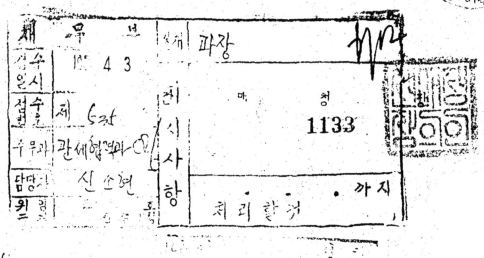

[별첨3]

"주한 미군인에 의한 밀수 사범 방지

회의 자료

1971. . .

0980

195

3. 위 체사의 문제점

1. 주한 미군인 군속및 그들 가족의 밀수등에 의한 협정또는 관세법 위반
현황
가. 양연초의 유출현황
1) P.X에 근무하는 지배인과 모-타풀 근무 한국인 운전수와 결탁하여 미군차량으로 인적드문곳 까지 완전 포장된 양담배를 BOX 채 운반 대기중인 뿌러커 상인들의 자가용 차량에 매매운반중 적발되는 경우
2) 미군차량이 통금시간중에 인적드문곳을 통과할때 대기중인 암거래 상인에게 떨어뜨려 주면 줏어 갖이고 가는 방법
3) 미군들이 위안부들에게 써비스 댓가로 양담배를 선물로 하고 있으며 그 수량도 또한 적지않은 수량을 차지하고 있다.
상기 외에도 타 방법이 있을줄 사료되나 그중 위와같은 방법이 대부분을 차지하고 있으며 인근 미군측의 양담배 판매시 과다하게 하여 수요인원에 대한 담배외 사용량을 무시하고 판매한 실증이 될수 있다고 생각 됩니다.
나. 양담배 부정유출 추정량 산출
별표(특수사건)와 같음.
3. 취체상의 문제점
미군인이 친면의 양부인을 옹호키 위하여 압수연초를 자기 소유라고 할 경우
3. 합리적인 예방책
가. 미8군 당국과의 협조로서 주한 미군인 원수에 비교 연초류를 적정량 수입판매
나. P.X 에서 판매시 1인당 1일 적정량을 정하여 과다하게 판매치 못하도록 규정을 지을것.
4. 관계부처간의 협조 사항
가. 전방지구 유엔군 주둔지역 내의 감시단속시 인원 부족등 제반 지원 사항이 요할시 신속히 응하여 주시기 바랍니다
196 나. 합동단속.

"별 표"

(1) 양담배 판매실적 (미군측에 통보)

월별	판매수량	금액	비고
1	6,912,130 갑	1,036,820 $	갑당 15 ¢
2	6,383,430 "	957,515 "	"
3	6,084,902 "	933,568 "	"
4	5,976,272 "	896,440 "	"
5	5,747,235 "	882,760 "	"
6	5,604,116 "	860,383 "	"
7	5,506,231 "	845,714 "	"
8	5,352,600 "	822,133 "	"
9	5,246,240 "	910,438 "	"
10	5,065,800 "	884,908 "	"
월평균	5,835,676 "	903,062 "	15

(2) 년간판매 추정량

수량 5,835,676갑 × 12월 =70,028,112 갑

(3) P.X 이용권자수

가. 미군인 및 군속과 그의 가족수 약 70,000명

(4) P.X 이용권자수의 년간 소비 추정량

가. 1인 1일 1갑의 경우

70,000명 × 1갑 × 365일 = 25,550,000 갑

나. 1인 1일 2갑의 경우

70,000명×2갑×365일 =51,100,000갑

(5)

197

(5) 년간과다 유출 추정량

가.1인 1일 1갑소비의 경우

70,028,112갑 – 25,550,000갑 =44,478,112 갑

나.1인1일 2갑의 경우

70,028,112갑 – 51,100,000갑 =18,928,112 갑

(6) 월평균 유출량

가.1인 1일 1갑의 경우

44,478,112갑 ÷ 12월 ≒ 3,706,509 갑

나.1인 1일 2갑의 경우

18,928,112갑 ÷ 12월 ≒ 1,577,342 갑

198

71년도 200갑 이상 특수사건 검거 실적

(1월-2월)

관서	건수	물량	비고
서울	14	5,454 갑	
추원	2	2,604 "	
인천	2	1,600 "	
남원	1	300 "	
계	19	9,958 갑	

(71년도 1,000갑 이상 검거 실적)

검거일시	검거장소	피의자	압수물량	검거관리
2.11	성동구 신평화시장	[redacted]	1,360갑	행정서기 고창순외2명
2.22	시흥군과천면 갑현리	[redacted]	1,200갑	한중석외 4명
2.12	수원시 남촌동	[redacted]	2,400갑	조병문외 2명

199

(5) 년간과다 유출 추정량

가.1인 1일 1갑소비의 경우

70,028,112갑 - 25,550,000갑 = 44,478,112 갑

나.1인1일 2갑의 경우

70,028,112갑 - 51,100,000갑 = 18,928,112 갑

(6) 월평균 유출량

가.1인 1일 1갑의 경우

44,478,112갑 ÷ 12월 ≒ 3,706,509 갑

나.1인 1일 2갑의 경우

18,928,112갑 ÷ 12월 ≒ 1,577,342 갑

266

양담배 대량 압수 사례

P05

201

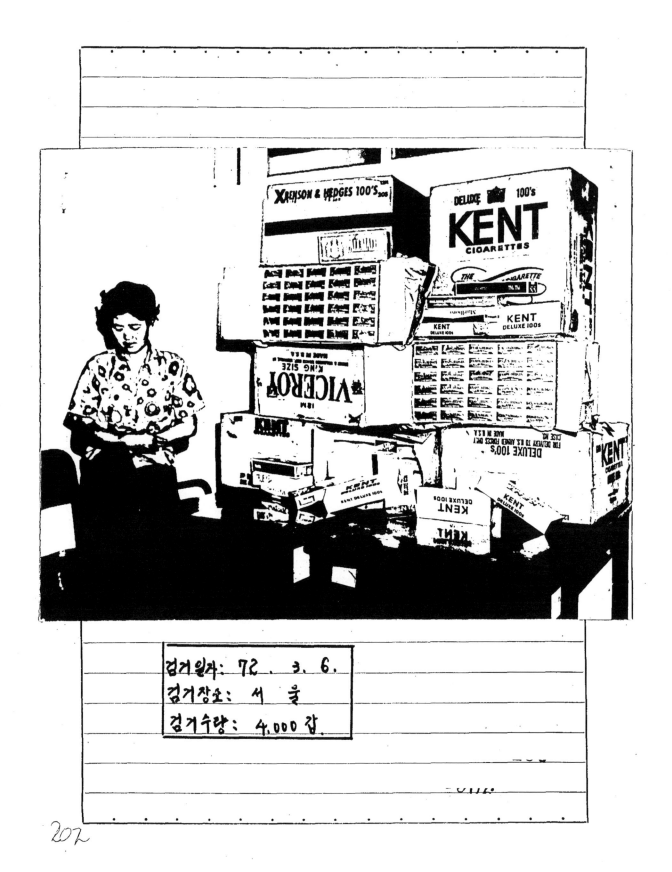

검거일자: 72. 3. 6.
검거장소: 서 울
검거수량: 4,000 갑

202

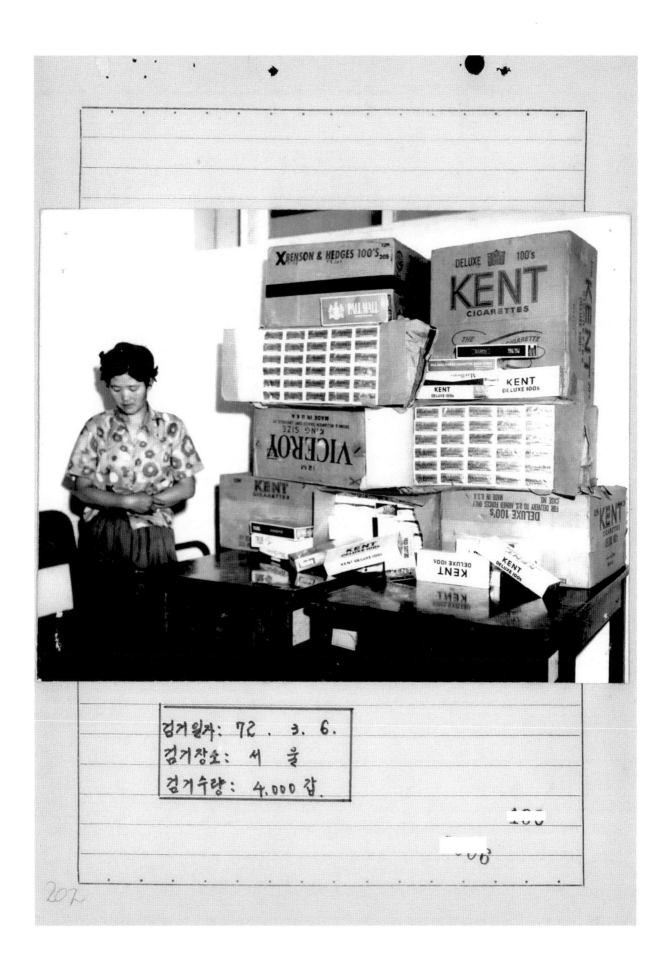

검거일자: 72. 3. 6.
검거장소: 서 울
검거수량: 4,000 갑.

[redacted]

[redacted]

202

검거일자	: 71. 12. 16
검거장소	: 인 천
검거수량	: 10.400갑

203

검거일자 : 71. 12. 16
검거장소 : 인 천
검거수량 : 10.400갑

203

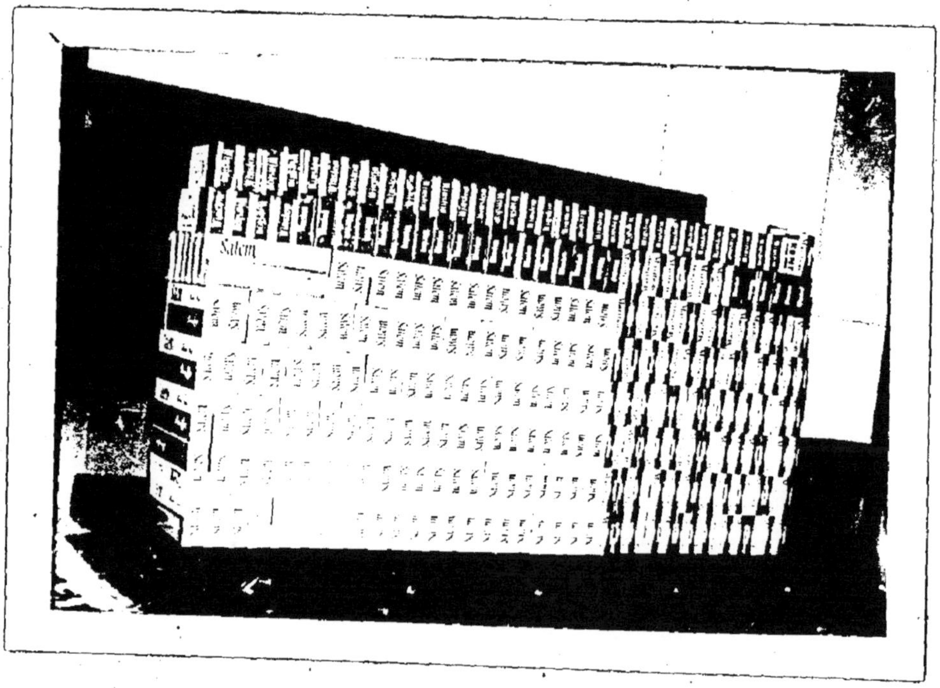

검거일자: 73. 4. 17.
검거장소: 인 천
검거수량: 2,806 갑

204

검거일자 : 73. 4. 17.
검거장소 : 인 천
검거수량 : 2,806 갑

204

검거일자 : 72.2.14
검거장소 : 서 울
검거수량 : 8,400 갑

검거일자 : 72.2.14
검거장소 : 서 울
검거수량 : 8,400 갑

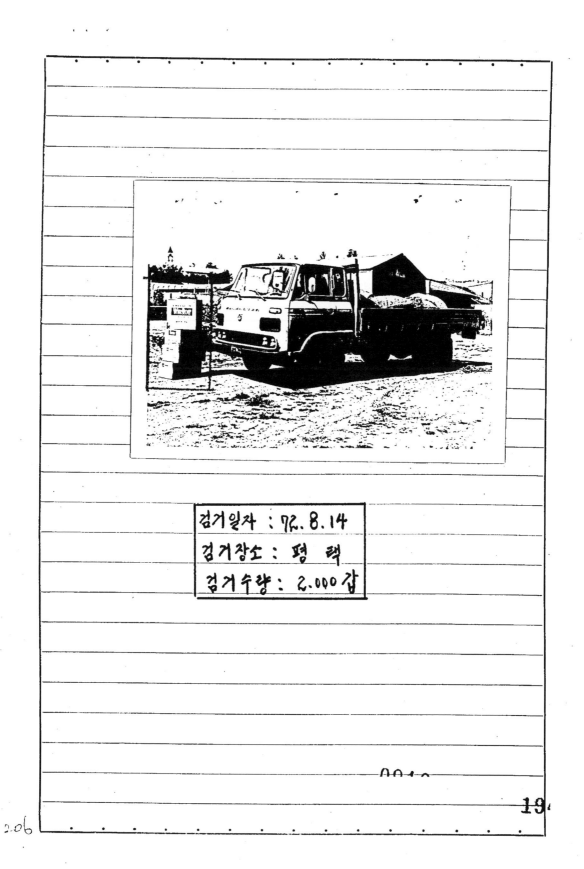

검거일자 : 72.8.14
검거장소 : 평 택
검거수량 : 2,000갑

검거일자 : 72. 8. 14
검거장소 : 평 택
검거수량 : 2.000갑

기 안 용 지

분류기호 문서번호	미이 723 -	(전화번호)	전결규정 9 조 2 항 국장 전결사항
처리기간			
시행일자	1973. 5. 9.		
보존년한		국 장	
보조기관	과 장		협조
기안책임자	변승국	북미 2 과	
경유 수신 참조	전매청장	발신 1973. 5. 9 16080 외무부	통제
제 목	양담배 부정유출 방지		

1. 귀청 공문 판매 823.73 - 131 (73. 4. 3.)과 관련됩니다.

2. 귀청에서 요청하신 양담배 부정유출 방지를 위한 대미 교섭건에 관하여는 SOFA 합동위원회 사무국을 통하여 일차적인 실무협의를 시작한바 있으며, SOFA 재무분과위원회에 대한 과제 부여를 위한 재무부 요청에 대하여는 별첨과 같이 회신하였음을 알려 드리오니 참고하시기 바랍니다.

첨부 : 재무부에 대한 회신 공문 1 부. 끝.

정서 관인 발송

공통서식1-2(갑)
1967. 4. 4. 승인

190mm×268mm(1급인쇄용지70g/m²)
조달청 (500,000매 인쇄)

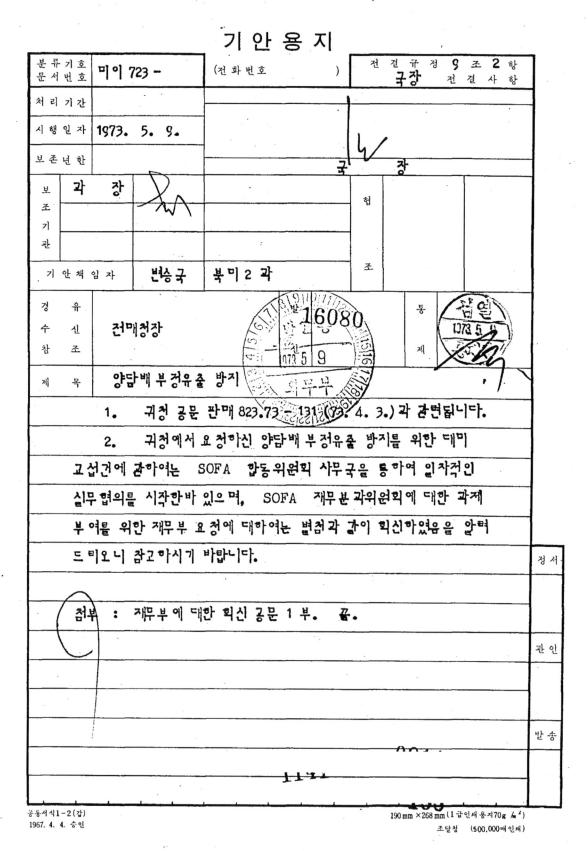

기 안 용 지

분류기호 문서번호	미이 723 -	(전화번호)	전결규정 9 조 2 항 국장 전결사항
처리기간			
시행일자	1973. 5. 9.		
보존년한		국 장	
보조기관	과 장		협조
기안책임자	변승국	북미 2 과	
경유 수신 참조	재무부장관	발신 1973 5 9 16079 외무부	통제
제 목	양담배 부정유출 방지를 위한 정보 제공 요청 추가		

1. 귀부 공문 협력 1243 - 318 (73. 4. 20.)과 관련됩니다.

2. 미군 PX 및 Commissary 를 통하여 국내 암거래 시장에 부정유출되는 양담배의 유출방지를 위한 귀부의 요청에 관하여는 SOFA 한미 합동위원회 사무국을 통하여 일차적인 대미 협의를 시작하여 재무분과위원회에 대한 과제부여에 별첨과 같이 합의한 바 있음을 회신하오니 참고하시기 바라며, 금후의 협의 진행을 위하여 다음 사항을 회보하여 주시기 바랍니다.

가. 1972년도 부정유출 추정량 (산출근거 명시)

나. 1972년도 압수실적

다. 200갑 이상 대량압수 건수 (72년도)

라. 기타 참고사항

첨부 : SOFA 재무분과위원회에 대한 과제부여안 1부 끝.

정서 관인 발송

공통서식1-2(갑) 1967. 4. 4. 승인

190mm×268mm(1급인쇄용지70g/m²) 조달청 (500,000매인쇄)

208

양담배 유출방지를 위한 SOFA 과제 부여

(1) 문제의 제기

주한미군용 양담배의 부정유출이 대규모화하는 최근 현상에 대비, 효과적 단속방안의 하나로 주한미군의 총 연초반입량을 SOFA 규정 제9조 합의의사록 3항에 의거 통보하여 줄것을 건매청이 요청.

(2) 관계 규정 운용현황

주한미군 당국은 제65차 합동위원회 (71. 8. 26.) 합의에 의거, 35개 품목 (양담배가 제외되어 있음)의 반입량을 월별로 통보.

(3) 신규과제 부여

전기 35개 통보대상 품목에 양담배를 추가하기 위하여 관계 분과위원회에 과제부여 예정.

209

공 란

공 란

공 란

공 란

공 란

공 란

공 란

공 란

공 란

공 란

공 란

공 란

공 란

공 란

공 란

10 [illegible]

전 매 청

판매 823.73_ 227 (75_5807) 1973. 5. 23.

수신 외무부 장관

참조 미주국장

제목 양담배 부정 유출 방지를 위한 정보 제공 품목 추가

미이 723_16080(73. 5. 9) 및 협력 1243_354(73. 5.15)에 의거 별첨과 같이 자료를 제출 합니다.

첨부 1. 72년도 부정 유출 추정량

2. " 양담배 압수실적

3. " 200갑 이상 압수실적

4. 기타 참고사항. 끝.

공람	73년 5월 24일	담당	과장	국장	참관보	차관	장관

발송 No. 1973. 5. 24 전매청

전 매 청

전매청장인

지우수[illegible]

225

별첨 1

72년도 양담배 부정 유출량 추정량 조서

72년도 양담배 부정 유출 추정량 = 26,172,000갑으로 추정함.

산출근기

1. 가. 70년도 양담배 부정 유출량 18,908,000갑
(미군측 P.X 판매량 통보 자료에 의함 ..... 산출근기 별첨)
나. 70년도 전매청 압수물량 ..... 87,650갑 (총 유출량의 0.4%에 해당함)

2. 가. 72년도 전매청 압수물량 121,321갑
나. 압수물량을 유출량의 0.4%로 보았을때 72년도 총 유출량은 26,172,000갑으로 추산함.

* 주한 미군수는 감소되었으나 양담배 국내 반입량은 감소되지 아니하고 부정 유출량이 증가 되는 것으로 사료됨.

226

* 70년도 년간 양담배 부정 유출량 추정 근거

구분 / 월별	총 판매량 (1)	이용권자 수요량 (1일 2갑 소비경우) (2)	부정 유출 추정량 (3)	비 고
1	6,912,130갑	4,200,000갑	2,712,130갑	
2	6,261,241	4,200,000	2,061,241	
3	6,084,902	4,200,000	1,884,902	
4	5,976,272	4,200,000	1,776,272	
5	5,747,235	4,200,000	1,547,235	
6	5,604,116	4,200,000	1,404,116	
7	5,506,231	4,200,000	1,306,231	
8	5,352,600	4,200,000	1,152,600	
9	5,246,240	4,200,000	1,046,240	
10	5,065,800	4,200,000	865,800	
계	57,756,767갑	42,000,000갑	15,756,767갑	
월평균	5,775,676 "	4,200,000 "	1,575,676 "	

주 (1) P.X 홍보 자료에 의함 (70.1월 _ 10월)

(2) P.X 이용권자 수(미군인 및 군속과 그의 가족 포함) 약 70,000명

(3) P.X 이용권자 수의 소비 추정량(월간)

1인 1일 2갑 소비의 경우

2갑 × 1일 × 30일 × 70,000 = 4,200,000갑

(4) 월간 부정 유출 추정량(평균)

(1) _ (2) = (3) 5,775,676갑 _ 4,200,000갑 = 1,575,676갑

(5) 년간 부정 유출 추정량

1,575,676갑 × 12월 = 18,908,112갑

2217

별첨 2　　　72년도 양담배 압수실적

총 검거건수	양 담 배		벌 과 금	비 고
	건 수	압 수 물 량		
5,731건	4,856건	(121,321갑) 2,426,425본	119,600,494원	

* 72년도 총 검거건수중 양담배 적발 건수가 85%임.

228

붙첨 3. 72 년도 200갑 이상 압수실적

단위 { 건수 : 건
　　　물량 : 갑

월별 / 구분	1		2		3		4		5		6		7		8		9		10		11		12		계	
	건수	물량	건수	물량	건수	물량	건수	물량	건수	물량	건수	물량	건수	물량	건수	물량	건수	물량	건수	물량	건수	물량	건수	물량	건수	물량
수량	13	24.488	10	13.177	5	1.280	11	14.108	3	1.040	4	13.452	6	4.319	9	5.789	3	1.900	.	.	1	840	4	2.990	69	83.[illegible]

229

별첨 4 기타 참고사항

1. 유출 근원별

가. 미국인과 국제 결혼한 양부인들을 세포로 하여 중간 도매 상인이 조직을 펴고 있는 경우, 이들은 티켓(P.X 사용 허가표) 소지하고 있어 P.X 의 자유로운 출입이 허용되고 있으며 담배는 1인당 하루의 구입 규정량이 있지만 실제로는 얼마든지 초과해서 구입할 수 있음.

나. 암상인 직접 P.X 와 관련을 맺고 있는 경우, 대체로 미군 부대에 근무하는 한국인을 앞잡이로 하거나 그들이 당사자인 예가 많으며 량적으로 최대의 루트이면서도 가장 손대기 어려운 조직으로 미군이 직접 개입하여 운반을 특수 차량으로 하기 때문에 포착하기 어려운 실정임.

2. P.X 로 부터의 양담배 부정 유출 경로

가. 한국인 종업원과 "부로카"의 사전 모의로 P.X 의 운반 차량을 이용하여 "부로카"가 지정한 장소에 운반 매각.

나. P.X 에서 미군과 P.X 이용권자가 매입한것을 위안부를 통하여 중간 상인 또는 보따리 상인에게 매각.

다. 보따리 상인이 제 차량(뻐스, 택시등)을 이용하여 시중에 반입후 시장 또는 가정에 매각.

3. 유출의 형태(도표)

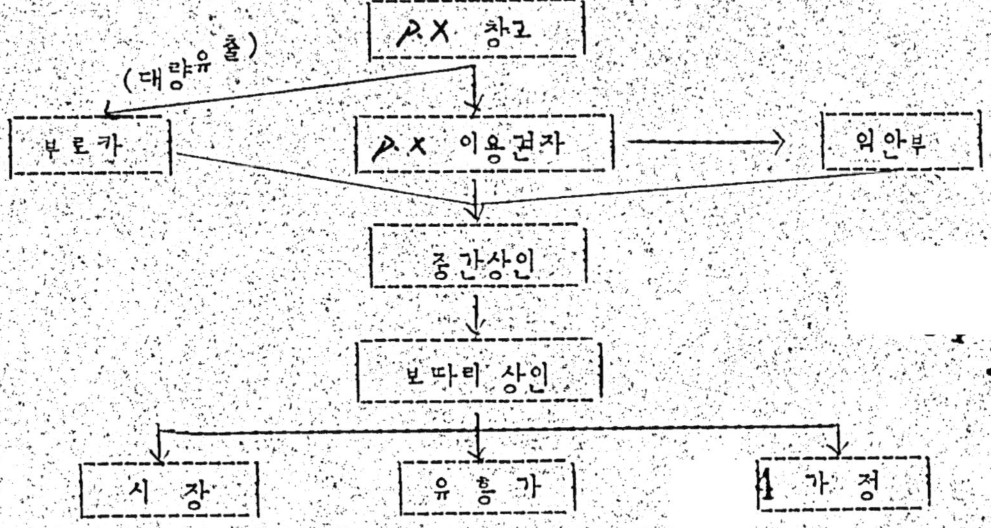

217

230

4. 부정 유출 방지 대책

가. 주한 미군의 P.X 및 Commissary에서 면세 담배가 계속 다량(BOX)으로 유출되고 있는 실정임.

나. 당청 감시 공무원으로 하여금 집중 단속을 하고 있으나 제한된 공무원으로는 근절시키기 어려운 실정이며 양담배의 원천은 P.X 임으로 근본적인 대책은 미군 P.X에 실수요량만을 반입하고 한국인에 유출이 없도록 하는 것임.

다. 한·미 군대 지위 협정에 의하여 설치된 한·미 합동 위원회를 통하여 미군측의 이해와 자발적인 협조가 이루어 지도록(P.X 총 판매량 통보) 적극적인 협조가 요망됨.

라. 당청 감시 공무원에 의하여 양담배 200갑이상 적발 검거량 수량만 하더라도 상당한 량에 달하고 있으며 전매권의 침해는 물론 전매 세입에 막대한 지장을 초래하고 있는 실정임.

5. 년도별 양담배 단속 실적

단위 { 건 수 : 건 / 물 량 : 천본 / 벌과금 : 천원

년도 / 구분	68	69	70	71	72
건 수	2,570	4,992	3,950	4,436	4,856
물 량	646	1,773	1,753	2,658	2,426
벌과금	12,671	44,520	73,478	90,592	119,600

218

231

25 May 1973

MEMORANDUM FOR: Mr. Robert A. Kinney, J5

SUBJECT: Import Declaration Forms for Personal Imports by USFK Personnel

1. On 24 February 1972 a task was assigned the Finance (Personnel Affairs) Subcommittee to review "current procedures in effect for the declaration and certification of imports consigned by name to persons who are subject to the ROK-US SOFA." Negotiations on the task revealed that:

a. The ROK intent was to revise the USFK Form 2, used to declare and certify property entering Korea under the provisions of paragraph 2, Article IX, ROK-US SOFA (commonly referred to as USFK imports).

b. The ROK side was extremely desirous of USFK personnel using the new ROK import document since the document was designed to interface with their Electronic Data Processing System program of recording items cleared through ROK customs.

2. The subcommittee agreed on a revised USFK Form 2 on 8 September 1972, which was approved by the Joint Committee on 5 October 1972, and implemented for use on 1 December 1972.

3. Efforts to resolve procedures to declare and certify paragraph 3, Article IX, ROK-US SOFA, imports have become bogged down due to ROK insistence that examination procedures for household goods and personal effects be included in the agreed procedures.

4. Ancillary to the above actions the US side interposed no objection to utilizing the ROK Import Document (inclosure 1) for paragraph 3, Article IX imports, provided ROK side provided the forms for USFK usage free of charge. On 18 October 1972 the ROK Office of Customs Administration advised the EAPM that the ROK Import Document would be required for paragraph 3 imports commencing 1 November 1972 (inclosure 2). On 27 October 1972 US Component Chairman objected to the unilateral ROK action on imposing a new form when the subcommittee was engaged in formalizing not only the form, but procedures (inclosure 3). In response the ROK Component Chairman, on 1 November 1972, stated the forms would be provided free to the USFK (inclosure 4, paragraph 2).

232

Based upon free supply of the forms, and to foster a spirit of cooperation, the US agreed to using the new import declaration form. Since initial receipt of the forms for use problems in obtaining additional stocks have arisen. The ROK customs houses in Seoul and Pusan state the only means of acquiring the forms is to buy them at 500 won per 100 forms. To prevent delays in delivering goods Pusan has purchased some. On 14 May 1973 I contacted Mr. Kang Yang Joo, a ROK component subcommittee member, in the Customs Cooperation Section, Bureau of Customs, regarding the problem and explained the ROK commitment to provide the forms free. He stated that he would contact the Office of Customs Administration to resolve the matter and for me to contact Mr. Lee Churl Hee (75-2723), Director of the Import Section, Office of Customs Administration later in the week. I contacted Mr. Lee on 17 May 1973 and he acknowledged the problem, indicating that apparently there had been a mix-up somewhere. He verified that the forms should be provided USFK free and said they could be obtained if the personnel in Pusan contacted Mr. Cho Yong So, Chief of the Baggage Section at Pusan Customs House and in Seoul contact Mr. Yang Jae Ho, Chief of the Baggage Section at Seoul Customs House. I gave Mr. Lee the names of the USFK personnel who would receive the forms for the USFK at both locations and he stated he would pass them and additional instructions to Pusan and Seoul customs houses.

5. On 17 May 1973 SGT Rouse at Pusan POV processing and Mr. Pak (EA customs clearance section) were advised of who to contact to acquire the forms.

6. On 24 and 25 May 1973 I checked with both Pusan and Seoul to see if the problem had in fact been resolved. The answer from both was no change and the ROK's refuse to furnish the forms free.

7. Your assistance in resolving the matter is requested in order that it not become a major issue.

Robert E. Spydell

ROBERT E. SPYDELL
CDR, USN
Secretary, US Component
Finance (Personnel Affairs)
Subcommittee

233

대 한 민 국 세 관
KOREAN CUSTOMS SERVICE
수(반입)입 신 고 서
IMPORT DECLARATION
(갑지)

1 신고기간 197 . . .(일간)	부호
2 입항 Date of Entry 197 . . .	
3 ※선하증권번호 B/L No	
4 ※선(기)명 적재선(기) Name of Vessel (Aircraft)	
선 국 적 Nationality of Vessel (Aircraft)	
5 ※ 적출국 Country of Shipment	
6 ※ 입항지 Place of Entry	
7 ※ 원산국 Country of Production	
8 ※ 장치장소 Place of Storage	

11※ 세관부호	12※ 수입채권번호	13 신고번호

※ 기관
14 수입허가 번호
년월일 197 . . .
15 신 고 197 . .
16 검 사 197 . .
17 조 정 197 . .
18 면 허 197 . .

9※ 주소	10※ 수입 형태 별		19※ 주소
수 Importer address	① 면허전반출	⑤ 면허전반출완결분	신 Declarant Address
주민등록번호	② 보세공장반입	⑥ 보세공장 수입 면허분	주민등록번호
입 상호 및 무역등록No.	③ 보세건설장 반입	⑦ 보세건설장수입면허분	고 상호
자 성명인 Name and Signature	④ 보세전시장반입	⑧ 보세전시장수입면허분	자 성명인 Name and Signature

20 ※ 품명 및 규격 DESCRIPTION OF ARTICLES & GRADE	21※ 중량 WEIGHT / 22※ 수량 QUANTITY	23※ 단위 UNIT	24※ 신고가격 DECLARED VALUE / 25 감정가격 APPRAISED VALUE	26 세번 / 27 특관세종	부호	28※ 세율 / 29 세율	30 관세액 / 31 특관세액	32 용관근기 부호 / 33 관세면제 근거부호
(1)	kg		CIF, $			%	W	
			W	( )				
			특		종	%	W	
(2)	kg		CIF, $			%	W	
			W	( )				
			특		종	%	W	
34 비고	합		CIF, $	35 환율			W	
	계		W 특				W	

36 내국세					37 증지 증인	38 세번계	(가) 고지번호	(나) 세액
① 과세가격	② 세번	③ 세종	④ 세율	⑤ 세액	매	① 관세		
W			%	W	계	② 특관세		
W			%	W	매 계	③ 물품세		
⑥ 원천과세 표준 W				합계	매 계	④ 세		
. 비고						⑤ 영업세		
						⑥ 소득세 법인세		

39 신고서 배 란
40 허가서 분할 □원본은
신고번호______(. . .)접수
41 검 사
생 략□
검 사 장□
장치장소□
검 정 시□
수입인지 첨부란

43 ※ 기호, 번호, 포장 종류와 개수 Markings, Numbering, Type and Number of Packages

44 ※ 보세운송
목적지:
경유지:
수송: ①육로□ ②해로□ ③공로□
기간: . . . 부터
도착일: . . . 까지

45 면허일

46 ※ 첨부서류 Attached herewith, if any
수입허가서 ( ) □ Import License
송 품 장 ( ) □ Invoice
포장명세서 ( ) □ Packing List
원산지증명 ( ) □ Certificate of Origin
운임명세서 ( ) □ Freight Sheet
보험영수증 ( ) □ Receipt of Insurance
선하증권사본 ( ) □ copy of B/L

221

접 수	검 사	주 무	과 장	주 무	과 장	장
	2774					

Incl 1

Office of Customs Administration

Taxation Section 1242-2702 (75-3703) 18 October 1972

TO: Commanding General
Eighth United States Army
ATTN: EAPM
APO 96301

SUBJECT: Imports Declaration of Paragraph 3, Article 9, SOFA

In accordance with the Paragraph 3, Article 9 of the SOFA, members of the United States Armed Forces, DAC and their dependents customs declaration for household goods and personal effects, should used the attached imports declaration form (sample), effective date 1 November 1972. Inform all of your units, your cooperation is required for preventine of problem.

Director
Customs Administration

Incl 2

235

REPUBLIC OF KOREA - UNITED STATES
FINANCE (PERSONNEL AFFAIRS) SUBCOMMITTEE
SEOUL, KOREA

27 October

Mr. PARK Dong Hee
Chairman, ROK Component
Finance Subcommittee

Dear Mr. Park:

The letter with the attached form at Inclosure 1 was passed, by the Provost Marshal, Eighth US Army, to me yesterday as being a matter under our subcommittee cognizance. At Inclosure 2 is a translation of the Office of Customs Administration letter.

In view of the negotiations which have been in progress for the past two and one-half months regarding forms for declaration and certification of Article IX, paragraph 3 imports and the long standing task to determine procedures for examination of household goods and personal effects, I feel that unilateral action, as indicated by the letter at Inclosure 1, is unwarranted and not in consonance with the past history of mutual consultation and agreement prior to implementation.

In our prior negotiations I have pointed out the following basic problem areas with the form:

1. Block 17, date of examination, is not satisfactory for household goods and personal effects until we reach mutual agreement on the task which was assigned on 25 May 1967, which placed the issue of examination of household goods and personal effects before the subcommittee for resolution. Further, I believe I have made clear the problems confronting the US Government in authorizing the examination of household goods and personal effects at any point other than the point of delivery.

236 Incl 3

Mr. PARK Dong Hee 27 October 1972

2. No designated block for USFK Customs Clearance Officer certification of entitlement for duty-free entry. This is required to protect both our interests and prevent abuse of the customs/duty-free privilege enjoyed by USFK.

3. There is no agreement as to who will provide the form for USFK usage. During the joint subcommittee meeting on 8 September 1972, it was directed that the component secretaries work together and attempt to resolve the problem areas. At their last meeting on 28 September 1972, my LCDR Spydell told Mr. LEE that he would draft procedures and we would submit them to your side for consideration. We expect to have these proposed procedures for Article IX, paragraph 3, imports ready for submission to your side by 8 November 1972.

Since the subcommittee is actively involved in resolving the Article IX, paragraph 3, declaration and certification process, I must ask that you have the letter at Inclosure 1 rescinded. If you feel a joint subcommittee meeting will assist in resolving the matter, please inform me and we will schedule it at the earliest practicable time.

Sincerely,

JOSEPH T. FORDHAM
Colonel, USAF
Chairman, US Component
Finance (Personnel Affairs)
Subcommittee

2 Inclosures
As stated

2

237

MINISTRY OF FINANCE
THE REPUBLIC OF KOREA
SEOUL, KOREA

1 November, 1972.

JOSEPH T. FORDHAM
Colonel, USAF
Chairman, US Component
Finance (Personnel Affairs) Subcommittee

Dear Col. FORDHAM:

In response to your letter, dated 27 October 1972, I would like to make clear our position regarding some problem areas with the form for declaration and certification of Paragraph 3, Article IX, "Imports".

1. No declaration form for personal effects has been stipulated in the SOFA and related regulations. This should be construed to use the generalized forms designed by the Office of Customs Administration. The Office of Customs Administration is scheduled to adopt the newly designed import declaration forms for personal effects beginning on 1 November 1972. Accordingly, it is, I believe, warranted to apply the above forms for your personal effects.

2. Import declaration forms are provided and sold by the Korean Tariff Association, a civil organization apart from the Government. This does not fall within the category of exemption of charges described in Paragraph 3, Article IX, SOFA. However, the Office of Customs Administration has negotiated with the above association to furnish the forms free to USFK.

3. Block 19 (Declarant) may be used as USFK customs clearance officer certification of entitlement for duty free entry.

4. As for current customs clearance procedures which have been suspended since the task assignment on 25 May 1967 by the Joint Committee, customs clearances for personal effects have been performed without trouble as described in the present SOFA, except the exemption from customs examination described in Paragraph 5, Article IX, SOFA. Accordingly, I don't believe it is necessary

238 Incl 4

1 November, 1972

to establish any special customs examination procedures for personal effects.

Your kind understanding in this matter will be appreciated.

Sincerely yours,

Park Dong Hee
Chairman, ROK Component
Finance Subcommittee

239

협 조 문

응신기일

분류기호 및 문서번호	미이 723-51	제 목	SOFA 규정 해석
수 신	방고국장	발신일자	1973. 6. 13. (협조제의)

북미2과	이○교 재	73년 6월 13일	담당	과장	국장	차관보	차관	장관

발신명의 미주국장

(제 1 의 견)

연 : 협조문 미이 723-35 (73. 4. 16.)

미군 화물 수송을 위하여 국내 수송업체가 사용하는 유류에 대한 면세조치의 타당성 여부에 관하여 미측은 별첨과 같은 의견을 제시하고 있으므로 이를 주가 송부하오니 관계 규정 해석에 참고하시고 6. 18.까지 귀국의 의견을 회보하여 주시기 바랍니다.

(제 2 의 견)

첨부 : 미측 각서 1 부. 끝.

0201-1-2B
1969. 11. 10승인

190mm×268mm(신문용지)
(조달청) 300.000매 인쇄

240

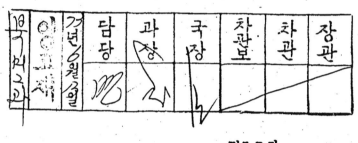

JAJ

LEGAL MEMORANDUM FOR: FINANCIAL AFFAIRS SUBCOMMITTEE CHAIRMEN

SUBJECT: Immunity of Certain Fuel Purchased by Trucking Contractors From the ROK Petroleum Taxes

1. A legal question has arisen in connection with the purchase of gasoline by local contractors for use in certain trucking contracts with the US forces. Normally, a petroleum tax is imposed by ROK law on the sale of all petroleum products by petroleum sellers. The contracts were concluded with an assumption by the parties thereto that the motor fuel to be purchased for the contracts was to be exempt from ROK petroleum taxes in view of provisions of Article XVI, SOFA. In fact, one ROKG governmental element has stated that the subject fuel was exempt from the petroleum tax; however, the ROKG tax authorities have concluded that the subject fuel purchased for the contracts was not exempt and was not being procured by or for the use by the United States armed forces within the meaning of the US-ROK SOFA.

2. Article XVI, paragraph 3 of the SOFA is the legal ground on which the substantive issue of this matter must be resolved. This states, in pertinent part:

241

"Materials, supplies, equipment and services procured for official purposes in the Republic of Korea by the United States armed forces including their authorized procurement agencies, or procured for ultimate use by the United States armed forces shall be exempt from the following Korean taxes upon appropriate certification in advance by the United States armed forces:

(a) commodity tax;
(b) traffic tax;

(c) petroleum tax;
(d) electricity and gas tax;
(e) business tax.

* * * * * (emphasis supplied.)

3. Paragraph 4 of the Agreed Minutes Re Article XVI, also provides a specific definition of what is meant by procurement for ultimate use:

"Materials, supplies, equipment and services procured for ultimate use" refers to procurement by contractors of the United States armed forces from Korean suppliers of items to be incorporated into or necessary for the production of the end product of their contracts with the United States armed forces.

4. It would seem that the tax exemption can be legally supported in the subject cases on either of two possible major legal grounds: one, that the procurement is directly by the US armed forces themselves, on the theory that the contractors are merely acting as agents for the US armed forces and two, that this is a pure case of indirect procurement, as defined in the SOFA, and that the contractors must be granted immunity from the ROK petroleum taxes otherwise applicable to the purchases provided they comply with the procedural provisions laid down by the

2

242

SOFA. The first ground of exemption, i.e., the theory of agency, would seem to be applicable to the situation only in the event that the SOFA had no provisions directly in point, or were vague and ambiguous. In such a case, general principles of international law bearing on the question of interpretation of international treaties and agreements, as well stated by the Harvard Research in International Law in a draft convention on Treaties, Art 19 (29 Am J. Int'l L. Supp 937), would indicate that the SOFA should "be interpreted in the light of the general purpose which it is intended to serve. The historical background of the treaty, the Travaux Preparatoires... are to be considered in connection with the general purpose which the treaty is intended to serve." Since it is a fact that it has been a well established general policy of the US, made well known to the ROKG during the negotiating period of the SOFA, that the US would under no conceivable circumstances pay for identifiable foreign taxes in its contracts with local firms, the theory of agency would under the assumed circumstances be usable for the subject exemption.

5. However, the rather specific provisions regarding the situation of indirect procurement in Article XVI of the SOFA lead to the tentative conclusion that the issues in this case should be resolved finally on the grounds of the "procurement for ultimate use" phrase, as used in the SOFA. For this reason, it would seem to be essential to determine, based on the requirements of the Agreed Minute quoted above, two questions; (1) whether the subject fuel has in fact been purchased by

243

contractors from Korean sources and whether it is necessary for the production of the "end product" of the contracts with the US. If the answers
to these questions are positive, the conclusion follows that the tax
exemption is warranted, unless it can be shown that this result is
inconsistent with the negotiating history or the subsequent conduct of the
parties.

6. There seems to be no logical basis to doubt that the fuel is an item
procured by contractors from Korean suppliers. That the fuel will be
incorporated into end products for the benefit of the US does seem to
require brief discussion. The contracts in these cases are for trucking
services, and it is obvious that a service can be an end product within
(a service is an item procured for the production of the end product)
the meaning of paragraph 4, in view of the provisions of paragraph 1,
Article XVI, quoted in paragraph 3, above, indicating that the US may
contract for "services." The only other question under paragraph 4 of
the Agreed Minute is whether or not the fuel in question is necessary
for the service being procured. The answer seems obvious that a
trucking contract cannot be accomplished without motor fuel being used.

7. The negotiating history of Article XVI, carefully examined, quite
strongly supports the above conclusions. Article XVI received a very
detailed analysis by the negotiators in view of an ROK concern that its
provisions could be so implemented as to require exemptions from ROK
taxes at very remote stages of the production of procured items (27th

Meeting). The US position was in effect that the US neither could nor would pay for any significant and readily identifiable taxes on any Korean procured materials, supplies, equipment and services.* . The issue was resolved on the basis of an understanding that no real problem existed when ROK taxes were levied in the last stage of procurement. In any earlier stage, if the tax were identifiable and a significant part of the purchase price, an exemption would be sought in the Joint Committee (53rd Meeting). This might indicate the necessity of a Joint Committee agreement on our question if it were not for the fact that the ROK negotiators, at the 27th Meeting, clearly stated that the problem of primary or intermediate stages could never arise in the case of petroleum taxes because these were readily identifiable at the point of ultimate use. Certainly, when fuel is purchased for use in a trucking contract, this is the "ultimate" use of such fuel and within the scope of the ROK statement at the 27th Meeting. Nor has it ever been questioned that petroleum taxes are readily identifiable and do constitute a substantial portion of the contract price for the service of transportation in the cases at issue.

8. The remaining questions are procedural and require consideration of the impact of paragraph 3 of the Agreed Minuteto Article XVI which was designed to establish the procedure whereby tax exemptions would be granted on purchases for US ultimate use. Paragraph 3 establishes a

*This "significant and readily identifiable" test was in fact incorporated into the provisions of Article XVI in connection with all taxes not specifically referred to in the Article.

245

system whereby an authorized representative of the US forces takes delivery of the goods, and collection of the taxes is "held in abeyance" until assurances are furnished that the goods are to be actually consumed or incorporated into articles or facilities used by the US armed forces. As the negotiating history indicates, paragraph 3 was intended to reflect the procedure existing at the time of negotiations, i.e., the period circa 1965. There does not appear to be any issue at this stage of the question as to the willingness of the US to comply with paragraph 3 procedures if the ROKG so desires. However, the issue as posed by the ROKG thus far is not based on the provisions of paragraph 3 - which are procedural - but on those other provisions of Article XVI which are substantive in nature. From the legal view, it is not material whether fuel is purchased by the contractor - as is apparently the present practice and consistent with paragraph 4 of the Agreed Minute - or is received from the manufacturer or distributor by an authorized representative of the US and later turned over to the contractor - as appears to be contemplated by paragraph 3 of the Agreed Minute. In both cases, the substantive nature of the tax exemption is based on Article XVI and cannot be denied by procedural rules developed on the basis of past practices. One more factor to note in connection with the procedural problem of conformance with paragraph 3 (a) of the Agreed Minute to Article XVI is that the subject contracts all come within the category of contracts intended to serve for the maintenance or operation of US military facilities and areas

246

referred to in Article V of the SOFA.

9. Based on the foregoing discussion, it may be concluded that (a) the ROKG is legally obligated under the provisions of paragraph 3, Article XVI, as amplified by paragraph 4 of the Agreed Minute to Article XVI, to accord exemption from the ROK petroleum taxes on fuel purchased by local contractors for use in contracts of transportation with the US armed forces in the ROK and (b) that the procedural requirements of paragraph 3(a) of the Agreed Minute may, but need not, be followed to obtain the subject exemptions.

2017

협 조 문	응신기일

분류기호 및 문서번호 방조 740-147 제목 SOFA 규정 해석

수 신 미주국장 발신일자 1973. 7. 4. (협조제의)

북미2과	공람	년 월 일	담당	과장	국장	참관보	차관	장관

발신명의 방 교 국 장

대 : 미이 723-35(73. 6. 13) (제 1 의견)

대호건 미군의 화물 수송을 위하여 국내 수송업체가 사용하는 유류에 대한면세조치의 타당성 여부에 관하여당국의 의견을 다음과 같이 회시합니다.

- 다 음 -

1. SOFA 제 16조는 미군의 최종소비를 위하여 조달되는 materials, supplies, equipment 와 service 는 (제 2 의견) 미리 미군의 적절한 증명이 있으면 한국 유류세로 부터 면제된다고 규정하고 있으며,

2. 동 16조에 대한 합의의사록은 "미군의 최종소비를 위하여 조달되는 materials, supplies, equipment 와 service 라

0201-1-2 B
1969. 11. 10승인

190mm×268mm(신문용지)
조 달 청(200,000매 인쇄)

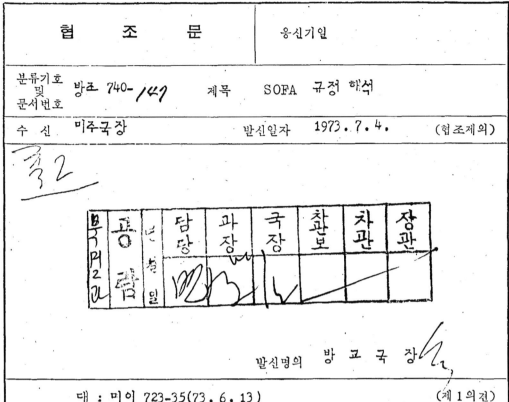

함은 미군의 계약자가 한국공급자로 부터 미군과 계약된 최종생산물을 생산하기 위하여 통합되거나 필요한 조목을 조달함을 말한다" 라고 되어 있으므로,

3. 미군과 화물 수송계약을 체결한 국내 수송업자에 대한 유류세 면세에 있어서

가. 여사한 업자는 상기 합의의사록에서 말하는 "미군의 계약자"에 해당되며,

나. 여사한 수송은 상기 합의의사록에서 말하는 "최종 생산물"에 해당되고,

다. 수송에 소요되는 유류는 상기 합의의사록에서 말하는 materials 에 해당되고,

라. 수송을 위하여는 유류가 "필요"한 것이므로, 이러한 경우 유류세 면제를 요청하는 미군측의 주장은 SOFA 규정의 해석상 이유가 있다고 사료됩니다. 끝.

249

1회 보고 통제
No. 12-1136
1973. 8. 14
최초작성기관
전체 보고 통제 국

내 무 부

세정 1234.9 - 1863 '73. 8. 14

수신 외무부장관

제목 주민세 특별징수에 대한 협조

1. 미8군에 근무하는 종업원에 대한 주민세 특별징수에 있어서 지방세법 제76조 제1항의 규정에 의하여 소득세(갑종근로 소득세) 원천징수의무자는 주민세 특별징수의무자로 하고 있으며 동법시행령 제54조의 규정에 의하여 주민세 특별징수 범위속에 갑종근로소득세에 대한 주민세도 포함하고 있으므로 응당 법에 의하여 미8군 특별징수의무자가 종업원에게 급료를 지급할 때는 국세인 갑종근로소득세와 지방세인 주민세(소득할)를 동시에 특별징수하여야 함에도 불구하고 별첨 서울특별시장의 공문사본과 같이 주민세에 관하여는 한국정부와 행정협정된바 없어 주민세 특별징수에 협조할수 없다는 의견인바 조속히 주민세 징수에 차질이 없도록 미8군당국과 협조하여 주시고 당부에 조치결과를 회보하여 주시기 바랍니다.

1973. 8. 14. 외무부

첨부 서울특별시 공문사본 1부. 끝

내 무 부 장 관

2361E

Lee Sang Hee, Chief, Local Tax Section
250 시경과 2478, 99. 김정국

외 무 부

접수일시	197 . 16 ... 43867 14 : 22
접수번호	제

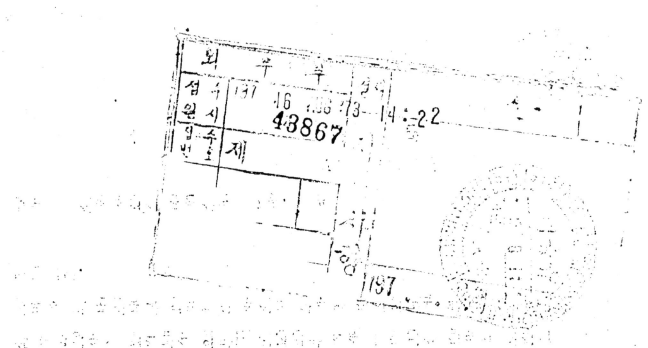

서 울 특 별 시

세정 1234 - 722 1973. 8. 9.

수신 내무부장관

참조 세정과장

제목 미8군 한국인 종업원의 주민세 특별 징수을 위한 조치

1. 미8군 산하 외국인 종업원에 대한 주민세 특별징수및 납입을 미8군 사령관 (한미 행정 협회 사무국)에 협조의뢰 하였으나 다음과 같은 이유로 협조할수 없다고 하오니 조속 조치하여 주시기 바랍니다.

2. 이 유

가. 한미 행정 협정상에 국세인 근로소득세는 협정이 되어 있으며

나. 지방세인 근로소득세할 주민세는 한국정부와 행정 협정사실이 없으므로 협조 할수 없음.

첨부 : 주민세 특별징수납입 협조 의뢰 사본 1부. 끝.

서 울 특 별 시 장

251

세무2 1234.9-13873 73. 8. 2.

수신 미8군 사령관 귀하 한미행정협의 사무국 (5)

제목 주민세 특별징수 납입협조 의뢰

42-1415
세무과장

1. 소득세를 원천 징수할 경우 소득세액의 $\frac{5}{100}$ 에 해당한 금액을 주민세 소득할로 징수하고 징수한달의 다음달 10일까지 관할구청에 납입하게 되었읍니다. 국세의 원천징수 의무자는 주민세의 특별징수 의무자로 되어 있읍니다. (지방세법 제76조 특별징수)

2. 귀 기관에서는 매월 소득세를 원천징수하여 관할 세무서에 납입하고 있읍니다. 주민세 소득할도 상기와 같이 관할구청에 일괄납입 하여 주시기 바랍니다. 본부에서 일괄 집중 납입하시면 산하 기관별 납입을 피할수 있읍니다.

3. 특별징수한 주민세 소득할 납입은 납입서에 계산서를 (명세서생략) 첨부하여 납입 하시기 바랍니다. (시행령 55조 2항)

4. 납입서 계산서는 시행규칙 제37조에 규정된 서식에 의하여야 합니다. 이것은 이미 특별징수 사무취급요령 책자를 보내드렸읍니다. 주민세 소득할 특별징수 납입에 적극 협조하여 주실것을 거듭 부탁드립니다. 끝.

용 산 구 청 장

262
6월 복리 징수 조항

증산 수출 건설

재 무 부

협력 1243-628 1973. 8. 16.

수신 수신처참조

제목 SOFA 재무분과 위원회 (한국측) 대책회의

SOFA 재무분과 위원회에 계류중인 아래 과제에 대한 토의를 위하여 다음과 같이 한국측 대책회의를 개최하고자 하오니 필히 참석하여 주시기 바랍니다.

1. 의제

가. 비세출 자금기관에 탁송되는 화물에 관한 정보제공

나. 별송품및 이사화물에 관한 세관 검사절차

다. 면세물품 양도 양수절차

2. 회의일시

1973. 8. 17(금) 15:00

3. 장소

재무부 관세협력담당관실

4. 참석범위

외무부 SOFA 재무분과 위원

관세청 "

전매청 감시과장

첨부 : 미측 초안 각1부. 끝.

발송 No. 1973. 8. 16 재무부

재 무 부 장 관

253

내집살림 나라살림 저축으로 부강하자

수신처 : 외무부장관, 관세청장, 전매청장

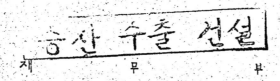

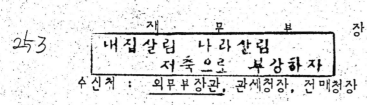

발송

No.

접수

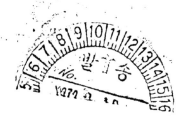

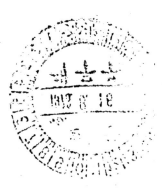

공 란

공 란

공　　　란

공 란

공 란

공 란

공 란

공 란

공 란

공 란

공 란

공 란

공　　란

공 란

공　란

대 한 민 국 세 관
KOREAN CUSTOMS SERVICE

수(반입) 입 신 고 서 (갑지)
IMPORT DECLARATION

1 처리기간 197 . . . (일간)

2 ※ 입항 Date of Entry 197 . . .

3 ※ 선하증권번호 B/L No

4 ※ 선(기)명 Name of Vessel (Aircraft)

선(기)국적 Nationality of Vessel (Aircraft)

5 ※ 적출국 Country of Shipment

6 ※ 입항지 Place of Entry

7 ※ 원산국 Country of Production

8 ※ 장치장소 Place of Storage

14 ※ 수입허가 기관 / 번호 / 년월일 197 . .

15 신고 197 . .

16 검사 197 . .

17 조정 197 . .

18 면허 197 . .

국비처리 [illegible]

9 ※ 수입자	
주소 Importer address	
주민등록번호	
상호 및 무역등록No.	
성명인 Name and Signature	

10 ※ 수입 형태 별	
(1) 면허전반입	(5) 면허전반출된것분
(2) 보세공장반입	(6) 보세공장수입면허분
(3) 보세전신장반입	(7) 보세건설장수입면허분
(4) 보세전시장반입	(8) 보세전시장수입면허분

19 ※ 신고자	
주소 Declarant Address	
주민등록번호	
상호	
성명인 Name and Signature	

20 ※ 품명 및 규격 DESCRIPTION OF ARTICLES & GRADE	21 ※ 중량 WEIGHT / 22 ※ 수량 QUANTITY	23 ※ 단위 UNIT	24 ※ 신고가격 DECLARED VALUE / 25 감정가격 APPRAISED VALUE	26 세번 / 27 특관세종	부호	28 세율 / 29 세율	30 관세액 / 31 특관세액	32 / 33
(1)	kg		CIF, $ / W / 과	( ) 종		% / %	W / W	
(2)	kg		CIF, $ / 과	( ) 종		% / %	W / W	
34 비고		합계	CIF, $ / W / 과	35 환율			W / W	

36 내국세					37 소지 증인
(1) 과세가격	(2) 세번	(3) 세종	(4) 세율	(5) 세액	
W			%	W	매 / 계
W			%	W	매 / 계
(6) 원천과세 표준 W				합계	매 / 계

38 세번계	(가) 고지번호	(나) 세액
(1) 관세		
(2) 특관세		
(3) 물품세		
(4) 세		
(5) 영업세		
(6) 소득세 법인세		

39 신고서 매

40 허가서 불참 □

신고번호 (. .

41 검사

성 단 □

검시장 □

검사장소 □

검정시 □

42 비고

43 ※ 기호, 번호, 포장 종류와 개수 Markings, Numbering, Type and Number of Packages

44 ※ 보세운송

목적지 :

경유지 :

수송 : ①육로□ ②해로□ ③공로□

기간 : . . . 부터 . . . 까지

도착인 : . . .

45 면허인

46 ※ 첨부서류 Attached herewith,

수입허가서 (Import License

송품장 (Invoice

포장명세서 (Packing List

원산지증명 (Certificate of Ori[illegible]

운임명세서 (Freight Sheet

보험인수증 (Receipt of Insura[illegible]

선하증권사본 (copy of B/L

(Others

접수	검사	주무	과장	주무	과장	장

269

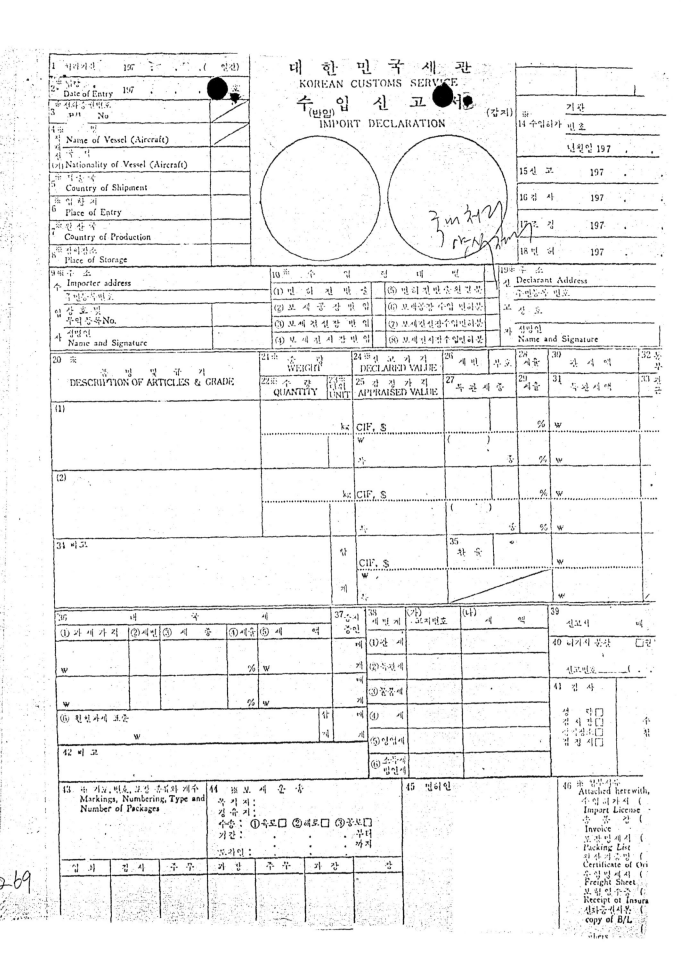

DRAFT

Notification of Delivery and Availability of Furniture, Household Goods and Personal Effects for Customs Examination

FROM: ______________________ (US Transportation Officer Concerned)　　TO: ______________________ (ROK Collector of Customs)　　DATE: ____________

1. Notification is hereby made of the intended delivery to the consignee and availability of the below indicated shipment for ROK Customs examination.

2. If examination is desired a customs official should be at this office not later than ________ (Time) on ______________ (Date) for transportation to the delivery location.

ORIGIN OF SHIPMENT	CONSIGNEE (Name & Grade)	GBL NUMBER	NO OF CONTAINERS IN THE SHIPMENT	GROSS WEIGHT	TYPES OF SHIPMENT[1]		
					Household Goods	Furniture	Personal Effects

1. Check Appropriate Column(s)

____
(Signature)

270

DRAFT

REPUBLIC OF KOREA - UNITED STATES
FINANCE (PERSONNEL AFFAIRS) SUBCOMMITTEE

MEMORANDUM FOR: The Joint Committee

SUBJECT: Review of Existing Procedures for the Disposal in the Republic of Korea of Duty-Free Goods

1. SUBCOMMITTEE MEMBERS:

UNITED STATES	REPUBLIC OF KOREA
COL Louis E. Herrick, USAF, Chairman	Mr. PARK Bong Whan, Chairman
CDR Robert E. Spydell, USN	Mr. KIM Kee In
COL Jeffrey R. McDougall, USAF	Mr. YANG Sei Hoon
LTC William H. Carnahan, USAF	Mr. WON Yoon Muk
COL George M. Gallagher, USA	Mr. KANG Yung Joo
LTC Glenn D. Spradlin, USA	Mr. LEE Jin Moo
LTC John D. Granger, USA	Mr. LEE Churl Hee
LT Miriam J. Lockard, USA	Mr. YANG Sung Bum
Mr. Samuel Pollack	Mr. BYUN Hyung
Mr. Francis Cook	Mr. BYUN, Seung Kook

2. Reference: a. Joint Committee's memorandum, dated 3 May 1972, subject as above.

b. Inclosure 6 to the Minutes of the Tenth Meeting of the Joint Committee, 22 June 1967.

DRAFT

271

DRAFT

3. In accordance with reference 2a, the procedures for disposal of goods imported into, or purchased in, the Republic of Korea free of duty by US Forces Korea personnel, as contained in reference 2b, have been reviewed. The existing procedures are considered to be adequate and no revision is necessary.

4. RECOMMENDATION: That the procedures contained in reference 2b, continue in effect without revision.

5. This completes the task assigned by reference 2a.

Mr. PARK Bong Whan Chairman, Republic of Korea Component Finance (Personnel Affairs) Subcommittee	COL Louis E. Herrick, USAF Chairman, United States Component Finance (Personnel Affairs) Subcommittee

DRAFT

272

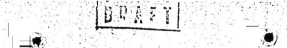

SOFA 재무분과위원회 (한국측) 대책회의

1. 일시및장소 : 1973. 8. 17.(금) 15:00 재무부 관세협력담당관실
2. 참석자 : 재무부 관세협력담당관 김기인
   " 관세협력담당관실 사무관 원윤묵
   전매청 감시과장
   외무부 북미2과 변승국
   관세청 심리과 사무관 엄낙용
   " 수입과 사무관 허노준

3. 합의내용 :

가. 비세출 자금기관에 탁송되는 미군화물에 관한 정보제공 문제

1) 현재 미군측으로 부터 한국 관계당국에 정기적으로 통보되고 있는 35개 미군화물 품목에 담배를 추가하는 문제(73. 5. 24. 제 84차 합동회의에서 과제부여)에 관하여는 담배이외에 또다시 커피를 추가하기로 함.

2) 현행 판매량 통보에 재고량 통보를 추가하도록 미측에 요청하기로 함.

나. 미군 개인화물에 관한 세관검사 절차문제

1) 세관검사 장소에 관하여 미측은 "at the point of delivery to the consignee" 로 할것을 주장하고 있으며, 한국측은"at port of entry" 로 할것을 주장함으로써 이문제는 장기간 미해결 상태에 있었으나 양측 주장을 완화하여 "at the point agreed between ROK-US appropriate authorities" 로 할것으로 합의.

273

2) 미군 개인화물 수입신고 양식은 별도로 제작하지 않고 현행 국내용 수입신고서 양식으로 쓰도록 대미 협의하기로 함.

3) 동 수입신고서 양식은 민간협회인 관세협회에서 유료로 판매하고 있으나 미측에 대하여는 필요 매수를 무료로 제공키로 함.

다. 면세물품 양도 양수절차 문제

1) 면세로 수입된 미군 사유차량의 판매창구를 관광공사로 일원화 하는 문제는 (72. 5. 30. 제 74차 합동회의에서 과제부여) 현행절차를 그대로 쓰도록 하고 기 부여된바 있는 과제는 철회하도록 함.

북미2과	공람	73년 8월 24일	담당	과장	국장	차관보	차관	장관
			(서명)	(서명)	(서명)			

274

면 담 기 록

(북미 2과)

1. 제 목 : 주한미군의 한국인 종업원 주민세 징수 문제

2. 일 시 : 73. 8. 24. 14:00 - 14:10

3. 면 담 자 : 양세훈 서기관
Mr. Kinney (SOFA 미측간사)

4. 내 용 :

가. 아측은 북미 2과장 (SOFA 한국측 간사)의 귀임을 기다려 공식 논의할것임을 전제하고, 비공식 의견 교환으로서 지방세법에 의거, 한국인 종업원의 주민세를 미측이 징수하여주는 문제에 대한 의견을 타진함.

나. 미측은 소득세에 관한 한 SOFA 제 17조 합의 의사록 3항에 의거, 징수하고 있으나, 주민세에 관하여는 하등의 의무규정도 없고 또한 미측의 인력사정으로 보아 협조할수 있는 전망이 희박하다고 말함.

다.

양

2175

공 란

공　　　란

공 란

공 란

기 안 용 지

분류기호 문서번호	미이723-	(전화번호)	전결규정 조 항 국 장 전결사항
처리기간			
시행일자	73. 9. 19.		
보존년한			국 장

보조기관	과 장		협조	
기안책임자	정의용	북미 2과	발송 No. 1973 9 ... 외무부	통제 검열 1973 9 .0 통제관

경 유	
수 신	재무부장관
참 조	세제국장
제 목	긴급과제 부여

미 8군 근무 한국인 종업원에 대한 주민세(소득할) 특별 징수건에 관한 내무부로 부터의 협조요청(별첨 공문사본)에 의하여, 별첨 각서내용과 같이 73. 9.12. SOFA 합동위원회 재무분과 위원회에 긴급과제 부여 되었음을 통보하오니, 조치하시기 바랍니다.

첨 부: 1. 내무부 요청공문 사본 1부.
2. 긴급과제 부여 각서 사본 1부. 끝.

정서

관인

1214

0201-1-8A (갑)
1969.11.10. 승인

190mm×268mm(특급인쇄용지40g/m²)
조 달 청 (1,500,000매 인 쇄)

280

기 안 용 지

분류기호 문서번호	미이723-	(전화번호)	전결규정 조 항 국장 전결사항
처리기간			
시행일자	73. 9. 19.		
보존년한		국 장	

보조기관	과 장		협조	
기안책임자	정의용	북미 2과		

경 유 수 신 참 조	내무부장관	발송 No. 1973 9 20 외무부	통제	검열 1973 9 20 통제관
제 목	주민세 특별징수에 대한 협조			

대: 세정 1234.9-1863 (73. 8.14.)

대호 미 8군 근무 한국인 종업원에 대한 주민세(소득할) 특별징수 건에 관하여 별첨 내용과 같이 73. 9.12. 자로 재무분과 위원회에 긴급과제로 부여되었음을 통보하오니 양지하시기 바랍니다.

첨 부: 긴급 과제부여 각서 사본 1부. 끝.

정서

관인

발송

0201-1-8A (갑)
1969. 11. 10. 승인

190mm×268mm(부급인쇄용지40g/m²)
조 달 청 (1,500,000매 인 쇄)

281

증산 수출 건설

재 무 부

협력 1243-644 (70-3225) 1973. 9. 7.

수신 외무부장관

제목 SOFA 한미합동위원회에 대한 건의

1. 미이 720-11882(72.4.20), 미이 720-15719(72.5.22) 및 미이 723-21196(73.6.14)에 대한 것입니다.

2. 제 72차, 제 73차 및 제 84차 SOFA 한미합동위원회에서 재무분과위원회에 과제부여한

가. P.X 통제품목추가

나. 면세물품 양도 양수 절차

다. P.X 판매정보 제공절차의 3개 사안이 SOFA 재무분과위원회에서 합의 되었기에 별첨과 같이 송부하오니 합동위원회에서 승인되도록 조치하여 주시기 바랍니다.

첨부 한미재무분과위원회 합의 각서 2건. 끝.

0088

재 무 부 장

정부공문서규정 제27조 제2항의 규정에 의하여
관 세 국 장 송 병 순 전결

새마을 나라살림
저축으로 부강하자

282

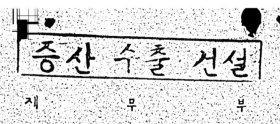

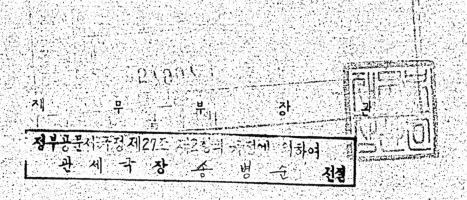

외 무 부

일 시	1967. 3. 13 15 24	
일 시	57907	
접수번호	제	
주무과		
담당자		

[illegible]

처리할것

[illegible]

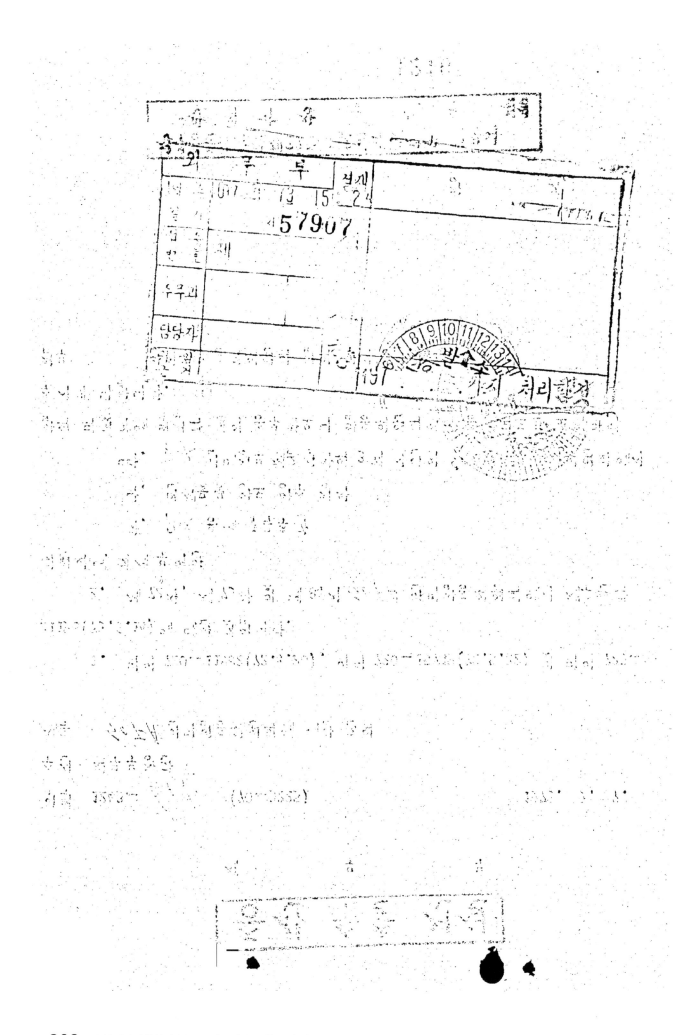

공 란

공 란

공 란

공 란

공 란

공 란

공 란

공 란

기 안 용 지

분류기호 문서번호	미이 723 -	(전 화 번 호)	전 결 규 정 조 항 국장 전 결 사 항
처 리 기 간			
시 행 일 자	1973. 10. 5.		
보 존 년 한			국 장

보 조 기 관	과 장		협

| 기 안 책 임 자 | 양세훈 | 북미 2 과 | |

경 유		발	통
수 신	재무부장관		
참 조	관세국장	신	제

제 목	SOFA 합동위원회의 건의 승인

대 : 협력 1243 - 644

　　　1.　당부는　SOFA　재무분과위원회에서 합의, 건의한 P.X.

통제품목 추가, 판매정보제공 절차 및 면세물품 양도　양수절차에 관한

3개 사안을 73. 10. 4. 개최된 제 88차 합동위원회에 회부하였든 바,

동 건의안이 원안대로 승인되었음을 통보하여 드립니다.

　　　2.　이에 관한 제 88차 합동위원회의 회의록은 추후 송부하여

드리겠읍니다.　끝.

	정 서
	관 인
	발 송

75

공동서식1-2(갑)
1967. 4. 4. 승인

190 mm ×268 mm (1급인쇄용지70g /m²)
조달청　(500,000매인쇄)

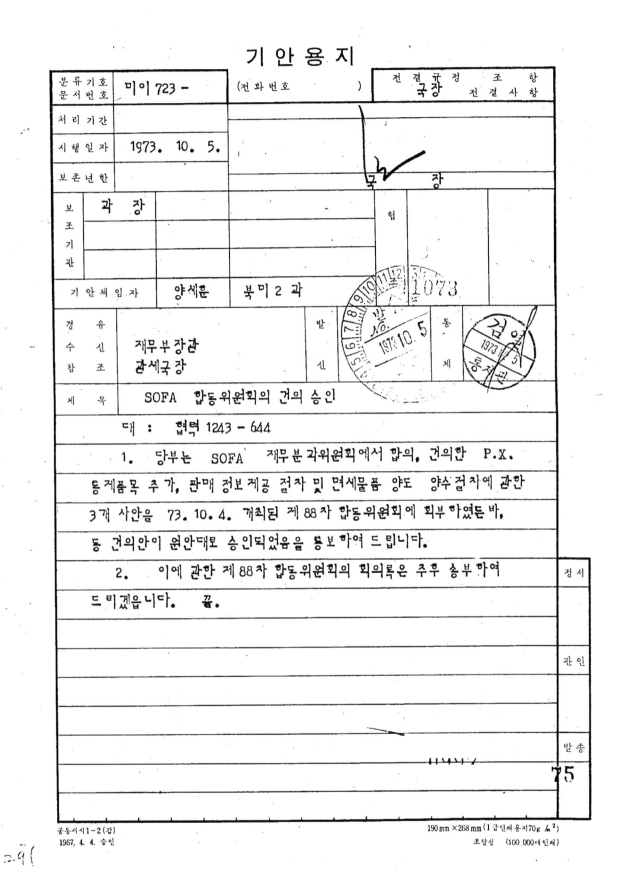

공 란

공　　　란

공 란

기 안 용 지

분류기호 문서번호	미이 723 -	(전화번호)	전결규정 조 항 전결사항 국장
처리기간			
시행일자	73. 11. 29.		
보존년한		국 장	
보조기관	과 장		협조
기안책임자	정의용	북미 2과	
경유 수신 참조	재무부 장관 관세국장		통제
제목	P.X. 통제 품목 재조정		

대 : 협력 1243 - 644 (73. 9. 7.)

연 : 미이 723 - 41073 (73. 10. 5.)

주한 미군 당국은, 73. 10. 4. 제 88 차 SOFA 합동위원회에서 승인된바 있는 SOFA 재무 분과위원회의 건의안중 P.X. 통제 품목의 재검토, 조정을 위하여 별첨과 같이 동 분과위원회에 대한 과제 부여를 제의하여 왔는 바, 이에 대한 귀부의 의견을 조속 회시 바랍니다.

첨부 : 미측 제의안 사본 1부. 끝.

정서 관인 발송

공용서식1-2(갑)
1967. 4. 4. 승인

190mm×268mm (1급인쇄용지70g/m²)
조달청 (300,000매인쇄)

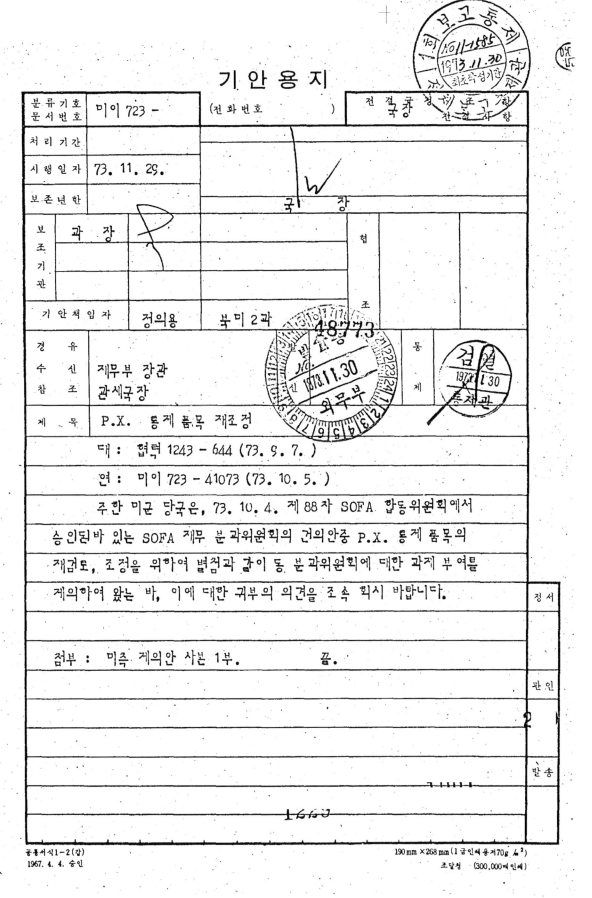

외 무 부

미이 723 - 73. 11. 29.

수 신 : 재무부 장관

참 조 : 관세국장

제 목 : P.X.통제 품목 재조정

대 : 협력 1243 - 644 (73. 9. 7.)

연 : 미이 723 - 41073 (73. 10. 5.)

주한 미군 당국은, 73. 10. 4. 제 88차 SOFA 합동위원회에서 승인된바 있는 SOFA 재무 분과위원회의 건의안중 P.X. 통제 품목의 재검토, 조정을 위하여 별첨과 같이 동 분과위원회에 대한 과제 부여를 제의하여 왔는 바, 이에 대한 귀부의 의견을 조속 회시 바랍니다.

첨부 : 미측 제의안 사본 1부. 끝.

외 무 부 장 관

296

증산 수출 건설

재 무 부

협력 1243 - 883 (70-3227) 1973. 12. 3.

수신 외무부장관

제목 P.X. 통제품목 재조정

585

1. 미이 723 - 48773 (73. 11. 29.) 에 대한 회신입니다.

2. 당부는 P.X. 통제품목의 재검토와 조정을 위하여 미측이 재무분과위원회에 대한 과제 부여를 제의한데 대하여 동의함을 통보합니다. 끝.

1973.12.

공람	73 12 5일				차관	장관

재 무 부 장관

재무부장관인

정부공문서규정 제27조 제2항의 규정에 의하여
관 세 국 장 송 병 순 전결

1231

내집살림 나라살림
저축으로 부강하자

외무부	1973 NOV 28
접수 일시	1973. 11. 28
접수번호	제71483호
주무과	
담당자	
일자	

지시사항

197 . . .까지 처리할

1004

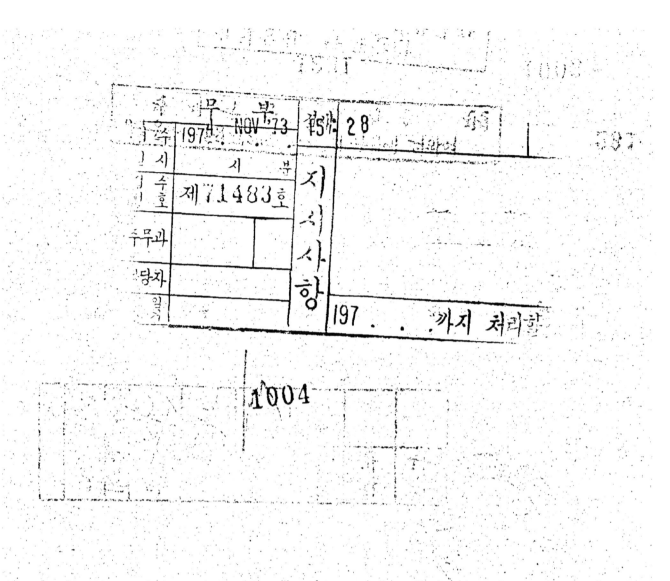

정/리/보/존/문/서/목/록					
기록물종류	문서-일반공문서철	등록번호	18108 6166	등록일자	2001-12-19
분류번호	729.415	국가코드		주제	
문서철명	SOFA-한.미국 합동위원회 재무분과위원회 - 주한미군 APO(미국군사우체국)를 통한 군사우편 소포 검사 절차 개정, 1973.12.13				
생산과	안보담당관실	생산년도	1971 - 1973	보존기간	영구
담당과(그룹)	미주	안보	서가번호	--	
참조분류					
권차명					
내용목차	1. 1971 2. 1972 3. 1973 * 1973.12.13 미국 군사우편 소포에 대해 관세 부과조치 결정 * 기타 미군용 수입신고서 양식개정 비세출자금기관(PX) 및 COMMISARY통제물품 추가 합동수사반 증설 면세물품 양도양수				

마/이/크/로/필/름/사/항				
촬영연도	*롤 번호	화일 번호	후레임 번호	보관함 번호
2007-09-21	Re-07-09	1	1-293	

결 번

넘버링 오류

결 번

넘버링 오류

1, 1971

4

공 란

공 란

공 란

공 란

공 란

증산 수출 건설

재 무 부

협력 720-627 1971. 6. 17.

수 신 외무부장관

제 목 SOFA재무분과 위원회 회의 일정 통보

1. 주한 미군에 의한 밀수방지를 위한 SOFA재무분과 위원회 회의를 1971. 6. 24. 14:00 당부 회의실(6층) 에서 개최키로 결정하였으니 양지 하시기 바라며

2. 동 회의에 대비하여 미측에서 제공하는 PX「레이숀」통제제도에 대한「브리핑」을 청취한후 한국측 대책회의를 열고자 6. 22 10:00 주한 미군사령부 SOFA 회의실에서 실시하는「브리핑」에 관계관이 참석할수 있도록 조치를 취하여 주시기 바랍니다.

1971. 6. 17

재 무 부 장 관

단결하면 방첩하고 건설하여 승공하자

10

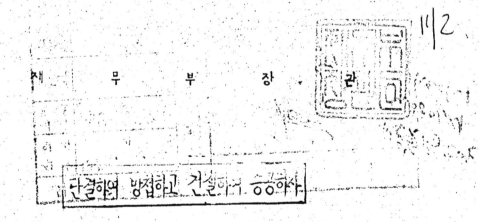

외 무 부		결재	
접수일시	197 . 19 Jul 시 분	지시사항	6. 결
접수번호	제24837호		
주무과			
담당자	K		
처리			197 . . 까지 처리할것

政策局 안보 사항안전 check.

[illegible]

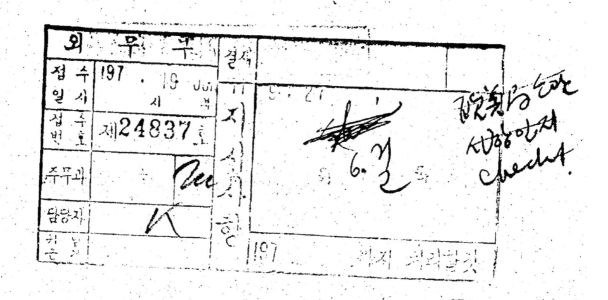

증산 수출 건설

재 무 부

북미2과

협 력 720-663　　　　　　　　　　1971. 6. 25.

수 신 외무부장관

제 목 SOFA재무분과 위원회 회의 연기

1971. 6. 24 14:00 당부회의실에서 개최 예정이던 SOFA 재무분과 위원회 회의를 미국측 요청에 의거 1971. 6. 28 14:00로 연기 하였으니 양지 하시기 바랍니다. 끝.

재 무 부 장

혼란속에 간첩오고 안정속에 번영온다

1971. 6. 25
재무부

11

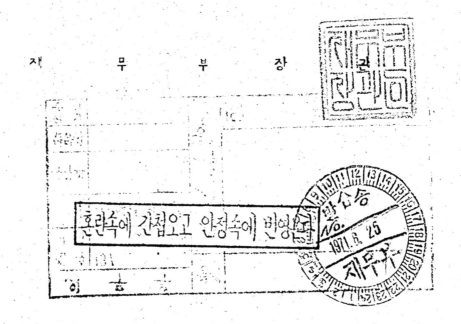

외 무 부		결재	
접수 일자	197 . . .	지시사항	
접수 번호	제26039호		
주무과			
담당자			
처리 기한			197 . . . 까지 처리할것

[illegible]

[illegible]

[illegible]

1973 . . 30 .

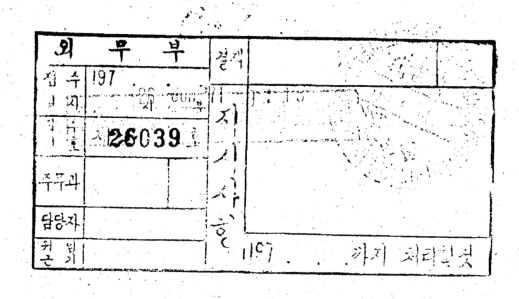

북미표2

증산 수출 건설

재 무 부

협력 1243.1 - 700　　　1971. 7. 12.

수신 외무부장관

제목 SOFA 재무분과 위원회 회의 일정통보

1971. 7. 15. 14:00 APO 및 PX 부정유출 방지를 위한 SOFA 재무분과 위원회를 주한 미군사 SOFA 회의실에서 개최하오니 양지 하시기 바랍니다. 끝.

발송
No.
1971. 7. 12
재무부

재 무 부 장

재무부장관인

단결하여 방첩하고 건설하여 승공하자

12

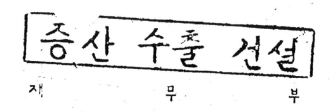

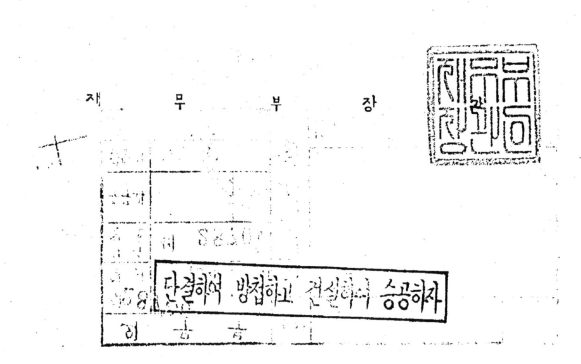

외 무 부		결재	
접수 일시	197 . . . 13 JUL 74 10 : 02		
접수 번호	제 28707 호	지시사항	
주무과			
담당자	金		
처리 근거		197 . . .까지 처리하였음	

[illegible]

[illegible]

[illegible]

SOFA 재무분과 위원회 회의자료(관세분야)

問題区分	関係規定	韓國側立場	備考
1. APO 関係			
가. 検査比率引上	金浦에서의 검사는 수입되는 비공용 소포량의 5% 이내의 표본 검사로 하여야 한다. 검사는 항공기 도착후 6시간 이내에 완료하여야 한다. SOFA. Art. IX Agreed Understanding, Paragraph 5, (1) (2) (3) (4) sample check	1. 김포 및 인천에서의 세관검사를 다음과 같이 한다. (가) 미국지역 발송우편물 5% 이내 (나) 미국 이외지역 발송우편물 : 50% 이내 2. 부차적 문제 (가) 검사원 및 포장원 증원 (나) 검사시설 확장 (다) 검사소포의 발췌기준 : Bag 또는 Package 별 (라) 소포검사 가능수량 산출을 위한 도착 우편물에 대한 통보	
	인천 및 김포의 미군우편책임장교는 우편물의 양과 세관검사 가능한 시간등을 사전에 세관당국에 통보하여야 한다.		
나. 合理·不合理의 數量與否決定 AM. J.C. Agreement 5(c) It is mutually agreed that the determination as to what constitutes a reasonable/unreasonable quantity of any given item rests with U.S. officials.	합리 불합리한 수량의 결정은 수한주의 사명, 가족상황, 수입경위, 기타 적절하다고 사료되는 것등을 고려하여 미군관계관에 의하여 결정된다.	1. 합리 불합리의 수량결정은 한·미 관계관의 합의로 결정한다. 2. 반입 빈도가 많은 주요 품목에 대한 합리적수량은 별첨과 같이 합의 결정한다.	

13

問題區分	關係規定	韓國側立場	備考
2. 非歲出資金機関 (PX) 関係			
가. 情報提供	정기적으로 제공될 비세출 자금기관에 탁송된 화물에 관한 정보는 특정품목수입보고(Selected items) 및 특정품목 매상 분석 초록(Selected items sales extract analysis) 만으로 구성한다는 것에 (3 paragraph [illegible] cargo consigned to NAFO)	매월 정기보고를 다음과 같이 한다. (가) 보고양식 : 단위 품목번호 품명 반입액 재고액 매출액 (나) 보고단위 : 3人 以上의 종업원이 근무하는 PX (다) 보고계통 : 주한미군 J-1 → 관세청 (직송) (라) 보고기한 : 보고기간 종료후 15일 이내	$1,600 computer cost: 832 hrs (5,000) $3500 per month. $44000 per year
나. 합리적 수량	SOFA Art. IX, Agreed Minutes. 1 paragraph. (shall be limited to the extent reasonably required for such use)	(1) 주요 PX 물품의 합리적 수량은 별첨과 같이 합의 결정한다. (참조 : PX 및 APO 물품의 합리적 수량 일람표) (2) 통제품목의 영외사용에 대하여는 소속 부대장의 허가를 받도록 한다.	
다. 세관 직원의 PX 파견		한 미 양측이 합의하에 선정하는 주요 PX에 PX 물품 유출 방지를 위해 활동할수 있도록 세관직원 1인을 배치한다.	

14

問題區分	関係規定	韓國側立場	備考
3. 合同团束班 增設	서울. 의정부. 동두천. 파주. 평택. 부평 (8) 대구. 부산 등 8개 지역 외에도 추후 양 당국간의 상호 합의 하에 합동 단속반을 설치 할수있다.	대전. 군산. 광주. 왜관. 김포. 인천 등 6개지역에 합동단속반을 증설하고 본부반을 신설한다. effective Date	

15

Reasonable Quantities of Important Items Consigned through APO and PX

No.	Descriptions	Q'ty	No.	Descriptions	Q'ty	No.	Descriptions	Q'ty
1	Air-Conditioner	1 set	18	Amplifier Tuner	1 set	35	Receiver	1 set
2	Dryer	1 ea	19	Typewriter	1 ea	36	Carpet	1 set
3	Electric Fan	1 ea	20	Washing Machine	1 ea	37	Mink (Coat, Shawl Collar)	1 pair
4	Hunting Gun	1 ea	21	Binocular	1 pair	38	Handbag (alligator)	1 ea
5	Freezer	1 ea	22	Ring (Precious metal, Pearls & diamond)	1 ea	39	Medicines	for family use only
6	Water Heater	1 ea	23	Stereo music system	1 set	40	Cosmetics	"
7	Movie Camera	1 ea	24	Watch	1 ea	41	Clothes	"
8	Gramophone	1 set	25	Mixer	1 ea	42	Textiles	"
9	Turn Table	1 set	26	Rice cooker	1 ea			
10	Radio	1 ea	27	Toaster	1 ea			
11	Gas Range	1 ea	28	Coffee pot. Coffee maker	1 ea			
12	Refrigerator	1 ea	29	Fry Fan	1 ea			
13	Speaker system	1 set	30	Cleaner	1 ea			
14	Camera (Still)	1 ea	31	Golf set	1 set			
15	Tape deck	1 ea	32	Iron	1 ea			
16	Tape Recorder	1 ea	33	Car cooler	1 set			
17	Television	1 ea	34	Car Radio	1 set			

* The above reasonable quantities are prepared on the basis of each unit of family staying in Korea under SOFA.

* It shall be considered not to be reasonable when the items unnecessary for a bachelor within barracks are purchased or consigned through PX or APO.

controband

provident parks proposal:

16

재 무 부 관 세 국

Selected Items for Furnishing of Information Pertaining to US Forces Non-Appropriated Fund Cargoes

A. Electric Goods

1. Refrigerator
2. Air-Conditioner
3. Television Set
4. Radio
5. Gramophone
6. Fan
7. Blanket
8. Amplifier
9. Tape Recorder
10. Coffee Maker
11. Rice Cooker
12. Iron
13. Mixer
14. Blender
15. Toaster
16. Cleaner
17. Record Player

B. Cosmetic Goods

1. Powder
2. Lipstick
3. Cold Cream
4. Perfume
5. Lotion

C. Liquor

D. Miscellaneous Goods

1. Ring(includes pearls, diamond and precious metal goods)
2. Necklace
3. Gold-Goods
4. Wrist Watch and others
5. Coffee

17

6. Cigarettes and Cigars	15. Textile (Men)
7. Hunting Gun	16. Textile (Women)
8. Battery for Automobile	17. Carpet
9. Candy	18. Record
10. Beverages	19. Recording Tape
11. Cameras	20. Playing Cards
12. Golf Requisites	21. Fountain Pen
13. Clothes	22. Sun-glasses
14. Fishing Requisites	23. Lighter

Selected Items Sales Report(Monthly)

Name of PX: ______________

Date Prepared: ______________

Item Number	Description	Unit Price	$ Value Received	$ Value Sales	$Value on Hand	Q'ty on Han

18

No. 64次 J.C. APO 改正修理 72-47-5
73.6.

1. APO 소포검사율 5% → 10% 인상.
2. 소포 발췌는 韓·美 職員의 共同作業으로 수행.
3. 시설확장과 人員增加 問題는 계속 檢討.
4. APO 主要品目의 合理的인 基準量 책정.
Ring, Watch, Textiles
(1 - $100 value) (1 - $100 value) (25 yd per shipment)
5. PX 화물의 情報提供은 종래의 총체적 매상보고 대신에 특정품목(specified items)에 대한 地域別 매상보고 제출.
제출.
6. 韓·美 合同 수사반 증설 — 7개지역. 와 (기존 9개지역)

19

증산 | 예규 | 전결

재

	기안	과장	국장	차관보	차관	장관
보고						
재						

협 력 720-733 1971. 7. 24.

수 신 외무부장관

제 목 SOFA 한, 미 합동 위원회에 대한 건의

1. 미이 720-8432(1971. 5. 10)에 대한 회신 입니다.

2. SOFA 재무분과 위원회에 부여된 과제 2건중 군사우편 소포 검사비율 인상과 이에 관련되는 절차는 첨부 1과 같이 재무분과 위원회에서 합의되었으며 그 요지는

가. APO 를 통해 반입되는 비공용 소포의 표본 검사율을 현행 5%에서 10%로 인상하며, 동시에 표본 발취를 한, 미 직원의 공동작업으로 행하도록 명문화 하고 검사비율 인상에 따른 시설 확장과 인원증가에 대해서는 재무 분과 위원회에서 계속 검토키로 하였고,

나. APO를 통해 반입되는 군사우편소포의 주요품목에 대한 합리적 기준량을 책정한 점이며,

3. 두번째 과제인 비세출 자금기관(P.X)을 통해 탁송되는 화물의 정보제공에 관한건은 현존의 선정품목에 대한 총체적 매상보고 대신에 통제품목에 대한 지역별 매상보고 제도를 채택하기로 하였으나 이에 관련되는 세부 절차가 확정되지 않아서 추후 확정되는 대로 보고될것이며,

1971.7.24 재무부

20

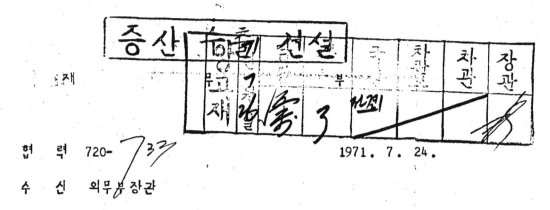

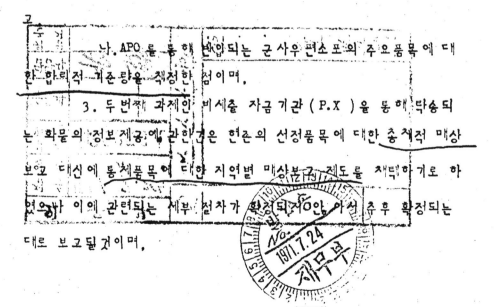

외 무 부		결재	
접수일시	1971. 7. 24.	지시사항	
접수번호	제30356호		
주무과			
담당자	[illegible]		1971. . .까지 처리할것
위임근거			

[illegible]

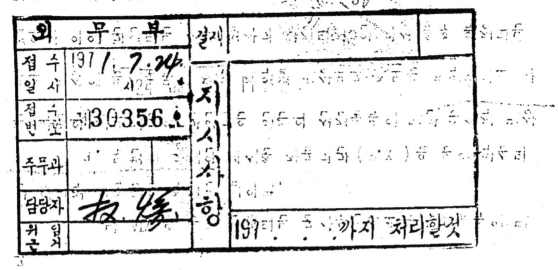

4. 합동위원회 제19차 회의의 회의록 별첨 12에 규정된 바와 같이 한.미 관계 당국의 합의에 의해 추가로 설치할수 있는 한.미 합동 수사반은 기존의 9개반(본부반. 서울. 의정부. 동두천. 파주. 평택. 부평. 대구. 부산) 외에 71. 7. 15일자로 7개 지역(인천. 대전. 왜관. 군산. 광주. 진해. 춘천)에 합동 수사반을 증설 하기로 첨부 2와 같이 합의하였으니 이를 합동위원회 기록에 등재 공식화하여 주시기 바랍니다.

첨부 : 1. APO 군사우편 소포 검사절차에 관한 재무분과 위원회 각서 1부.

2. 합동 수사반 증설에 관한 재무분과 위원회 각서 1부. 끝.

재 무 부 장 관

다결하여 방첩하고 건설하여 승공하자

21

공 란

공 란

공 란

공 란

공 란

공 란

공 란

공 란

공 란

공 란

공 란

DEPARTMENT OF THE ARMY
HEADQUARTERS, EIGHTH UNITED STATES ARMY
APO SAN FRANCISCO 96301
Office of the Provost Marshal

EAPM 7 July 1971

US MEMBERS JOINT ROK-US CUSTOMS TEAMS

Central Office of Joint Investigations Team	Mr Brain	293-8049
	Mr Rainaldo	293-8049
	Mr Adkins	293-8049
	Mr Chong	293-8049
Yongsan	Mr Calvino	293-3251
Uijongbu	Mr Davey	277-3709
Tongduchon	Mr Ellis	276-3258
Munsan	Mr Coste	275-3191
Chunchon	Mr Rehders	2915-320
Bupyong	Mr Woods	292-3228
Inchon	Mr Chipman	2925-207
Pyongtaek	Mr Snyder	283-3800
Taejon	Mr Snyder	283-3800
Taegu	Mr Asten	264-4690
Waegwan	Mr Stovall	265-8613
Pusan	Mr Luketic	263-3588
Chinhae	Mr Bolton	2635-300
Kwangju	Mr Scheel	Kwangju 4027
Kunsan	Mr Wollaston	282-4522

Kriwanek
ROBERT J. KRIWANEK
Colonel, MPC
Provost Marshal

33

SOFA 재무분과 위원회 회의자료 (관세분야)

問題區分	韓國側提議 (1.2次會議)	美側意見	韓國側 position (3次會議)
I. APO 관계			
가. 檢査比率 引上	1. 金浦 및 仁川 에서 의 小包의 稅關檢査를 다음과 같이 한다.	1. 発送地域 區別 없이 一律的으로 小包의 標本檢査比率을 現行 5% 에서 10%로 引上한다	
	(가) 美國地域 발송우편물 : 5% 이내		
	(나) 美國 以外 地域 : 50% 이내		
	2. 副次的 問題	2. 부차적 문제	
	(가) 檢査施設 擴張 : 美側負担	(가) 검사시설확장 : 확장을 위한 검토를 하고 있음.	
	(나) 檢査員과 包裝員 增員 및 包裝材料 調達 : 韓國側負担		
	(다) 檢査小包 반송 選擧 : Bag 또는 package 別		
	(라) 小包檢査 可能 數量 算出을 爲한 到着 郵便物 에 對한 通報		
나. 合理 不合理 의 數量 如否決定	1. 合理 不合理 의 數量決定은 韓美 關係官의 합의로 決定한다.	1. 檢討中	
	2. 搬入 빈도가 많은 主要品目 에 対한 合理的 數量을 別添 과 같이	2. 주요품목 에 대한 合理的 數量表 採択 에 合議 하며	

재 무 부 관 세 국

SOFA 재무분과위원회 회의자료 (관세분야)

問題區分	韓國側提議 (1.2次會議)	美側意見	韓國側 position (3次會議)
	合意 決定한다 (添付 1 參照)	1表의 內訳은 別添과 같다 (添付 3. 參照)	
2. 非歲出資金機關 (P.X) 關係			
가. 情報提供	1. 選定品目에 對한 月別 賣上報告를 다음과 같이 한다 (添付 2 參照)	1. 選定品目賣上報告	
	(가) 報告樣式 단가, 품목별로 품명 반입액 재고액 매출액	a. 3人 以上 P.X는 44個 이며 現在보다 費用, 人力, 時間의 消耗가 44倍로 되어 韓國側 提議를 따르기 困難하다	
	(나) 報告單位: 3人以上의 從業員이 勤務하는 P.X	b. 統制品目에 대한 地域別 (20個地域) 月別 賣上 報告提供을 考慮하고 있다	
	(다) 報告系統: 駐韓美軍 → 關稅廳(直送)		
	(라) 報告期限: 報告期間 終了後 15日 以內		
나. 合理的數量	1. 主要 P.X 物品의 合理的 數量을 別添과 같이 合意 決定한다 (添付 1 參照)	1. 合同委員會로부터 부여된 課題가 아니다	
	2. 統制物品의 營外使用에 대	2. 營外使用은 個人의 自由이며	

35

—2—

재무부 관세국

SOFA 재무분과위원회 회의자료 (관세분야)

問題區分	韓國側提議(1.2次會議)	美側意見	韓國側 position (3次會議)
	하여는 所屬部隊長의 許可를 받도록 한다	文書에 의한 許可는 위조의 우려조차 있다	
다. 稅關職員의 P.X 派遣	1. 韓美兩側의 合意下에 選定하는 主要 P.X에 販賣狀況 把握을 爲하여 稅關職員 1人을 配置한다	1. 反對한다	
3. 合同開束班 增設	大田, 群山, 光州, 倭館, 金浦, 仁川 等 6個 地域에 合同開束班을 增設한다	合同開束班 美側要員 配置表를 參照할 것 (別添 4)	

36

- 3 -

재 무 부 관 세 국

#1

Reasonable Quantities of Important Items [illegible] through APO and PX

No.	Descriptions	Q'ty	No.	Descriptions	Q'ty	No.	Descriptions	Q'ty
1	Air-Conditioner	1 set	18	Amplifier Tuner	1 set	35	Receiver	1 set
2	Dryer	1 ea	19	Typewriter	1 ea	36	Carpet	1 set
3	Electric Fan	1 ea	20	Washing Machine	1 ea	37	Mink (Coat, Shawl, Collar)	1 pair
4	Hunting Gun	1 ea	21	Binocular	1 pair	38	Handbag (all[illegible])	1 ea
5	Freezer	1 ea	22	Ring (Precious metal, Pearl & Diamond)	1 ea	39	Medicines	for family use only
6	Water Heater	1 ea	23	Stereo music system	1 set	40	Cosmetics	"
7	Movie Camera	1 ea	24	Watch	1 ea	41	Clothes	"
8	Gramophone	1 set	25	Mixer	1 ea	42	Textiles	"
9	Turn Table	1 set	26	Rice cooker	1 ea			
10	Radio	1 ea	27	Toaster	1 ea			
11	Gas Range	1 ea	28	Coffee pot, Coffee maker	1 ea			
12	Refrigerator	1 ea	29	Fry Pan	1 ea			
13	Speaker system	1 set	30	Cleaner	1 ea			
14	Camera (Still)	1 ea	31	Golf set	1 set			
15	Tape deck	1 ea	32	Iron	1 ea			
16	Tape Recorder	1 ea	33	Car cooler	1 set			
17	Television	1 ea	34	Car Radio	1 set			

* The above reasonable quantities are [illegible] on the basis of each unit [illegible] family staying in Korea under SOFA.

* It shall be considered not to be reasonable when the items unnecessary for a bachelor within barracks are purchased or consigned through PX or APO.

376

재 무 부 관 세 국

Selected Items for Furnishing of Information Pertaining to US Forces Non-Appropriated Fund Cargoes

A. Electric Goods

1. Refrigerator
2. Air-Conditioner
3. Television Set
4. Radio
5. Gramophone
6. Fan
7. Blanket
8. Amplifier
9. Tape Recorder
10. Coffee Maker
11. Rice Cooker
12. Iron
13. Mixer
14. Blender
15. Toaster
16. Cleaner
17. Record Player

B. Cosmetic Goods

1. Powder
2. Lipstick
3. Cold Cream
4. Perfume
5. Lotion

C. Liquor

D. Miscellaneous Goods

1. Ring(includes pearls, diamond and precious metal goods)
2. Necklace
3. Gold-Goods
4. Wrist Watch and others
5. Coffee

38

6. Cigarettes and Cigars
7. Hunting Gun
8. Battery for Automobile
9. Candy
10. Beverages
11. Cameras
12. Golf Requisites
13. Clothes
14. Fishing Requisites
15. Textile (Men)
16. Textile (Women)
17. Carpet
18. Record
19. Recording Tape
20. Playing Cards
21. Fountain Pen
22. Sun-glasses
23. Lighter

Selected Items Sales Report(Monthly)

Name of FX: ____________

Date Prepared: ____________

Item Number	Description	Unit Price	$ Value Received	$ Value Sales	$Value on Hand	Q'ty on H

39

APO통해 金塊밀수

女人구속 千萬원어치…녹음기로 가장

71.7.29 조선

관세청은 28일 금괴30개 (1천만원어치)를 APO를통해 밀수한 강순자(姜順子·32·서울신당동373의19)여인을 관세법위반혐의로 구속했다.

강여인은 70년7월 홍콩에서 주한미군의 부인 베스 후자(32)여인을 만나 1천만원상당의 금괴를 녹음기라고속여 한국으로 보내달라고 부탁, 후자여인은 미군사우편으로 남편친구인 데이후트, 로렌스 제임스씨등 2명앞으로 이를 보냈다고 한다.

그러나 연락이 잘못되어 이들 2명의 미군들이 수취를 거부함으로써 세관검사에서 적발된것이다.

1971. 7. 29 조선일보

40

71.7.30 신아

APO통한密輸

철저히團束키로

韓美合同委

韓·美合同委員會는 29일 낮 제64차회의를 열고 美軍事郵便(APO)을 통한 密輸등을 막기위해 小包貨物에대한 韓國稅關員의 檢査절차를 강화, 標本검사의 비율을 종래보다 2배로 늘리기로 합의했다.

한편 이날회의는 최근 平澤동 美軍基地근처에서의 일어난 韓國人과 美軍과의 충돌사건도 議題로 다루었는데 美國측은 犯法者를 軍法會議에 넘겨 처벌하고 앞으로 이같은 不祥事가 일어나지 않도록 各級하부대에 지침을 내렸다고 韓國측에 설명했다.

1971. 7. 30 신아일보

41

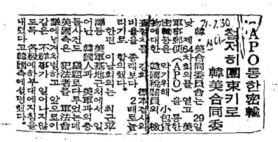

증산 수출 건설

재 무 부

협 력 1243.1- 948 1971. 9. 22.

수 신 외무부장관

제 목 SOFA 합동위원회에 대한 건의

1. 1971. 8월말 김포소재 주한 미 공군기지의 오산으로의 이동에 따라 김포를 통해 반입되던 군사우편소포의 일부가 오산 미 공군기지를 통해 반입되게 되었으므로

2. 제9차 주한 미군지위협정 한미 합동위원회에서 제정되고 제64차 한미합동위원회에서 개정된 APO 군사우편소포에 대한 한국세관 검사절차 규정을 첨부와같이 검사장소로서 오산을 추가토록 개정조치하여 주시기 바랍니다.

첨부 : APO 군사우편 소포 검사절차개정에 관한 한미합동위원회 각서 1부. 끝.

재 무 부 장

66차 회의에서 승인

完

어둠에서 떨지말고 ... 찾자

42

공 란

공 란

2. 1972

45

주산 수출 진실

재 무 부

협 력 1243.1-1200 1972. 2. 3.

수 신 외무부장관

제 목 미군사우체국을 통한 우편소포 검사절차 개정

1. 제 64 차 SOFA 합동위원회 합의에 의거 미군사우체국을 통하여 반입되는 비공용 일반소포에 대한 검사비율이 종전의 배로 인상됨에 따라 강화된 세관 검사를 피하고자 비검사 대상으로 규정된 등기 소포를 이용한 밀수가 발생하고 있는 바.

2. 이에 대하여서도 세관검사를 실시할수 있도록 별첨과 같이 문제점을 제기하오니 SOFA 회의를 통하여 조속히 해결되도록 필요한 조치를 취하여 주시기 바랍니다.

첨부 : 협의사항 1부. 끝.

재 무 부 장

46

1972 2 3
재무부

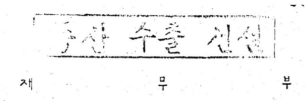

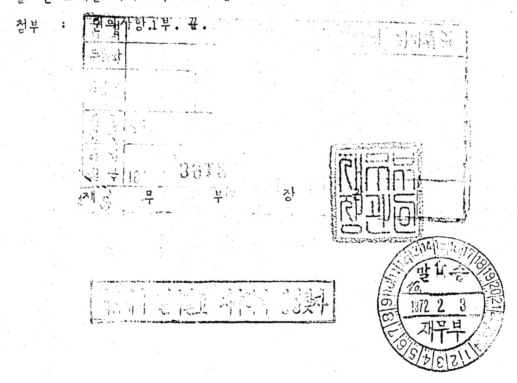

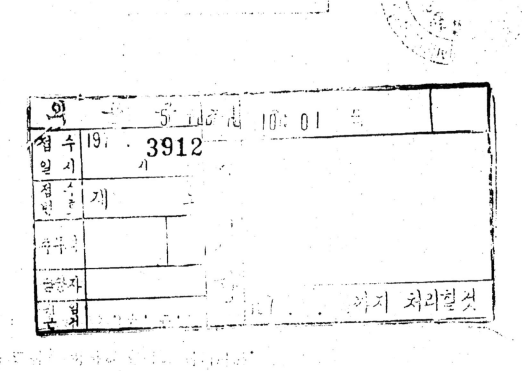

외	10 01
접수 일시	197 . 3912 시
접수 번호	제
주무과	
담당자	
처리 기한	197 . . 까지 처리할 것

의제	관계규정	문제점	건의사항
미군사 우체국(A.P.O)를 통한 우편소포 검사절차 개정	1) 협정 제9조에 대한 합의 양해사항 2) 제9차 합동위원회에서 제정되고 제64차 및 제66차 합동위원회에서 부분 개정된 A.P.O.를 통한 군사우편 소포 검사절차: 미군사 우체국을 통한 우편소포는 다음에 지적된것을 제외하고는 한국 세관의 검사를 받어야 한다 가. 주한 미대사관, U.S.O.M 및 미군사 고문단의 인원과 그의 가족에게 우송된것 나. 미정부기관 또는 공용계인이 있는 소포및 사령관, 책임장교 단위부대장 또는 참모부와 부대 자금관리관을 포함하는 조기관으로 우송되는 소포 다. 사진첩 또는 녹음된 전령으로 명백히 표시된것 및 제1종 우편물 또는 등기우편물로 표시된것	1) A.P.O를 통하여 반입되는 일반 군사 우편 소포에 대하여서는 종전 5% 표본 검사를 하였으나 제64차 합동위원회(1971. 7. 29) 합의에 따라 10%로 검사비율을 인상하였고 이에 따라 검사가 보다 철저하게 됨으로써 반입 규정에 위배되는 물품이 보류 반송 또는 적발되는 사례가 많아지고 있음. 2) 그러나 등기소포는 관계 규정에 의거 검사대상에서 제외되고 있어 등기소포를 이용하여 귀금속류 및 고가 사치품을 밀수입하는 사례가 발생하고 있으므로 "등기소포"에 대한 검사 제외 규정을 개정하여 이에 대해서도 10% 표본 검사를 실시할 필요가 있음. 3) 관세청 조사에 의하면 A.P.O를 통해 반입되는 월평균 군사우편물량은 66만 파운드이고 그 구성내역은 세관 검사 대상 일반소포 18.8%, 등기우편물 3%, 기타 공용우편물등이 78.2%라고 함 (1971년도의 경우)	제9차 합동위원회에서 제정된 A.P.O.를 통한 군사우편 소포 검사 절차: 검사 제외 대상에서 "등기우편물(Registered matter)"을 삭제하여 이에 대하여서도 검사를 할수 있게 한다.

47

재 무 부 관 세 국

기 안 용 지

분류기호 문서번호	미이 723 -	(전화번호)	전결규정 조 항 국장 전결사항
처리기간			
시행일자			
보존년한		국	장
보조기관	북미2과장		협
기안책임자	권 찬	북미2과 (72. 2. 21)	
경유 수신 참조	수신처 참조	발신	통제
제목	주한미군 지원사령부내의 재산손실 통계		

1972. 2. 21 외무부 5394

1972 2. 21

주한미군 당국은 주한미군 지원사령부내에서 발생한 1971. 11 - 12월분 재산손실에 관한 통계를 당부에 전달하여온 바, 동 자료를 별첨 송부하오니 업무에 참고하시기 바랍니다.

점부 : 동 자료 1 부. 끝.

수신처 : 내무부장관 (치안국장)

법무부장관 (검찰국장)

정서

관인

발송

공통서식1-2(갑)
1967. 4. 4. 승인

190mm ×268mm (1급인쇄용지70g/m²)
조달청 (500,000매인쇄)

48

외 무 부

미이 723 - 72. 2. 21.

수신 :

참조 :

제목 : 주한미군 지원사령부내의 재산손실 통계

주한미군 당국은 주한미군 지원사령부내에서 발생한 1971. 11 - 12월분 재산손실에 관한 통계를 당부에 전달하여온 바, 동 자료를 별첨 송부하오니 업무에 참고하시기 바랍니다.

첨부 : 동 자료 1 부. 끝.

외 무 부 장 관

49

Chief of Staff Memo

28 January 1972

To: Provost Marshal

1. Attached copy of letter from CG KORSCOM is furnished for additional action. The CG desires that in addition to bringing this to the attention of the SOFA Committee, that follow up in the form of a letter to the CO of Cp Grant and letter to C/S ROKA be prepared.

2. Specifically, the CG takes issue with the report in as much as it admits that the vehicle departed Cp Grant without an adequate check by the MP gate guard and KATUSA gate guard. Prepare a letter through channels to the CO of Cp Grant for my signature indicating the comments concerning this breach of policy and requiring a report as to what action has been taken against the MPs, assuming they are US MPs. Request also that you prepare a letter for CG's signature to C/S ROKA outlining the problem of the failure of the KATUSAs and also the action of the ROKA CID Corporal who did not perform satisfactorily.

3. SUSPENSE: 4 February

WHB

50

DEPARTMENT OF THE ARMY
HEADQUARTERS, U.S. ARMY KOREA SUPPORT COMMAND
APO SAN FRANCISCO 96212

EAKS-CS

12 January 1972

SUBJECT: Matters of Importance to the Joint United States/Republic of Korea SOFA Committee

Commanding General
Eighth United States Army
APO 96301

1. It is requested that the below shown information be furnished to the Joint United States/Republic of Korea SOFA Committee for their information.

2. At 1000 hours, 6 January 1972, the below listed Korean trash collectors were stopped as they attempted to exit the main gate, Camp Grant, in the trash truck. A routine search of the truck revealed four Relay Test Sets valued at $463 each (total value $1,852) on the back of the truck. SIR #1-24-72 (Larceny of Government Property).

KIM, Sin Kil, KN(M), #478 Chuan Dong, Inchon City, Korea
KIM, Hyon Myong, KN(M), #504 Bupyong-dong, Inchon City, Korea
PAK, U Yong, KN(M), #240 Tohwa Dong, Namgu, Inchon City, Korea
O, Song Yong, KN(M) #277 Bupyong-dong, Puk-ku, Inchon City, Korea
KIM, Jong Su, KN(M), #8 Chuan Dong, Inchon City, Korea

3. At 1530 hours, 4 January 1972, (CAM) Point, Camp Grant, MSG Song, ROK CID agent, observed a ROK three-quarter ton military vehicle depart the main gate, Camp Grant, without being checked by MPs or KATUSA gate guards. Song followed the vehicle to #173 Sipjong Dong, Puk-ku, Inchon City, Korea, where numerous vehicle parts were unloaded. A check of the occupants of the vehicle revealed that Chae, Kyu Yong, Corporal, KA #61016592 Pupyong Depot ROKA, attached to Pupyong ROKA CID, Pupyong, Korea, and Kun, Sung Woo (KN) (address: #1 San, Puk-Dong, Book, Inchon City, Korea), had no documentation for the property. SIR #1-25-72 (Larceny of Government Property).

GIMCH 01345

51

EAKS-CS
SUBJECT: Matters of Importance to the Joint United States/Republic of Korea SOFA Committee

FOR THE COMMANDER:

L. P. PERNA
Colonel, GS
Chief of Staff

2

52

DEPARTMENT OF THE ARMY
HEADQUARTERS, U.S. ARMY KOREA SUPPORT COMMAND
APO SAN FRANCISCO 96212

EAKS-PM

20 JAN 1972

SUBJECT: Property Losses Within USAKORSCOM's Area of Responsibility

Commanding General
Eighth United States Army
ATTN: EADCS
APO 96301

1. This Headquarters is greatly concerned over the alarming number of larcenies and housebreakings occurring throughout the command's area of responsibility. During this calendar year larceny losses of this type have been occurring at the average rate of approximately $80,000 per month. During the month of December, however, 293 larcenies with a total value of $180,000 were reported. Of this total, 185 or 63% of the larcenies and $150,000 or 83% of the dollar loss occurred in the ASCOM area. A breakdown of major losses, showing location, items lost, dollar value and method of entry for the months of November and December 1971, appear at Inclosure 1.

2. I am making every member of my command fully aware of his responsibilities with regard to this situation, and I have directed that stringent actions be taken by sub-area commanders to reduce these losses. However, this command's unilateral efforts without the co-operation of the Government of the Republic of Korea, can only be partially successful, since the main outlet for stolen US goods and equipment is normally the local Korean economy. This situation exists mainly because US goods and equipment often exceed their actual value by as much as 300% on the local economy. This ready opportunity for large profits attracts both US and Korean criminals.

53

20 JAN 1972

EAKS-PM
SUBJECT: Property Losses Within USAKORSCOM's Area of
Responsibility

3. I strongly recommend the Joint US/ROK SOFA Committee study the larceny situation, with particular emphasis on ASCOM, in order to offer appropriate assistance and/or solutions to these pressing US/ROK problems.

1 Incl
as

JOSEPH W. PEZDIRTZ
Major General, USA
Commanding

74

2

DATE	TIME	LOCATION	ITEMS	TYPE SECURITY	MOE	AMOUNT
6 Nov 71 23 Nov 71	1300 hrs 1300 hrs	TMP, USAAD	(25) Tek Tires	Unknown	Unknown	1,565.00
8 Dec 71	1200 hrs 1430 hrs	Bldg 833, Cp Grant	(1) Refrigerator (1) Motor Drinking Fountain	Padlock	Forced	400.00
8 Dec 71 9 Dec 71	2400 hrs 0630 hrs	Bldg T-770, Cp Grant	(2) TV Sets (1) Cash Register	Unknown	Removed Window	1,100.00
8 Dec 71 9 Dec 71	1800 hrs 0740 hrs	Bldg T-768, Cp Grant	(4) Comm telephones (1) Fire Extinguisher	Padlock	Forced	Unknown
7 Dec 71 9 Dec 71	Unknown	Bunker #570, Cp Howard	4,800 rds of ammo (shotgun)	Fence and Contract Guard	Forced Lock	432.00
7 Dec 71 9 Dec 71	Unknown	Bunker 508, Cp Howard	250 Carrying Plugs, 57 Carrying Plugs, 9,375 Carrying Plugs	Fence and Contract Guard	Faulty Lock	Unknown
10 Dec 71	0010 hrs 0030 hrs	Bldg T-998, Cp Grant	Unknown Misc. Items	Fence	Unsecured Window	Unknown
10 Dec 71 11 Dec 71	2000 hrs 0800 hrs	Bldg 1535, Cp Market	(4) High speed hand pieces (2) cauilitions (4) Low speed hand pcs	Padlock	Cut Lock	2,010.00
11 Dec 71	0915 hrs	Bldg 795, Cp Grant	(4) Field phones (1) pr wire cutters (4) Log Books	Padlock	Cut Lock	Unknown
12 Dec 71	1500 hrs - 1800 hrs	Bldg T-798	Unknown	Fence	Forced	Unknown
12 Dec 71 13 Dec 71	Unknown [illegible] hrs	Bldg 2439, Cp Hays	Misc Items	Padlock	Cut Lock	[illegible]

55

DECEMBER 1971

DATE	TIME	LOCATION	ITEMS	TYPE SECURITY	MOE	AMOUNT
2 Dec 71	1830 hrs	Bldg 1210, Cp Market	Unknown	Padlock	Forced	Unknown
3 Dec 71	0100 hrs	Bldg 1210, Cp Market	Unknown	Padlock	Forced	
3 Dec 71	1200 hrs	Bldg 798, Cp Grant	Unknown amount of Misc Equip	Padlock	Cutting hole in Fence and Bldg.	Unknown
5 Dec 71	0015 hrs	Bldg 798, Cp Grant	Unknown amount of Misc Equip	Padlock		
6 Dec 71	0745 hrs	Bldg 1604, USAAD	(4) Typewriters	Padlock	Pried off Hasp	$918.00
20 Nov 71	1615 hrs	Bldg 1928, USAAD	(4) Typewriters	Padlock	Forced	1,272.00
4 Dec 71	1000 hrs	Bldg T-786 55th Cmpd, 96220	(1) RT-A23 AN-AEC	Padlock	Cut Lock	3,056.49
5 Dec 71	1230 hrs	Bldg T-786 55th Cmpd, 96220	131 FM Radio	Padlock	Cut Lock	
3 Dec 71	1700 hrs	Bldg 903, Cp Grant	(87) Carrier Assy	Security Guards	Unknown	55,245.00
6 Dec 71	1030 hrs	Bldg 903, Cp Grant				
6 Dec 71	1300 hrs	Bldg 960, Cp Grant	Handriven Dispensine pump	Padlock & Security Guard	Cut Lock	Unknown
7 Dec 71	0700 hrs					
6 Dec 71	1700 hrs	Bldg 1407, Cp Market	(2) Typewriters	Padlock	Cut Lock	Unknown
7 Dec 71	0740 hrs					
7 Dec 71	1:00 hrs	Bldg T-12, Cp Mercer	(2) Sewing machines (1) Iron (1) Civ Shirt (1) Yellow Shirt (3) pr Fat Trousers (1) Radio (2) Hair Clippers (1) Hair Dryer (10) Civ Jackets	Padlock	Cut Lock	314.95
8 Dec 71	1300 hrs					

20TH SUPPORT GROUP

NOVEMBER 1971

DATE	TIME	LOCATION	ITEMS	TYPE SECURITY	MOE	AMOUNT
29 Oct & 1 Nov 71	1645 hrs 0800 hrs	Bldg T-982, Cp Grant	42 pr trousers, AG 44/37 pr trousers, AG 344, 14 flt jkts 8 flyers coveralls, 1 typewriter	Padlock	Forced entry	$1,341.12
20 Oct & 3 Nov 71	1630 hrs 0900 hrs	POL Pipeline T-2, Inchon	8 non-raising gaye valves	Fence	Unknown	1,200.00
6 Nov & 9 Nov 71	1000 hrs 1030 hrs	Storage and MCR Room 20th Support Group TMP	Misc motors & parts	Padlock	Forced	1,179.58
16 Nov & 17 Nov 71	1700 hrs 0745 hrs	Sign Paint Shop, Cp Mercer	(1) typewriter, (2) Vacuum Pump Assy w/1/2 HP elec motors	Padlock	Forced	2,618.00
8 Nov & 9 Nov 71	1740 hrs 0740 hrs	Bldg 1477, HHC ASCOM Depot	9 typewriters	Padlock	Forced	2,215.00
21 Nov 71	0315 hrs	Bldg 4416 1st AG MMT Seattle Co.	U. S. Mail	Fence	Cut Hole	Unknown
23 Nov 71	2030 hrs 2215 hrs	Bldg 1535, Cp Market	Unknown	Padlock	Cut Lock	Unknown
28 Nov 71	0400 hrs	Bldg 1780, Cp Market	Unknown	Fence	Cut Wire Broke Window	Unknown
29 Nov & 30 Nov 71	2300 hrs 0730 hrs	Bldg T-2560, Cp Eiler	(1) TV (1) Speaker (1) Phonograph	Padlock & Fence	Cut Fence broken hasp	Unknown

67

23D SUPPORT GROUP

DECEMBER 1971

DATE	TIME	LOCATION	ITEMS	TYPE SECURITY	MOE	AMOUNT
6 Dec 71	1630 hrs	Camp Humphreys	(1) Oscilloscope Tek-442	Unknown	Unknown	$1,500.00
13 Dec 71	1700 hrs	Bldg 682, Cp Humphreys	(2) Oscilloscopes	Padlock	Forced	
14 Dec 71	0815 hrs	Bldg 682, Cp Humphreys	(1) Threading Set	Padlock	Forced	$2,986.00

23D SUPPORT GROUP

.58

NOVEMBER 1971

DATE	TIME	LOCATION	ITEMS	TYPE SECURITY	MOE	AMOUNT
1 Nov & 7 Nov 71	1730 hrs 0730 hrs	Bldg T-7, Stonestown Compound Bldg T-7, Stonestown Compound	Nonappropriated Fund Money Nonappropriated Fund Money	Padlock Padlock	Removed Plaster Board	$2,020.11
7 Nov 71	0730 hrs	Bldg T-7, Stonestown Compound	Misc Exchange Merchandise	Padlock	Removed Plaster Board	$474.90
25 Jun - 16 Nov 71	1700 hrs 1100 hrs	Area #4 Near Bldg 522 USA Depot 053 96271	560,016 Rds of 7.62 MM ball-type ammo	Fence	Unknown	$41,131.28

23D SUPPORT GROUP

증산 수출 건설

재 무 부

협력 1243-722 1972 .8. 25

수신 수신처참조

제목 P. X 및 COmmissary의 월판매 금액및 수량통제

미군측 SOFA 재무분과 위원회가 보낸 P. X및 Commissary 의 1인당 및 1가구당 월판매 수량및 금액통제표를 송부하오니 업무에 참고하시기 바랍니다.

첨부 : SOFA 자료 1부 (영문) 끝.

0358

재 무 부 장

수신처 : 외무부 장관. 관세청 장

내집살림 나라살림 저축으로 부강하자

발송 1972. 8. 25 재무부

0717 964

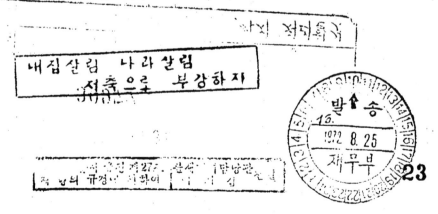

EXCHANGE RATIONING LIMITATIONS

1. MONTHLY DOLLAR LIMITATIONS. Primary control on purchases shall be exercised through a fixed monthly dollar amount which may be spent in the exchange. This dollar amount is determined by the size of the household in Korea.

a. The monthly dollar limitations are computed on the following basis:

Status	Monthly Dollar Limitation
Sponsor or unaccompanied individual	$75.00
Spouse	$50.00
Dependent (over 18 years of age)	$50.00
Dependent (under 18 years of age)	$25.00
Sponsor or spouse with limited privilege (no controlled items)	$50.00

b. Purchases totaling $0.99 or less will not be counted toward the monthly dollar limitation.

c. Purchases which have a unit value of $25.00 or more will not be counted toward the monthly dollar limitation.

d. Purchases of military uniforms and accessories by military personnel will not be counted toward the monthly dollar limitation.

e. Purchases of books and periodicals will not be counted toward the monthly dollar limitation.

f. The aggregate household limitation can be determined by adding the applicable monthly dollar limitations for each status of person in the household.

2. CONTROLLED ITEMS. These items, listed below, may be purchased once during a tour in Korea. Those items indicated by an asterisk (*) require a Letter of Authorization (LOA) for initial purchase. Subsequent purchase of any item listed will require an LOA.

CONTROLLED ITEMS

23 - Still Camera over $40
24 - Still Camera under $40

*31 - Television
32 - Radio over $25
34 - Stereo Music System
35 - Tuner/Amplifier/Receiver
36 - 2 Speakers over $25
38 - Turntable
39 - Phonograph over $25

41 - Tape Deck
42 - Tape Recorder over $25

52 - Typewriter
*53 - Firearm
*54 - Diamond Ring
55 - Watch over $50 (excluding costume jewelry watches)

61 - Electric Blender
62 - Electric Rice Cooker
63 - Electric Toaster
64 - Electric Coffee Pot
65 - Electric Skillet
66 - Electric Fan
67 - Electric Steam and/or Dry Iron

*71 - Washing Machine
*72 - Clothes Dryer
*73 - Range
*74 - Vacuum Cleaner
*75 - Floor Polisher
*76 - Refrigerator
*77 - Freezer
*78 - Water Heater
*79 - Air Conditioner
*95 - Special Purchases for clubs or organizations

3. LIMITED ITEMS. Those items in temporary short supply or unusual demand on a local basis. The purchase quantity limitations will be determined by local exchange management and will be posted at the stockage/display point and enforced at the checkout counters.

0720 25

COMMISSARY RATIONING LIMITATIONS

1. MONTHLY DOLLAR LIMITATION.

a. Primary rationing control will be accomplished by limiting the amount of money which may be spent in the commissary during each month. The amount which may be spent is determined by the number of authorized patrons supported within a household in Korea. The monthly dollar limitations are:

Number of Patrons Supported	*Monthly Dollar Limitation
1 (Unaccompanied Personnel on subsistence/separate rations/LQA)	$ 70.00
2	140.00
3	170.00
4	205.00
5	230.00
6	255.00
7	265.00
8 or more	280.00

* Includes surcharge

b. Unaccompanied personnel not on subsistence/separate rations/LQA will be limited to fifty percent of the unaccompanied personnel on subsistence/separate rations/LQA monthly dollar limitation.

2. CONTROLLED ITEMS. Items which are limited in purchase quantity on a monthly basis. Procedure to receive authorization for excess purchases of controlled items is contained in Annex G. The quantity limitations on controlled items are scaled by the number of patrons supported and are as follows:

EA Reg 60-1
314th AD Reg 147-
CNFKINST-4066.1B

CONTROLLED ITEMS LIST

ITEM	UNIT	Number of Patrons Supported: 1	2-3	4-5	6-7	8+
		QUANTITY AUTHORIZED PER MONTH				
*Baby Formula, Liquid	cn	0	8	8	8	8
Chocolate/Cocoa	16 oz cn	2	3	4	5	6
Ground Coffee	lb	6	8	8	8	8
or						
Instant Coffee	oz	30	40	40	40	40
Mayonnaise	32 oz qt	1	2	3	4	5
Olive Oil	16 oz	1	2	2	3	3
Pepper	4 oz cn	1	2	2	2	3
Salad Oil	32 oz qt	1	4	8	8	8
Soluble Cream	16 oz jar	1	2	2	2	4
Tang	26 oz jar	2	3	4	5	6
Salt	26 oz	1	1	2	2	2

*One (1) baby will receive eight (8) units of baby formula per month. One unit is equal to:

4 cns of 13 oz concentrated liquid
3 cns of 32 oz ready to use liquid
12 bottles of 8 oz ready to use liquid
24 bottles of 4 oz ready to use liquid
1 cn of 16 oz powder

This items list was based on an average factor of 720 oz that a baby (1-4 months) will consume a month.

0722 96827

Appendix 2 to ANNEX F

64

3. LIMITED ITEMS. Those items in temporary short supply or unusual demand on a local basis. Determination of items to be so designated will be made by local management. Purchase quantity limitations will be posted at stockage/display points and enforced at checkout counters.

0723

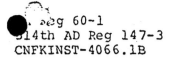

EA[illegible] 60-1
314th AD Reg 147-3
CNFKINST-4066.1B

ALCOHOLIC BEVERAGE RATIONING LIMITATIONS-
PURCHASE CONTROL

1. ALCOHOLIC BEVERAGES. Primary control on purchases shall be exercised through monthly limitations on the amount of alcoholic beverages which may be purchased. These limitations are:

a. Active duty military personnel in the grade of 06 and above and U.S. civilian employees, grades GS-15 and above (or equivalent): No purchase limitations.

b. Active duty military personnel in the grade of 05 and below, U.S. civilian employees, grades GS-14 and below (or equivalent) and all others authorized Class VI store privileges:

(1) Accompanied: Ten (10) quarts/fifths of alcoholic beverages per month.

(2) Unaccompanied: Five (5) quarts/fifths of alcoholic beverages per month.

2. BEER/MALT LIQUOR. Twenty-four (24) bottles/cans per day. Malt liquor may only be purchased by personnel twenty (20) years of age or older.

0724

Appendix 3 to ANNEX F

970

29

66

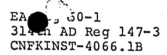

JOINT COMMITTEE
UNDER
THE REPUBLIC OF KOREA AND THE UNITED STATES
STATUS OF FORCES AGREEMENT

22 February 1972

MEMORANDUM FOR: Chairmen, Finance Subcommittee

SUBJECT: Procedures for Examination by ROK of Parcel Post Packages delivered through U.S. APO

1. Reference:

(a) Article IX, Paragraph 5.

(b) Article IX, Agreed Minute #4.

(c) Article IX, Agreed Understanding.

(d) Procedures for Examination by ROK of Parcel Post Packages delivered through U.S. APO (9th Joint Committee, May 5, 1967) and Revision Thereof (64th Joint Committee, July 29, 1971).

2. Since the adoption and implementation of above referred procedures, further violation of the Korean custom legislation and pertinent SOFA provisions have been reported to the Korean authorities. Recent such cases are those of smuggling into Korea of golds, precious stones and other luxurious commodities through "Registered matter" mail or parcel which has so far not been subjected to the inspection by Korean custom officials.

3. The Subcommittee is requested to study this matter with a view to prevent smuggling of such items referred to above and recommend appropriate measures to the Joint Committee.

결재 공람	담 당	과 장	국 장

ROBERT N. SMITH
Lieutenant General
United States Air Force
United States Representative

KIM DONG WHIE
Republic of Korea
Representative

67

Uw Mr. Chung

증산 수출 건설

봉. 4/2 권

재 무 부

협력 1245-258 (70-3227) 1972. 3. 13.

수신 외무부장관

제목 미군사우체국을 통한 마약등의 부정유입방지

1. 제71차 SOFA 합동위에서 APO 를 통한 마약 및 습관성 의약품의 부정유입을 방지하기 위한 노력을 강화하도록 합의한바 있으며,

2. 이에따라 미군사우체국을 통한 마약 및 습관성 의약품에 대한 세관검사를 강화할수 있도록 별첨과 같이 문제점을 제기하오니 SOFA 회의를 통하여 조속히 해결되도록 소요조치를 취하여 주시기 바라며,

3. 또한 협력 1245-60(72.1.22)로 건의한 세관원 상주에의한 비세출자금기관의 판매상황에 대한 조사및 감시권확보에 관해서는 주요지구(서울, 부평(인천포함), 동두천, 의정부, 평택 부산 대구 지구등)의 PX 에 세관원상주, 기타지구, (파주 왜관, 대전, 군산지구등)의 PX 에 수시 출입감시할수 있도록 조치하여 주시기 바랍니다.

발송 No. 1972. 3. 13 재무부

첨부 건의사항 1부. 끝.

재 무 부 장 관

68

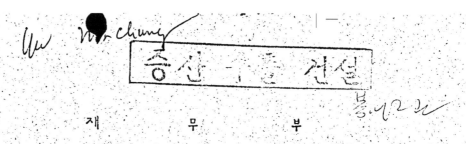

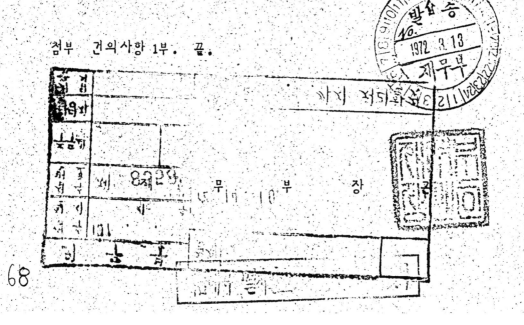

외 무 부		결재	
접수 일시	197 . . . 45 12 14 : 10		
접수 번호	제 8558 호		
주무과			
담당자			
처리 일시			. . 까지 처리할것

[illegible]

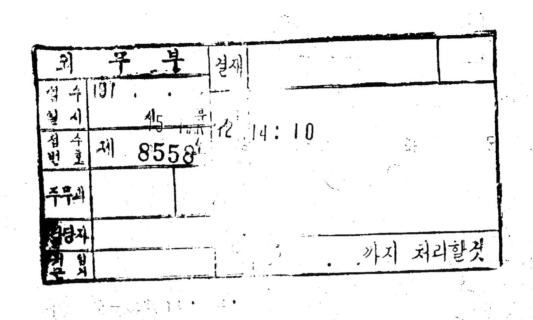

의제	관계규정	현황	건의사항
APO를 통한 마약 및 습관성 의약품 부정유입 방지	I. 협정 제9조에 대한 합의양해사항. II. 제9차 합동위원회에서 제정되고 제64차 및 제66차 합동위원회에서 부분 개정된 APO를 통한 군사우편 소포 검사 절차 : 3. 검사의 구체적 절차. 다. 협정 제9조에 따른 합의 양해사항에 완전한 합치를 위하여 우편물의 지연 및 우편당국의 행정적 부담의 증가는 최소한으로 하여야 한다. (1) 검사는 수입되는 비공용 소포량의 10% 이내의 표본 검사로 하여야 한다. (2) 검사는 우편물을 계획대로 발송하게끔 계획된 적재시간 이전에 완료하여야 한다. 5. 검사한 소포의 처리 나. 한국세관 관리와 미군 우편관계 대표자간에 합의에 의하여 금수품으로 인정되는 물품이 있는 소포는 한미관계 당국의 처리 결정이 있을 때까지 미군 우편 당국의 관리하에 둔다	1. 기지촌 정화등을 위하여 설치된 군민관계 임시분과 위원회는 마약 및 습관성 의약품의 부정유입 및 상습적 사용을 근절하기 위해서 다음의 사항을 건의했으며 제71차 합동위원회 (1972. 2. 24)에서 채택된바 있다 가. 미군 당국은 APO를 통한 마약및 습관성 의약품의 반입을 방지하기 위한 노력을 강화한다 나. 마약 및 습관성의약품 상습사용자에 통제강화 (1) 미군당국 : 상습사용자의 식별 및 격리수용 (2) 한국당국 : 기호자에 대한 취업 기회박탈 다. 마약의 소개인등에 대한 적절한 제재조치 2. 제71차 합동위원회 회의에서 채택된 군민관계 임시분과 위원회는 군수품 부정유출에 관련된 미국인 범법자에 대해 취해진 제재 조치의 내용을 한국정부에 통고하도록 하고 있다. 3. APO를 통하여 반입되는 비공용 소포의 10%에 대하여 개장 검사를 실시하고	1. 제9차 합동위에서 제정된 APO 군사우편 소포 검사절차 등을 다음과 같이 개정 보완하여 APO를 통한 마약 및 습관성 의약품의 부정유입을 방지한다. 가. 마약 및 습관성 의약품 사용상습자, 군용및 개인용 면세물품 부정유출 관련자 등의 명단 및 그들에 대해 취해진 제재 조치의 내용을 관세청에 통보한다. 나. 상기 "가" 항에 해당되는 자에게 송부되는 우편소포에 대해서는 전량 개장 검사를 실시하도록 한다. 다. 마약 감식견 2두씩을 APO 우편소포 검사장 (인천 김포, 오산)에 배치하여 마약등의 포함 혐의가 있는 소포를 식별 개장 검사 하도록 한다. 라. 습관성 의약품에 대한 분석 감정제도를 채택 실시한다.

재무부 관세국

69

의제	관계규정	현황	건의사항
		있으나 마약류등의 단속을 위해서는 불충분 하므로 검시반을 인상이 요망된다.	
		4. APO를 통하여 반입되는 소포가 마약 및 습관성 의약품을 포함하고 있는지 여부를 Check 하기 위해서는 특수한 장비 (예 : 마약 감식견) 또는 실험 분석이 요구된다.	

재무부 관세국

070

공 란

81

COMMANDER IN CHIEF PACIFIC
FPO SAN FRANCISCO 96610

11
Ser 1558
04 APR 1972

From: Commander in Chief Pacific
To: Distribution List

Subj: Review of Proposed CINCPACINST 5840.3A (Customs Inspection Within the PACOM)

Ref: (a) Draft DOD Regulation 5030.49-R (Customs Inspection)

Encl: (1) Proposed CINCPACINST 5840.3A

1. Reference (a) was approved on 28 February 1972 for immediate implementation within the PACOM. Copies of reference (a) are being air mailed directly to you by Department of the Army.

2. Enclosure (1) (CINCPAC's proposed implementing instruction to reference (a)) is forwarded for your review and comments, as appropriate. Request comments/recommendations be furnished, by electrical means, to CINCPAC (J113) by 12 April 1972.

BERNARD B. SAPP
Assistant Chief of
Staff Personnel

Distribution:
COMUSMACV
COMUSMACTHAI
COMUSJAPAN
COMUSKOREA
COMUSTDC
CHDLG INDONESIA
CHMEDT CAMBODIA
CINCPACREPRYUKYUS
CINCPACREPPHIL
CINCPACREPGUAM/TTPI
CINCPACREPAUSTRALIA

	ROUTING	INITIAL
J-1		
DEPUTY		
ADMIN BR.		
PERS MGT BR.		
PERS SVC BR.		
REMARKS:		

담당	과장	국장	차관보	차관	장관

172

DRAFT 4 APR 1972

CINCPACINST 5840.3A
11

CINCPAC INSTRUCTION 5840.3A

Subj: Customs Inspection within the PACOM

Ref: (a) DOD Regulation 5030.49-R

1. Purpose. To establish policy, prescribe procedures, define responsibilities, insure compliance with United States customs laws, and outline customs inspection and entry requirements within the Pacific Command (PACOM) in order to preclude the movement of controlled substances and other contraband through DOD Channels in the CINCPAC area of responsibility. This Instruction implements reference (a) within the PACOM.

2. Cancellation. CINCPAC Instruction 5840.3

3. Definitions. For the purpose of this Instruction the definitions outlined in Chapter 2 of reference (a) apply.

4. Background.

a. Criteria for customs inspections and/or examinations within the PACOM have differed considerably among the Services due to differences in command emphasis, resources available and density of assigned strength. As a result of these differences throughout the PACOM, there has been a general lack of acceptance by the Bureau of Customs of inspections/examinations conducted within the major part of the PACOM.

73

b. An increase in the credibility of inspections/ examinations performed by military customs inspecting officers within the PACOM should decrease the intensity of inspections in the United States and thereby minimize inconvenience to personnel and delays in movement of mail, personal property and cargo which is now caused by such enforcement of customs regulations.

c. ~~In addition to eliminating the flow of controlled substances and contraband into the United States, an effective customs inspection program is necessary to eliminate the flow of such materials between oversea areas.~~

5. Policy. It is the policy of Commander in Chief Pacific (CINCPAC) to:

a. Prevent the flow of controlled substances and other contraband from the PACOM into the United States and between overseas countries.

b. Encourage the development of country-oriented customs programs which incorporate appropriate United States military and civil elements coordination with country customs and enforcement officials will be encouraged.

c. Coordinate and supervise the activities of all Bureau of Customs personnel assigned to support the Program within the PACOM.

74

d. Advise and assist PACOM Service Commanders, Subordinate Unifed Commanders and/or CINCPAC Single Senior Military Representatives (SSMR) in the development of effective customs programs; training of military customs personnel; maintenance of quality control procedures; and perpetuation of effective information programs.

e. Ensure that proposals for implementation of special or one-time programs designed to prevent drug smuggling are forwarded to CINCPAC prior to implementation for further forwarding to JCS and OASD(C), as appropriate.

f. Minimize inconvenience to DOD personnel and delays of DOD cargo, aircraft, ships and mail caused by the enforcement of customs regulations and directives.

g. Ensure compliance with the procedures outlined in reference (a) and this Instruction.

75

6. Inspection/Examination Requirements. Within the PACOM, as further amplified in the following paragraphs, customs inspections and/or examinations will be performed on the following in order to interdict prohibited items and to determine presence of items subject to import duties whenever any trans-ocean or international cross-border movement is about to begin:

a. Military passengers (including troop movements)

b. Civilian passengers

c. Accompanied baggage

d. Crews of ships, watercraft and aircraft

e. DOD sponsored cargo

f. Official mail

g. Personal mail

h. Naval ships

i. Naval aircraft

j. Air Force aircraft

k. Army aircraft

l. Army watercraft

m. Household goods

n. Privately owned vehicles

o. Unaccompanied baggage

p. Armed Forces Courier Service Couriers

q. Command Couriers

r. Privately owned firearms and ammunition

76

7. Inspection/Examination Responsibilities

a. Responsibility for customs inspections and/or examinations will be as follows:

(1) Passengers and Accompanied Baggage. Inspection/Examination will be accomplished by the Service which is responsible for the operation of the aerial port or seaport through which passengers and accompanied baggage normally process prior to departure from areas outside the customs territory of the United States.

(2) Crews of Ships, Watercraft, and Aircraft. Inspection/examination will be accomplished by the Service to which the ships, watercraft, and aircraft are assigned.

(3) DOD Sponsored Cargo. Inspection/examination of DOD sponsored cargo will be accomplished by the Service which is accountable for such cargo.

(4) Official and Personal Mail. Inspection/examination or forwarding to the Bureau of Customs for examination will be accomplished by the Service which is responsible for operation of the APO/FPO where the mail first enters the military postal system.

(5) Ships, Watercraft, and Aircraft. Inspection/examination will be accomplished by the Service to which the ships, watercraft, and aircraft are assigned.

(6) Household Goods and Unaccompanied Baggage. Inspection/examination will be accomplished at the point of origin by the Service to whom the owner of the goods and baggage is assigned. Deviations from this procedure must be

approved by th(■)appropriate CINCPAC Subo(■)nate
Unified Commander/Single Senior Military Representative (SSMR).

 (7) <u>Privately Owned Vehicles.</u> Inspection/exami-
nation will be accomplished by the Service which
operates the port from which the vehicle will be
shipped.

 (8) <u>Armed Forces Courier Service and Command
Couriers</u>

 a. Each Service entering materials into
the ARFCOS and/or a Command Courier service will be
responsible for establishing procedures to insure that
these services are used solely for the transmission
of qualified material.

 b. Inspection/examination of personal
property of both ARFCOS and command couriers and the
individuals themselves will be accomplished by the
Service which is responsible for the operation of the
aerial port or seaport through which such couriers
process prior to departure from an oversea area.

 (9) <u>Privately Owned Firearms and Ammunition.</u>
Each Service will establish inspection/examination
procedures to insure that privately owned firearms and
ammunition of its members meet eligibility requirements for
importation into the United States or other foreign areas.

8. Inspection/Examination Procedures.

Reference (a) primarily contains customs inspection and examination requirements for entry into the customs territory of the United States. This paragraph amplifies those requirements and expands applicability to include intra-theater and inter-theater movements. The procedures outlined in reference (a), as applicable, will be utilized in addition to the procedures outlined below.

a. Passengers and Accompanied Baggage.

(1) Military Passengers and Accompanied Baggage.

(a) An inspection of all military passengers' and an examination of all accompanied baggage will be accomplished immediately prior to departure from an oversea area on a DOD controlled ship or aircraft destined to cross international boundaries.

(b) An examination of military personnel will be undertaken only when there is probable cause that contraband or controlled substances may be concealed on the member's person and when the examination has been approved by the senior military customs inspecting officer present in the embarkation facility. In all cases where examination is conducted, the dignity and privacy of the individual will be preserved, no force will be applied, and no harsh language will be used. When an

79

examination has been approved by the senior military customs inspecting officer and the member persistently refuses examination duly appointed law enforcement elements may employ minimum force necessary to examine the member.

(2) Civilian Passengers and Accompanied Baggage.

(a) An inspection or examination (where necessary) of all civilian passengers and an examination of all accompanied baggage will be accomplished immediately prior to departure from an oversea area on a DOD controlled ship or aircraft, regardless of final destination.

(b) Civilian personnel who refuse to submit to an inspection or examination will be denied access to the DOD controlled ship or aircraft. They will be provided transportation by other practicable means as authorized by appropriate directives. U.S. Customs representatives at the first port of entry will be notified.

(3) Security of Passengers and Baggage. All passengers and baggage will be isolated in a sterile area from the time of inspection/examination until departure.

b. DOD Sponsored Cargo.

(1) All DOD sponsored cargo being relocated

from an oversea area to a destination in the customs territory of the United States or another oversea area will be examined at the time it is placed into appropriate receptacles for movement. After examination, such cargo will be secured until departure for its destination.

c. Official Mail.

(1) Military postal personnel will conduct examinations, on a random basis, of all official matter presented for entry into the military postal system as official mail to insure that no contraband or controlled substances are contained therein. Particular attention will be given to official mail which is addressed to civilian addresses or to individuals by name at official addresses.

(2) Official mail will be accepted at military post offices solely from individuals who can be positively identified as authorized agents or unit mail clerks of an organization or activity. Official mail entering the military postal system by any means other

86

than an authorized agent or unit mail clerk will be returned to the origin activity or organization for verification of its authenticity.

(3) Mail which upon examination is found to contain contraband or a controlled substance will be turned over to the appropriate investigative agency.

(4) Official mail entered into the military postal system by authorized non-DOD agencies and suspected of containing contraband or controlled substances will be forwarded under an indicia label to Chief Administrative Officer, U.S. Customs Mail Division, 1675 7th Street, Oakland, California 94615 for examination.

d. Personal Mail

(1) Letter and Parcel Mail

(a) All first class letter and parcel mail, regardless of its final destination, will be inspected by military postal personnel to determine its potential for containing contraband or controlled substances. Such mail, determined to be suspect, will be forwarded under an indicia label to Chief Administrative Officer, U.S. Customs Mail Division, 1675 7th Street, Oakland, California 94615 for examination.

(b) All second, third and fourth class mail, regardless of its final destination, which is suspected of containing contraband or controlled substances will be examined by military postal authorities or military customs inspectors (excepted) where such inspectors are available. Such mail found to contain contraband or controlled substances will be reported to appropriate military investigative agencies for action.

(2) Parcel Mail

To positively identify mailers of all parcels, postal clerks in military post offices in overseas areas within the PACOM will:

(a) Identify the mailer by checking his identification card.

(b) Ensure that a complete and legible return address is entered on each parcel.

(c) Ensure that mailers sign parcels below the return address at the time of mailing.

(d) Ensure that any person mailing parcels for another individual places his name, grade, social security account number, and signature below the return address of the actual sender.

(e) Verify the information required in paragraph (d) above by checking the identification card of the person mailing the parcel.

(3) Cassettes and Film Mailers

(a) All voice tape cassettes and film mailers destined for the United States or its territories, except Hawaii, will be pouched, labeled, and forwarded to CAO U.S. Customs Mail Division, 1675 7th Street, Oakland, California 94615 for examination.

(b) All voice tape cassettes and film mailers destined for Hawaii will be pouched, labeled, and forwarded to U.S. Mail Section, Post Office Annex, 530 Rodgers Blvd, Honolulu, Hawaii 96819 for examination.

(c) Voice tape cassettes and film mailers addressed to an individual which are mailed from one oversea area to another will be considered suspect mail and forwarded to CAO U.S. Customs Mail Division, 1675 7th Street, Oakland, California 94615 for examination.

(4) Detection Equipment

Fluoroscope and other detection equipment including marijuana detector dogs will be used by military postal personnel as directed by the appropriate Service which operates the military post office.

e. Ships and Aircraft

(1) On-board inspection of ships and inspection of naval aircraft traveling between oversea areas within the PACOM will be conducted in accordance with procedures established by the Commander in Chief United States Pacific Fleet.

84

(2) Inspection of Air Force aircraft traveling between oversea areas within the PACOM will be conducted in accordance with procedures established by the Commander in Chief Pacific Air Forces.

(3) Inspection of Army watercraft and aircraft traveling between oversea areas within the PACOM will be conducted in accordance with procedures established by the Commander in Chief U.S. Army Pacific.

(4) Customs inspections of all ships and aircraft returning from oversea areas within the PACOM to the customs territory of the United States will be conducted in accordance with appropriate Departmental regulations.

f. Personal Property (Household Goods, Privately Owned Vehicles and Unaccompanied Baggage).

(1) Inspection and/or examination is required for all personal property shipments moved from one oversea area to another oversea area within PACOM. The purpose of this inspection/examination is to preclude the possibility of contraband material or controlled substances being transported from one oversea area to another.

85

(2) Inspection/examination should be performed in the presence of the owner and at a time when he will not again have access to the personal property prior to its shipment.

LOCAL CUSTOMS INSPECT?

(3) Military customs inspecting officers will inspect/ examine all household goods and unaccompanied baggage at the point of packing.

(4) DD Form 1252 will be prepared in original and five (5) copies for all shipments moved by the Military Airlift Command when Through Government Bill of Lading service is used. The six copies will be utilized as follows:

(a) The original will be attached to the Government Bill of Lading.

(b) One copy will be attached to the number one (1) container of the shipment.

(c) One copy will be turned over to the aerial port to be attached to the cargo manifest.

(d) One copy will be turned over to the owner.

(e) One copy will be retained by the Customs Inspection Office.

(f) One copy will be retained by the Transportation Office.

(5) Privately owned vehicles will be inspected and/or examined at the port of embarkation in accordance with procedures established by the Service responsible for operation of the port.

g. Armed Forces Courier Service (ARFCOS) and Command Couriers.

(1) The movement through courier service channels of any property not owned or controlled by the United States is strictly prohibited.

(2) The commander of each organization or activity within the PACOM which enters materials into ARFCOS and/or utilizes a Command Courier service will establish controls to assure that these services are used solely for the transmission of qualified material and that contraband/controlled substances is not entered into the courier service systems.

(3) Military customs inspecting officers will not examine or impound ARFCOS or command courier pouches.

(4) Personnel having knowledge of material entered into ARFCOS, which is suspected or known to be unqualified or unauthorized, will forward a letter report to the Director, Armed Forces Courier Service, 3511 Carlin Springs

Road, Falls Church, Virginia 22041, furnishing all particulars, including ARFCOS control number, originator and addressee.

(5) Reports concerning material which is entered into a command courier system and is suspected or known to be contraband or controlled substances will be forwarded to the commander who designated the courier.

(6) The personal property of ARFCOS and/or command couriers and the individuals themselves will be inspected/examined immediately prior to departure from an oversea area within the PACOM regardless of final destination.

h. Privately Owned Firearms and Ammunition.

(1) Chapter 10, reference (a) prescribes procedures, assigns responsibility and outlines eligibility requirements for the importation into the United States and the interstate movement of privately owned firearms and ammunition by DOD personnel.

(2) In addition to insuring compliance with the provisions of chapter 10, reference (a), commanders at all levels within the PACOM will conduct inspections/examinations to insure that privately owned firearms and

ammunition of their members meet eligibility requirements for importation into other oversea areas.

9. Selection, Training and Appointment of Military Customs Inspecting Officers.

a. General. Military personnel who perform customs inspections and/or examinations on any of the categories listed in para 6 will, in general terms, be called Military Customs Inspecting Officers. Within this general category, there will be two basic types of inspectors: Military Customs Inspectors (Excepted) (MCI-E) and Military Customs Inspection Officers (MCIO).

(1) Personnel selected for training as MCI-E will be trained by the Bureau of Customs or by other MCI-E who have previously received the requisite training under a program approved by the Bureau of Customs. Under ideal conditions, the majority of military customs inspecting officers will be MCI-E.

(2) Where the number of MCI-E is insufficient to accomplish mission requirements, selected personnel may be designated by a commander as MCIO to serve on a full-time or part-time basis. Under ideal conditions, only a small portion of military customs inspecting officers will be MCIO.

b. Selection.

(1) Personnel selected for training as MCI-E must meet the following minimum criteria.

(a) Possess only the highest degree of personal integrity.

(b) Have at least one-half of the normal overseas tour remaining.

(c) If possible, have previous experience as a Military Customs Inspection Officer.

(d) Be a commissioned officer, warrant officer, enlisted person (E-4 or above) or United States citizen who is a DOD civilian employee (GS-7 or above).

(e) Not be an officer on the active list of the Regular Army, Regular Navy, Regular Air Force or Regular Marine Corps.

(2) Personnel selected for designation as MCIO should have some experience in the general area in which they will perform duties as MCIO.

c. Training.

(1) MCI-E will be trained by the Bureau of Customs or under programs approved by the Bureau of Customs.

(2) MCIO will be trained in accordance with the requirements of their specific duties, i.e., Passenger and Baggage Inspector, etc.

(3) Training courses will include, but not be limited to, the subjects outlined in paragraph B-1.b, Appendix B, reference (a).

d. Appointment.

(1) MCI-E will be appointed on written orders by the appropriate CINCPAC Subordinate Unifed Commander/ SSMR in coordination with the Bureau of Customs advisor in the PACOM.

(2) MCIO will be appointed on written orders by the designated representative of the appropriate PACOM Service Commander.

e. Military Customs Inspection Stamps. Military Customs Inspection Stamps (as portrayed in figure B-1, Appendix B, reference (a)) will be issued to personnel upon appointment as Military Customs Inspecting officers. Stamps will be controlled at the lowest possible operating level consistent with ensuring their absolute security. Stamps will be numbered in accordance with the block of numbers assigned by country below. A rubber stamp signature will not be acceptable on the signature line of

19

91

the military customs inspection stamp. Handwritten signature is required.

COUNTRY	NUMBERS
India	I 0001 - 0500
Pakistan	PP 0501 - 0999
Aleutian Islands	AA 1000 - 1499
Ryukyus Islands	R 1500 - 1999
Japan	J 2000 - 2999
Korea	K 3000 - 3999
Taiwan	TT 4000 - 4999
Vietnam	V 5000 - 5999
Thailand	T 6000 - 6999
Philippines	P 7000 - 7999
Guam/TTPI	G 8000 - 8999
Australia	A 9000 - 9499
Other Areas	X 9500 - 9999

f. Training Assistance.

(1) Requests for Bureau of Customs training teams and training materials will be routed through the appropriate CINCPAC Subordinate Unifed Commander/SSMR to CINCPAC.

(2) Requests for approval of one-time training programs involving other than PACOM military and civilian personnel will be routed through the appropriate CINCPAC Subordinate Unified Commander/SSMR to CINCPAC.

10. Resource Requirements. Fiscal and personnel requirements developed as a result of compliance with reference (a) and this Instruction will be satisfied within existing resources, to the extent possible. If, after redistribution of existing resources, a validated need for additional resources exists to ensure mission accomplishment, such requirements and adequate justification will be forwarded through Service channels with an information copy to CINCPAC. CINCPAC will be kept informed of the status of all such requests.

11. Command Responsibilities. In addition to the customs inspection/examination responsibilities outlined in preceding paragraphs, the following responsibilites are assigned in connection with the PACOM Customs Inspection Program (hereinafter referred to as "the Program").

a. The Commander in Chief Pacific will:

(1) Provide policy guidance on PACOM customs matters to PACOM Service Commanders and CINCPAC Subordinate Unifed Commanders/SSMRs.

(2) Maintain liaison with the Bureau of Customs, Department of the Treasury, through the Department of the Army (DA) as DOD executive agent for customs matters.

(3) Coordinate and supervise the activities of all Bureau of Customs personnel assigned to support the program within the PACOM.

98

(4) Ensure compliance with the procedures outlined in reference (a) and this Instruction.

(5) Designate the level of appointment of military customs inspecting officers.

(6) Inform DA of any major problem areas in the program.

(7) Furnish such information as from time-to-time may be required by DA concerning the Program.

b. PACOM Service Commanders will in addition to the responsibilities outlined in above paragraphs.

(1) Ensure the implementation and enforcement of the customs inspection procedures and entry requirements outlined in reference (a) and this Instruction.

(2) Develop an information program designed to inform all personnel of the prohibitions, restrictions, requirements and penalties pertaining to the importation of controlled substances and contraband material into the customs territory of the United States and into oversea areas.

(3) Ensure that personnel selected for training as Military Customs Inspecting Officers meet the criteria outlined in paragraph 9b above.

(4) Advise all personnel that examination of locked containers may be necessary at the United States

port of entry even though such containers have been previously examined by military customs inspecting offices within the PACOM.

(5) Establish standards of performance to ensure the overall effectiveness of the Program.

(6) Conduct normal day-to-day operations in the Program.

(7) Forward four copies of implementing instructions to CINCPAC within 60 days of the date of this instruction.

(8) Furnish such information as from time-to-time may be required by CINCPAC concerning the Program.

(9) Inform CINCPAC of major problem areas encountered within their commands which relate to the Program.

c. CINCPAC Subordinate Unifed Commanders and/or CINCPAC SSMRs will in addition to the responsibilities outlined in above paragraphs.

(1) Coordinate individual Service customs programs within their respective countries to ensure uniformity of operations.

(2) Develop and conduct, in cooperation with a Bureau of Customs advisor, a training program for military customs inspecting officers.

95

(3) Establish monitorship procedures designed to ensure compliance with the provisions of reference (a) and this Instruction.

(4) Develop country-oriented customs programs which incorporate appropriate United States military and civil elements. As a part of such programs, designate a single point of contact on their staffs for customs matters.

(5) Coordinate with host country customs and enforcement officials.

(6) Forward four copies of implementing instructions to CINCPAC within 60 days of the date of this Instruction.

(7) Furnish such information as from time-to-time may be required by CINCPAC concerning the Program.

12. Modifications. Personnel using this Instruction are invited to forward comments and recommendations for its improvement to CINCPAC. Modifications will be forwarded to the field initially via electrical means. Subsequently, all such modifications will be included in printed revisions of the instruction.

13. Reports. This Instruction requires no formal recurring reports; however, CINCPAC will be informed via electrical means when:

a. There is a sizable seizure of controlled substance, or

b. New techniques of smuggling controlled substances and/or contraband are discovered by customs inspecting officers.

DISTRIBUTION: (CINCPACINST 5605.1B)
List I (A only)
List II (less D5)

Copy to: (2)
SECDEF (ASD/Admin)
DA (DALO-TRT-P)
JCS
CG, FMFPAC
USAF Postal & Courier Service (Pacific Region)

증산 수출 건설

재 무 부

협력 1241-364 1972. 4. 18.

수신 외무부장관

제목 미군사우체국을 통한 우편소포 검사 장소변경

1. 미군사우체국 (APO)를 통한 군사우편 소포의 검사절차에 의하면 반입 소포에 대한 세관 검사 장소는 항공편인 경우 김포및 오산, 선박편인 경우 인천으로 지정되어 있읍니다.

2. 그러나 1972년 3월 인천기지 APO 의 김포 이동후 미측에서는 한국측에 사전 통고도 없이 선박편을 이용 부산에 반입되는 소포를 세관검사를 받지 않고 단위부대 APO에 직송하는 사례가 발생하고 있다고 하는바,

3. 별첨과 같이 문제점을 제기하오니 이러한 사태의 시정과 아울러 세관검사 장소의 즉각적인 변경조치를 취하여 주시기 바랍니다.

4. 아울러 협력 1245-258(1972. 3. 13) 및 협력 1243·1 -120(1972. 2. 3)로 건의한 APO를 통한 마약류 부정유입 방지와 등기소포에 대한 세관검사 적용 건의에 대해 조속히 조치하여 주시기 바라며

5. 협력 1243·1 - 116 (1972. 2. 2)로 문의한 [illegible] 통관에 관한 귀부의 의견을 조속히 회시하여 주시기 바랍니다.

첨부 : 미군사우체국 반입우편소포에 대한 세관검사장 변경. 끝.

접수 1972. 4. 18 재무부

TSJ23

재무부장관

정부 공문서 규정 제27조 제2항의 규정에 의하여	관세국장 박동희 전결

이등에서 떨지말고 자수하여 광명찾자

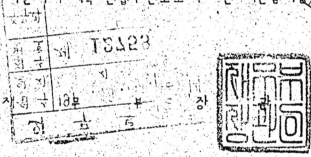

외 무 부	
접수 일시	197 .18.APR. 72 14:31
접수 번호	제 12753
주무과	
담당자	
처리 근거	

처리할 것

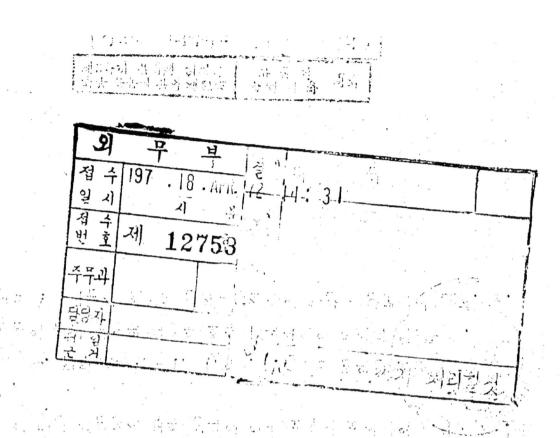

미군사 우체국(APO) 반입 우편소포에 대한 세관검사장 변경

I. 관계규정

가. 한 미주둔군 지위 협정 제9조에 대한 합의 양해 사항

나. 제9차 합동위원회에서 제정되고 제 64 차 및 제 66차 합동위원회에서 부분 개정된 APO를 통한 군사우편 소포검사절차 (발췌):

2. 우편물의 도착 통지

인천소재 미군 제 1 우체국과 김포 및 오산공항 미군우편책임 장교는

우편물의 양과 세관검사 가능한 시간등을 사전에 세관 당국에 통보하여야 한다.

3. 검사의 구체적 절차,

가. 한국 세관의 표본 검사를 받아야 하는 수입소포의 검사는 인천 미 제 1 우체국내 및 김포와 오산의 미군 우편 당국에서 마련하는 시설내에서 행하는 것에 합의한다.

II. 문제점

가. APO를 통하여 반입되는 소포에 대한 한국세관 검사는 항공편으로 반입되는것은 김포 및 오산에서

재무부 관세국

99

선박편으로 반입되는것은 인천에서 검사를 행하도록 관계규정에 의거 검사 장소가 지정되어있음.

나. 1971년 9월 인천 미군 수송대가 부산으로 이동한 후에는 종전 인천항을 통해 반입되던 군사우편 소포가 부산항을 통해 한국에 반입 Container 편으로 육로수송되어 인천 미군기지 우체국에서 세관 검사를 받았음.

다. 1972년 3월 인천기지 APO가 김포로 이동되었으므로 미군측은 관계규정에 의거 검사 장소를 한미 상호합의하에 변경 지정하여야 됨에도 불구하고 한국측에 사전 통보도 없이 부산항을 통해 반입된 소포를 세관검사도 받지 않고 세관 검사장이 설치되어 있지않은 단위부대 APO에 직송하는 사례가 발생하고 있다고 함.

III. 건의사항

미측의 일방적 조치를 시정토록하고 APO를 통한 군사우편 소포 검사 절차를 개정하여 선박편으로 한국에 반입되는 군사 우편 소포에 대한 세관 검사 장소를 변경한다.

재무부 관세국

100

검사장소 변경에 있어서는 다음의 두가지 방안이 대체적으로 선택될수 있다.

가, 제 1 안 :

선박편으로 한국에 반입되는 군사 우편소포의 세관 검사 장소를 종전의 인천에서 부산으로 변경한다.

나, 제 2 안 :

부산항을 통해 반입된 군사우편 소포를 Container 편을 이용, 김포로 육송.

김포에서 세관검사를 받도록 한다.

이 경우 부산에서의 발송 및 김포 도착에 대한 세관 확인 절차가 보장되어야 할것이다.

재무부 관세국

0101

공 란

공 란

공 란

tion should not have accrued as soon as the initial decision was rendered, whether that decision was favorable or unfavorable.

Hawaiian's final contention on this appeal is that Friendly did not sustain its burden of proof on the question of whether it was entitled to specific performance.

[8] Where there has been a threatened or actual breach of a contract of sale, the determination of whether specific performance should be granted rests within the sound discretion of the trial court. McFarland v. Gregory, 2 Cir., 322 F.2d 737; 5A Corbin on Contracts, § 1136, pages 92–96.

[9] The property to be sold under the contract here in question was unique in the sense that it pertained to one of only four television stations in Honolulu. Presumably the station in question had both programming, and an established clientele of viewers, not wholly shared by the other Honolulu stations. We do not think Friendly was required to prove it could not buy one of the other Honolulu stations before it could enforce the contract in question. All we need to hold, and do hold, however, is that the trial court did not abuse its discretion in decreeing specific performance.

Affirmed.

UNITED STATES of America, Appellee,

v.

Gerritt Johannes VAN LEEUWEN, Appellant.

No. 23449.

United States Court of Appeals Ninth Circuit.

May 29, 1969.

Certiorari Granted Oct. 27, 1969.

See 90 S.Ct. 175.

Defendant was convicted before the United States District Court for the Western District of Washington, Northern Division, William T. Beeks, J., of illegally importing gold coins into United States, and he appealed. The Court of Appeals, Solomon, District Judge, held that detention of first-class mail packages for 29 hours, without warrant authorizing detention, was unreasonably long, and the seizure of packages, which contained gold coins, violated Fourth Amendment rights of defendant even though customs officer, who knew that addressee of one of packages was suspected of trafficking in gold coins, had probable cause to search the packages.

Reversed.

1. Post Office ⇨47

First-class mail is protected by the Fourth Amendment. U.S.C.A.Const. Amend. 4.

2. Post Office ⇨47

Detention of first-class mail packages for 29 hours, without warrant authorizing detention, was unreasonably long, and the seizure of packages, which contained gold coins, violated Fourth Amendment rights of defendant, who was convicted of illegally importing gold coins into United States, even though customs officer, who knew that addressee of one of packages was suspected of trafficking in gold coins, had probable cause to search the packages. 18 U.S.C.A. § 545; U.S.C.A.Const. Amend. 4.

3. Post Office ⇨47

Defendant, who mailed two packages within the United States as first-class mail, but who was not the addressee or return addressee of packages containing gold coins, had standing, in prosecution for illegally importing gold coins, to object to seizure of the packages. 18 U.S.C.A. § 545; U.S.C.A. Const. Amend. 4.

Craig G. Davis (argued), Bellingham, Wash., for appellant.

William H. Rubidge (argued), Asst. U. S. Atty., Eugene G. Cushing, U. S. Atty., Seattle, Wash., for appellee.

105

Before CHAMBERS and KOELSCH, Circuit Judges, and *SOLOMON, District Judge.

SOLOMON, District Judge:

Gerritt Johannes Van Leeuwen was convicted of illegally importing gold coins into the United States in violation of 18 U.S.C. § 545. He asserts the post office violated the Fourth Amendment when it detained two first class packages without a warrant. He also asserts an affidavit in support of a search warrant was insufficient. We reverse on the basis of Appellant's first claim.

On March 28, 1968, at about 1:30 P.M., Appellant mailed two twelve-pound packages at the post office in Mount Vernon, Washington. He sent both packages by first class mail and insured each for $10,000. Appellant told the postal clerk that the packages contained coins. As Appellant was leaving the post office, the clerk told Captain Belgard of the Mount Vernon police that he was suspicious of the packages. Captain Belgard noticed that Appellant's car had British Columbia license plates and that the return address on the packages was a vacant housing area of a neighboring junior college.

Captain Belgard called Sergeant McKenzie of the Canadian police, who, in turn, called R. J. O'Hearn, Customs Officer-in-charge at Seattle, Washington. At about 3:00 P.M. O'Hearn called the Customs office in Van Nuys, California, the destination of one of the packages. He learned that the addressee was under investigation for trafficking in illegal coins. O'Hearn could not reach the Customs office at Nashville, Tennessee, the destination of the other package, because of the time difference. When he called the next morning, he learned that the addressee of the second package was also suspected of trafficking in gold coins. O'Hearn secured a search warrant and opened the packages at 6:30 P.M. on March 29. The Mount Vernon post office detained the packages for 29 hours, between the time they were mailed and the execution of the warrant. No judicial officer authorized this detention.

[1] First class mail is protected by the Fourth Amendment. Ex parte Jackson, 96 U.S. 727, 24 L.Ed. 877 (1878). Oliver v. United States, 239 F.2d 818, 61 A.L.R.2d 1273 (8th Cir.1957). In Lustiger v. United States, 386 F.2d 132 (9th Cir.1967), the Court said:

> "The protection against unreasonable search and seizure of one's papers or other effects, guaranteed by the Fourth Amendment extends to their presence in the mails. * * * Thus, first class mail *cannot be seized and retained,* nor opened and searched, without the authority of a search warrant." 386 F.2d at 139. (Emphasis added.)

The Fourth Amendment protects "the right of the people to be secure * * * in their papers and effects, against unreasonable searches and seizures." The information known to Captain Belgard immediately after Appellant mailed the packages would reasonably have justified a brief detention, without a warrant, while a further investigation could be made. Terry v. Ohio, 392 U.S. 1, 20–21, 88 S.Ct. 1868, 1879, 20 L.Ed.2d 889 (1968); *cf.* Warden, Md. Penitentiary v. Hayden, 387 U.S. 294, 87 S.Ct. 1642, 18 L.Ed.2d 782 (1967).

[2] By 3:00 P.M., O'Hearn knew that the addressee of one of the packages was under investigation for trafficking in gold coins. This additional fact supplied probable cause to search the packages. Instead, O'Hearn decided to wait until the following day so he could call the customs office at the destination of the second package. This decision represents an understandable exercise of caution. Nevertheless, as a result of this delay, the packages were detained for 29 hours at the post office. This period was unreasonably long, and the officers should have obtained a war-

* Honorable Gus J. Solomon, United States District Judge, District of Oregon, sitting by designation.

106

rant authorizing the detention. Katz v. United States, 389 U.S. 347, 88 S.Ct. 507, 19 L.Ed.2d 576 (1967); Lustiger v. United States, *supra*; *see* Davis v. Mississippi, 394 U.S. 721, 89 S.Ct. 1394, 22 L.Ed.2d 676 (1969); Camara v. Municipal Court, 387 U.S. 523, 87 S.Ct. 1727, 18 L.Ed.2d 930 (1967).

In *Katz*, the Government urged the Court to "retroactively validate" the conduct of its agents who had eavesdropped on the defendant's telephone conversations. The Government argued that the agents "did no more than they might properly have done with prior judicial sanction." 389 U.S. at 356, 88 S. Ct. at 514. The Court rejected this argument:

> "It is apparent that the agents in this case acted with restraint. Yet the inescapable fact is that this restraint was imposed by the agents themselves, not by a judicial officer. * * * Searches conducted without warrants have been held unlawful 'notwithstanding facts unquestionably showing probable cause,' * * * for the Constitution requires 'that the deliberate, impartial judgment of a judicial officer * * * be interposed between the citizen and the police * * *.'" 389 U.S. at 356–357, 88 S.Ct. at 514.

In the present case, the length of time that the packages were retained by the post office made prior judicial authorization necessary.

The Government cites United States v. Beckley, 335 F.2d 86 (6th Cir.1964). There, the package involved was mailed from outside the country and was not in first class mail.

[3] The Government also contends that Appellant has no standing to object to the seizure because he was not the addressee or the return addressee of the packages. There is no merit to this contention. Jones v. United States, 362 U. S. 257, 80 S.Ct. 725, 4 L.Ed.2d 697 (1960).

The seizure of Appellant's packages violated his rights under the Fourth Amendment and the gold coins should not have been admitted in evidence. Weeks v. United States, 232 U.S. 383, 34 S.Ct. 341, 58 L.Ed. 652 (1914).

Reversed.

CHAMBERS, Circuit Judge (concurring):

I think I am as sensitive as anyone to the Fourth Amendment in protecting one's person and one's home. But the detention of Van Leeuwen's "hot money" at the post office for 29 hours does not offend me very much. Someone in the post office holds up much of my mail over 29 hours.

I concur in the reversal only because I think precedent, which we must follow, requires us to reverse.

UNITED STATES of America, Appellee,
v.
John E. MANFREDONIA, Appellant.
No. 646, Docket 33289.

United States Court of Appeals
Second Circuit.

Argued June 11, 1969.

Decided Aug. 5, 1969.

Defendant was convicted by a jury sitting in the United States District Court for the Southern District of New York, Marvin E. Frankel, J., of violation of the federal perjury statute, and he appealed. The Court of Appeals, Anderson, Circuit Judge, held that fact that defendant's conviction on wagering tax charge was overturned because of unconstitutionality of wagering tax statutes did not render untenable conviction for perjury occurring during wagering tax prosecution and reversal did not operate nunc pro tunc to make immaterial testi-

107

cooperative projects without the authorization in § 116.2.

PART 117—MAIL TREATED IN CONFIDENCE

§ 117.1 Mail treated in confidence.

Sealed first-class mail while in the custody of the Post Office Department is accorded absolute secrecy. No persons in the Postal Service, except those employed for that purpose in dead-mail offices, may break or permit the breaking of the seal of any matter mailed as first-class mail without a legal warrant, even though it may contain criminal or otherwise unmailable matter, or furnish evidence of the commission of a crime.

(R.S. 161, as amended, sec. 1, 62 Stat. 782; 5 U.S.C. 301, 18 U.S.C. 1717, 39 U.S.C. 501) [26 F.R. 11513, Dec. 6, 1961. Redesignated at 31 F.R. 15350, Dec. 8, 1966; 32 F.R. 9629, July 1, 1967]

PART 118—COOPERATION WITH RED CROSS DURING NATURAL DISASTERS [1]

§ 118.5 Cooperation with Red Cross during natural disasters.

(a) *Application of these instructions.* This section applies only to natural disasters such as those caused by floods, tornadoes, hurricanes, earthquakes, fires, explosions, etc., and not to those caused by enemy action.

(b) *Objective of instructions.* Both the Post Office Department and the Red Cross realize the importance to the individual and the community of maintaining communication during times of disaster. These procedures will help maintain this essential communication.

(c) *Action by the Red Cross.* (1) The American National Red Cross will encourage its chapters to establish and maintain contact with the postmaster(s) within the chapter jurisdiction in the interest of disaster planning.

(2) The Red Cross will arrange to use the "Change of Address Order," Form 3575 as a standard item in Red Cross disaster operations. It will also arrange to distribute these forms as needed to disaster-displaced persons in all Red Cross field facilities such as registration centers, feeding centers, mobile canteens, disaster shelters, etc. The chapter concerned will arrange with the postmaster concerned for the disposition of the completed forms for the establishment of a postal locator file.

(3) The Red Cross will arrange for the distribution of postal cards or other suitable stationery as needed by individuals or families in areas affected by disaster for mailing to relatives and friends as notification of the whereabouts and safety of the senders.

(4) The Red Cross will in disaster situations include in its Public Information releases an appeal to affected families and individuals to obtain and complete "Change of Address Order" forms, along with an appeal to write to relatives and friends immediately concerning their whereabouts and safety.

(5) The Red Cross will include all necessary instructions in operating procedure manuals and training programs to guide its field staff and volunteers in cooperating with local postmasters in implementing this arrangement.

(6) The Red Cross has advised all of its chapters concerning these instructions and has urged that they include postmasters in their disaster preparedness planning.

(d) *Action by the Post Office Department.* (1) The Post Office Department will make available to the American National Red Cross "Change of Address Order," Form 3575, in a manner mutually agreeable to both agencies.

(2) Post offices that receive completed "Change of Address Order" forms following a disaster will maintain them as a central locator file to provide directory service whereby mail may be promptly forwarded to individuals and families displaced by the disaster.

(3) The Post Office Deparment will permit postmasters to make available the information on these "Change of Address Order" forms to authorized Red Cross disaster workers. This information will be used by the Red Cross in locating individuals and families, only to answer inquiries from relatives and friends concerning the whereabouts and welfare of residents of the disaster community, or to make contact with residents who have made application for assistance from the Red Cross but who cannot be located because of a change of address.

(4) Regional Directors and Postal Inspectors in Charge are responsible for seeing that the post offices concerned implement these cooperative arrangements in disaster situations. Postmasters are encouraged to participate in community and Red Cross disaster preparedness planning.

[1] 32 F.R. 20811, Dec. 27, 1967.

108

공 란

공　　　란

증산 수출 건설

재 무 부

협력 1243-695 1972. 8. 14.

수신 외무부장관

제목 SOFA 재무분과 위원회 회의개최 및 대책회의

1. SOFA 재무분과 위원회 회의를 1972년 8월 18일 14:00 주한 미군 SOFA 회의실에서 개최 하오니 각위원들은 필히 참석하여 주시기 바랍니다.

의제: 1) 미군용 수입신고서 양식 개정

2) APO 우편물 검사장

3) P.X 및 COMMISARY 통제물품 추가

4) 면세물품 양도 양수

2. 1972년 8월 16일 14:00시 동회의에 대한 대책회의를 재무부 관세협력담당관실에서 개최 하오니 각위원들 께서는 필히 참석하여 주시기를 바랍니다. 회의자료는 추후 송부 위계입니다. 끝.

재 무 부 장 관

내집살림 나라살림 저축으로 부강하자

정부공문서 규정 제27조 제2항의 규정에 의하여 | 관세 박동희 전결

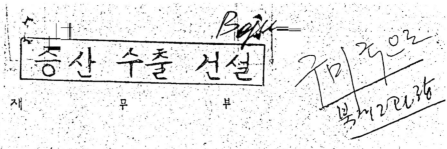

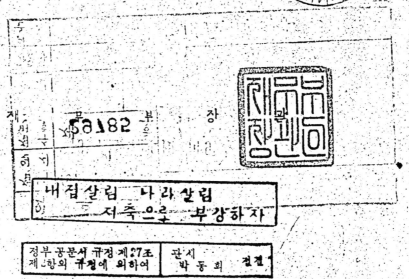

접수일시	197 . . .
접수번호	제 29785 호
처리담당자	
처리결과	

197 . . . 까지 처리할 것

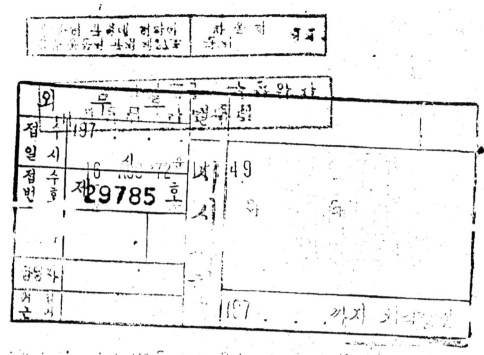

[대책회의 자료]

〈의제 2〉 국제연합군용 수입신고서 양식 개정

1. 관계규정

제 5차 합동위원회 제정 SOFA 제9조 2항의 운용을 위한 절차 : 합중국 군대가 수입하는 각종화물의 적절한 증명서의 양식및 제출 방법.

2. 경위

가. 세관행정의 EDPS 화에 따라 일반수출입 신고서 양식이 1972年 초부터 개정되었으며 이에따라 SOFA 제9조 2항에 의한 국제연합군용 수입신고서의 양식을 개정토록 조치해줄 것을 관세청으로 부터 건의하여 왔음.

나. 협력 1245-60호 (1972. 1. 22) 로 외무부에 이를 건의함.

다. 제 71차 SOFA 한미 합동위원회에서 재무분과 위원회에 과제부여됨 (첨부 1 참조)

라. 미측에 한국측 의견을 송부함 (첨부 2 참조)

가, 재무부 관세국

2

0686

943

112

마. 미측의 대안을 제시받음 (첨부 3 참조)

3. 대책

가. 주한미군 지위협정의 적용을 받은 개인이 한국에 반입하는 물품의 수입신고에 대해 지금까지 SOFA 제9조 2항의 군사화물에 대한 증명 양식을 사용하여 왔으나 SOFA 및 동 관계 규정에 의하면 개인용품에 대해서는 한국 정부가 정하는 어떠한 수입신고 양식도 사용할수 있게 되어있음.

나. 따라서 협정 제9조 2항의 군사화물 증명 양식을 개정 이를 협정 제9조 3항의 개인용품 수입신고에 대해서도 겸용하도록 하는 최초의 방침 대신에, 협정 제9조 2항의 군사화물 증명 양식은 개정하지 않고 협정 제9조 3항의 개인용품에 대해서는 한국 정부가 정하는 양식을 사용토록하고 이를 미측에 통보하여 그 협조를 구하도록 함.
(첨부 4 참조)

재무부 관세국

3 944

113

다. 그 이유는 미측의 대안에 의하면 개인용품의 면세 여부를 미군 통관 장교가 확인 하도록 되어있고 차후 개인용품에 대한 수입 신고서 양식을 개정할 필요가 생길때 마다 일일이 미측과의 합의를 얻어야 하도록 되어있음.

0098

4

재무부 관세국

945

114

공 란

	부호 Code No	
1. 입항 Date of Entry		
2. 선하증권번호 B/L No		
3. 적재선(기)명 Vessel (Aircraft)		
4. 적재선(기)국적 Flag		
5. 적출국(지) Place of Shipment		
6. 입항지 Place of Entry		
7. 생산지. 원산국(지) Place of Production		
8. 장치장소 Place of Storage		

대한민국세관
Korea Customs Service

국세연합군수입신고서 Card
Import Declaration [redacted] USFK
certification

9. 세관부호 Customs Code No	10. 수입종별 Sort of Import	11. 신고번호 Declaration No

12. 신고서 Date of Declaration 19 . . .

~~13. 검사 Date of Examination 19 . . .~~

~~14. 조정 Date of Levy 19 . . .~~

~~15. 면허 Date of Permit 19 . . .~~

결재	계	주무	과장

16. 품명 및 규격 Description of Articles & Grade	17. 중량 Weight / 18. 수량 Quantity	단위 Unit	20. 신고가격 Declared Value / 21. ~~감정가격 Appraised Value~~	22. 세번 Heading / 23. 부호 Code No	~~24. 세율 Rate~~	25. ~~관세액 Amount of Customs Duty~~	26. 관세면세근거 및 부호 Duty Exemption Code No
(1)		Kg	CIF$		%	₩	
			₩				
(2)		Kg	CIF$		%	₩	
			₩				
27. 비고 Remark		계 Total	CIF$ / ₩	환율 Exchange Rate		₩	

28. 기호.번호.포장종류와 개수 ~~Mark Number, Type of Package~~
Markings:

~~30. 내국세~~

1. 과세가격	2. 세별	3. 세종	4. 세율	5. 세액
(1)			%	₩
(2)			%	₩

29. 신고서 매란 Declared Paper Sheet Column

원천과세표준

31. 비고 Remarks

32. 첨부서류 Attached herewith if any
송품장 ( ) Invoice
포장명세서 ( ) Packing List
원산지증명 ( ) Certificate of Origin
운임명세서 ( ) Freight Sheet
보험영수증 ( ) Receipt of Insurance
선하증권사본 ( ) Copy of B/L
Others ( )

~~상기 각항에는 허위가 없을뿐아니라 당해물품은 개인용품, 업무용품으로서 결코 판매 또는 교환등의 방법에 의하여 타용도에는 사용하지 않겠기 자이 서약함.~~

~~The above statement is true and correct to the best of my knowledge and I hereby affirm that the above articles are not for resale, exchange or other such purpose and will be used as personal or official items only:~~

상가 물품에 대하여 수입통관면허를 신청함.
국제연합군통관관리장교 certify
I hereby make application for permission to import the above goods for the use of [redacted] USFK

33. 면허인 Signature of Permit

0706

947

신고자성명 Name and Signature of Declarer	통관장교 서명 Signature of Customs clearance Officer
신고자주소 Address of Declarer	부대명 Department of the Army

116

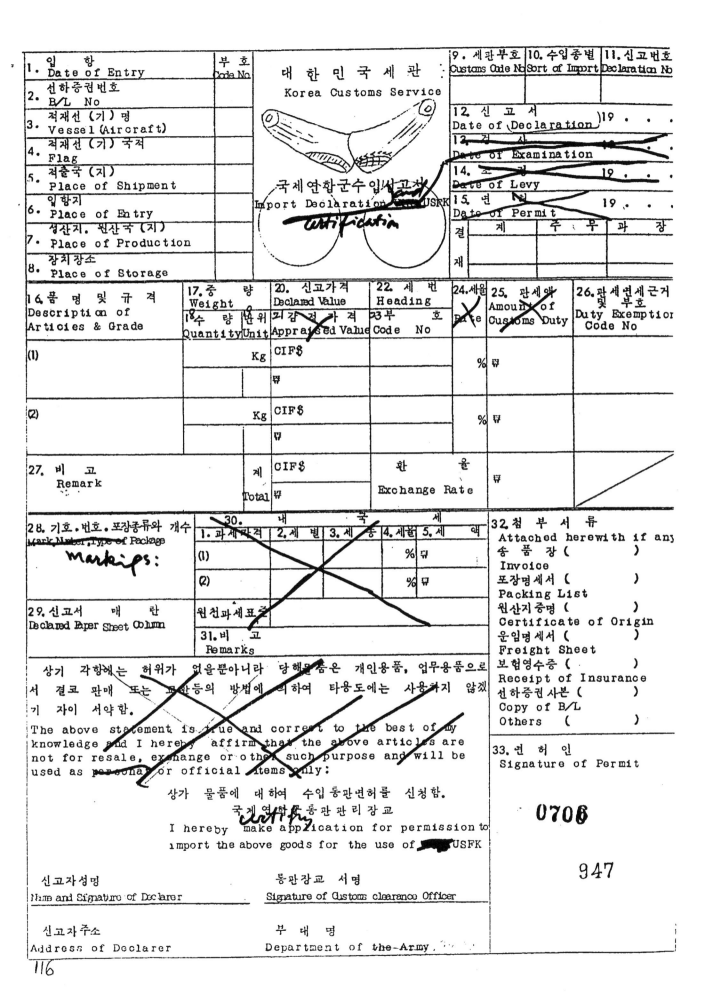

공 란

공 란

공 란

공 란

공 란

공 란

공　　란

공 란

공　란

공 란

공 란

공 란

공 란

공 란

SOFA 재무분과위원회 회의 자료

의 제	관 련 규 정	배 경	대 책
1. AFO의 이동에 따른 군사우편소 검사 설치 개정	제9차 합동위원회에서 지정되고 제64차 및 제66차 합동위원회에서 수정 개정된 AFO 를 한국군사우편소로 검사 절차	가. 현지 규정상의 AFO 우편소로 검사장 : 선박편 (인천), 항공편 (김포, 오산) 나. 인천기지 AFO ⟶ 평택으로 이동 : 선박편으로 반입되는 군사우편소로 검사장의 신규 지정이 요구됨	1) AFO 우편소로 검사장 : 부산, 김포, 오산 2) 시설분과는 한·미 양측관계자의 현지조사 방의 의 오조 시 시정 개정
2. 주한 미군용 수입신고서 양식 개정	가. 5차 합동위원회 설정 SOFA 제9조 2항의 운용은 위한 면세 수입되는 군용화물에 관한 증명서의 양식 및 제출방법	가. 재판관할의 FDIS 화에 따라 SOFA 제9조 2항에 의한 군화물 증명 양식의 변경이 요구되었음 나. 미측은 협정 제9조 5항의 규정에 의한 제9조 2항의 개인용품 수입신고 이동 사용할 것을 요청하고 있음	1) 협정 제9조 2항에 의한 미군사 화물 증명 양식은 쌍방간의 합의에 의하여 개정 2) 협정 제9조 3항의 개인용품 수입신고서는 관계측이 일방적으로 개정 상시
3. 미군재산의 처리	가. 협정 제9조의 규정 위의 배제를 하는 합중국 군대의 비세출 자금 기관에 수입되는 물품 중 이러한 사용을 위하여 합리적으로 소요되는 한도에 한정되어야 한다. 나. 제65차 합동위 거상 : 비세출자금 기관에 반송되는 화물이 과다 일정 제공	가. 위 [illegible] 외의 제품은 초기되고 기관의 합리적소요량을 초과한 물품이 한미 부정유출되는 것을 방지하기위한 검사를 강조하기로한 군관계 임시 분과위원회의 합의에 따라 재무분과위원회에 검토요청된 사안임	1) 수도 연초 [illegible] 계 미군 통제방으로 추가 한다. 2) 상기 추가 품목의 관한 수량에 대한 이월의 사용고의 감퇴는 요구한다. 3) 현지의 15개 품목을 승인 (LOA) 하되 중복 있는 건만 요구한다.

0715

962

재 무 부 관 세 국

의 제	관 계 규 정	배 경	비 고
5. 면세품을 양도 양수 절차 검토	가. 협정 제9조 6항(면세물품의 처분) 나. 제10차 합동위 채택 면세 물품 양도조건 절차	외자 사업의 인수 창구를 관광공사로 일원화 함에 따라 제10차 합동위원회에서 채택된 면세물품의 양도 양수 절차를 재검토 한다.	외자차량 인수창구 일원화 문제와의 확정으로 인하여 당 위원회는 보류함

0716

963

재 무 부 관 세 국

22

122

공 란

SOFA 재무분과 위원회 대책회의 결과 보고

1. 참석자: 외무부 북미 2과장 김 기조
   " 북미2과 변 승국
   재무부 관세협력과장 이 재섭
   " 관세협력과 강 영주
   관세청 세무과 윤 필수
   " " 정 기성
   " 심리과 김 재흡

2. 회의일시: 72. 8. 16. 14:00-16:40

3. 회의장소: 재무부 관세협력과 사무실

4. 토의및 합의내용

(의제 1): APO 의 이동에 따른 군사우편 소포검사 절차 개정

가. 문제점:

APO 를 통하여 반입되는 소포에 대한 한국세관 검사는 항공편으로 반입되는것은 김포 및 오산에서, 선박편으로 반입되는것은 인천에서 검사를 행하도록 지정되어 있으나, 72년 3월 인천기지 APO 가 김포로 이동되었으므로 해상을 통해 반입되는 우편 소포에 대한 검사장소의 변경 지정이 요구됨.

북미2과	공람	72년 8월	담당	과장	국장	차관보	차관	장관
			(서명)	(서명)	(서명)	출장중	(서명)	

0727

972 31

134

나. 합의 대책

제 1안: 부산항에 입항하는 모든 우편 소포에 대하여 반입 직후 세관 검사를 실시함.

* 71년 9월 인천 미군 수송대가 부산항으로 이동한 후에는 종전 인천항을 통해 반입되던 군사 우편 소포가 부산항을 통해 반입되고 있음.

제 2안: 부산항 입항시 우편 소포를 적재한 Container 에 대한 점검만 실시한 후 육로로 수송, 김포 및 오산에서 세관검사를 실시함. 단 부산 인근지역에 배부될 우편소포에 대하여는 부산에서 세관검사 실시

(의제 2): 주한 미군군용 수입 신고서 양식 개정

가. 문제점:

세관 행정의 EDPS 화에 따라 일반 수출입 신고서 양식이 72년초부터 개정되었으며 이에따라 주한 미군 군용수입(군용 선편 제외) 신고서 양식을 개정하여야 할것임.

나. 합의 대책:

(1) SOFA 제 9조 2항의 군사화물에 대한 수입(일반상용 선편에 의한) 신고 양식은 별첨 양식과 같이 개정함.

32

973

0728

135

(2) 지금까지 SOFA 제9조 2항의 군사화물 수입신고 양식을 준용해 오던 개인용품 수입(군용선편 또는 상용선편에 의한) 신고에 대해서는 한국정부가 새로히 정하는 양식을 사용토록하고 미측에 통보하여 그 협조를 구하도록 함.

(의제 3): 통제 품목의 추가

가. 문제점:

PX 및 Commissary 의 통제품목을 추가하고 물품의 부정 유출을 방지하기 위한 절차를 검토하기로 재무분과위원회에 과제 부여된바가 있음.

나. 합의 대책:

(1) 주류, 연초, 커피를 통제품목으로 추가한다.

(2) 상기 추가 품목의 판매 수량에 대한 미측의 자율규제 강화를 요구한다.

(3) 현재의 35개 통제 품목을 승인 (LOA: Letter of Authorization) 품목으로 전환 요구한다.

(의제 4): 면세 물품 양도 양수절차 검토

가. 문제점:

의제 차량의 인수 창구를 관광공사로 일원화함에 따라 제 10차 합동위원회에서 제정된 면세물품의 양도 절차를 재 검토하도록 재무분과 위원회에 과제 부여된바 있음.

33

974

0729

136

나. 합의 대책

관광회사에서 일괄 매수 준비가 완성되지 않았음으로 대미측 교섭을 보류하기로 함.

(기타 의제)

1. 초청 계약자 업무용 장비의 면세 통관 여부

미측은 SOFA 제9조 2항 및 제15조 5항의 규정을 원용하여 건설 장비등의 면세 통관을 주장하고 있으나 이러한 건설장비 등을 제9조 2항의 "물품, 시설등에 합체될 자재"등으로 보기는 어렵고 제15조 5항의 "조세"는 내국세를 의미하는 것이므로 (영문 표기로는 Taxes 로 되어 있음) 관세의 부과가 면제될 수는 없음. 이 문제 검토를 위한 과제 위촉을 하기로함.

2. APO 우편 소포검사 절차 개정

등기 우편 소포를 검사 대상으로 추가하는 문제와 마약류등에 대한 세관 검사를 강화하는 문제에 대하여는 불법 내용물이 내재한다고 의심되는때에 한하여 검사를 실시하되 시행과정에서 양측의 견해에 차이가 발생할 때에는 그때에 다시 문제를 제기하기로 함.

3. 세관 직원에게 PX 등 비세출 자금기관에 대한 출입 및 검사권을 부여하는 문제는 미측에 자율적인 통제를 강화하도록 요청하는 선으로 우리측 주장을 완화함.

4. 미측은 차량등 면세물품 양도에 관하여 수입면장이 불필요하다고 주장하고 있으나 모든 수입물품은 면세 또는 과세 여부에 불구하고 수입면장을 필요로 하는것이므로 일선 세관에서 필히 수입신고를 받아 면장을 발부케 하도록 제도를 개선한다.

34 975

0730

137

1. 입 항 Date of Entry	부 [redacted] Code No	대 한 민 국 세 관 Korea Customs Service
2. 선하증권번호 B/L No		
3. 적재선 (기) 명 Vessel (Aircraft)		
4. 적재선 (기) 국적 Flag		
5. 적출국 (지) Place of Shipment		국제연합군수입신고서 Import Declaration ~~UNC~~/USFK or certification
6. 입항지 Place of Entry		
7. 생산지, 원산국 (지) Place of Production		
8. 장치장소 Place of Storage		

9. [redacted] 부호 Custom[redacted] No	10. 수입종별 Sort of Import	11. 신고번호 Declaration No

12. 신 고 서 Date of Declaration	19 . . .
13. 검 사 Date of Examination	19 . . .
14. 조 정 Date of Levy	19 . . .
15. 면 허 Date of Permit	19 . . .

결재	계	주 무	과 장

16. 품 명 및 규 격 Description of Articles & Grade	17. 중 량 Weight		20. 신고가격 Declared Value	22. 세 번 Heading	24. 세율 Rate	25. 관세액 Amount of Customs Duty	26. 관세면세근거 및 부호 Duty Exemption Code No
	18. 수 량 Quantity	단위 Unit	21. 감정가격 Appraised Value	23. 부 호 Code No			
(1)		Kg	CIF$		%	₩	
			₩				
(2)		Kg	CIF$		%	₩	
			₩				
27. 비 고 Remark		계 Total	CIF$ ₩	환 율 Exchange Rate		₩	

28. 기호. 번호. 포장종류와 개수 Mark, Number, Type of Package	30. 내 국 세				
	1. 과세가격	2. 세 별	3. 세 종	4. 세율	5. 세 액
	(1)			%	₩
	(2)			%	₩
29. 신고서 매 란 Declared Paper Sheet Column	원천과세표준				
	31. 비 고 Remarks				

32. 첨 부 서 류
Attached herewith if any
송 품 장 ( )
Invoice
포장명세서 ( )
Packing List
원산지증명 ( )
Certificate of Origin
운임명세서 ( )
Freight Sheet
보험영수증 ( )
Receipt of Insurance
선하증권사본 ( )
Copy of B/L
Others ( )

상기 각항에는 허위가 없을뿐아니라 당해물품은 개인용품, 업무용품으로서 결코 판매 또는 교환등의 방법에 의하여 타용도에는 사용하지 않겠기 자이 서약함.

The above statement is true and correct to the best of my knowledge and I hereby affirm that the above articles are not for resale, exchange or other such purpose and will be used as personal or official items only.

상기 물품에 대하여 수입통관면허를 신청함.

국제연합군통관관리장교

I hereby make application for permission to import the above goods for the use of UNC/USFK

33. 면 허 인
Signature of Permit

0731

35

976

신고자성명
Name and Signature of Declarer

통관장교 서명
Signature of Customs clearance Officer

신고자주소
Address of Declarer

부 대 명
Department of the Army

138

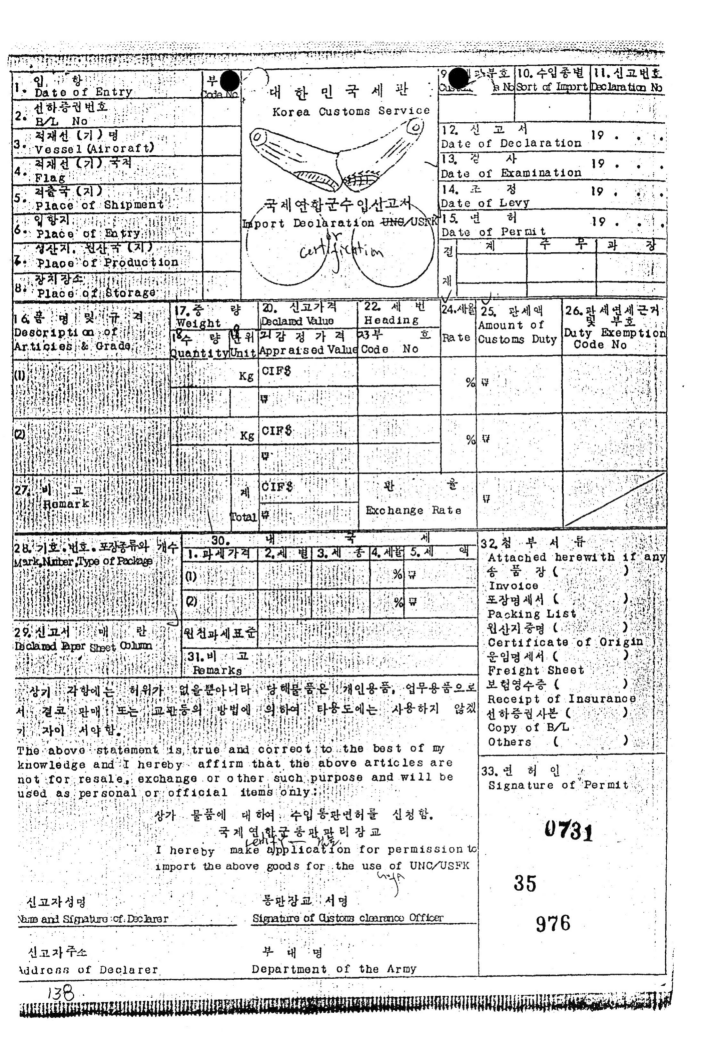

移徙貨物 및 別送貨物 稅関檢査 節次

經緯
① 1967. 5. 25 第8次 JC에서 課題賦与됨
② 韓·美間의 見解差異로 継続未決 状態
1969. 5月 以後에는 美側에서도 [illegible] 하지 않고 있음.

美側意見	韓國側意見	関係規定
檢査与否 및 時間 場所		SOFA 第9條 1項 (協定에서 規定된 경우를 除外하고는 大韓民國 稅関 当局이 집행하고 있는 法令에 따라야 한다)
a. 移徙貨物 (Household Goods)		
① 韓国政府가 원한다면 到着後 開装하는 동안에 檢査할수 있다	i) 物品을 輸出入하고자 할 때에는 稅関長에게 輸出入 申告를 하고 그 免許를 받아야 한다	関稅法 第137條 (輸出入의 免許)
	ii) 前項의 規定은 当該物品이 関稅法에 規定한 蔵置場所에 있는 경우에 限하여 이를 할수있다	関稅法 第138條 (申告의 要件)
0739	iii) 申告人은 申告한 物品에 対하여 稅関公務員의 檢査를 받아야 한다 다만 稅関公務員이 必要없다고 認定하는 경우에는 檢査를 省略할수있다	関稅法 第140條 (物品의 檢査)
② 檢査는 貨主 또는 貨主指名人 立会下에 貨主가 정한 時間과 場所에서 実施한다	i) 관세법 規定의 蔵置場所에서 하여야 함	관세법 第138條 (申告의 要件)
	ii) 原則的으로 稅関開庁 時間内에 檢査하여야 한다	관세법 第236條 (稅関의 開庁時間)

42

983

139

	iii) 物品의 檢査를 받는 者는 檢査에 參与하고 物品의 開装 및 再包裝을 하여야 한다	関稅法 施行令 第124條 (申告物品에 대한 檢査)
b 别送貨物 (Unaccompanied Baggage)		
① 個人의 别送貨物은 韓美関係当局이 그 檢査가 両國의 最上의 利益이 된다고 相互 合意하는 경우를 除外하고는 檢査하지 않는다	i) 物品을 輸出入하고자 할때에는 輸出入申告를 하고 그 免許를 받아야 한다	関稅法 第137條 (輸出入의 免許)
	ii) 前項의 申告는 当該物品이 関稅法에 規定한 藏置場所에 있는 경우에 限하여 이를 할수 있다	関稅法 第138條 (申告의 要件)
	iii) 申告人은 申告物品에 対하여 稅関公務員의 檢査를 받아야 한다	関稅法 第140條 (物品의 檢査)
② 檢査는 韓國및 美國関係官 立会下에 実施한다	i) 物品의 檢査를 받는 者는 檢査에 参与하고 物品의 開装및 再包裝을 하여야 한다	関稅法 施行令 第124條 (申告物品에 対한 檢査)

0740

43

984

재무부 관세국

140

2. 韓國稅関에 開裝時間通報	上記條件下에서 貨主가 원하는 時間에 檢査 可能함	
① 稅関은 開裝 1日 以前에 時間과 場所를 通報 받는다.	(要 削 除)	
② 通報는 口頭 또는 文書로써 指定된 稅関 官吏에게 通知 되었을때 成立한다.	(要 削 除)	
③ 韓国 당국은 開裝時間을 稅関 官吏에게 通報 하는데 必要한 정보를 美軍司令官에게 提供한다.	(要 削 除)	
④ 稅関檢査 官吏가 指定時間에 出頭치 않아도 開裝을 延期하지 않는다.	(要 削 除)	
3. 檢査費用 負担 기타.		
① 稅関 檢査로 因해 直接 発生하는 費用은 韓国이 負担한다.	세관 檢査로 인해 直接発生하는 費用은 檢査를 받는 者가 負担한다.	

0741

985

44

재 무 부 관 세 국

14

② 税関当局은 美軍司令官의 同意없이는 美軍構成員 등의 家事用品 또는 別送貨物로부터 여하한 品目도 押收하지 않는다	輸入禁止品은 押留한다.	関税法 第146條 (輸出入의禁止) SOFA 第9條 9項 (b): (합중국 군대는 한국세관에 의하여 압류될 물품을 인도하도록 확보하기 위하여 그의 权限内의 모든 援助를 提供하여야 한다.)
0742	986	45

재무부 관세국

142

중간 수출 [illegible]

법 주미국
출 2

재 무 부

협력 1243- 741 1972. 9. 4.

수신 외무부장관

제목 SOFA재무분과 위원회 회의 및 대책회의 개최 통보

1. 1972. 9. 8 14:00 재무부 회의실에서 SOFA 재무분과 위원회 회의를 개최하오니 각위원들은 필히 참석하여 주시기 바라며

2. 이에 관련하여 1972. 9. 7일 16:00시 재무부 관세협력담당관실에서 대책회의를 개최하오니 각위원들은 필히 참석하여 주시기 바랍니다. 끝.

발송 1972. 9. 4 재무부

재 무 부 장

내집살림 나라살림 저축으로 부강하자

문서 규정 제27조 규정에 의하여 관세국장 박동희 전결

0725

971

30

143

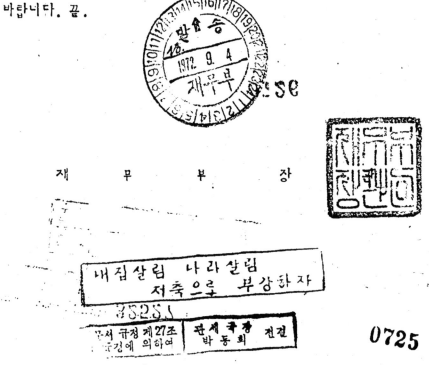

SOFA 재무분과위원회 회의 합의내용

(1972. 9. 8.)

1. APO 의 이동에 따른 군사우편소포검사 절차 개정문제

미측 주장 :

김포 및 오산으로 반입되는 우편소포는 개인용품이 대부분이나, 부산으로 반입되는 우편소포는 대부분이 군사화물이며 부산을 새로운 검사장으로 지정하기 위하여는 검사시설을 새로히 갖추어야 하는 문제가 있으므로 부산항에 입항하는 우편소포 (군사화물)에 대하여는 Container 에 한.미 공동으로 jointly sealing 을 한다음 김포, 오산으로 보세운송하여 이곳에서 개장 검사하도록 한다.

한국측 주장 :

1) 군사화물의 반입이 주로 되더라도
2) 부산을 검사장으로 부터 제외할수는 없고
3) 장래의 필요한 경우에 대비되어야 한다.

합의 결과 :

부산항을 possible designated location 으로 지정한다.

72

1013

0771

144

SOFA 재무분과 합의내용 (72. 9. 8.)

2. 주한미군용 수입신고서 양식 개정

가. 군사화물 ~~증명서~~ 수입신고서 양식 개정 (협정 9조 2항)

양식중 ㊽번의 수입면허난은 "import permitted, date and signature"의 문구를 삽입하기로 합의.

나. 개인용품 수입신고서 양식 제정

미측 주장 :

(제8차 회의)
67. 5. 27. 과제부여된 household goods and unaccompanied baggage 에 대한 검사절차에 대한 토의가 선행되어야 할것임.

한국측 주장 :

이 문제는 다시 양측 간사의 실무적인 검토에 맡기는 것이 좋을것임. 한국측 주장에 미측도 동의.

3. PX 통제품목의 추가

주류, 연초, 커피를 통제품목으로 할것을 주장하고 주류는 월간 1인당 현행 5 bottles 에서 3 bottles 로 하고 연초는 100 packs 에서 50 packs 으로, 커피는 6 lbs 에서 3 lbs 로 각각 판매수량을 줄일것을 주장. 이에 대하여 미측은 예산상의 이유등으로 난색을 표명하고 한국측은 다시 연초, 커피를 판매량 보고 품목으로 할것으로 주장을 완화하였으나, 이에 대하여서도 미측은 합동위원회로부터의 과제부여가 필요하다는 이유로 결정을 보류, 합의를 보지 못함.

73

1014 0772

145

SOFA 재무분과위원회 합의 자료

의 사	관 계 규 정	미 측 의 견	한 국 측 의 견	비 고
1. APO 의 이용에 의한 군사우편소포 검사 절차 개정	제10차 합동위원회에서 지시되고 제14차 및 제66차 합동 위원회에서 부분 개정된 APO 를 통한 군사우편 소포 검사 절차	1) 우편소포 검사장: 김포, 오산 2) 시설문제의 해결에 따라 "부산"도 검사장으로 추가 가능 (possible 군사화물만 반입)	1) 우편소포 검사장: 부산, 김포, 오산 2) 입항지 세관장의 승인을 얻은 경우 Container 로서 운송 가능 (특히 부산이 port of entry로 되는 경우) ~~3) 시설문제:~~ 한미 양측관계자 현지 조사후 조속한 조치.	
2. 주한미군용 수입신고서 양식 개정	제5차 합동 위원회 제정 SOFA 제9조 2항의 운용을 위한절차: 합중국 군대가 수입하는 각종 화물의 적절한 증명서의 양식및 제출방법	1) 협정 제9조 2항에 의한 미군사 화물 증명 양식 전 찬성 2) 협정 제9조 3항의 개인용품 수입신고 가) 수입신고서 양식: 검토중 나) 세관검사절차: 미측의 편의가 확보 되어야 함 (별첨 참조).	1) 협정 제9조 2항에 의한 미군사화물 증명 양식 개정: 합의안 작성. 2) 개인용품 수입신고 (5사(?)에서 ~~검사 일자~~) 가) 신고서 양식: 일반 수입신고서 양식 사용 나) 세관절차: ① 1967. 5. 25. 제8차 합동위원회에서 과제부여된 시안으로 당 외자와는 분리하여 다루어야 함. ② 개인용품의 세관검사 절차는 한국관세법의 규정을 준수하여야 함.	import permitted, date and signat

0773

1015

재무부 관세국

146

의제	관계규정	미측의견	한국측의견
3. PX 통제품목의 추가	가. 협정 제9조에 대한 합의 의사록 1항: 합중국 군대의 비세출 자금 기관이 ..... 수입하는 물품의 양은 이러한 사용을 위하여 합리적으로 소요되는 한도에 한정되어야 한다.	1) 현재 PX 등의 판매제도에 의해 충분한 통제가 가능하며 통제 제도의 개편은 예산상의 이유등 제 인에 의하여 곤란함.	1) 주류, 연초, 커피를 통제 품목으로 추가
	나. 제 65차 합동위 지정: 비세출 자금 기관에 탁송되는 화물에 관한 정보 제공		2) 상기 추가품목의 판매 수량에 대한 미측의 자율규제 강화 요구
			3) 현재의 통제품목을 승인 (LOA) 품목으로 전환 요구

0074

/47 1016 재무부 관세국 75

공 란

공　　　란

공 란

공 란

공 란

공 란

공 란

공 란

증산 수출 건설

별

재 무 부

협력 1243-741 1972. 9. 21.

수신 외무부장관

제목 미군 군사화물 증명 양식 개정

1. 미이 720-7962(1972. 3. 14)에 대한 것입니다.

2. SOFA제71차 합동 위원회에서 재무분과 위원회에 과제 부여된 미군사화물증명 양식 개정의 건에 대하여 재무분과 위원회에서 미측과 합의한 내용을 별첨과 같이 작성 송부하오니 합동위원회에서 승인 되도록 필요한 조치를 취하여 주시기 바랍니다.

첨부 : 미군사화물 증명양식 개정에 관한 재무분과 위원회 합의 각서1부. 끝.

0533

북미2과	공람	72년 9월	담당	과장	국장	차관보	차관	장관
					전결			

0732

재 무 부 장 관

문서 규정 제27조 ... 규정에 의하여
관리 박 ... 전결

저축으로 부강하자

156

36

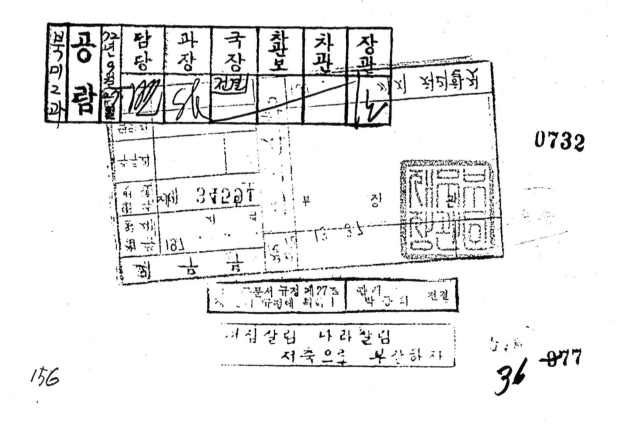

공 란

공 란

Monthly Average Sales for 1 Person

Years / Items	1970	1971. 8	Authorized quantity per month requested by Korea Government	Quantity authorized per month under the present control system
Cigarettes	108 packs	100 packs	50 packs	
Liqour	4.1 bottles	3.7 bottles	3 bottles	5 bottles per month for unaccompanied (Club)
Coffee	6.6 lbs. (3.3 bottes) PX authorized persons -55,000-	7.6 lbs. (3.8 bottles) PX authorized persons -40,000-	3 lbs.	6 lbs. of ground coffee per month for a unaccompanied (Commissary)

0236

39 980

159

Cigarettes

Unit : 1,000 packs

Year		1970	1971
Domestic products sold in Korea		2,012,719	2,285,483
Cigarettes imported by Korean importers		2,476	2,769
		($ 303,000)	($ 237,000)
Non - Appropriated - Fund - Cargo (PX)	Sales of Cigarettes	(A) 71,350	(C) 48,003 *
	Estimated Consumption of cigarettes by USFK persons	(B) 39,600	(D) 28,800
		(= 60 packs per month × 55,000 persons × 12 months)	(= 60packs per month × 40,000 persons × 12 months)
0737	Estimated outflow to black market	(A) - (B)	(C) - (D)
		31,750	19,203
Quantities of Confiscated cigarettes in black market		87	131

40

* Estimated by informations furnished by USFK pertaining to NAF cargoes

981

160

P X 판매 실적표

Cigarette unit: Carton

품 명	70 년 도		71 년 도 (8月末現在)		72년도 (6월말 현재)	
	금 액	수 량	금 액	수 량	금 액	수 량
양 주		2,707,487 병		1,797,468병		969,432 병
권 연 초	$10,555,010	6,485,965	$5,397,860	3,126,912		
엽 연 초	$ 315,432	481,059	$ 146,631	378,466		
커 피	$ 2,571,898	2,174,042	$ 680,332	953,926		

0738

982

41

161

1991

공 란

공 란

공 란

공 란

대 한 민 국 세 관
KOREAN CUSTOMS SERVICE

수(반입) 입 신 고 서 (갑지)
IMPORT DECLARATION

1 처리기간 197 . . .(일간)	
2 ※입항 Date of Entry 197 . . .	부 호
3 ※선화증권번호 B/L No	
4 ※선(기)명 적재선(기) Name of Vessel (Aircraft)	
국 적 Nationality of Vessel (Aircraft)	
5 ※적출국 Country of Shipment	
6 ※입항지 Place of Entry	
7 ※원산국 Country of Production	
8 ※장치장소 Place of Storage	

11※ 세관부호	12※ 수입재원별	13 신고번호

※ 14 수입허가	기관
	번호
	년월일 197 . . .
15 신 고	197 . .
16 검 사	197 . .
17 조 정	197 . .
18 면 허	197 . .

9※ 수입자	10※ 수 입 형 태 별		19※ 신고자
주 소 Importer address	① 면 허 전 반 출	⑤ 면허전반출완결분	주 소 Declarant Address
주민등록번호	② 보 세 공 장 반 입	⑥ 보세공장 수입 면허분	주민등록 번호
상 호 및 무역등록No.	③ 보 세 건 설 장 반 입	⑦ 보세건설장수입면허분	상 호
성명인 Name and Signature	④ 보 세 전 시 장 반 입	⑧ 보세전시장수입면허분	성명인 Name and Signature

20 ※ 품 명 및 규 격 DESCRIPTION OF ARTICLES & GRADE	21※ 중 량 WEIGHT / 22※ 수 량 QUANTITY	23※ 단위 UNIT	24※ 신 고 가 격 DECLARED VALUE / 25 감 정 가 격 APPRAISED VALUE	26 세번 / 27 특 관 세 종	부호	28 세율 / 29 세율	30 관 세 액 / 31 특 관 세 액	32 통관근거 부 호 / 33 관세 면제 근거 부호
(1)	kg		CIF, $			%	₩	
			₩	( )				
			특		종	%	₩	
(2)	kg		CIF, $			%	₩	
				( )				
			특		종	%	₩	
34 비고	합계		CIF, $	35 환 율			₩	
			₩					
			특				₩	

36 내 국 세					37 증지 증연
① 과 세 가 격	② 세번	③ 세 종	④ 세율	⑤ 세 액	
₩			%	₩	매 개
₩			%	₩	매 개
⑥ 원천과세 표준 ₩				합계	매 개
42 비 고					

38 세 별 계	(가) 고지번호	(나) 세 액
① 관 세		
② 특관세		
③ 물품세		
④ 세		
⑤ 영업세		
⑥ 소득세 법인세		

39 신고서 비 란

40 허가서 분할 □원본은

신고번호 ______(. . .) 첨부

41 검 사	
생 략□ 검사장□ 장치장소□ 검 정 시□	수입인지 첨 부 란

51

43 ※ 기호, 번호, 포장 종류와 개수 Markings, Numbering, Type and Number of Packages

44 ※ 보 세 운 송
목 적 지 :
경 유 지 :
수송 : ①육로□ ②해로□ ③공로□
기간 : . . . 부터
도착일 : . . . 까지

45 면허인

0748

992

46 ※ 첨부서류 Attached herewith, if any
수입허가서 Import License ( ) □
송 품 장 Invoice ( ) □
포장명세서 Packing List ( ) □
원산지증명 Certificate of Origin ( ) □
운임명세서 Freight Sheet ( ) □
보험영수증 Receipt of Insurance ( ) □
선화증권사본 copy of B/L ( ) □
others ( ) □

접 수	검 사	주 무	과 장	주 무	과 장	장

2509-9-1A-1 1971. 11. 승인 ※ 표시는 신고자 기입 210mm×300mm (백상지40g/m² 3매 백상지60g/m²

2. 입항 일 19 . . Date of Entry	부호 Code No.	대한민국 세관 Korean Customs Service	16. 세관부호 Customs Code No	
3. 선하증권번호 B/L No.			17. 수입종별 Sort of Import	
4. 적재선(기)명 Name of Vessel (Aircraft)			13. 신고번호 Declaration No.	
적재선(기)국적 Nationality of Vessel (Aircraft)			15. 신고 Date of Declaration 19 . .	
5. 선출국(지) Country of Shipment		주한미군용 수입신고서 Import Declaration /Certification and permit for use of USFK, ROK-US SOFA	계 / 주부 / 과장	
6. 입항지 Place of Entry			결재	
7. 생산지.원산국(지) Country of Production				
8. 장치장소 Place of Storage				

21. 품명및 규격 Description of Articles & Grade	22. 중량 Weight	23. 수량 Quantity	24. 단위 Unit	25. 신고가격 Declared Value	27. 세번 Heading	28. 부호 Code No.
(1)				CIF $		
(2)				CIF $		
(3)				CIF $		
35. 비고 Remarks	계 Total			CIF $		

45. 기호, 번호, 포장종류와 개수
Markings, Numbering, Type and Number of Packages

상기 물품은 SOFA 제9조 제2항에 의거 주한 미군용으로 수입되는 것임을 증명함.

I hereby certify the import of the above goods for use of USFK in accordance with the ROK-US SOFA, Article IX, Paragraph 2.

0749

신고자 성명
Name and Signature of Declarant

통관신고 서명
Signature of Customs Clearance Officer

신고자 주소
Address of Declarant

부 서 명
Department

993

46. 첨부서류
Attached herewith if any
송품장
Invoice
포장명세서
Packing List
원산지 증명
Certificate of Origin
운임명세서
Freight Sheet
보험영수증
Receipt of Insurance
선하증권 사본
Copy of B/L
기타
Other

52

47. 면허일및 면허일자
Entry under ROK-US SOFA Article IX, Paragraph 2
Certified, Signature and Date

~~Seal~~ Permit ~~Date~~ ~~Stamp~~ and Signature
import ~~imported~~ d
~~permit~~
date and stamp signature

167

〈의제 1〉 APO의 이동에따른 군사우편 소포 검사 절차 개정

1. 관계규정

제9차 합동위원회에서 제정되고 제64차 및 제66차 합동위원회에서 부분개정된 APO를통한 군사우편소포 검사절차

2. 문제점

가, APO를 통하여 반입되는 소포에 대한 한국 세관 검사는 항공편으로 반입되는것은 김포 및 오산에서, 선박편으로 반입되는것은 인천에서 검사를 행하도록 관계 규정에 의거 검사 장소가 지정되어 있음.

나, 1971년 9월 인천미군 수송대가 부산으로 이동한후에는 종전 인천항을 통해 반입 되던 군사우편 소포가 부산항을 통해 한국에 반입 Container 편으로 육로 수송되어 인천 기지 APO에서 세관검사를 받았음

다, 1972년 3월 인천기지 APO가 김포로 이동되었으므로 해상을 통해 한국에

재무부 관세국

168

반입되는 우편 소포에 대한 검사 장소의 변경 지정이 요구됨.

3. 경위.

부산항에서 선편으로 한국에 반입된 우편소포를 적재한 Container에 대한 점검을 행한 다음 육로로 수송, 김포및 오산에서 우편소포에 대한 세관검사를 행하자는 첨부의 합의안에 대하여 미측은 반대하지 않고 있음.

4. 대책.

가. 첨부의 합의안을 채택한다.

4. 시설 문제에 대하여는 한미 양측 관계자의 현지조사에 의해 요 조치 사항을 결정토록 한다.

재무부 관세국

169

공 란

공 란

외 무 부

정세보고처리전 　　　　　　　　　　1972. 10. 4.
(　　　　　)

담당	과장	국장	차관	장관	공람

발 신 인 　　　　　　　　　　SOURCE

요약및비고

제목 : 미군사우편소포 검사절차 개정에 관한 SOFA 재무 분과위원회 의결 내용.

1. 검사장의 변경 지정 :

종전의 검사장소인 인천, 김포, 오산을 김포, 오산으로 줄이고, 부산을 새로운 검사장 후보지로 정함.

2. 보세 운송 :

입항지로 부터 지정 검사장소까지의 보세 운송제도를 명문 규정함.

3. 조문 정리 :

상기 절차 개정에 따른 조문 정리.

172

제78차 합동위 승인 ('72.10.5.)

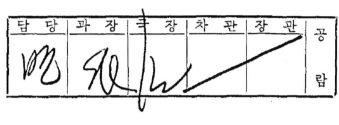

증산 수출 건설

변 미2

재 무 부

협력 1243-796 1972. 9. 28.

수신 외무부장관

제목 미군사 우편소포 검사 절차 변경

1. 미이 720-15719(72. 5. 22)에 대한 것입니다.

2. SOFA 제73차 합동 위원회가 재무분과 위원회에 과제 부여한 미군사 우편소포 검사절차의 검토에 대하여는 이를 다음과 같이 개정 코자 하며 미측과의 합의 내용을 별첨과 같이 송부 하오니 합동 위원에서 승인 되도록 필요한 조치를 취하여 주시기 바랍니다.

다 음

가. 검사장의 변경 지정

1. 종전에는 군사우편소포에 대하여 인천, 김포, 오산에서 검사 하던것을 김포, 오산만을 검사장으로 하여

2. 앞으로의 상황변경에 대비하여 부산을 검사장 후보지 (Possible designated location for examination) 로 정하였음

나. 보세운송

입항지로 부터 지정 검사장까지의 보세운송 제도를 명문 규정함.

다. 조문 정리

우편소포 검사절차의 본문에서 검사장을 [illegible] 있던 것을 별첨 1에서 이를 규정하며, 종전의 별첨 1을 2로, 별첨 2를 3으로 변경 하였음.

첨부 : 미군사 우편소포 검사절차 개정에 관한 재무분과 위원회 합의 각서 1부. 끝

재 무 부 장 관

(발송 1972. 9. 28 재무부)

(접수 1972 9 30 12:13)

규정에 의하여 | 관서 박동희 전결

1173

내집살림 나라살림 저축으로 [illegible]

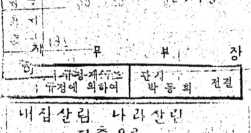

외		
접수 일시	197	
접수 번호	제 35313 28 SEP 72 15:13	
주국과		
담당자		
위임 근거		

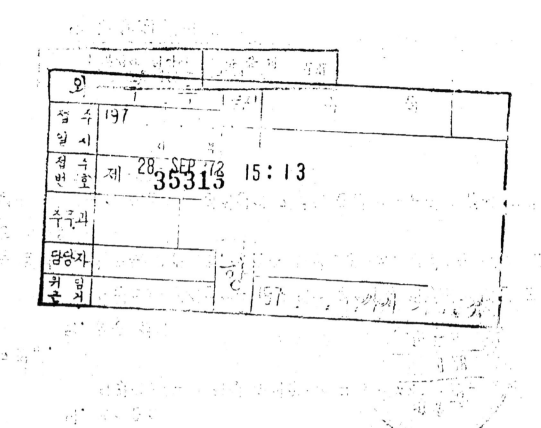

공 란

공 란

공 란

공 란

공　란

공 란

공　　란

공 란

공 란

공 란

공 란

공 란

공 란

공 란

공　　　란

공 란

공 란

공 란

공 란

공 란

통 신 두 문 ...

재 무 부

변
미2

협력 1243- 846 1972. 10. 25.

수신 외무부장관

제목 SOFA제9조 3항에 의한 수입신고서

관세청은 SOFA제9조 3항의 개인용품에 대하여 1972. 11. 1일 부터 일괄 수입신고서로써 수입신고 하도록 별첨과 같이 조치 하였기 이를 통보 하오니 참고 하시기 바랍니다.

첨부 : SOFA 제9조 3항의 수입신고서에 관한 관세청 공한 사본 1부. 끝.

북미2과	공람	72년 10월 29일	담당	과장	국장	차관보	차관	장관
			(서명)	(서명)	(서명)			

재 무 부 장 관

72 10 26 14:05
38766

정부 공문서 규정 제27조 제2항의 규정에 의하여
관세협력담당관 이재섭 전결

1972.10.25
재무부

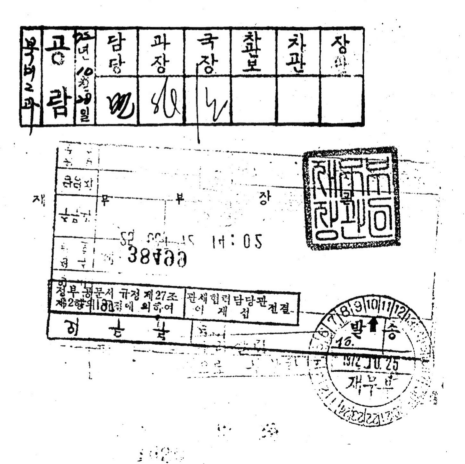

증산 수출 건설

관 세 청

세무 1242 - 2708 (75-3703) 1972. 10. 18.

수신 재무부장관

제목 SOFA 제9조 3항에 의한 수입신고

SOFA 제9조 3항에 의한 수입신고는 72. 11. 1 부터 일반 수입신고서로서 시행토록 별첨과 같이 각 세관에 시달하고 미8군에 조치토록 통보하였음을 보고 합니다.

첨부: 1. 각세관 시달공문 사본 1부.
2. 미8군 통보 공한사본 1부. 끝.

발송 No. 1972 10 18 관세청

국장 과장

재무부

접수일시	1972 10 18
접수번호	제 7083
주무과	관세협력과
담당	신 소관현

정부공문서규정 제27조 제2항의 규정에 의하여 세무국장 송 병 순 전결

관세청

서울 0123

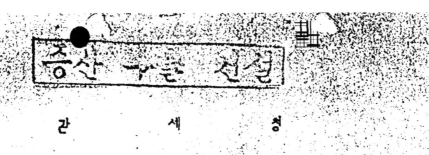

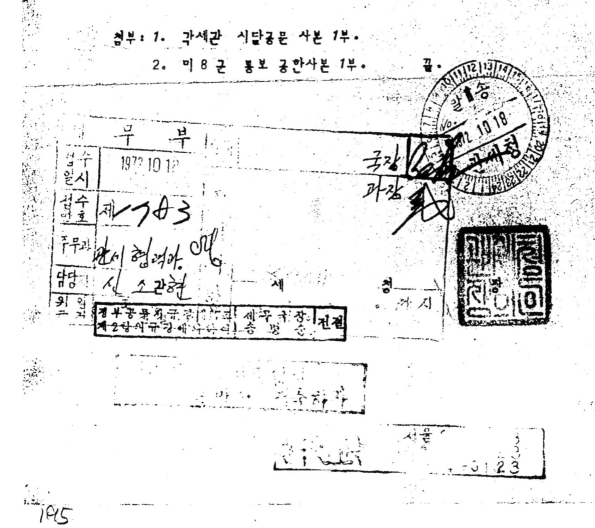

재무국

외 무 부

정세보고처리전
(　　　　　)

196 72. 11. 11.

담당	과장	국장	차관	장관	공람
(서명)	(서명)	(서명)			

발 신 인　　SOURCE

요약및비고　　주한미군 개인용품에 대한 수입신고서

1. 72. 11. 1. 부터 주한미군의 개인용품 반입에 대하여 일반수입 신고서 양식을 사용한다는 관세청의 대 미군측 통보에 대하여,

2. 미군측에서는 수입신고서 양식의 개정에 앞서 세관검사 절차의 검토가 선행되어야 할 것이라는 회한을 재무부에 발송한바 있음.

3. 이에 대하여 재무부는 다시 다음과 같은 내용의 대 미군측 공한을 발송함.

   (1) 개인용품에 대한 수입신고서 양식은 SOFA 내문제가 아니므로 한국 관세청이 제정한 일반 수입신고서 양식에 따라야 할 것이며,

   (2) 동 수입신고서 용지는 민간기관인 관세협회에서 팔고 있으나 관세청은 관세협회와 협의하여 미군에 무료로 배부할 수 있는 방안을 강구할 것임.

   (3) 세관검사 절차는 현행 SOFA 규정에 따라 실시될 것이며, 새로운 절차를 검토할 필요는 없을것임.

196

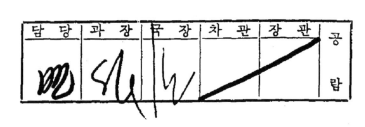

관 리 번 선 설

북미 2 2

재 무 부

관세 1245-870 1972. 11. 2.

수신 외무부장관

제목 주한 미군 ~~개인용품에 대한 수입~~신고서

72. 11. 1 부터 주한 미군의 개인 용품에 대하여 일반 수입 신고서 양식을 사용한다는 관세청의 대 미군측 통보에 의거 미군측에서 제기한 의견 (72. 10. 27) 에 대한 한국측 입장을 별첨 공한 사본과 같이 미측에 통보하였으니 참고 하기 바랍니다.

첨부 : 대 미측 재무분과 위원장 공한 사본 1부.

0125

재 무 부 장 관

군서 규정 제27조 규정에 의하여 | 관세 국장 박 풍 희 | 전결

300만원 남과 살림 저축으로 부강한 고

197

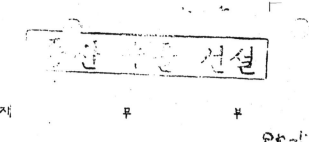

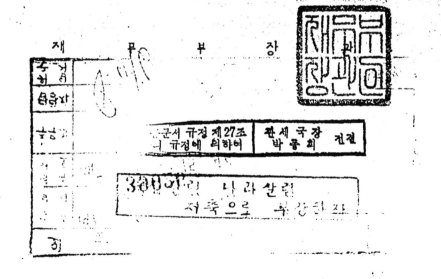

공 란

공 란

공 란

공 란

공 란

공　　란

공 란

공　　　란

공 란

공　　　란

대한민국세관
KOREAN CUSTOMS SERVICE
수(반입)입 신고서 (갑지)
IMPORT DECLARATION

1 ※접수일자 197 . . . (접수)

2 ※입항 Date of Entry 197 . . .

3 ※B/L No.

4 ※선명 Name of Vessel (Aircraft)

5 ※국적 Nationality of Vessel (Aircraft)

※적출국 Country of Shipment

6 ※입항지 Place of Entry

7 ※원산국 Country of Production

8 ※장치장소 Place of Storage

11※세관부호	12※수입재원별	13신고번

※ 14 수입허가 기관 / 번호 / 년월일 197 . .

15신고 197 . .

16검사 197 . .

17조정 197 . .

18면허 197 . .

수입자	
9※주소 Importer address	
주민등록번호	
상호 및 무역등록No.	
성명인 Name and Signature	

10※ 수입형태번	
①면허전반출	⑤면허전반출완결분
②보세공장반입	⑥보세공장수입면허분
③보세건설장반입	⑦보세건설장수입면허분
④보세전시장반입	⑧보세전시장수입면허분

신고자	
19※주소 Declarant Address	
주민등록 번호	
상호	
성명인 Name and Signature	

20 ※ 품명 및 규격 DESCRIPTION OF ARTICLES & GRADE	21※중량 WEIGHT / 22※수량 QUANTITY	23※단위 UNIT	24※신고가격 DECLARED VALUE / 25 감정가격 APPRAISED VALUE	26 세번 / 27 특관세종	부호	28 세율 / 29 세율	30 관세액 / 31 특관세액	32 통관근부 / 33 관세면근거부
(1)	kg		CIF, $			%	₩	
			₩	( )				
			특		종	%	₩	
(2)	kg		CIF, $			%	₩	
				( )				
			특		종	%	₩	
34 비고	합계		CIF, $	35 환율			₩	
			₩					
			특				₩	

36 내국세					37증지증연
①과세가격	②세번	③세종	④세율	⑤세액	
₩			%	₩	매 개
₩			%	₩	매 개
⑥원천과세표준 ₩				합계	매 개
42 비고					

38 세별계	(가) 고지번호	(나) 세액
①관세		
②특관세		
③물품세		
④ 세		
⑤영업세		
⑥소득세 법인세		

39 신고서 매

40 허가서 분할 □원본은

신고번호_____(. . .)

41 검사

생략□
검사장□
장치장소□
검정시□

수입인지 첨부란

43 수기호, 번호, 포장 종류와 개수 Markings, Numbering, Type and Number of Packages

44 ※보세운송
목적지:
경유지:
수송: ①육로□ ②해로□ ③공로□
기간: . . 부터
도착일: . . 까지

			과장	주무	계장	장

45 면허인

46 ※첨부서류 Attached herewith, if any
수입허가서 ( ) □ Import License
송품장 ( ) □ Invoice
포장명세서 ( ) □ Packing List
원산지증명 ( ) □ Certificate of Origin
운임명세서 ( ) □ Freight Sheet
보험영수증 ( ) □ Receipt of Insurance
선하증권사본 ( ) □ copy of B/L
( ) □

70

208

재 무 부

협력 1243-898 1972. 11. 10.

수신 외무부장관

제목 SOFA 비 적용 대상자에 대한 협정상의 특권 부여

1. 관세청으로 부터 별첨 보고에 의하면 주한 미군 지위 협정 (SOFA) 적용 대상자가 아닌 ① 주월미군 가족 ② 미군 제대군인 ③ 고용계약이 끝난 초청계약자와 그 가족에 대하여도 미군 당국은 비세출 기관 및 미군사우체국의 이용권과 SOFA 상의 차량 등록 번호 발급등의 조치를 취하고 있다고 하는바

2. 상기인에 의한 물품 부정유출의 우려가 특히 크다는 점에서 미군 당국에 이를 시정 조치토록 강구하여 주시기 바라며,

3. 특히 SOFA 제 28차 합동위원회 회의록에 의하면 미국측 대표는 "미군 제대군인 및 주월 미군 (가족)"을 SOFA 제 13조에 대한 합의의사록 (가) 항의 "통상적으로 이와 같은 특권이 부여되는 합중국 정부의 기타 공무원및 직원"으로 간주하여 비세출 자금기관을 이용케 하고 있다고 설명하고 있는바. 이와 같은 해석이 협정상으로도 타당 한지 여부를 회시하여 주시기 바랍니다.

첨부 : 관세청건의 공한 사본 1부. 끝.

재 무 부 장

문서 규정 제27조 단서에 의하여 | 관세국장 박동희 전결

0126

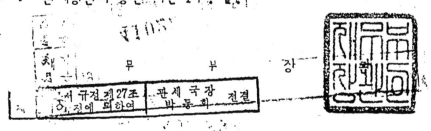

증산 수출 건설

관 세 청

심미 1245-12?? 1972. 10. 31.

수신 재무부장관

참조 관세국장

제목 SOFA 대상자에 대한 합동위원회 건의

SOFA 제1조에 의거 대한민국 영역안에 주둔한 현역에 복무하는 합중국 군대의 구성원, 군속 및 그들의 가족과 제15조에 의한 초청계약자에 한하여 제9조 및 제13조에 명시된 미군사우체국과 비세출자금 기관의 이용권을 부여하게 되어 있는바,

1. 미8군 당국은 다음에 열거한 비 SOFA 대상자에게 SOFA에 의한 "신분증과 레손류 메이드"를 교부하여 주고 SOFA대상자로 취급하고 비세출 자금기관과 미군사우체국의 이용권 및 SOFA에 의한 차량등록 등 면세특권을 부여 함으로서 면세특권을 악용하고 있고 SOFA 협정에 위배되는 처사이오니 이를 조속히 시정조치 하도록 한미 합동 위원회에 건의하여 주시기 바랍니다.

다 음

(1) 상당수에 달하는 주월 미군 가족

(주로 국제결혼한 한국출신 부인)

(2) 상당수에 달하는 미군제대 군인

(3) 상당수에 달하는 고용계약이 끝난 초청계약자와 그 가족

(미8군 초청계약회사인 A.A.E.O 회사에서 퇴사한 도저아이, 애디 및 피터 박, 유미오가 1971. 6. 30 퇴직하였음에도 불구하고 현재까지 계속 동사 직원으로 가장 APO 및 PX 이용권은 물론 면세차량

발송 1972 10 31 관세청

3-0123
4-0123

210

심리 1245-　　　　　　　　　　　　　　　　　1972. 10. 31.

도 계속 사용케 하고 있음을 적발 72. 9. 30 미8군 헌병부에 번호판을 이첩한 사례가 있음)

첨부 : 1. SOFA 차량 번호판 송부 공문 사본 1매.
　　　2. A.A.E.O 회사장 진술서 사본 1매. 끝.

관　　세　　청

서축의 날 나누 서축하자

접수시간

2410

공 산 출 선 설

관 세 청

심이 1245-1274 1972. 10. 31.

수신 주한 미8군 헌병부장

제목 SOFA 차량 번호판 송부

귀하의 당청 관세 행정업무에 협조하여 주신데 대하여 사의를 표하는 바입니다.

1. 주한 미8군 초청계약회사인 A.A.E.O. 회사에서는 1971. 6. 30까지 동사에 근무하다가 퇴직한바 있는 다음과 같은 사람에게 그후 계속하여 SOFA대상자로 취급하여 차량을 등록 사용케하고 있음을 적발하였음으로,

2. 앞으로는 비 SOFA 대상자에게 SOFA 에 의한 차량번호판의 교부 조치가 없도록 시정하여 주시기 바랍니다.

다 음

소속 : A.A.E.O. 회사

가. 성 명 : 로저 아이. 에디 (RODGER I. EDDY)

등록차량번호 : 2-2090

나. 성 명 : 피터 피. 쿠피크 (PETER P. KUPIEC)

등록차량번호 : 2-1206 (본인이 72. 10. 27 헌병대에 반납하였다고 함)

첨부 : 1. 번호판 (2-2090) 1조

2. 검사증 (2-1206) 1매. 끝.

관 세 청

60

2121

APO SAN FRANCISCO [illegible]

ENGINEERING · D[illegible] & [illegible] [illegible]SION OF CONSTRUCTION · INSPECTION · T[illegible]NICA[illegible] [illegible]S[illegible]ANCE · CONSULTATION

SEOUL, KOREA

TEL. 32-7803
YS 3737

STATEMENT

25 October 1972

Mr. Peter P. Kupiec and Mr. Rodger I. Eddy was dropped from the employ of AAE, according to the SOFA report, on 30 June 1971 and was again employed by me in May and June of 1972, also indicated on the SOFA report, terminating on 30 June 1972. According to records, Mr. Eddy was issued an ID Card on 17 March 1972 which appears to be in advance of his actual employment of record, resulting in a procedures violation. The reason for termination on 30 June 1972 was not receiving the award of contract expected to start on 1 July 1972, for which planning and preparatory work was in progress since March of 1972. Mr. Eddy was engaged in this phase of management duties, especially with regard to fact-finding research. Special care will be taken in the future to avoid any technical violations with regard to issuing ID Cards in advance of reported employment dates.

I wish to apologize on behalf of my company for the technical violation and will do my best to prevent this from happening again.

Sincerely,

Wayne G. Mayotte

WAYNE G. MAYOTTE
President
Associated American Engineers

CABLE ADDRESS: "ASAMEN, TOKYO" "ASSOCAMEN, SEOUL" "ASAMEN, OKINAWA" "ASAMEN, SAIGON"

213

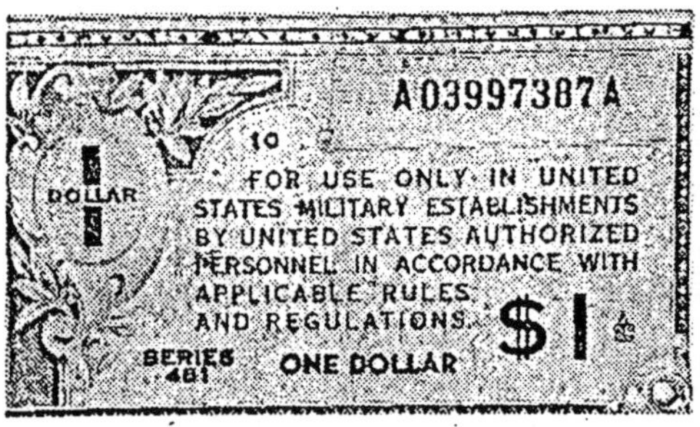

Series 461 (Sept. 1946 to March 1947)
The first MPC

Series 481 (June 1951 to May 1954)
This MPC was used during the Korean War.

U.S. Forces Pay

'72. 11. 12. <K.T.>

MPC Use Curbs Black Market

By Don C. Terrill

Although the U.S. greenback dollar is famous as a standard of international payment, foreigners in Korea may also encounter another type of U.S. paper money known as Military Payment certificates or MPC.

These notes are used as payment to U.S. forces personnel, and these personnel are forbidden by regulation to possess greenbacks. MPC is good only in certain overseas areas and worthless in the United States itself.

Before MPC was used, troops were paid in local currencies and were allowed to exchange that currency for greenbacks upon their departure. It became clear that some persons were redeeming far more money than they could have reasonably saved from their pay. As a result the first MPC's were issued on Sept. 16, 1946.

Authority to possess MPCs is officially restricted to persons having a current Eighth Army "Ration Control Plate."

Access to the PXs and commissaries is tightly restricted, and the transfer of funds to the United States is complicated and carefully controlled. Nevertheless, the blackmarketing of PX goods and MPC currency flourishes in the camp villages, and after army paydays there may very well be more MPCs in the hands of unauthorized persons than in the hands of authorized ones.

This situation has existed for as long as the U.S. forces have been in Korea despite "tight" control of MPCs combined with a fantastic succession of rationing schemes. Still, the military authorities regard MPCs as a valuable weapon against blackmarketing, and one can only suppose how much worse the situation would be if MPCs did not exist.

The current MPC series in Korea (Series 651) consists of $1, $5, and $10 notes, and until early 1967 MPCs here also included small notes of values 50, 25, 10, and 5 cents. Today, these small notes have been replaced by U.S. coins.

The current notes are initially printed on sheets of paper measuring 32 by 54 inches, so that a sheet will fit 70 one-dollar or 50 five- or ten-dollar notes. On the face of each MPC there is a small number, much smaller than the serial number, which indicates at what position that MPC was on the sheet at the time of printing.

There have been nine different MPC series used in Korea and four separate series used in Vietnam, and these notes follow an identifiable pattern.

First, each series number indicates the date of the design and whether it was the first or second design during that year. For example, U.S. Forces in Korea now use Series 651, indicating that it was designed in 1965 and was the first design of that year. U.S. Forces in Vietnam presently use Series 692, which was designed in 1969 and was the second design of that year.

Further, the serial numbers of MPCs begin and end with a letter, and every series has used a higher letter. For example, the first MPCs (in 1946) were "A", the next series was "B", and so on (with letter "I" omitted) until the letter "J" was used. Following "J", "A" was again reused (Korea now) followed by "B", "C," and "E" in Vietnam. The entire pattern of MPCs looks like this:

Series 461 "A"
Sep 16, 1946 to Mar 10, 1947
Series 471 "B"
Mar 10, 1947 to Mar 22, 1948
Series 472 "C"
Mar 22, 1948 to Jun 20, 1951
Series 481 "D"
Jun 20, 1951 to May 25, 1954
Series 521 "E"
May 25, 1954 to May 27, 1958
Series 541 "F"
May 27, 1958 to May 26, 1961
Series 591 "G"
May 26, 1961 to Jan 6, 1964
Series 611 "H"
Jan 6, 1964 to Apr 28, 1969
Series 641 "J" (Vietnam)
Aug 31, 1965 to Oct 21, 1968
Series 651 "A" (Korea now)
Apr 28, 1969 to now
Series 661 "B" (Vietnam)
Oct 21, 1968 to Aug 11, 1969
Series 681 "C" (Vietnam)
Aug 11, 1969 to Oct 7, 1970
Series 692 "E" (Vietnam now)
Oct 7, 1970 to now

As we can see from the pattern, Series 691 "D" is missing, and it is speculated by American and Korean collectors that 691 is destined to be used next in Korea. The date of the next MPC change is, of course, unknown, but the recent trend is to change MPC in Korea every three or four years.

MPCs are usually designed with an illustration of a woman's face. These women are imaginary and do not represent any real or famous person (except for certain designs showing the Statue of Liberty). An exception to this pattern was Series 681 which was used in Vietnam between August 1969 and October 1970. Series 681 featured well-designed pictures of soldiers and sailors and their equipment.

Although old MPCs are worthless after the series is changed, collectors (especially myself) have great difficulty locating old MPCs. This seems quite strange since it would be assumed that illegal money changers and other persons would be stuck with large quantities of MPCs during MPC changes. It is known, for example, that during the last MPC change in 1969 that more than one million dollars was not turned in to be redeemed.

Where did it all go? The idea staggers the imagination since it represents a quantity of money which (with $1 notes) if layed end-to-end would stretch from Osan Air Base all the way to Taejon City. The missing MPC could provide every American souvenir hunter in Korea with a lunchbox full of notes. Readers who enjoy solving mysteries might enjoy trying to solve that modern-day mystery which is right at their own doorsteps.

In summary, it is reasonable to suppose that the foreign and Korean readers of this newspaper who have a little patience will have the opportunity to see a new series of this colorful and peculiar currency issued in the near future.

* *

The writer resides in Taegu.

214

미군 화물수송에 사용되는 유류구입에 대한 면세문제

1. SOFA 제 16조 3항에 규정된 "현지조달" (local procurement) 에 따르는 석유류세등의 면세를 위하여는 다음의 요건을 충족하여야 함.

   (가) 합중국 군대 또는 그 공인 조달기관이 대한민국 공급자로 부터 직접 조달하는 품목 이어야 하며, (제 16조에 대한 합의의사록 4항)

   (나) 합중국 군대의 최종 소비 사용을 위하여 (for ultimate use)조달되는 품목 이어야 한다. 여기서 "최종 소비 사용을 위하여 조달되는 품목" 이라함은 (합중국 군대가 사용하는 물품 이나 시설에)"통합될 품목" 이거나 또는 "최종 생산품의 생산을 위하여 필요한 품목" 을 의미한다. (전기 합의의사록 4항)

2. 미군 화물 수송을 위하여 한국 상사등이 소비하는 석유류의 구입은,

   (1) 전기 (가)항의 합중국 군대가 대한민국 공급자로 부터 직접 조달하는 경우로 볼수가 없고,

   (2) 합중국 군대가 사용하는 물품 이나 시설에 "통합될 품목" 또는 "최종 생산품의 생산을 위하여 필요한 품목" 에도 해당되지 않음.

3. 따라서 전술한 유류구입은 국내과세 관계법령의 적용을 받게되며, SOFA 규정에 의한 면세는 허용되지 않는것으로 사료됨.

북미2과	공람	73년 11월 17일	담당	과장	국장	차관보	차관	장관
			(서명)	(서명)	(서명)			

국제조세과 3223

재무부 민종식 씨 4/10

215

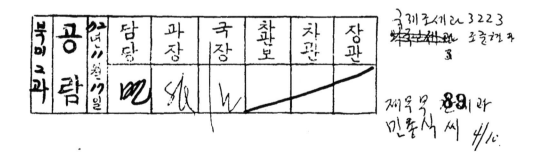

상산 수출 건설

재 무 부

간세 1235-1068 7?-???? 1972. 7. 16.

수신 서울특별시 중구 충무로 2가 9

건양기업주식회사 대표이사 손 종 빈

제목 석유류세 면제에 대한 질의

미군용물자수송에 소요되는 기름에 대한 면세 요청.

1. 건기관 제 4호 (72. 7. 1?)에 대한 회신입니다.

2. 본건의 경우 한미행정협정 제 11조 및 제 16조의 규정에 의한 석유류세 면세는 공인 조달기관을 포함한 합중국 군대가 대한민국 안에서 공용을 위하여 조달하는 석유류 또는 합중국 군대의 최종소비사용을 위하여 조달하는 석유류에 한하는 것이오니 양지하시기 바랍니다. 끝.

재 무 부 장 관

재무부장관인

접수 1972. 7. 19 재무국 90

저축의 날 날마다 저축합시다

216

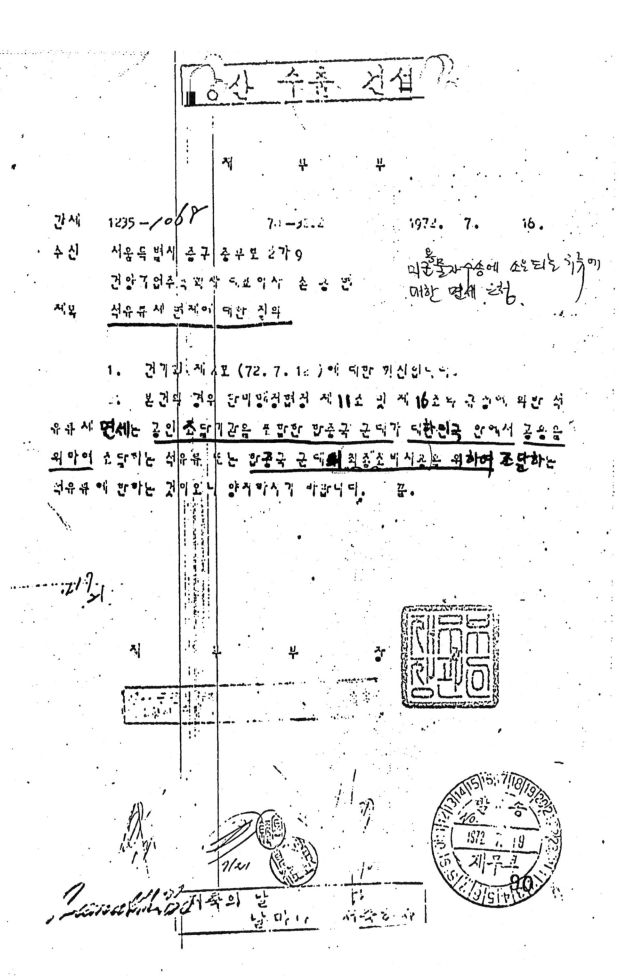

1451 (?)

미군 화물 수송을 위한 구입 연료의 면세 신청

1.한전 제 175호 (72.9.9)에 대한 회신 입니다.

2. 현행 법상 미군 화물 수송용 석유류의 면세는

관세국장
차 [illegible]

배부처 :

3210

217-

증산 수출 건설

관 세 청

세무 1242 - 2920 (75-3703) 1972. 11. 17.

수신 외무부장관

제목 SOFA 제78차 한.미 합동위원회 회의록

1. 미이 723 -34916 (72. 11. 6) 호에 관련된 것 입니다.

2. 본건과 관련하여 당청해당 사항을 별첨과 같이 각 세관에 조치 하였음을 통보 합니다.

첨부: 각세관 시달공문 사본 1부. 끝.

관 세 청

전부공무시규정제27조 제2항의규정에의하여	세무국장 송병순	전결

218

저축의 날 따로 없다

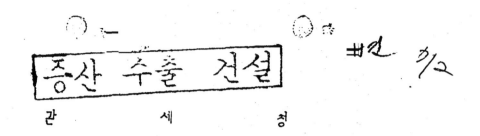

관 세 청

세무 1242 - (75-3703) 1972. 11. 16.

수신 수신처 참조

제목 SOFA 제 78 차 한. 미 합동위원회 회의록

1. SOFA 제 78 차 한. 미 합동위원회가 72. 10. 5 개최되었는바 동 위원회의 합의 사항중

가. SOFA 제 9 조 제 2 항 (주한미군 수입품)에 관한 수입신고서가 별첨과 같이 승인되어 72. 12. 1 부터 시행토록 합의되고

나. " SOFA 제 9 조 합의 양해사항 1-4 에서 규정한 APO 를 통한 우편소포에 대한 한국세관 검사절차" 가 별첨과 같이 개정 합의 되었음을 통보하니 업무처리에 차질이 없도록 할것.
(72. 11. 1 시행)

첨부: 1. 주한미군용 수입신고서 1 매

2. 한미군대 지위협정 제 9 조 합의 양해사항 1-4 에서 규정한 미군사우체국을통한 우편소포에 대한한국세관 검사절차 개정 원문 1부. 끝.

관 세 청 장

219

2. 입항 Date of Entry 19	Code No.	대한민국 관세청 Korean Customs Service	Customs Code No.
3. 선하증권번호 B/L No.			12. 수입종별 Sort of Import
4. 적재선(기)명 Name of Vessel(Aircraft)			13. 신고번호 Declaration No.
적재선(기) 국적 Nationality of Vessel(Aircraft)		주한미군용 수입신고서 Import Declaration/Certification USFK, ROK-US SOFA	15. 신고 Date of Declaration 19
5. 적출국(지) Country of Shipment			과 / 주무 / 과장
6. 입항지 Place of Entry			결
7. 생산지.원산국(지) Country of Production			재
8. 장치장소 Place of Storage			

21. 품명및 규격 Description of Articles & Grade	22. 중량 Weight	23. 수량 Quantity	24. 단위 Unit	25. 신고가격 Declared Value	27. 세번 Heading	28. 부호 Code No.
(1)				CIF $		
(2)				CIF $		
(3)				CIF $		
35. 비고 Remarks / 계 Total				CIF $		

45. 기호, 번호, 포장종류와 개수
Markings, Numbering, Type and Number of Packages

상기 물품은 SOFA 제9조 제2항에 의거 주한 미군용으로 수입되는 것임을 증명함.

I hereby certify the import of the above goods for use of USFK in accordance with the ROK-US SOFA, Article IX, Paragraph 2.

신고자 성명
Name and Signature of Declarant

통관심고 서명
Signature of Customs Clearance Officer

신고자 주소
Address of Declarant

부 대 명
Department

46. 첨부서류
Attached herewith if any
송품장
Invoice
포장명세서
Packing List
원산지증명
Certificate of Origin
운임명세서
Freight Sheet
보험영수증
Receipt of Insurance
선하증권 사본
Copy of B/L
기타
Others

47. 면허 및 면허일자
Import Permitted, Signature and Date

210mm × 300mm

220

공 란

공 란

공 란

공 란

공 란

공 란

공 란

공 란

PROCEDURES RELATING TO EXAMINATION BY REPUBLIC OF KOREA CUSTOMS INSPECTORS OF PARCEL POST PACKAGES, DELIVERED THROUGH UNITED STATES MILITARY POST OFFICE CHANNELS WITH REGARD TO ARTICLE IX, AGREED UNDERSTANDING, SUBPARAGRAPH I THROUGH 4 OF THE STATUS OF FORCES AGREEMENT.

개 정 전	개 정 후
I. a. . . . . the United States Operations Mission (USOM-K) 2. Notification of Mail Arrival The Commander, 1st Base post Office, Inchon, and the Commanding Officer in charge of postal affairs at Kimpo and Osan Air Bases will furnish the Republic of Korea Customs Officials with advance information of bulk mail arrival, and approximate volume, and the expected time mail will be available for customs inspection.	I. a. . . . . the United States Operations Mission-Korea(USOM-K) 2. Notification of Mail Arrival: a. Customs examination of parcel post packages by Republic of Korea customs officials will be made at mutually agreed upon designated locations. The listing of the designated and possible designated locations is attached as Inclosure I. b. The Commanding Officer in charge of postal affairs at the designated locations will furnish the Republic of Korea customs officials with advance information of bulk mail arrival, approximate volume, and the expected time such parcel post packages will be available for customs examination. c. Containers in which parcel post packages subject to customs exmination by Republic of Korea customs officials are located will be transported in bond between the port of entry and designated locations for exmination. The collector of customs, or his designated representative, at the port of entry shall permit transportation in bond and shall not delay movement of US parcel post in conjunction with issuing such permit.

229

개 정 전	개 정 후
3.	3.
a. . . . by the Republic of Korea customs inspectors will take place in facilities of the 1st Base Post Office at Inchon and in the space as the authorities of the United States Armed Forces shall provide at Kimpo and Osan Bases."	a. . . . by the Republic of Korea customs officials will take place in facilities as the authorities of the United States Armed Forces shall provide at the designated locations.
c.	c.
(2) At Inchon and at Kimpo and Osan Air Bases	(2) At the designated locations . . . . . .
4.	4.
. . . . " Form, at inclosure I, by	. . . . " Form, at Inclosure 2, by . . . . .
5.	5.
c. . . . . . as Inclosure 2.	c. . . . . . as Inclosure 3.

230

DESIGNATED LOCATIONS FOR CONDUCT OF REPUBLIC OF KOREA

INSPECTION AND EXAMINATION OF PARCEL POST PACKAGES

Kim Po

O San

POSSIBLE DESIGNATED LOCATION FOR CONDUCT OF ROK

INSPECTION AND EXAMINATION OF PARCEL POST PACKAGES

Pu San

(Incl 1)

231

개 정 전	개 정 후
Subject : Record on Condition of parcel (Incl 1) 35 개 지정품목 (Incl 2)	Subject : Record on Condition of parcel (Incl 2) 35 개 지정품목 (Incl 3)

2312

ITT International Electric Corporation
A Subsidiary of ITT

BOX 112 JUSMAG-K (AF SECTION)
APO SANFRANCISCO 96276

November 1972

Honorable Minister,
Ministry of Foreign Affairs
Republic of Korea
Seoul, Korea

Dear Sir:

ITT Far East Pacific, respectively request permission to give a donation of surplus electronic parts which was left over from our Up-Grade/Modification effort for the ROKAF under USAF Contract number F34601-71-C-0134 completed this year. This surplus parts etc. came in Country duty free in support of the above mentioned contract.

We wish to donate these electronic parts to the Korea Advanced Institute of Science and or to the Yonsei University. Please refer to a copy of Mrs. Gertrude Ferrar's letter which is attached for your information. We would like to make this presentation if at all possible sometime this month. These parts will not be used in any way contrary to or in violation of any existing ROK laws, regulations or customs.

Sincerely Yours,

Burton G. Schetzle
ITT/IEC Representative
Box 87
JUSMAG-K, AF Section
APO San Francisco 96483

233

공 란

공 란

3. 1.91)3

236

증산 수출 건설

재 무 부

협력 1243-672 (70-3227) 1973. 9. 17.

수신 외무부장관

제목 미군사우체국을 통한 우편소포검사절차 개정

1. 협력 1243-120(72.2.3)로 미군사우체국을 통한 우편소포검사절차를 개정하여 동 기우편물에 대하여도 세관검사가 가능하도록 조치하여 줄것을 건의한바 있읍니다.

2. 동 사안이 아직까지 해결되지 않고 있는바, 조속히 해결되도록 조치하여 주시기 바라며, 그 결과를 당부에 통보하여 주시기 바랍니다. 끝.

No. 1973. 9. 17 재무부

재 무 부 장

정부공문서규정 제27조 제2항의 규정에 의하여
관세국장 송병순 전결

근면검소 나라살림
저축으로 부강하자

237

외 무 부			
접수일시	197 . . . 18시 ... 15 16:18	결재	
접수번호	제 59223		
주무과	[illegible]		
담당자	[illegible]		
처리결과			

[illegible]

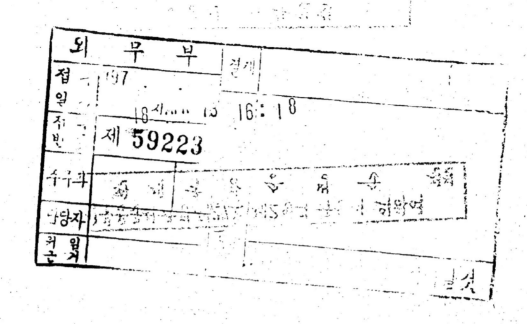

미 주 국

197 3 . 10 . 22 .

담 당	과 장	국 장	차관보	차 관	장 관
(서명)	(서명)	(서명)			

제 목 : 군사우편을 통한 미군인의 관세법 위반

요 약

1. 법무부는 미제 51통신대대 본부중대 소속 Marvin J. Wolf 대위에 의한 군사우편등을 통한 관세법위반 사건에 대하여 재판 관할권을 행사하기로 결정

2. 재무부는 상기 밀수입 사건과 관련 APO 등기소포 검사 절차를 개정 등 기우편물에 대한 세관 검사를 실시할 수 있도록 조치하여 줄것을 요청.

조치사항 : 재무분과위원회에 대한 신규 과제 부여를 검토중.

238

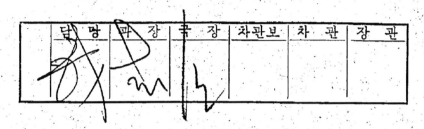

증산 수출 건설

재 무 부

협력 1243- 1763 (70-3227) 1973. 10. 19.

수신 외무부장관

제목 APO 등 기소포검사 시행 건의

1. 협력 1243-120 (72.2.3) 및 협력 1243-672 (73.9.17) 와 관련됩니다.

2. 당부에서 요청한바 있는 APO 등 기소포 검사시행에 관한 문제가 아직까지 해결되지 않고 있던중, 별첨과 같이 APO 등 기소포를 이용한 보석류등 고가품의 밀수입사건이 관세청 한미합동 단속 본부반에 의하여 73. 10. 4. 검거되었으므로, 동 사건에 관한 자료를 송부하오니, 한미합동위원회에 대한 건의 자료로 활용하여주시기 바랍니다.

첨부 : 1. 사건 개요 1 부

2. 사진 5 매. 끝.

발송 1973 10 20 재무부

재 무 부 장 관

재무부공문서규정 제27조 에 의하여
관 세 국 장 송 병 순 전결

내집살림 나라살림
저축으로 부강하자

239

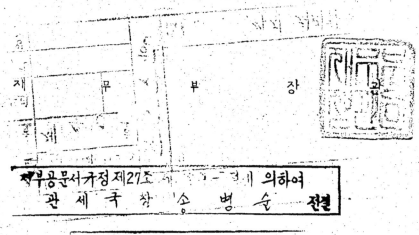

접수	20	2 30	
번호	제64205호	지시사항	
주무과			
		197 . . 까지 처리할것	

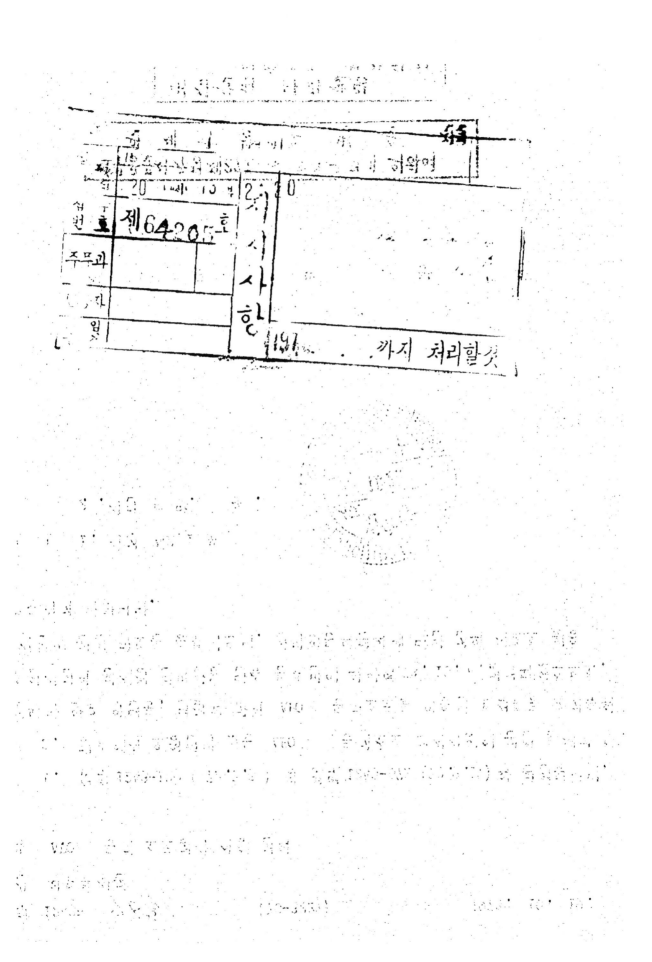

사 건 개 요

1. 피의자의 인적사항

(가)주소 : 홍콩 구룡시 나탄가 36-44

청킹 맨숀 7층

성명 : 엘.엠. 모하메드 메이딘

(보석상) (L.M. MOHAMED MAIDEEN) 당 50년

(나)주소 : 주한 미 제 51통신대 본부중대

(HQS CO. 51ST SIN.BN)

성명 : 마빈 쥴스 울푸 (MARVIN JULES WOLFH.) 당 32년

(미군 대위)

2. 검거일시 : 1973. 10. 4.

3. 검거장소 : 의정부 미제 1군단 장교 숙소.

4. 압수물품 및 금액

에메랄드, 오팔등 보석류 2903점.

시가 14,740,000원.

5. 조치사항

(가)피의자는 1973. 10. 12. 서울지검 구속고발.

(나)피의자는 " " " 불구속고발. (재판권 행사)

6. 범죄사실 : 별지와 같음.

240

범 죄 사 실

(1)피의자는 홍콩에 거주하는 인도 교포로서 주거지에서 모하메드 에이부라힘 앤드 썬스 (MOHAMED EBRAHIM & SONS.)보석상을 하는 자이고,

(2)피의자는 주한 미제 51통신 대대 본부 중대에 근무하는 미 육군 대위로써,

피의자등은 1973년 5월 17일 동경발 김포착 비행기에서 (2)피의자의 미군사 우편을 통하여 각종 보석을 밀수입 시중에 부정 유출할 것을 상호공모하여,

1973. 9. 9.(1)피의자는 김포공항으로 입국하면서 에메랄드, 오팔등 시가 470만원 상당품을 인삼 상자등을 가장하여 은익 밀수입 하여 숙소인 시내 충무로 3가 43번지 소재 대원호텔 216호에서 동년 10월 4일 적발 압수 되었으며 (2)피의자의 APO 주소로 홍콩에서 발송한 에메랄드 등 보석류 시가 1,000만원 상당품을 10월 4일 오전 12시경 (2)피의자가 소속부대 우편실에서 수취하여 영내 숙소에 은익해 놓고 (1)피의자에게 인도하기 직전에 적발 압수됨으로서 (1)(2)피의자는 공히 동 물품에 대한 소정의 관세 250만원 상당을 포탈 한자등 임.

241

"울푸" 大尉 명의로 발송된 등기 우편물 (#600)

242

"울푸" 大尉 명의로 발송된 등기 우편물 (₩600)

242

(APO)
등기우편을 이용 "보석"이 밀수입된 봉투

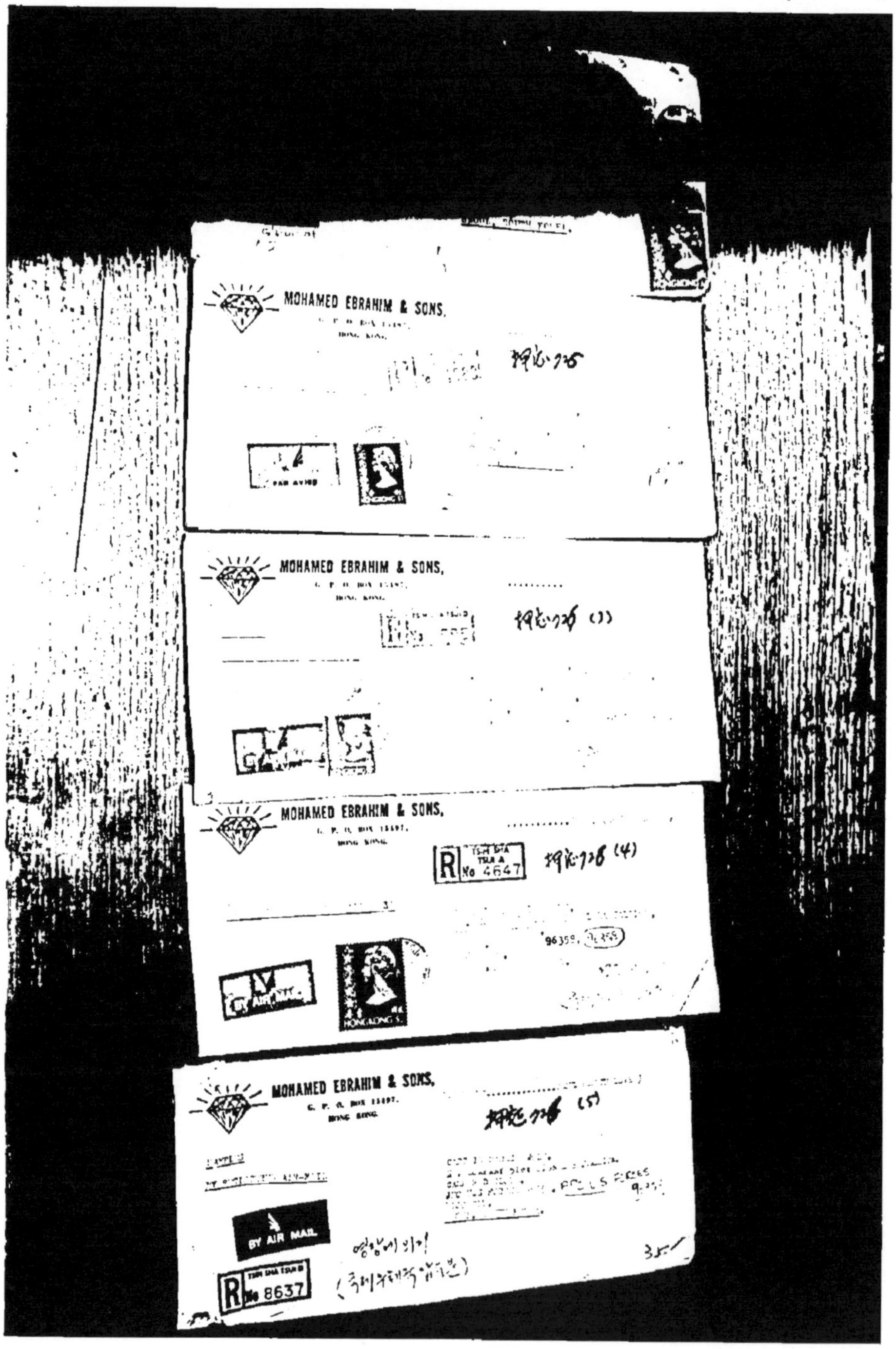

243

(APO)
등기우편을 이용 "보석"이 밀수입된 봉투

243

(APO)
등기소포를 이용 보석이 밀수입된 포장

244

(APO)
등기소포을 이용 "보석"이 밀수입된 포장

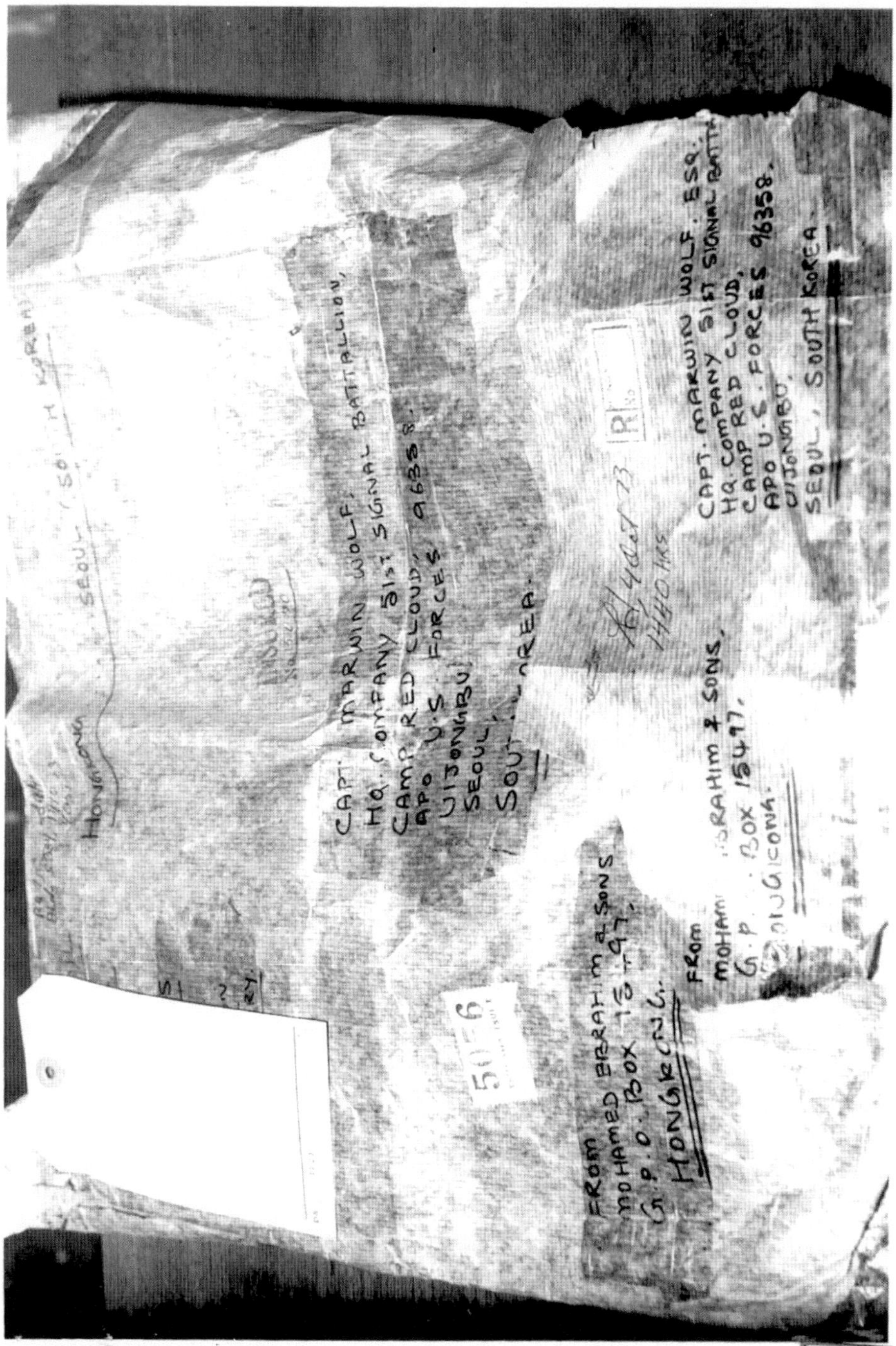

244

(APO)
등기우편을 이용 보석이 밀수입된 봉투.

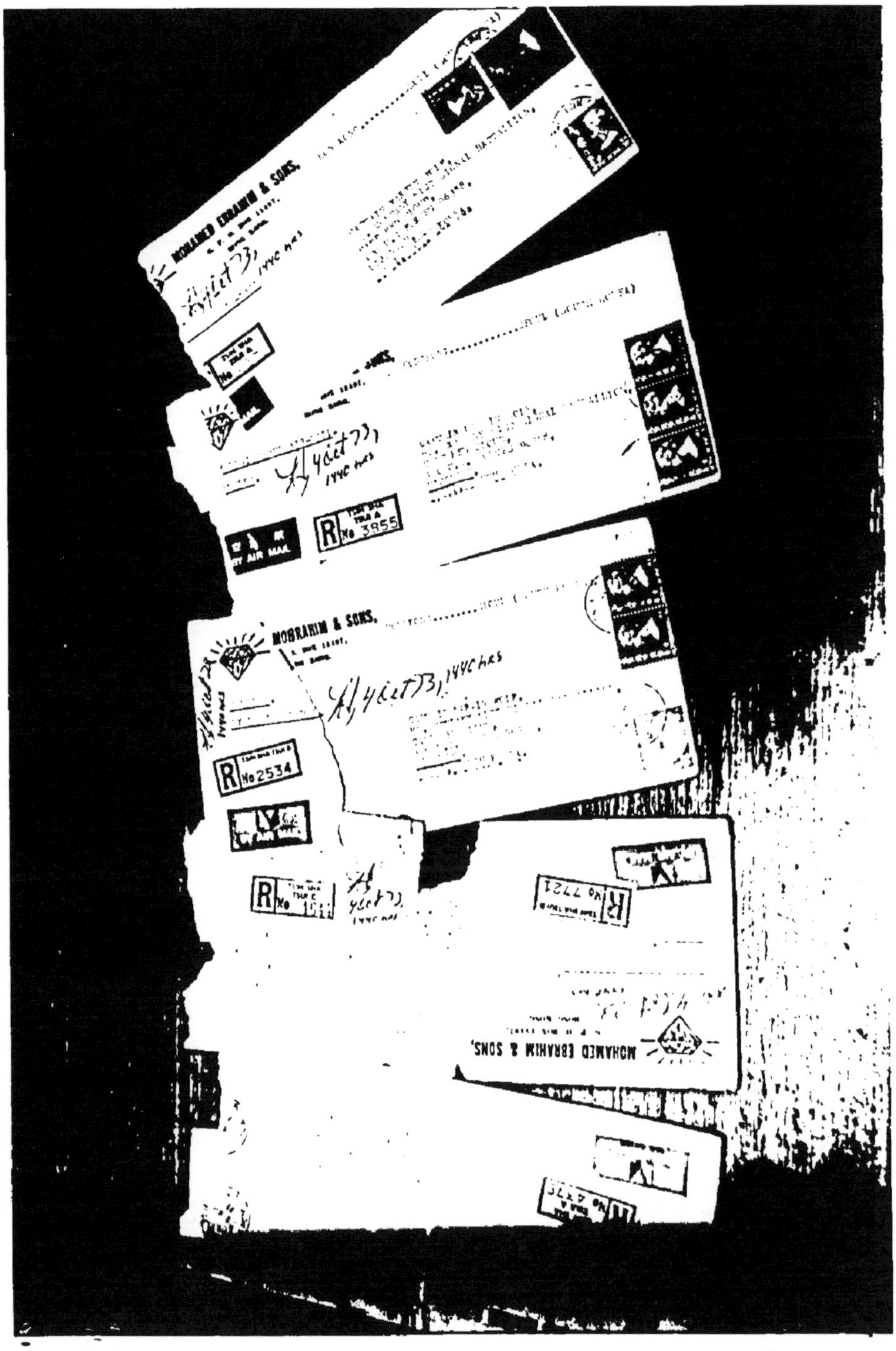

245

(APO)
등기우편을 이용 보석이 밀수입된 봉투.

245

(APO)
등기우편물 속에 들어있는 보석류

246

(APO)
등기우편물 속에 들어있는 보석류

246

DEPARTMENT OF THE AIR FORCE
HEADQUARTERS USAF POSTAL & COURIER SERVICE (HQ COMD USAF)
HOFFMAN BUILDING II
ALEXANDRIA, VIRGINIA 22332

26 OCT 1973

REPLY TO ATTN OF: DO

SUBJECT: Examination of Mail

TO: All USAFPCS Activities (Less ARFCOSTAS)

1. We recently asked the USPS for a determination on whether second, third and fourth class matter mailed at the priority (airmail) rate of postage, not indorsed first class, was considered sealed against postal inspection. We also asked the USPS if priority parcels should be indorsed "First Class" regardless of contents since the priority rate is same as the first class rate of postage.

2. The following is quoted from the USPS reply:

> "Our Law Department has advised that mail matter mailed at the priority rate of postage, not endorsed first-class or otherwise endorsed, is considered sealed against postal inspection and should not be inspected without a search warrant authorized by law.
>
> "It was further stated by the Law Department that matter sent at the priority rate and intended to be priority mail need only be endorsed 'priority mail'."

3. The above ruling creates major changes to past procedures as follows:

a. Prohibits our postal clerks from opening for contraband examination parcels mailed at the priority rate. However, such parcels suspected of containing explosives should be treated according to PCSM 182-3, paragraph 34-12.

b. Makes it essential that all suspect priority mail be forwarded to the appropriate customs officials for examination according to PCSM 182-3, paragraph 91-2.

247

SUPPORTING AEROSPACE FORCES WORLDWIDE

4. All activities should implement these procedural changes. These changes will be published in PCSM 182-3, Parts Four and Nine. This letter expires 15 Jan 74 unless sooner superseded or rescinded.

5. For Pacific Region. This answers your letter, 20 Jul 73, subject as above.

FOR THE COMMANDER

Robert L Meyer Jr

ROBERT L. MEYER, JR, Maj, USAF
Chief, Postal Operations Div

2

248

출2

미군사 우체국을 통한 우편 소포 검사 절차

10.25

1. SOFA 규정 제9조에 대한 합의 양해 사항에 의거 제9차 SOFA 합동위원회에서 제정하고 3차에 걸쳐 개정된 "미군사 우체국을 통한 우편 소포 검사 절차"에 의하면 다음 3가지 품목을 검사 대상에서 제외됨.

   가. 주한 미대사관, USOM 및 미군사고문단의 인원 및 그 가족에 우송된것.

   나. 공용 우편물

   다. 제1종 우편물 또는 등기 우편물로 표시된것.

2. 72. 2. 3. 재무부는 제64차 합동위원회(71. 7. 29.) 의결에 따라 표본 검사 비율을 10% (종전 5%)로 인상하여 철저한 검사를 실시한바, 반입규정 위배 사례가 증가하고 있으며 특히 등기우편을 통한 밀수입 사례 방지를 위해 동 등기 우편물의 10% 표본 검사 실시를 건의해옴. 당부는 미측에 SOFA 재무분과위원회에 동건 해결을 위한 과제부여를 제의.

3. 72. 3. 23. 미측은 미군사 우편 당국이 72. 4.중 새로운 검사 기기를 설치하여 자체 검사를 강화할 예정이며, 등기 우편물의 대부분이 공용 우편물이란 점등을 들어 등기 우편물의 검사 대상품목 추가를 반대.

4. 73. 10. 재무부는 APO 등기 소포를 이용한 보석류등의 밀수입 사건이 관세청 한미합동 단속 본부반에 의하여 검거된 사례를 들어 등기 우편물의 검사 대상품목 추가를 재차 요청.

249

처 리 방 안 :

SOFA 재무 분과위원회에 대한 신규 과제를 부여 함으로써 상기 "우편물 검사 절차"를 개정, 등기 우편물을 검사 대상 제외 품목에서 제외 하도록 해야 할것임.

APO (미군사 우체국)

1. 의 의

미국 군대의 공용을 위한 우편물과 미국 군대의 구성원, 군속 및 가족의 사용을 위한 우편물을 취급하는 미군사 우체국으로서 우편물 접수, 운송, 집배, 배달등 일체를 일반 우편 경로를 경유하지 않고 단독 처리하고 있음.

2. SOFA (한.미 주둔군 지위협정) 관계 규정

가. 본 협정 제9조 (통관과 관세)

(1) 3 항

군인, 군속 및 가족의 사용을 위하여 합중국안에서 통상적으로 구입되는 종류의 합리적인 양의 개인용품 및 가정용품으로서, 군사 우편국을 통하여 대한민국에 우송되는 것에는 관세 및 기타 과징금 면제

(2) 5 항

공용의 봉인이 있는 공문서와 공용의 우편 봉인이 있고 군사 우편 경로에 있는 제1종 서장 및 합중국 군대에 탁송된 군사 화물에 대한 세관 검사 면제

(3) 제9조에 대한 합의 의사록 3항

군사 화물에 대한 정의

251

74-2-33

(4) 제 9조에 대한 합의 양해 사항

(가) 소포에 대한 세관 검사는 내용물을 손상시키지 않으며 배달을 지연시키지 않음.

(나) 검사는 군사우체국 시설내에서 행함.

(다) 합의된 경우 이외는 여하한 소포도 합중국 우편 경로에서 제거되지 않음.

(라) 검사는 표본검사 (sample check) 기준에 따라 행함.

나. 미군사우체국을 통한 소포 우편 검사 절차 (합동위원회 합의 사항)

* 9차 합동위 회의시 (67. 6. 5.) 제정, 64차 (71. 7. 29.) 66차 (71. 9. 23.), 78차 (72. 10. 5.) 및 91차 합동위 회의시 (74. 1. 24.) 개정

(1) 세관의 검사 면제 품목

(가) 주한 미대사관, USOM, 미군사 고문단의 인원 및 가족에게 우송된 것

(나) 공용 우편물(軍部隊가 受取人인 公用小包)

(다) 제 1종 우편물 ~~또는 등기 우편물로 표시된 것~~

(2) 우편물 도착 통고

252

74 -2- 34

(3) 검사 절차

(가) 세관 검사 장소로서 항공편은 김포, 오산이며 선박편은 부산에서 container 점검후 김포, 오산으로 이송

(나) 검사는 비공용 소포량의 10% 이내에서 표본검사로 하여야 하며 우송에 지장을 초래하지 않도록 신속히 완료해야 함.

(4) 검사한 소포 처리

한.미간 합의에 의해 금수품으로 인정되는 물품이 있는 소포는 처리 결정시까지 미군 우편 당국이 관리 함.

3. 관련된 문제점

가. 관세 포탈

(1) 현재 주한 미군이 면세물품을 도입할 수 있는 경로로는 ①PX, commissary 등 물품 판매소에서 구입, ②APO 를 통한 탁송, ③부임시 이사화물 반입등 3가지가 있으며 상기 면세물품의 부정 시중 유출을 방지하기 위하여 PX 등 물품 판매에 대해서는 구입 통제 제도 (구입 상한선 설정, 부대장의 구매승인서 제도, 한국정부에 대한 통제물품 판매량 통보)가 있으며 이사화물에 대해서도 미군 통관 장교의 사전검토 및 통관 검사등의 제도가 있음.

253

74-2-35

(2) APO 에 대해서도 세관 검사를 하게 되어 있으나, 미군이 통보해 주는 우편물에 대해 검사를 하므로 반입량을 정확히 파악할 수 없고 검사 면세 품목이 많으며, 10%의 표본검사만 하게 되어 있고 우송에 지장을 초래하지 않도록 신속히 완료하여야 한다는 규정 때문에 사실상 전혀 통제되지 않고 있음.

최근 관세청에서 PX, 이사화물등에 대한 통제를 강화하자 APO 를 통한 밀수 사례가 많아지고 있음.

나. 마약 및 습관성 약품 부정유입

현재 기지촌 주변에서 유통되고 있는 마약 및 습관성 약품 중에서 LSD, 메스 카린등 환각제류 와 암페타민등 각성제류 및 바비츄 레이트등 수면제류는 국내에서 제조된 것이 아니며 APO 를 통해부정 유입되는 것이 많음.

다. 총기류 부정유입

4. 현행 조치

가. 우편 소포 검사 절차 개정

한국측은 수년간 비공용 APO 화물에 대한 전량 개장 검사를 추진해 왔으나 미측이 미국의 우편법, 우송의 지연, 내용물 파손 우려등을 이유로 극력반대 함으로서 관철되지 못하고

254

74-2-36

표본 검사 비율소폭 인상, (종래 5%에서 10%로 인상) 검사 제외대상에서 등기 우편물을 제외하는 정도에서 그쳤음.

나. 군민관계 임시분과위원회를 통한 마약 반입 통제 노력 촉구

기지촌 정화를 위해 설립된 군민관계 임시분과위원회에서 미군당국이 APO 를 통한 마약 및 습관성 의약품의 반입을 방지하기 위한 노력을 강화할 것을 합의한 바 있음.

5. 대 책

APO 우편물중 비공용 소포에 대한 현행 10% 표본 검사 제도를 전량 개장 검사 제도로 변경하기 위한 대미 교섭이 필요 함. 반입 물품중 고가품에 대해서는 기록을 한 후 출국시 반출을 확인하면 암거래가 방지될 수 있으며, 전량 개장 제도가 채택되면 마약 및 총기류 반입도 불가능해 질 것임.

첨부 : 1. SOFA 관계규정

2. 소포 우편 검사 절차 (개정분 포함)

끝.

255

74-2-37 (6)

HEADQUARTERS

UNITED STATES FORCES KOREA

APO San Francisco 96301

REGULATION

NUMBER__________

Status of Forces Agreement (SOFA)

ELIGIBILITY FOR AND GRANTING OF SOFA STATUS, RIGHTS AND PRIVILEGES

Supplementation of this regulation by major subordinate commands is not authorized.

1. PURPOSE: This regulation contains policies, procedures and guidance for determining eligibility for and granting of Status of Forces Agreement (SOFA) status, rights and privileges. The agreement under Article IV of the Mutual Defense Treaty between the United States of America and the Republic of Korea regarding facilities and areas and the status of United States Armed Forces in the Republic of Korea defines the categories of individuals who are covered by the SOFA. SOFA Article I addresses (a) "members of the United States armed forces", (b) "civilian component", and (c) "dependents". SOFA Article XV addresses "invited contractors".

2. SCOPE: Categories of personnel possessing SOFA status and their rights and privileges are as follows:

a. Active duty members of the US armed forces when in the territory of the ROK but excluding MAG personnel and miliary personnel attached to the American Embassy. It should be noted that SOFA coverage is not limited to US military personnel on assignment in Korea but includes all such military personnel physically present in Korea for whatever reason, i.e., leave, TDY, etc. Such personnel possess all rights defined by this regulation

2256

except for those which are solely applicable to members of the civilian component and may, at command option, be granted all privileges enumerated in this regulation.

b. Members of the civilian component defined in SOFA Article I(b) as civilian persons of US nationality in the employ of, serving with, or accompanying the US armed forces in the ROK but excluding invited contractor personnel provided for in SOFA Article XV and persons who are ordinarily resident in the ROK. Under the Agreed Minute to SOFA Article I, two categories of third-country nationals shall also be considered as members of the civilian component: (1) those who have been employed continuously since the entry into force of the SOFA in February 1967; and (2) those persons possessing certain skills determined to be unavailabe from US or Korean sources. From the referenced definitions, two clearly defined categories of civilian component members emerge:

(2) Direct-hire civilian employees of the USFK who possess US nationality and who are not ordinarily resident in the ROK.

(2) Direct-hire, third-country employees of the USFK who meet the qualifications specified in b above and who are, or who have been brought into, the Republic of Korea by the USFK solely for employment by the USFK.

To the above two categories of SOFA status personnel, a third is added comprising those US national employees of organizations normally accompanying, and serving with, US forces in overseas areas; namely, US citizen employees of the American Red Cross, the United Service Organization, the San Diego Navy Federal Credit Union and the United Seamen's Service organization. It should be noted in this connection that the Article I definition of "civilian component" is not confined to direct-hire US Government employees but extends to civilian persons serving with, or accompanying, the US armed forces in the ROK, providing they be of US nationality and not ordinarily resident in the ROK.

c. SOFA Article I defines dependents of all categories of SOFA personnel (active duty military personnel, the civilian component, invited contractors and technical representatives) as (1) spouse and children under 21; and (2) parents, children over 21, or other relatives dependent for over half their support upon a member of the US armed forces.

257

or civilian component. It is important to note that this SOFA definition draws no distinction between command sponsored and non-command sponsored dependents. All dependents, irrespective of type or nationality, therefore possess SOFA status and accompanying rights. As is the case for other categories of SOFA personnel, the extension of SOFA privileges to dependents, and the extent and nature of such privileges, is a matter of command determination, except to the extent that certain privileges, such as medical support, may be mandated by higher US authority.

d. Invited contractors are defined in paragraph 1 of SOFA Article XV. They comprise persons, including corporations organized under US law, their employees who are ordinarily resident in the US and their dependents, present in Korea solely to execute contracts with the USFK. Use of invited contractors is restricted by the SOFA to cases where Korean contractors cannot be used because of security considerations, technical qualifications required, unavailability of materials or services required by US standards, and limitations of US law. Invited contractor firms are designated as such by US authorities after consultation with the ROK Government, normally conducted through the US-ROK Joint Committee and its Commerce Subcommittee. Unlike other categories of SOFA personnel, invited contractors are accorded certain rights necessary or beneficial in the performanc of duties related to the execution of contracts. These include exemption from customs duties under Article IX for imports required in the performance of contracts; the use of military postal facilities under Article XX for official correspondence; the use of military banking facilities for corporate business; the right to transmit corporate dollar funds into and out of Korea under Article XVIII; the use of utilities and services in the execution of contracts, in accordance with provisions of SOFA Article VI; exemption from the laws and regulations of ~~Kxxxxx~~ the ROK with respect to terms and conditions of employment and licensing and registration of businesses and corporations; exclusion from ROK taxes on depreciable assets, except houses, used exclusively for the execution of contracts; exemption from taxation in the ROK on the holding, use and transfer of movable property; and exemption from liability to pay income or corporation taxes to the ROKG on income derived under a contract with the US related to the construction, maintenance or operation of US facilities and areas.

258

e. In addition to the foregoing benefits relating to functions excercised in the performance of duties in fulfillment of contract provisions, invited contractor personnel and their dependents are afforded, under the SOFA, many of the rights and privileges applicable to other individuals subject to the SOFA. These rights of individual invited contractor personnel and their dependents comprise: entry into the ROK under SOFA Article VIII; access to, and movement between, USFK facilities and areas, as provided for in SOFA Article X; exemption from payment of Korean customs and duties, to the extent provided in SOFA Article IX for other categories of SOFA personnel; the right of transmission into or out of the ROK of US dollars or dollar instruments realized as a result of service or employment as invited contractor personnel, the same as provided for armed forces and civilian component members under Article XVIII; exemption from Korean taxes applicable to the holding, use, transfer by death, or transfer to persons or agencies entitled to tax exemption under the SOFA, of movable property, tangible or intangible, which property is present in Korea due solely to the temporary presence of those persons in Korea but excluding property held for investment or the conduct of other business in Korea or any intangible property registered in Korea (essentially the same as provided for in SOFA Article (XIV); exemption from ROK income taxes on income derived under a contract with the US Government or on income derived from sources outside of Korea; the licensing and registration by the ROK Government of authorized vehicles of invited contractor personnel as provided for in Inclosure 17 to the minutes of the 32d Joint Committee meeting of 7 Nov 68; and limited protections in criminal jurisdiction matters confined to paragraphs 5, 7(b) and 9 and the related agreed minutes of SOFA Article XXII and applicable to US nationals only.

f. Privileges that may be granted invited contractor personnel and their dependents are identical with those contained in the definition in this regulation (para 5(c). It should be noted that the conferring of such privileges is at command option. They may be granted or withheld by command decision, unless the grant of any or all privileges is specifically required by higher authority. Privileges may further be restricted by the terms and provisions of individual contracts but may not be expanded beyond the scope of those privileges permissible under the SOFA.

g. The qualifying criterion in determining eligibility for invited contractor status is one of residence rather than nationality. This contrasts with that applicable to the civilian component, which specifies US nationality. To qualify for invited contractor status, one must be ordinarily resident in the US. There are two exceptions. Those third-country invited contractor personnel, wherever ordinarily resident, present in that capacity in Korea on the effective date of the SOFA (6 Feb 67) and who have served continuously in that capacity may continue to be accorded invited contractor status. A second exemption is contained in paragraph 2 of the Agreed Understanding regarding paragraph 1 (b) of SOFA Article XVII, which permits the USFK to bring into Korea third-country contractor employees who possess special skills not available from the Korean labor force, but without the privileges of the SOFA. Since the only contractor employees referenced under paragraph 1 (b) of SOFA Article XVII are those in Korea under Invited Contractor Article XV, referenced "contractor employees" can be accorded invited contractor status and attendant rights (which would appear in some degree necessary to fulfill contract provisions) but not the privileges normally accorded invited contractor personnel as described in this regulation. In addition to the use of third-country invited contractor personnel, third-country corporations may be designated as invited contractors, but only with the approval of the ROK Government.

h. Technical representatives constitute another category of SOFA personnel. There are no SOFA provisions governing technical representatives. Therefore, to establish SOFA status for this group, the US Joint Committee Representative, at the 14th Joint Committee meeting on 14 Sep 67, stated that he wished to clarify the status of technical representative He explained that the US Government employes technical representatives to serve as special instructors and advisors to US and ROK personnel in the operation and maintenance of complex military equipment where the particular skills required were not available from US military or other sources in the ROK. He proposed that the minutes of that Joint Committe meeting affirm that technical representatives were members of the civilian component of the USFK as defined in SOFA Article I (b). The ROK Representative agreed to that proposal, as reflected in paragraph 12 of the minutes of the 14th Joint Committee meeting. Hence, technical representatives have an established status as members of the civilian component, ~~as defined in this regulation.~~

260

with rights and privileges idenical to other elements of the civilian component, as defined in this regulations.

i. Part time employees working 75 percent of full-time as defined in this regulation are accorded SOFA status and its corresponding rights, and may be accorded the privileges normally attendant upon possession of SOFA status. Those working less than at least 75 percent of a full time schedule as defined by this regulation are accorded SOFA status and rights, but not SOFA privileges. In the case of invited contractors, the sponsor will verify the extent of full-time employment prior to extending SOFA privileges.

j. For purposes of clarification, all or specified SOFA privileges may be accorded the following persons or organizations who do not possess SOFA status:

(1) US personnel of the American Embassy and its affiliated organizations.

(2) Non-Korean armed forces personnel of the United Nations Command.

(3) Non-Korean members of the UNC Military Armistice Commission.

(4) Non-Korean members of the UNC Liaison Group.

(5) The Swedish and Swiss members of the Neutral Nations Supervisory Commission.

(6) Retired US military personnel.

(7) Widows of deceased active duty military personnel.

(8) Non-Korean persons whose presence in Korea is solely for the purpose of providing contract services financed by the US Government.

(9) Organizations and their non-Korean personnel present in Korea for the benefit and service of the US armed forces. Such organizations include the American Red Cross, the United Service Organization, the San Diego Navy Federal Credit Union and the United Seamens Service organization.

(10) Dependents of the above.

3. REFERENCES. a. The United States of America and the Republic of Korea Status of Forces Agreement with Related Documents, Fourth Edition, January 1978.

b. Index to Minutes of Official Meetings of the ROK-US Joint Committee, Status of Forces Agreement, 1 February 1979.

6

26 (10) FULLTIME DIRECTORS OF RELIGIOUS SERVICEMEN'S CENTERS, IF A US CITIZEN, TO THE EXTENT AND UNDER CONDITIONS SPECIFIED IN USFK REG 60-1.

c. USFK Regulation 550-7, Organization and mission of U.S./ROK Joint (SOFA) Committee.

d. USFK Regulation 527-1, Organization and Mission of U.S. Component of (SOFA) Subcommittees Established by U.S./ROK Joint Committee.

e. USFK Regulation 60-1, Exchange Services, Ration Control.

f. USFK Regulation 230-11, non-appropriated Funds and Related Activities - Alcoholic Beverage Activities.

g. USFK Regulation 643-1, Personal Property - Transactions Between SOFA Personnel and Personnel Entitled Duty Free Import Privileges in the Republic of Korea.

h. USFK Regulation 643-2, Transactions Between SOFA Personnel and Personnel Not Entitled Duty Free Import Privileges in the Republic of Korea.

4. RESPONSIBILITIES. a. Assistant Chief of Staff (ACofS), J-1 will develop, promulgate, and implement a flexible program for determining eligibility and granting of SOFA privileges.

b. As appropriate Army Criminal Investigation Command or the Air Force Office of Special Investigations will be responsible for investigating suspected illegal or unauthorized SOFA irregularities and will cause investigation when and where required.

c. The Assistant Chief of Staff (ACofS) for Acquisition Management is the staff proponent concerning invited contractors (IC) and technical representatives (TR) as defined by this regulation and will establish a system to monitor eligibility for and granting of SOFA status for all invited contractor and technical representative personnel. As staff proponent, this ACofS will verify IC/TR personnel's contract employment for ration control and SOFA purposes.

d. The appropriate Civilian Personnel Officer will authorize issuance of DD Form 1173, Uniformed Services Identification and Privilege Card for all members of the civilian component as defined by this regulation.

e. The ACofS, Comptroller is designated the command sponsor for employees of the San Diego Navy Federal Credit Union.

f. Component Commanders will:

262

(1) Assume responsibilities as the sponsor of those individuals performing services for the unit and eligible for SOFA status, rights, and privileges defined in this regulation to ensure compliance with this regulation and all reference USFK SOFA regulations affecting personnel sponsored.

(2) Assign a responsible officer as the individual tasked to determine eligibility of individuals requesting SOFA status, rights and privileges. This office will sign all appropriate documentation including USFK form 42 (Command Unique Personnel Information Data System (CUPIDS) Application); DD Form 1172 (Application for Uniformed Services Identification and Privilege Card); and will make determinations concerning status of employment (full time vs. part time), length of employment, and will assume responsibility for retrieval of USFK Ration Control Plates, Uniformed Services Identification and Privilege Card (DD Form 1173) and SOFA vehicle registration material including license plates upon termination of employment for any reason.

5. DEFINITIONS. a. SOFA Status. SOFA "status" refers to those categories of personnel, as enumerated in paragraph 2 of this regulation, who are subject to the provisions of the US-ROK Status of Forces Agreement (SOFA). Pertinent provisions of the SOFA concerning its applicability to individuals are to be found in SOFA Article I and XV and, for technical representatives, in paragraph 12 of the minutes of the 14th Joint Committee meeting held on 14 Sep 67.

b. SOFA Rights. SOFA "rights" comprise entitlements to be accorded mandatorily to persons subject to the SOFA. These include: (1) the right of entry into, and exit from Korea under SOFA Article VIII; (2) exemption from payment of Korean customs and duties as delineated in SOFA Article IX; (3) access to, and movement between, USFK facilities and areas as stipulated in SOFA Article X; (4) exemption from Korean taxes on income received as a result of their service or employment with the USFK, or on income derived from sources outside of the Republic of Korea; (5) exemption from Korean taxes applicable to the holding, use, transfer inter se or transfer by death of movable property, tangible or intangible, which property is present in Korea due solely to the temporary
263 presence of those persons in Korea, but excluding property held for investment or the

conduct of business in Korea or any intangible property registered in Korea (SOFA Article XIV); (6) For civilian component members only, exemption from ROK laws or regulations of the ROK with respect to their terms and condition of employment (SOFA Article XVII); (7) the right of transmission into or out of the ROK of US dollars or dollar instruments realized as a result of service or employment with USFK or obtained from sources outside of Korea (SOFA Article XVIII); (8) various protections afforded in criminal jurisdiction matters under SOFA Article XXII, with particular reference to the entitlements accorded SOFA persons under paragraph 9 of that article and agreed minutes and understandings thereto; and(9) the licensing and registration by the ROKG of authorized, privately-owned vehicles of SOFA personnel (SOFA Article XXIV)..

c. SOFA Privilgges. SOFA "privileges" involve access to, and use of, logistic support facilities and financial institutions, including NAF activities. "Privileges" differ from "rights" in two important respects. First, privileges may be granted or withheld at command option (except as may be directed by higher authority, as in the case of certain medical services). No individual, whether possessing SOFA status or not, may invoke a right to the use of such facilities. Secondly, "privileges" may, under specified conditions, be accorded to persons lacking SOFA status. "Privileges" consist of: (a) the use of NAF activities and commissaries (SOFA Article XIII), except as limited by command policy, capacity limitations or restrictions contained in the charter or by-laws of certain organizations, especially military clubs; (b) the use of military banking facilities and credit union (SOFA Article XIX); and (c) the use of military post offices (SOFA Article XX).

6. POLICY. a. Reference documents provide guidance concerning SOFA privileges and procedures to prevent SOFA abuse. The purpose of this regulation is to clearly define eligibility criteria for granting SOFA status, rights and privileges; procedures for granting SOFA status; identification of all categories of personnel granted SOFA status; and conduct of initial investigation prior to granting SOFA status and retrieval of identification cards, ration control plates, vehicle registration data and license plates upon termination of employment; and other related responsibilities.

264

b. SOFA status can be granted to those individuals defined in reference (a) and paragraph (2) of this regulation. Only those employees certified as "full time" employees will be granted SOFA privileges. Full time employment is defined as working at least 3/4 time, or 60 hours per two-week pay period in all cases except those where the individual is an employee of an academic institution. Employees of academic institutions are considered full-time employees when scheduled to teach nine classroom hours of instruction or two classes weekly.

c. The sponsor of all individuals eligible for SOFA privileges is the Commander of the agency for which the individual is accomplishing full time work. In the case of invited contractors and technical representatives, the sponsor is the agency responsible fo monitoring contract compliance. In the case of NAF personnel, the agency designated sponsorship is the staff principal assigned liaison responsibility for USFK/EUSA.

7. PROCEDURES. The sponsor will ensure that all employees designated full-time by the originator or employing agent meet the definition of full time employment stipulated in this regulation prior to authorizing issuance of DD Form 1173, Ration Control Plates or vehicle registration. Upon termination of employment of the individual for any reason the sponsor will retrieve all documentation authorizing SOFA privileges including DD Form 1173, Ration Control Plates, for disposition in accordance with reference document In addition, the sponsor will ensure that vehicle registration and license plates are returned to the Provost Marshal as required by reference documentation. Action will be taken by the sponsor to establish a system whereby the employees supervisor notifies the sponsor upon learning of the intent to resign or reaching a decision to release or terminate the employee to ensure retrieval of all materials prior to the individual's departure from the command. Enforcement responsibilities for ration control and investigation of such irregularities are established by USFK 60-1. More specific information as to other areas of responsibility/procedures involving the granting and monitoring of SOFA status, rights and privileges are provided by reference documents listed in paragraph 3 of this regulation.

265

미군사우체국을 통한 우편소포 검사 절차

1. 관계규정및 문제점

관 계 규 정	문 제 점
가. SOFA 제9조에 대한 합의 양해 사항 나. 제9차 합동위제정, 제64차, 66차 합동위 부분개정및 제78차 합동위 (72.10.5.) 개정 의 "미군사 우체국을 통한 우편소포 검사 절차" 주요내용 1) 검사대상에서 제외되는 품목. 가) · · · · · · · 나) - - - - - 다) · · · · · 및 제1종 우편물 또는 등기우편물로 표시된것. 2) 수입되는 비공용 소포량의 10% 이내만 표본검사를 함. (동표본은 한미관계관에 의해 합동으로 선정됨)	가. 반입규정에 위배되는 물품이 보류, 반송또는 검거되는 사례가 늘어나고 있음. 특히 마약류등의 단속을 위해 표본검사 비율(현1%)의 인상이 요망됨. 나. 등기소포를 통한 밀수입사례의 방지를 위한 10%의 표본검사 실시가 필요함. (73.10.4. 한미합동단속반에 의한 현역미군장교의 APO 등기소포 이용 보석류 밀수입 혐의 검거 사건등) 다. APO를 통한 월평균 우편 반입량 (72년도기준, 관세청 추산) : 약 65만 파운드 1) 일반소포 (검사대상) - - - 18.8% 2) 등기우편물 - - - - 3 % 3) 기타공용물 - - - - - 78.2% ↓ 간지원사무관

266

2. 규정개정을 위한 노력

재무부측 요청	당부 조치 사항	SOFA	결 과
가. 72.2.3. 우편소포검사 절차개정요청	가. 72.3.8. 과제부여 제의		
나. 72.3.13. 마약등의 부정 유입 방지 요청	나. 72.3.23. 미측 간사의 서한 접수		
다. 72.4.18. 우편소포 검사장소 변경요청	다. 72.4.22. 과제부여 제의	가. 72. . . 73차 합동위에서 재무분과위에 과제 부여	
라. 72.8.16. 대책회의 개최		나. 72.8.18. 재무분과위 개최 → 주요의제	의결내용 1. 검사장의 변경지정: 오산을 줄이고, 부산을 검사장 후보지로 규정 2. 보세 운송: 입항지로 부터 지정 검사장소 까지의 보세 운송제도를 규정 3. 조문정리: 상기절차 개정에 따른 조문정리.
마. 72.9.28. 재무분과위의 합의사항에 대한 합동위승인요청		다. 72.10.5. 78차 합동위에서 승인	
바. 73.9.17. 등기우편물에 대한 세관검사 제의 →	라. 재무부에 대하여 충분한 증거등 자료 제시토록 구두요청.		
사. 73.10.19. 밀수입건 증거물 2건 제시.			

회 의 록

1. 제 목 : APO 를 통한 등기우편물의 세관 검사

2. 일시및장소 : 73. 10. 30. (화) 16 : 45 - 17 : 30
외무부 북미2과

3. 참 석 자 : 외무부 북미2과 양세훈 서기관, 정의용 사무관
재무부 관세협력과 강지원 사무관
관세청감시국심리과 엄낙용 사무관 (73 - 2877)

4. 회의내용 :

북미2과 : 가. APO 를 통한 등기우편물의 10% 표본 검사 실시를 위한 SOFA 합동위원회의 과제부여에 대하여 당부에서는 73. 10. 25. 미측에 정식 제의한바 있음.

나. 동 문제와 관련, 재무부 및 관세청에서 제시한 증거물 (울푸대위건)이 사실상 APO 등기우편물로 볼수있겠는지와 APO 우편물의 범위 및 처리 절차 등을 구체적으로 설명하여 주기바람.

다. 상기 증거물 외에 참고 자료등 (예 : APO 를 통한 우편량 및 세분항목별 비율과 일반소포중 밀수 적발 건수 및 비율등)을 제공 바람.

268

관 세 청 : 가. 울푸대위건의 증거물에 대하여 관세청에서는 명백히 APO 우편물로 보고 있음.
APO 우편물의 분류 기준은 다음과 같음.

1) 순수한 APO 우편물
발신부터 APO channel 을 통한 것으로 이는 순전히 APO 에 의해 집배에서 배달까지 하고 있음.

2) 일반 우편물중 주소를 APO 로 기재한것, 이에 대해서 외국에서 한국으로 들어오는 경우 국제 우체국에서 분류하여 세관 검사를 실시치 않고 APO 로 즉시 넘겨주고 있음.

나. APO 에 관한 각종 통계는 사실상 집계가 불가능하며 71년도 경우도 관세청의 추산에 불과한것임.

북미2과 : APO 로 주소가 기재된 일반우편물을APO 를 통한 우편물로 분류하는 기준이 확실치 않은것 같음. 동건에 대하여 관세청에서 재확인 통보 바람. 만일 상기 경우 APO 우편물이 아니라면, 세관 검사를 실시치 않은 것은 우리측의 잘못임.

관 세 청 : 가. 동 APO 우편물 분류기준에 대해서는 당청에서 재확인 통보하겠으나, 당청에서는 지금까지 상기 2항의 경우도 APO 우편물로 취급하여 왔음.

269

나. 사실APO 주소로 기재된 일반 우편물도 문제는 되고 있으나, 순수한APO 우편물중 전혀한국측 세관 검사를 못하고 있으며, 반입량조차 추산할수 없는 등기 소포를 통한 밀수입량은 상당할 것으로 예상되며, 미측의 자체 검사는 한국으로 반입되는 것보다는, 국외로 반출되는 우편물에 치중하고 있는것으로 알고 있음.

다. 이번 과제부여 기회를 통하여 등기소포에 대한 적어도 10% 표본 검사가 실현되도록 귀부에서 적극 협조하여 줄것을 요청함.

270

관세청 엄낙용 사무관 전화 73. 11. 7. 16 : 45.

통화내용

가. 관세청 실무진과 미 APO 실무자와 접촉, 검사 재개에 대하여 합의 (11. 7.)

나. 동건은 일단 해결된것으로 사료됨으로, 명일 Mr. Kinney 가 외무부 방문시 거론할 필요가 없음.

271

지급

기 안 용 지

분류기호 문서번호	미이 723 -	(전화번호)	전결규정 국장 전결사항
처리기간		국 장	
시행일자	73. 11. 9.		
보존년한			
보조기관 과 장		협조	
기안책임자	정의용	북미 2과	
경유			
수신	재무부 장관		
참조	관세국장		
제목	미군사우체국을 통한 우편소포의 검사절차 개정		

보고통제 1941-14688 1973. 11. 9 최초작성기관

발송 45858 1973. 11. 9 외무부

대 : 협력 1243 - 763 (73. 10. 19.)

협력 1243 - 672 (73. 9. 17.)

대호 건과 관련하여, 당부에서는 별첨 1 과 같이 SOFA 합동위원회 재무분과위원회에 대한 과제부여를 미측에 제의하였으며, 미측은 우리측의 과제부여 각서 문안을 별첨 2 와 같이 수정 제의하여 왔는바, 이에 대한 귀부의 의견을 회시하여 주시기 바랍니다.

첨부 : 1. 아측 과제부여 각서 사본 1부.

2. 미측 수정제의 문안 사본 1부. 끝.

정서 / 관인 / 발송

공통서식 1-2 (갑)
1967. 4. 4 승인

190mm×268mm 중질지 70g/㎡
조달청 1000,000매 인쇄)

272

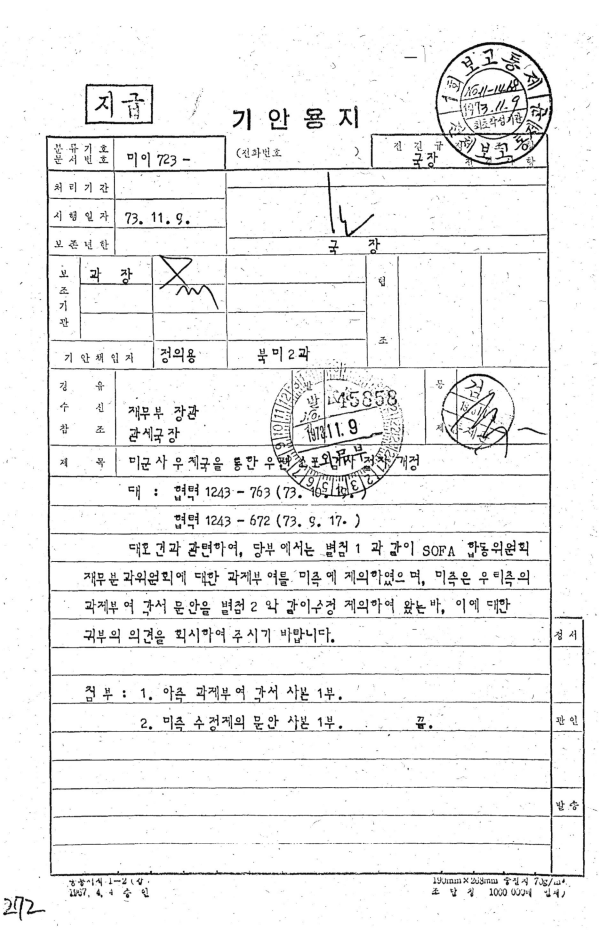

공 란

공 란

증산 수출 건설

재 무 부

지 급

협력 1243-820 (70-3227) 1973. 11. 14.

수신 외무부장관

제목 미군사우체국을 통한 우편소포 검사 절차 개정

1. 미이 723-45858(73.11.9)에 대한 회신입니다.

2. A.P.O 등기소포의 세관검사실시 문제에 관한 미측의 과제부여각서 문안에는 Registered Matter 에 대한 구체적인 언급이 없으므로 이에 따라 재무분과위원회에서 논의하더라도 그 실효를 얻기 힘들것으로 사료됩니다.

3. 따라서 "미군사우체국을 통한 우편소포에 대한 한국세관검사절차" 규정제 1 항(다)중 Registered Matter 의 삭제(deletion)문제를 구체적으로 명시하여 주시기 바랍니다. 끝.

과장	담	과	국	관	차관	

재 무 부 장 관

-215

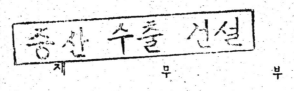

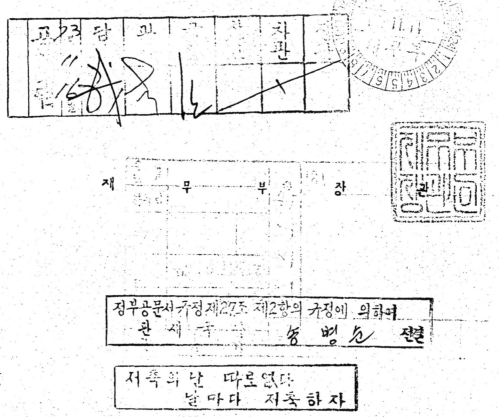

외 무 부			지시사항	
접수일시	197 . . .			
접수번호	제 68568 호			
주무과				
담당자				
취급 일자				197 . . . 까지 처리

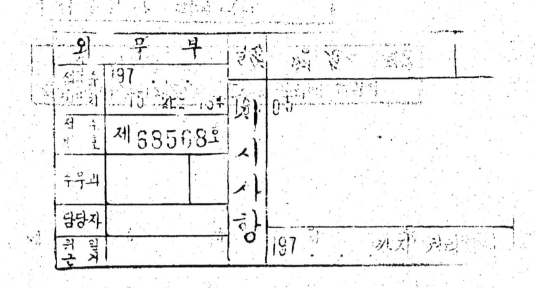

공 란

공 란

기 안 용 지

분류기호 문서번호	미이 723 -	(전화번호)	전결규정 국장 전결사항
처리기간			
시행일자	73. 11. 29.		
보존년한		국 장	
보조기관 과 장			협조
기안책임자	정의용	북미 2과	
경유 수신 참조	재무부 장관 관세국장		
제 목	미군사우체국을 통한 우편소포 검사		

(1회 보고용 No. 11-1586 1973. 11. 30 최초작성기관 국장 회 보고사항)

(발송 No. 48774 1973. 11. 30 외무부)

(검열 1973. 11. 30 통제관)

대 : 협력 1243 - 820 (73. 11. 14.)

연 : 미이 723 - 45858 (73. 11. 9.)

대호건과 관련하여 미측은 동 과제부여 각서 문안을 별첨과 같이 재수정 제의하여 왔는바, 이에 대한 귀부의 의견을 조속 회시 바랍니다.

첨부 : 동 미측안 사본 1부. 끝.

정서
관인
발송

공통서식1-2(갑)
1967. 4. 4. 승인

190mm×268mm (1급인쇄용지70g/m²)
조달청 (300,000매인쇄)

278

외 무 부

미이 723 - 73. 11. 29.

수 신 : 재무부 장관

참 조 : 관세국장

제 목 : 미군사우체국을 통한 우편소포 검사 절차 개정

대 : 협력 1243 - 820 (73. 11. 14.)

연 : 미이 723 - 45858 (73. 11. 9.)

대호 건과 관련하여 미측은 동 과제 부여 구서 문안을 별첨과 같이 재수정 제의하여 왔는 바, 이에 대한 귀부의 의견을 조속 회시 바랍니다.

첨부 : 동 미측안 사본 1부. 끝.

외 무 부 장 관

279

공 란

증산 수출 건설

재 무 부

협력 1243 - 882 (70-3227) 1973. 12. 3

수신 외무부장관

제목 미군사 우체국을 통한 우편 소포 검사절차 개정

1. 미이 723 - 48774 (73. 11. 29) 에 대한 회신입니다.

2. 당부는 미측이 수정 제의한 각서 문안에 대하여 동의합니다. 끝.

고	담	과			차관	장관
	12. 5					

재 무 부 장

정부공문서규정 제27조 제2항의 규정에 의하여
관세국장 공병순 전결

새집살림 나라살림
저축으로 부강하자

281

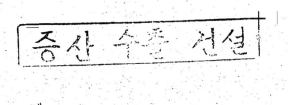

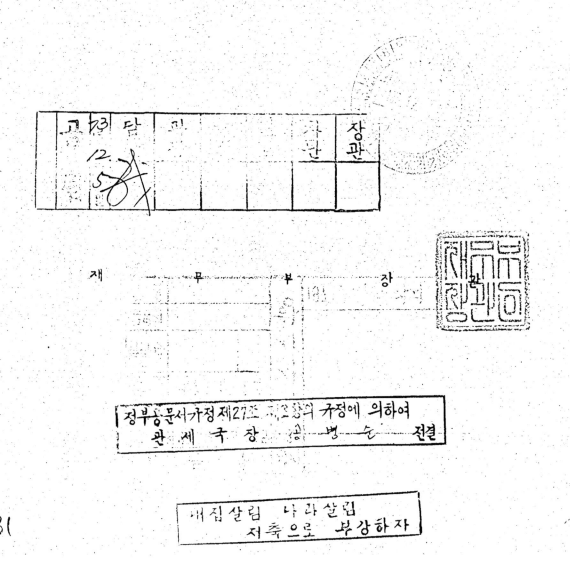

외 무 부		결재	
접수	1971 NOV 23 ... 15 : 28	지시사항	
접수번호	제71484호		
주무과			
담당자			
접수일자			197 . . . 까지 처리할 것

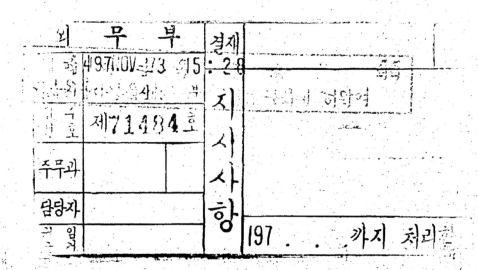

공 란

증산 수출 건설

재 무 부

협력 1243 - 896 (70-3227) 1973. 12. 5

수신 외무부장관

제목 재무분과 위원회 대책회의

당부가 재무분과위원회에 대한 긴급과제 부여에 동의한 2개 안건 (A.P.O 등기소포 검사시행 및 P.X. 통제품목 재조정)에 대한 아측 보지선을 검토하기위한 대책회의를 다음과 같이 개최하고자 하니 아측 재무분과 위원은 필히 참석하시기 바랍니다.

다 음

1. 일시 : 1973. 12. 7일 오후

2. 장소 : 재무부 관세협력담당관실.

공람	담	과	국	차관보	차관	장관
73 12						

재 무 부 장

재무부장관인

정부공문서규정 제27조 제2항의 규정에 의하여
관 세 국 장 송 병 순 전결

의심나면 다시보고 수상하면 신고하자

283

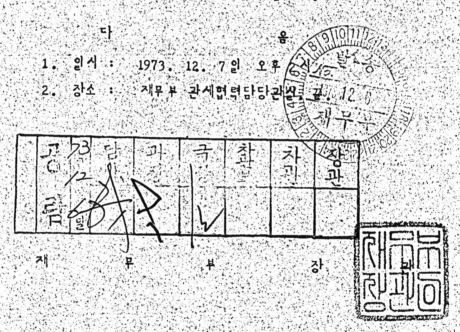

대책 회의록

1. 제　　목 : SOFA 재무분과위 개최에 따른 관계부처 실무자간의 대책 회의

2. 일　　시 : 1973. 12. 7. (금) 14 : 00 - 15 : 00
재무부 관세협력과

3. 참 석 자 : 외무부 정의용 사무관,
재무부 강지원 "
관세청 엄낙용 "

4. 회의내용 요지 :

재무부 : 가. 12. 6. 긴급과제 부여된 통제품목 재조정 (미측)과 APO 등기 소포에 대한 세관검사 실시 (한국측)에 관한 2개의 과제에 대하여 논의코자 함.

나. 미측은 아측 과제부여 제의 (APO 건)에 대하여 그 대응책으로 다른 문제를 제기한것으로 보이며, 양측의 상호 양보시 동 과제는 원만히 해결될 것으로 예상됨.

다. 미측은 동 2건의 과제에 대한 재무분과위의 건의를 90차 합동위 (12. 13.)에 제출할것을 요청하였으나, 내주부터 실무접촉키로 한것을 고려할때 금년중 처리는 곤란할것임.

284

외무부 : 가. APO 등기 소포물에 대한 세관검사 실시건은 미측이 동 과제부여 최종 문안에 "registered" 삽입을 동의한것등은 일단 아측의 요청이 관철된 것으로 생각할수 있으며,

나. 미측의 제의한 과제는 현재의 통제품목 (Controlled Item)을 현실화하자는 것이므로, 이번 기회에 아측이 희망하는 품목도 추가토록 노력하면 좋을것임.

재무부 : 아측이 추가 희망하는 통제품목으로는, 보석류, 모피류, 광학기기류 및 기타 고가품목($100 이상) 등이나, 과거 상기와 같은 아측 요청에 대하여 미측은 동 품목 통제를 위한 EDP System 재수정의 곤란한점 (예산등)을 들어 반대해오고 있는 실정이므로 기대하기가 힘들것임.

관세청 : 가. 사실상 미측의 Controlled Item 에 관한 정기적인 판매량 통보는 무의미한 것임. 그보다는 L.O.A. (중대장 승인서) Item (현재 12개)의 확보 내지는 추가가 요망되고 있음. 이는 미군 자체의 견제효과가 있다고 봄.

285

나. 따라서 이번 과제 부여된 문제 해결에 있어 관세청이 요청한 " APO 등기 소포에 대한 세관검사 실시"는 반드시 쟁취되야 될것이며, "통제품목 재조정"은 미측 요청에 따라 어느 정도 현실화 하여도 무방할것으로 사료됨.

다. 특히, 동 과제와 직접적 관련은 없으나 PX 등의 고가품 구매자 명단을 통보하여 주거나 또는 열람할수 있도록 미측에 요청하여야 할것임.

재무부 : 고가품 구매자 명단 열람과 관련하여, 재무부에서는 특히 최근 문제된바 있던 Chosun Gift Shop 에서의 고가품 구매자 명단 열람을 요청하였던바 미측이 조만간 이에 응해줄것이 예상되고 있으며, 과제부여 없이 실무접촉으로 해결할 방침임.

공람	73. 12. 10	담당	과장	국장	차관보	차관	장관

286

a.	Binoculars	X
b.	Movie camera	X
c.	Still camera over $ 40	Still camera over $ 80
d.	Still camera under $ 40	Still camera under $ 80
✓ e.	Television set	Television___
f.	Radio over $ 25	Radio over $ 50
g.	Radio under $ 25	X
h.	Stereo music system	Stereo music system
i.	Tuner / amplifier / receiver	Tuner / amplifier / receiver
j.	Two speakers over $ 25	4 Speakers
k.	Two speakers under $ 25	
l.	Turntable	Turntable
m.	Phonograph_____	Phonograph over $ 50
n.	Tape deck	Tape deck
o.	Tape recorder over $ 25	Tape recorder
p.	Tape recorder under $ 25	
		Carpets over $ 50

287

q.	Watch ____	Watch over $ 75 (Excluding costume jewelry watches)
r.	Typewriter	Typewriter
s.	Firearm	Firearm
t.	Diamond ring	Diamond ring
u.	Electric blender	Electric blender
v.	Electric rice cooker____	Electric rice cooker or steam cooker
w.	Electric toaster	Electric toaster
x.	Electric coffee pot	Electric coffee pot
y.	Electric skillet	Electric skillet
z.	Electric fan	Electric fan
		Electric steam / or dry iron
aa.	Washer____	Washer machine
bb.	__Dryer	Clothes dryer
cc.	Range____	Range or microwave oven
dd.	Vacum cleaner	Vacum cleaner

288

✓ ee.	Floor polisher	Floor polisher
✓ ff.	Refrigerator	Refrigerator
✓ gg.	Freezer	Freezer
✓ hh.	Water heater	Water heater
✓ ii.	Air conditioner	Air conditioner
		Special purchases for clubs and organizations

✓ LOA items (12)

1) jewelry
2) fur
3) 광학 기기
4) 기타 high priced items

※ 美側 EDPS 에게 ~~재검~~ 재수정이 必要.

289

[redacted]

美軍事郵便 소포 韓國稅關 거쳐야

주한미군지위에 관한 협정(SOFA)운용을위한 한미합동위원회는 주한미군및 군속이 미군사우편(APO)을 통해 등기소포를 수발하는 경우 한국세관을통해 관세를 물도록 결정했다고 十四일 발표했다。

이같은 조치는 APO를 통한 빈번한 밀수행위를 근절시키기 위한 조치인것으로 알려졌다。

한미합동위는 또 종래 미군영내의 「피 엑스」를 개방, 면세특혜를 주던 「언커크」회원국 외교관들에 대해서도 「언커크」해체에 따라 특혜를 주지않기로 했다。

[redacted]

'73. 12. 14. <동아>

[redacted]

APO 小包에도 關稅물리기로

주한미군 군사우편(APO)을통한 개인소포에 한국세관을 거쳐 관세를 부과하게됐다。

주한미군 지위에관한 협정의 시행을위한 한·미합동위원회가 13일 이같이 합의했는데 이러한조치는 미군우편을통해 밀수행위가 일어날수 있는 소지를 없애기위해 취해진 것이다。

한·미합동위는또「언커크」의 해체에따라「언커크」회원국 (호주·태국·「필리핀」·「터키」·화란) 외교관에게 허용했던 미군영내의 PX사용을 중지시키기로 결정했다。

[redacted]

<중앙>

공람	담당	과장	국장	차관보	차관	장관

290

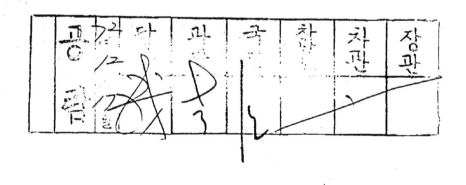

재 무 부

협력 1243 - 2

(70-3227) 1974. 1. 11

수신 외무부장관

제목 SOFA 한미합동위원회에 대한 건의

1973. 12. 7 SOFA 재무분과 위원회에 긴급과제부여된 " APO 를 통한 우편소포검사절차 개정 "의 건에 대하여 별첨과 같이 합의 되었기에 이를 송부하오니 SOFA 합동위원회에서 승인 되도록 조치하여 주시기 바랍니다.

첨부 SOFA 재무분과위원회 합의각서 사본 1부.

1974. 1. 12 재무부

공	73 년 / 일	담당	과장	국장	참관보	차관	장관

재 무 부 장 관

291

의심나면 다시보고 수상하면 신고하자

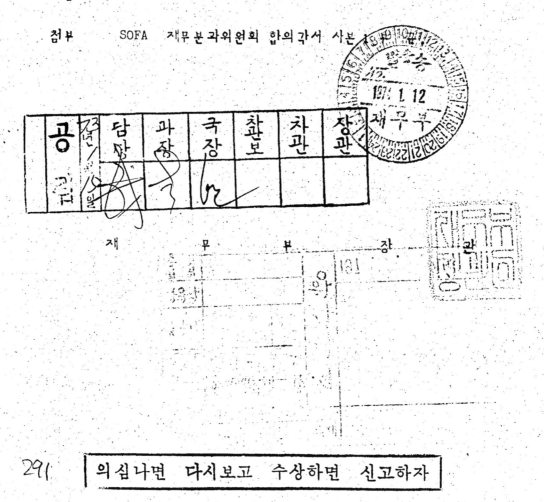

미안 496-1(10)

접수일시	197 . . . 12 JAN 74 12:04	결재	
접수번호	제 1801 호	지시사항	
주무과			
담당자			
처리기일			197 . . . 까지 처리

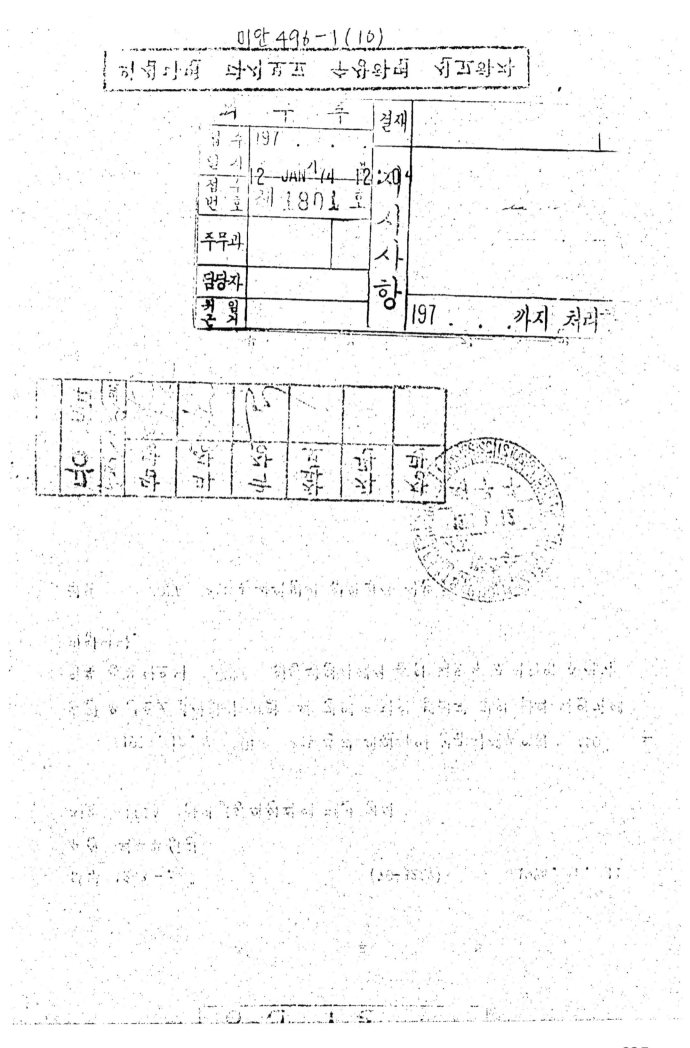

공 란

공 란

정/리/보/존/문/서/목/록

기록물종류	문서-일반공문서철	등록번호	19784	등록일자	2003-09-25
분류번호	729.419	국가코드		주제	
문서철명	SOFA - 한.미국 합동위원회 면세물품 불법거래 임시위원회 회의, 제5-6차, 1975				
생산과	안보담당관실	생산년도	1975 - 1975	보존기간	영구
담당과(그룹)	미주	안보		서가번호	--
참조분류					
권차명					
내용목차	1. 제5차, 2.3 2. 제6차, 4.2				

마/이/크/로/필/름/사/항

촬영연도	*롤 번호	화일 번호	후레임 번호	보관함 번호
2005-10-03	G-42		7/1-81	

색 인 목 록

분류번호	등록번호	생산과	생산년도	필름번호		화일번호	후레임번호		
				주제	번호		시작		끝
729.419 1975	8341 (19784)	북미2과	1975	G	-0042	07	0001	~	0081

기 능 명 칭 : **SOFA-한·미국 합동위원회 면세물품 불법거래 임시위원회 회의, 제5-6차, 1975**

일 련 번 호	내 용	페 이 지
1	제5차, 2.3	0004
2	제6차, 4.2	0020

2

결 번

넘버링 오류

1. 제 5차, 2. 3

4

관 세 청

임분위 1148 28-7698 75. 1. 30.

수신 외무부장관

참조 북미2과장 이 상훈.

제목 임시분과위원회 제5차 회의개최

한.미 면세물품의 불법거래에 관한 임시분과위원회 제5차 회의가 다음과 같이 개최되오니 참석하여 주시기 바라며, 동회의 의제(안)를 별첨과 같이 송부하오니 참고하시기 바랍니다.

다 음

1. 회의일시 : 1975. 2. 3.(월)14:00

2. 장 소 : 관세청 회의실

3. 참 석 자 : 임시분과위원회 위원 및

첨부 제5차 회의 의제(안) 1부. 끝.

(접수 1975. 1 30 관세청)

관 세 청 장

부공문서 규정 제27조 제 항의 규정에 의하여 전결

감사국장 김 진 우

민원신고는 서울 28-0123 인천 3-0123 부산 4-0123

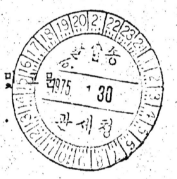

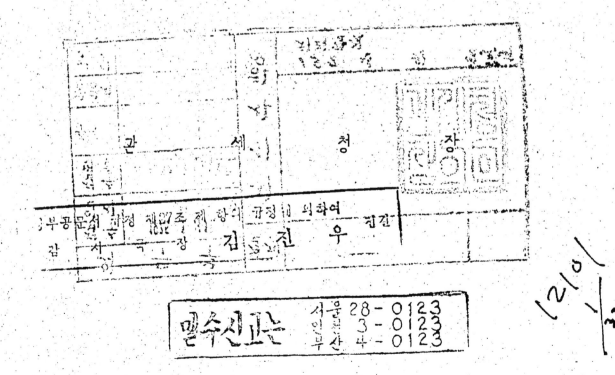

외 무 부		결재		
접수 일시	1975. 1. 31			
접수 번호	제 2490 호	지시사항		
주무과				
담당자				
인 임			197 년 월 일까지 처리할것	

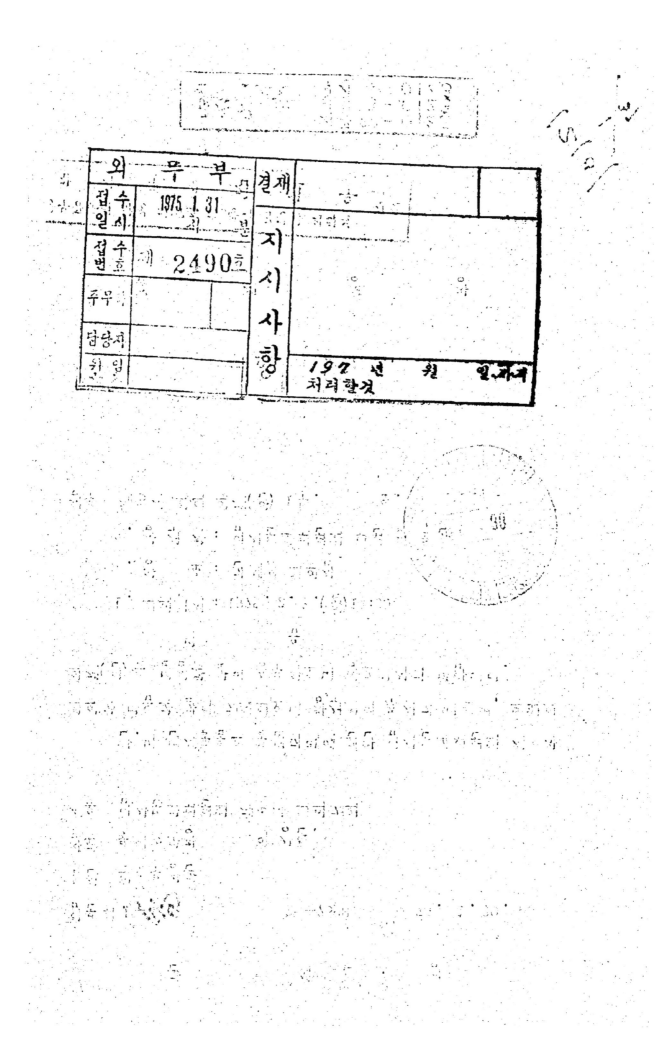

의 제(안)

(제5차 회의)

1. 환영사 : 한국측 위원장
2. 미측 인사말 및 한.미합동단속반 고문관 미측 대표 소개
   : 미측 위원장
3. 한.미 합동단속본부반 실적에 대한 브리핑을 위하여 한국측 고세관사 이재병씨를 소개
   : 한국측 위원장
4. 단속실적에 대한 브리핑 : 한국측 고세관사
5. 한.미합동단속반의 현안에 대한 보고를 위하여 미측 중령 싱글톤을 소개
   : 미측 위원장
6. 한.미합동단속반 현안보고 : 미측 중령 싱글톤
7. 공동관심사에 대한 일반토의
8. 제6차회의 일시 선정
9. 폐회선언 : 한국측 위원장.

6

제 5 차 회의

의 제

1. 환영사 : 한국측 위원장.

2. 미측 인사말 및 한.미 합동단속반 고문단 미측대표 소개
   : 미측 위원장.

3. 한.미 합동단속 본부반 실적에 대한 브리핑을 위하여 한국측 고체간사 이 제병씨를 소개.
   : 한국측 위원장.

4. 본부반 단속 실적에 대한 브리핑 : 한국측 고체간사.

5. 한.미 합동 단속반의 현안에 대한 보고를 위하여 미측 중령 싱글톤을 소개 : 미측 위원장.

6. 한.미합동 단속반 현안 보고 : 미측 중령 싱글톤.

7. 한.미 공동 관심사에 대한 일반토의.

8. 제 6차 회의 일시 선정.

9. 폐회선언 : 한국측 위원장.

7

(의제 1)

헤리크 대령,

준비 되셨으면 면세물품의 불법거래에 관한 임시분과 위원회 제 5차 회의를 개최 하겠읍니다.

토의에 앞서 오늘 당청에 찾아주신 미측위원 여러분에게 심심한 감사의 뜻을 표하며 이자리를 빌어 한국측 고문단 대표 양 성범씨와 김 철수씨 후임으로 한국측 신임 고제간사로 지명된 이 제병씨를 소개하고자 합니다.

미측 위원장께서 한미합동 단속반 고문단 미측대표를 소개하여 주시기 바랍니다.

(2. 미측인사말 및 소개)

감사합니다.

- 의제 3으로 넘어 가겠읍니다. -

2

(의제 3)

다음으로 지난 12월 17일 부터 활동을 개시한 한.미합동 단속 본부반의 그 간의 실적에 관하여 한국측 한.미 반장인 이 제범씨가 브리핑을 하겠읍니다.

(4. 본부반 단속 실적에 대한 브리핑).

- 다음 의제 5로 넘어 가겠읍니다 -

미측 대표 께서 한.미합동 단속반의 현안 문제를 말씀하여 주실분을 소개하여 주시기 바랍니다.

9

(5. 한.미 합동단속반 현안 문제 보고를 위하여,
미측 대표는 중령 싱글톤을 소개).

(6. 중령 싱글톤의 합동단속반 현안 보고).

- 미측의 한.미합동 단속반 현안 보고에 대하여 감사하며,
다음 의제 7로 넘어 가겠읍니다 -

10

(의제 7)

헤리트 대령,

지금부터 일반적인 토의에 들어가기로 하겠읍니다.

금일 현재 제 5차 회의를 개최하기 까지 면세물품의 불법거래 방지를 위한 한.미 양측위원들의 성원으로 부정 외래품 단속에 훌륭한 성과가 있었읍니다만 아직도 부정외래품은 완전히 근절되지 않고 있으며, 많은 문제점이 남아있는 것으로 생각 합니다.

이 기회에 양측 위원들께서 면세물품의 불법거래 방지를 위하여 좋은 대안이 있으시면 기탄없이 토의를 하여 주시기 바랍니다.

첫째, 한미 합동단속반이 설치되어 현재 운영중에 있읍니다만 PX 등의 판매고 추세를 알 수 없으므로 그 구체적인 성과파악이 거의 불가능한 실정에 있읍니다. 따라서 전국 각지의 PX , 콤미서리등의 월별 판매고를 입수할 수 있다면 한.미합동단속반 활동의 구체적 성과 파악은 물론 전국지구반의 효율적인 운영방안을 수립하는 유용한 자료로 활용할 수 있을 것입니다.

따라서 본인은 미 8군 당국이 전국 각 PX , 콤미서리등의 월별 판매고를 익월까지 관세청에 통보해 주실것을 건의하는 바 입니다.

또하나 미제대군인이 계속 한국에 체류하면서 PX 등을 이용하고 있는데 이들은 대부분 일정한 직업없이 생활비 조달책으로 PX 및 커미서리에서 구입한 면세물품을 불법 유출하는 경향이 있으므로 이들 제대군인에 대한 명단을 한미 합동단속반에게 제공하여 이들의 불법행위를 방지할 수 있게 하는 한편, 미군 당국에서도 이들에 대한 PX 등 미군 면세물품 판매업소 이용권을 제한할 수 있는 방안을 연구하여 주시기 바랍니다.

- 더 제의할 안건이 없으시면

다음 의제로 넘어 가겠읍니다.

11

(의제 8)

헤리크 대령.

임시분과 위원회 제 6차 회의 일시 및 장소에 대하여 의견을 말씀하여 주십시요.

12

(의제 9)

그러면 이것으로서 임시분과 위원회 제 5차 회의를 전부 마치겠읍니다.

감사 합니다.

13

지금부터 한.미합동단속 본부반의 운영 상황을 보고 하겠읍니다.

운영상황의 보고에 앞서 한국측은 그간 헤리스대령이하 여러 미8군 관계관들이 본부반 운영에 대하여 보여주신 협조에 대하여 심심한 사의를 표하는 바입니다.

(1)

아시다시피 부정외래품은 일부 SOFA 대상자들이 불법으로 판매하는 PX 물품으로서 중간상인들을 통하여 지내 각 시장으로 유출되고 있읍니다. 따라서 관세청이 작년 7월 1일부터 시작된 부정외래품 단속도 이처럼 시중에 유출된 부정외래품의 단속과 아울러 이 물품의 유출근원인 SOFA 대상자와 중간상에 대한 단속을 병행하고 있는 것입니다. 전자가 관세청 자체의 시장단속이며 후자가 바로 한미합동단속의 내용이라 할수 있읍니다.

(2) 본부반 운영상황

오는 면세물품의 불법거래에 관한 임시분과 위원회 제5차 회의에 대한 본 브리핑은 단지 1개 단속반의 한달간 검거실적을 보고함에 있다기보다는 오히려 본부반의 경험을 앞으로의 한.미합동 단속의 방침과 정책의 Model case로 삼고자 하는데 그 주요목적이 있음을 먼저 말씀 드립니다.

한.미합동 단속본부반은 관세청 수사요원 6명과 미8군 헌병요원 3명으로 구성되어 작년 12월 17일 부터 SOFA 대상자및 중간상들의 주요 거래처인 미8군 용산지구 인근의 우범지역을 중심으로 단속을 실시하여 왔읍니다.

14

(표 1)

구 분 ＼ 유 별	계	SOFA 대상자		기 타	
		실 적	%	실 적	%
건 수	54	7	13	47	87
인 원	74	9	12	65	88
금 액(단위: 천원)	3,070	741	24	2,329	76
벌금 추징액	1,831	105	6	1,726	94

(대상기간: 1974. 12. 17-75. 1. 24)

(표 1) 에서 보시다시피 본부반은 작년 12. 17. 부터 금년 1. 24. 까지의 한달간 총 54건,74명을 검거하고, 3,070천원 상당의 물품을 압수하였읍니다.

즉, 일평균 1.8건 2.5명을 검거하였으며 이중에는 SOFA 대상자도 12% 인 9명에 24% 인 741천원을 차지하고 있읍니다.

15

(표 2)

가. (금액 : 천원)

구분 / 월별	PX			APO			기타			계		
	건수	인원	금액	건수	인원	금액	건수	인원	금액	건수	인원	금액
1	16	17	1,137	9	13	2,090	28	34	10,334	53	64	13,561
2	9	14	1,405	4	4	967	32	39	3,834	45	57	6,206
3	15	26	1,916	9	12	4,674	42	48	4,025	66	86	10,615
4	8	10	1,754	4	6	650	21	30	10,291	33	46	12,695
5	6	13	1,861	1	1	28	28	30	2,560	35	44	4,449
6	4	13	2,720	1	4	560	22	29	3,595	27	46	6,875
7	5	7	501	2	4	91	82	85	5,263	89	96	5,855
8	10	18	8,122				23	16	1,187	33	34	9,309
9	16	25	978	1	3	59	43	42	1,532	60	70	2,569
10	4	6	1,181	1	2	700	37	37	3,850	42	45	5,731
11	3	12	880				16	13	1,584	19	25	2,464
12	4	8	15710	2	13	8,934	43	33	2,940	49	54	27,584
계	100	169	38165	34	62	18,753	417	436	50,995	551	667	107,913
월평균	8	14	3,180	3	5	1,536	35	36	4,250	46	55	8,993

(주 : 현 본부반 실적은 제외)

나.

	전국 계(월평균)	본부반	대비
건 수	46	54	117%
인 원	55	74	135%
금 액	8,993,000	3,070,000	34%

16

가) 표 2 에서 보시는 것처럼 본부반의 한달간 실적은 작년도 전국세관이 범인 외국인 가지은 정화사업 실적의 1 개월분에 해당하는 것 입니다. 1 개월의 실적이 전국 이아범의 총실적과 같을수 있었던 것은 비록 대상지역이 서울지구라는 특수성도 있겠지만, 한미 양국의 적극적인 성원과 단속요원의 노고에 크게 기인한 것이라 말할수 있읍니다.

나) 동 실적을 분석할때 건수 및 인원에서는 본부반 실적이 전국누계를 약간 상회하고 있으나, 금액은 1/3 정도에 그치고 있읍니다.

본부반 실적중 가액이 이처럼 적은것은 부정외래품의 근원을 봉쇄하기 위하여 금액의 다과에 불문하고 관계자를 철저히 적발한것에 기인하는 것으로 볼수 있읍니다.

다) 또하나 표에는 나타나 있지않으나 본부반 한달간의 활동중 가장 중요한것의 하나는 8군인근의 부정외래품 관계자에게 심리적 압박감을 주어 그들의 활동을 크게 위축시켰다는 점입니다. 물론 수년래 고질화 되어온 부정외래품 거래가 근절되었다고는 말씀드릴수 없으나 적어도 대낮에는 그들의 활동이 거의 완전히 정지되고 있으며 또한 많은 중간상인들이 그들의 활동을 스스로 제한하고 있음은 그간의 경험에서 알수 있었읍니다.

본부반은 가급적 이러한 추세를 확고한 것으로 하기위해 앞으로도 계속 우범지역의 순찰, 용의자의 불심검문등을 강화하겠으며 나아가 i) 심야내지 야간활동 ii) 보다 철저한 수색으로 이에 임하고 있으며 대규모의 유출사태 및 동 기품목의 유출적발에도 주력할 예정입니다.

17

(3) 문 제 점

이상 간단히 본부반의 운영실적에 대해서 말씀드렸읍니다마는 그간의 과정에서 노출된 몇가지 문제점을 말씀드리고자 합니다.

1) 정보의 부족

첫째 구체적인 정보의 부족입니다. 말씀드린것처럼 암거래 활동이 극히 음성화함에 따라 종전의 방법에 따른 단속은 쉽게 한계에 부딪히게 되며, 또한 본부반 자체의 영내수사도 어떠면에서 극히 제한됨에 따라 자칫 주먹구구식의 방법에만 의존할 우려가 있읍니다.

2) 구체적 성과의 파악 곤란

본부반의 활동은 용산 Main PX 를 중심으로 한 암거래의 근절에 주력해 왔읍니다. 따라서 정보에 따르면 일부 중간상들은 비교적 단속이 덜한 변두리 PX 등으로 그활동무대를 옮기고 있는것으로 알려져 있읍니다. 그러나 그 구체적인 동태에 대하여는 본부반의 인적기약등으로 파악이 곤란하며 또한 면밀단속의 결과에 따른 구체적 성과의 측정도 거의 불가능한 실정에 있읍니다.

18

(4) 건의사항

따라서 다음과 같은 사항을 개선사항으로 건의하고자 합니다.

구체적 정보의 제공

부정외래품의 유출을 근원에서 부터 봉쇄하는 조직적 이고도 효과적인 방법은 구체적인 정보의 사용이다 함은 이미 말씀드린바와 같읍니다. 미 8군 당국은 이에 대하여 최선의 협조를 약속한바 있으며, 또한 상당한 준비도 되어있는 것으로 알고 있읍니다.
이 기회를 빌어 가급적 정확하고 신속한 정보를 단속반에 제공해 줄것을 부탁 드립니다.

이상 본부반의 운영상황에 대하여 말씀 드렸읍니다.
감사 합니다.

19

2. 제 6차, 4. 2

20

관 세 청

심리 1245- 620 (28-7698) 1975. 3. 31.

수신 외무부장관

참조 북미 2 과장.

제목 입시분과 위원회 제 6차 회의

한.미 면세물품의 불법거래에 관한 입시분과 위원회 제 6차 회의가 다음과 같이 개최 되오니 참석하여 주시기 바라며, 동 회의 의제(안)를 별첨과 같이 송부하오니 참고하시기 바랍니다.

다 음

1. 회의일시 : 1975. 4. 2.(수) 14:00.
2. 장 소 : 미군 SOFA 회의실.
3. 참석자 : 입시분과 위원회 위원 및 고문.

첨부 제 6차 회의 의제 (안) 1부. 끝.

1975. 3. 31 관세청

관 세 청 장

정부공문서 규정 제27조 제 항의 규정에 의하여
감시국장 김 진 우 전결

서울 28-01순

21

면세물품의 불법거래에 관한 임시분과위원회
제 6차 회의 의제

1975. 4. 2.

1. 환영사 : 미국측 위원장.
   미국측 신임위원 (미8군 헌병참모 웨인스 데인 대령)소 개.

2. 한 국측 신임위원 소 개 : 한국측 위원장.

3. "일부 대상자에 대한 특전제한"에 관하여 전번 회의시 제기된 문제에 대한 연구결과 설명 : 미국측 위원장.

4. 상기의제에 대한 일반토론.

5. 공 개토론에 의거, 동 문제에 관한 분석 및 공동목표의 성취를 위한 조치를 다룬 건의안 제출 : 미국측 위원장.

6. 적절한 검토 및 토의후, 분과위원회가 동 건의안을 채택하여 합동 위원회에 검토승인차 제출할 것을 건의 : 미국측 위원장.

7. 차기 회의 일시 및 장소 선정.

22

AGENDA 2 April 1975

Ad Hoc Subcommittee On
Illegal Transactions In
Duty-Free Goods

6th Meeting

1. Welcome Remarks by COL Herrick, Chairman, U.S. component.
Introduce COL Weinstein, PMJ.

2. Remarks by Mr. KIM, Chairman, ROK component.
Introduce new members.

3. COL Herrick discuss the results of the review initiated by the question concerning limitation of privileges to certain categories of personnel discussed by the Subcommittee at the last meeting.

4. General discussion on the above comments/subject.

5. Based on the results of open discussions COL Herrick present the recommendation which covers the analysis of the problem and the action that can be taken to achieve mutual objectives.

6. After appropriate review and discussion COL Herrick propose that the Subcommittee approve the recommendation for forwarding to the Joint Committee for their consideration and approval.

7. Nothing further being brought before the Subcommittee adjourn the meeting to convene at the call of the ROK component chairman at a place and time mutually acceptable to all members.

23

DEPARTMENT OF CUSTOMS ADMINISTRATION
REPUBLIC OF KOREA

1. Preface

The ROK component presents two recommendations to the US component in relation to the repression of blackmarketing and smuggling; one is the quantity limitation on imports for certain items, the other is to record costly imported goods and to check whether the possessor keeps it at the time of exportation.

With these recommendations, it is not our intention to sqeeze the daily life of the USFK personnel who are stationed in Korea for the maintenance of peace in the far east and the protection of South Korea from the infiltration from the north, nor to harass USFK personnel by employing severe controls, such as investigative or punitive actions, but to prevent the abuse of duty-free import privileges.

The reason we present these recommendations are threefold; first, to solve the blackmarketing problems by clearly defining the provisions and the spirits of SOFA; second, to reduce the involvement of USFK personnel in such violations and minimize inducements by certain sectors of our society; and third, to promote genuine friendship and mutual understanding between the Republic of Korea and the United States of America.

Since last year, the efforts to repress the abuse of duty-free import privileges have been strengthened more than ever before, and satisfactory results seem to have been gained. The Ad-Hoc Subcommittee on Illegal Transactions in Duty-Free Goods was newly established and the activities of ROK-US joint investigative team were strengthened.

But the scale of blackmarketing and its quantity show increasing trends, an increasing number of SOFA personnel, about 1% of the total, and Korean blackmarketeers are apprehended yearly. This situation substantially increases the work load and administrative

24

burden of enforcement agencies of both countries and causes many diplomatic problems affecting the friendship and mutual understanding between the peoples of the ROK and US.

According to the information we receive from US authority, more than 100 million dollars in merchandise is sold in PXs and commissaries, equivalent almost to $200 per month per capita; 16,812 music components; 10,316 rice cookers; 7,017 cameras; 3,519 TV sets; 2,675 refrigerators; 1,169 air conditioners and 5,660 tape recorders were sold at PXs during Fy 74. A more or less similar quantity of these items seem to have been imported through APO mail channels or as household goods. More than half of those items are funneled to the domestic market, while investigators apprehended only 1% of them.

2.Quantity Limitation on Imports for Certain Items

The control system utilized in the retail outlets, such as dollar allowance limits and quantity limits, does not seem to produce satisfactory results. For example, 60 ounces of coffee per capita per month were purchased during the FY 74. Everyone on US installations can see long lines in front of PXs and commissaries everyday, they also can see the patrons returning back into the store for a second round of shopping. It is easy to see a man buy 8 cases of beer at the beverage store, who purchased the same amount just the preceding day and then drank several glasses of beer at the club on the same night. Black-market operations conducted through USFK commissaries and PXs at the retail level are operations to which all patrons of such facilities are continuously exposed. Such operations have an impact far beyond that tangible effects of the depletion of USFK

25

supply levels, the substantial loss of US appropriated funds, and the avoidance of ROK taxes and duties, these activities also have a negative effect on ROK-US relationships. Furthermore, this situation which is observed daily by the law-abiding majority of USFK military personnel and dependents is a continuing source of Korean-American misunderstanding and tension. It is also a source of corruption of previously law-abiding USFK personnel who are enticed into this racket in part by the ease with which they apparently can make quick profits. USFK personnel are actively encouraged by the Korean blackmarket operators to become a part of this organized racket, even to the extent of utilizing marriage contracts to facilitate such illegal activities.

One of the things that we should mention is the work load and administrative burden on law enforcement activities of both governments. The investigation activities, of course, should continue even after the recommendation is approved and becomes effective. But the capability in investigative activities cannot cope with blackmarketing organizations on equal terms. Customs, along with their US counterparts, confiscated approximately 500 thousand dollars of duty-free items, which is equivalent to only 1% of the blackmarket amount.

These results were gained during a period in which ROK customs and US counterparts had strengthened their activities even stronger than it had been. Yet this strengthening and use of more equipment and manpower only produced small results. Customs will willingly provide as many investigators and as much equipments as necessary to prevent and destroy blackmarketing activities. But even with all the resources of ROK Customs and US law enforcement agencies a huge barrier remains; namely the lure for easy money. With 15,000 Korean dependents, their families

26

and scores of blackmarketeers the competition with law enforcement personnel is decidedly in favor of the wrong doer. Depending only on investigative activities in eradicating blackmarketing and expecting a good result from them is merely a desk theory.

The reason why the duty-free items are sold in unreasonable quantity, such as coffee for 60 ounces per capita per month, is that the present modus operendi of activities importing duty-free goods is to import goods to satisfy the demand without taking into account what is a reasonable amount to satisfy the legitimate needs of SOFA personnel. This results in an almost unlimited supply of many items having a high resale value on the blackmarket. A ready supply of these items coupled with a ready market inadvertently induce personnel to become involved in highly lucrative blackmarketing activities and it is this after the fact violation that is difficult to pin point and control. In other words, the efforts to repress the abuse of duty-free import privileges is a matter after the fact attempt to control violations.

It is the opinion of the ROK component that effective control can only be effected at the source. Accordingly, it is recommended that imports of certain items, such as coffee, liquor, cigarettes, beer and cosmetics, having a high resale value on the blackmarket and sold in the retail outlets in unreasonable quantity, be limited to quantities reasonably required for the legitimate use of SOFA personnel, in accordance with SOFA provisions which provide that; "The quantity of goods imported by non-appropriated fund organizations of the United States armed forces for the use of persons authorized shall be limited to the extent reasonably required for such use."

It is recommended that the above-mentioned items of imports be limited to a monthly quantity based on a reasonable per capita account multiplied by the total number of eligible SOFA personnel in Korea. Per capita account can be modified after the discussion

27

between the appropriate members of the Subcommittee on Illegal Transactions in Duty-Free Goods. This recommendation, though, surely will accompany some difficulties in distributing the items. But this could be easily solved if patrons are required to use only one PX, commissary and Class IV store, even though a few exceptions be allowed for specific individual problem. Then, if only US retail outlets and patrons are furnished with the same brief record of how many items the patron purchased per month, there's no more needed action.

3. Recommendations to prevent blackmarketing activities involving expensive and durable goods

A serviceman, who was apprehended by ROK customs officials, complained when he was examined, "I was arrested because I was too simple and unsophiscated. Though I cannot name who they are, almost everyone in my unit is involved in blackmarketing and they are profiting from it. They don't transact small ones, but electric items or controlled items which give them a big profit at one time. Transacting with blackmarketeers is also a chance to meet girls without money. I've been in Korea only for a month but was induced by some Koreans and I felt relieved because my friends do the same things without being checked. Some of them imported a lot of color TV sets from Japan or Hongkong through APO channels, and some of them ask retired personnel to give them the power of attorney to import and ship household goods from United States. I was really UNLUCKY!"

"Do you think that GIs who are supposed to leave Korea take all their items back to the states? Definitely No! It takes him a lot of money to ship it back, besides the items which he used are worn out and no longer useful. But if he sells it to

28

a Korean, he gets more money than he paid to buy it. It is very safe to sell controlled items to a Korean, if you make a bill of sale saying you sold it to a GI who is supposed to leave Korea in a few days. Nobody checks, no investigation could be initiated! I heard that a GI who went to the states after his tour in Korea conspired with his friends in Korea and sent a lot of household goods to make profits. Who it was? I can let you know the names but you cannot do anything, because no one keeps the records of what was imported through APO channels. They knew that only 10% of the mail through APO channels is checked, and that the customs clearance officer is too busy to conduct a detailed examination as to whether the household goods are exempted from customs or not.

I was really simple! I was encouraged by my friends and induced by Koreans, I was also relieved when my unit commander OK'd my application for an LOA without any hesitation and without studying it. I heard that if anyone is involved in blackmarketing, the punishment will be very severe. Who will be responsible for that?"

The serviceman was 21 years old.

There are three ways to import duty-free items into Korea; PX purchases, APO channels and household goods shipments. Controlled items at the PXs are recorded at the time of purchase, while the same items through the other two channels are not recorded and not checked.

The only system that checks the expensive and durable items is the LOA system utilized by US authorities. A letter of authorization is required for purchase of controlled items, to prevent and control the blackmarketing of highly lucrative merchandise. US regulations provide that when the unit commander or supervisor makes the

29

determination whether to approve or disapprove the application, he should consider such factors as; a bona fide need exists for the applicant to purchase the item, applicant's DEROS, and whether or not the applicant has previously purchased a like item. This system is apparently very effective to control the blackmarketing for certain items. But if this kind of system lacks the correct and careful attention of the unit commander or supervisor, it cannot be effective. When US authority expanded the scope of controlled items to 32 in June, last year, the sales record showed an 80% decrease in quantity and 75% decrease in value. But after 2 or 3 months, the records climed higher than before. Furthermore, in some instances, some applicants change the contents of the LOA form, such as camera to refrigerator. No examination follows for such action nor is appropriate action to remedy the situation taken.

The LOA itself is not considered to be a very desirable system to prevent blackmarketing, because it depends wholely upon the humanbeing's discretion and continuous attention. The reason that the above-mentioned quantity of items were sold last year, 16,872 music components, etc., can be referred to the non-effectiveness of LOA system.

Though controllied items at PX can be controlled by the LOA system or investigation activities, the same items that are imported through APO channels or as household goods cannot be controlled.

In connection with APO mail channels, the inspection will consist of 10% of the incoming bags/containers of non-official parcel mail. No component knows how much and what items are imported. If the item is not inspected at the time of arrival, it's free for the consignee to dispose of it; as no further investigative

DEPARTMENT OF CUSTOMS ADMINISTRATION
REPUBLIC OF KOREA

action follows. We all are very familiar with what is conducted through APO channels and how much smuggling is involved in the mails. But we haven't devised appropriate measures to prevent such activities. Gold ingots, jewellery and expensive merchandise are still smuggled.

On August 15, last year, a communist Korean-Japanese shoot the wife of President Park and killed her. After that accident, ROK customs examined all import baggage and personal effects to check for visitors or cargo containing the parts of deadly weapon. But very surprisingly, although all other mail items entering Korea were examined, only 10% of APO mail items were made available for search. No one can say that deadly weapons, which could be used to harm Korean VIPs, will not imported through APO channels, and perhaps be in the 90% of the mail that is not checked.

It is not our intention to harass the USFK or SOFA personnel. We will willingly exempt customs for items imported, and not care how many items are considered a reasonable quantity by USFK. What we want to is to know what items are imported and to have a record of all the items imported for personal use and more than $25 in value. We will provide as many inspectors as necessary so as not to delay delivery. The number of inspectors needed can be requested by USFK and all the expenses for rewrapping the package can be the ROK's.

The same can be referred to imported household goods, which amount to 5 million pounds per year. In connection with household goods imported, no inspection either by US nor ROK authorities are allowed since these goods were shipped on United States Government Bill of Lading. The only action that USFK takes is the documentary examination by USFK customs officials, who handle hundreds of applications a day.

31

DEPARTMENT OF CUSTOMS ADMINISTRATION
REPUBLIC OF KOREA

After both ROK and US authorities strengthened their investigative activities on PX and US retail outlets, blackmarketing through the shipment of household goods increased considerably. 5 cases were revealed for the month of August this year, which involved approximately 150 thousand dollars. These 5 cases involving household goods were the first in Korea. One of the female suspects who resides in the United States but came to Korea for this kind of operation confessed that she and her husband had difficulty in finding a new job after discharge, so they came to Korea to make money by blackmarketing.

Furthermore, the number of household goods imported are increasing at a rate double of that last year, while outblound household goods shows a 10% decrease. To break it down further, household goods shipments for persons E-5 and below increases 12 times as much, NCO's 2 times as much, while officers showed no changes in quantity.

If we don't take proper measures to prevent the abuse of duty-free import privileges and correct this deplorable situation; many items will be smuggled, many SOFA personnel will be ruined by investigative activities, many diplomatic problems will arise.

Again, it is not our intention to harass the USFK and its personnel. What we need is to find out whether the imported goods are exported. This recommendation will not harass personnel, nor cause delays; but will allow records of items being brought or purchased for personal use, and find out whether SOFA personnel are taking these items out when they leave Korea. If this recommendation become effective, no one will be involved in blackmarketing, no one will be ruined, then no blackmarketing problem will reflect negatively on relations between the people of the United States and the Republic of Korea.

32

DEPARTMENT OF CUSTOMS ADMINISTRATION
REPUBLIC OF KOREA

*NOTES:

This recommendation will not need any new action by USFK. The PX purchases are already recorded individually by the Central Processing Facilities(CPG). The need is only to record, in a same way, merchandise with a value of $25 or more, which will be in hands of SOFA personnel.

To check household goods, the recommendation requires only to have the ROK customs officials present at the time of pack out, where only US inspectors are presently used.

33

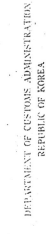

QUANTITY LIMITATION ON IMPORTS OF CERTAIN ITEMS

I. INTRODUCTION

Present Situation	Imports Control	Blackmarketing Control	Problems	Recommendation	Effects
Import Quantities for PX and commissary; $100 mil per year	The quantity of goods imported shall be limited to the extent reasonably required for such use IAW SOFA provisions		Unlimited orders	Define the limit of goods by quantity as described in SOFA provision	1) Effective control at the source 2) Obedient SOFA pers are not induced to become involved in blackmarketing
		Control by US Army: 1)dollar allowance limit 2)quantity limit 3)patron limit	Ineffective		
To Blackmarket; $50 mil per year		Investigation Activity	Insufficient and ineffective		
For the use of SOFA personnel; $50 mil per year					

34

II. Present Situation

Unreasonable purchase amount & its increasing trend - - - - - - -

	Average Monthly Purchase	Average Per Capita Purchase	
		Monthly	Yearly
Post Exchange	$7,093,858	$157	$1,884
Commissary	1,604,488	35	420
Total	8,698,346	192	2,304

*Note: 1) Statistics for FY 75
2) Sales at the Class IV & Beverage Store deleted

(a) Post Exchange Sales Amount Koreawide

Year	Average Monthly Sales	Average Per Capita Purchase		Increasing Trend
		Monthly	Yearly	
1973	$5,154,247	$114	$1,368	100%
1974	5,725,097	127	1,524	111%
1975	7,093,858	157	1,884	138%

(b) Commissary Sales Amount Koreawide

Year	Average Monthly Sales	Average Per Capita Pur.		Increasing Trend
		Monthly	Yearly	
1974	$1,360,200	$30	$360	100%
1975	1,604,488	35	420	117%

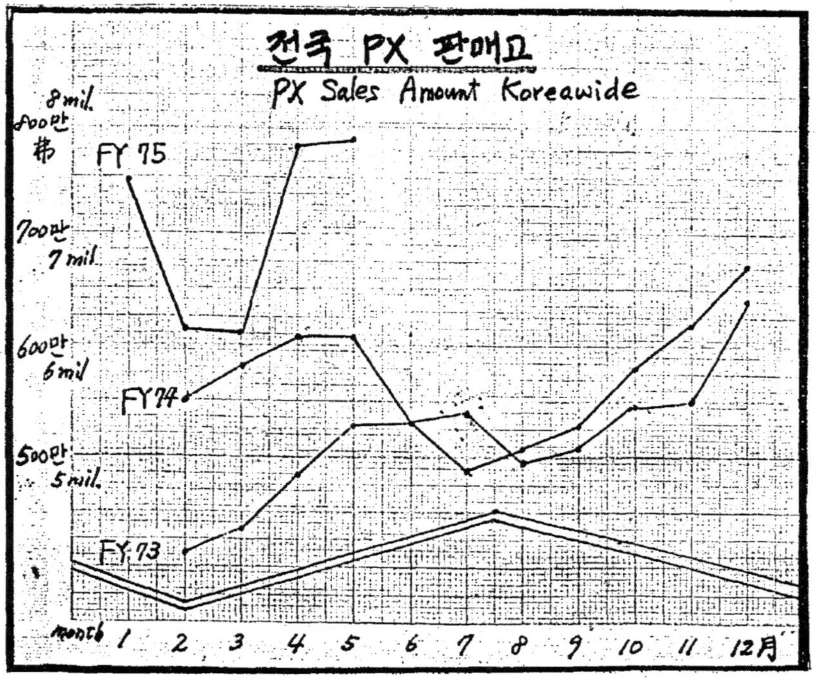

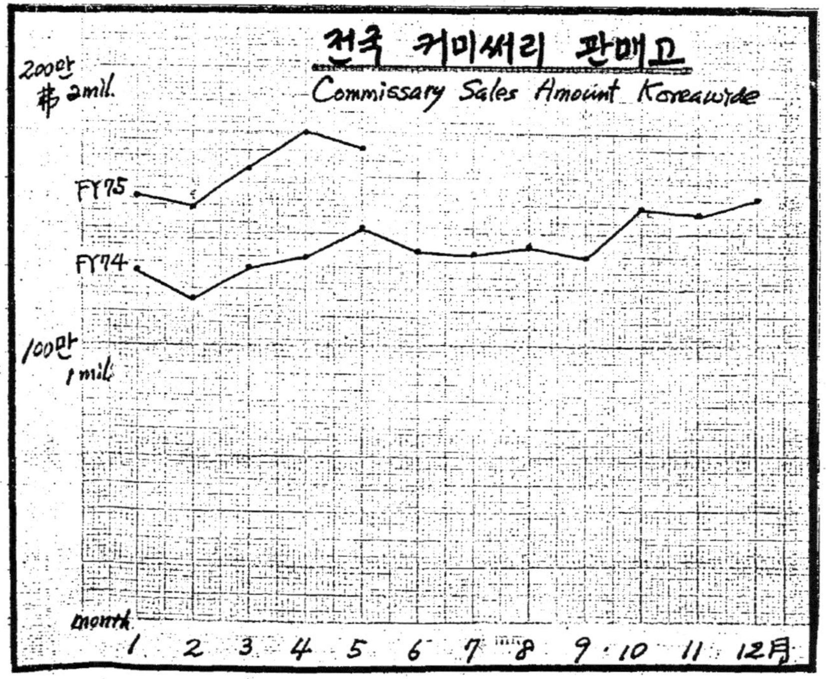

III. Problems

A. Imports Control - - - - - Unlimited Orders

B. Blackmarketing Control - - Insufficient and Ineffective

(a) Ineffective Control at the Retail Outlets

*Post Exchange

PRESENT SYSTEM	POSSIBLE MAXIMUM SALES	UNDERSTANDABLE SALES
Monthly Dollar Limitation	(1) $85 X 45,000 = $3,825,000	(1) $50 X 45,000 =$2,250,000
Plate Code / Limitation: A, B $85; D, E 50; C, F 25		
Items not counted toward limit		
Purchase of controlled items	(2) Average Monthly Sales for FY 75 = $867,000	(2) 50% of Average Monthly Sales for FY 75 = $434,000
Purchase of a unit value of $25 or more, $1.99 or less, or that of military uniforms, accessories and books, etc.	(3) 10% of (1) + (2) = $469,000	(3) 10% of (1) + (2) = $268,000
Total	$5,161,000	$2,952,000

Plate Code	Limitation
A, B	$85
D, E	50
C, F	25

*Average Monthly Sales for FY 75 = $7,094,000 — $7,094,000 - $5,161,000 = $1,933,000 — $7,094,000 - $2,952,000 = $4,142,000

Consequently, PX items valued from approximately $2 mil to $4 mil seem to be channeled to the blackmarket due to inadequate and ineffective control at the retail outlets

*Illegal RCP or forged RCP

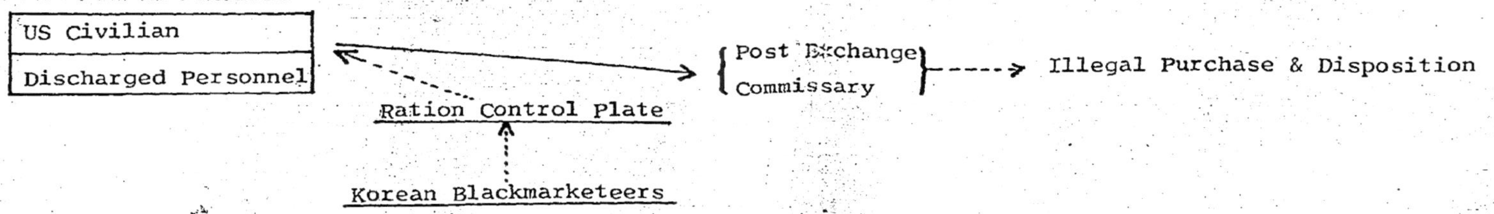

*5,000 - 10,000 illegal (forged) Ration Control Plates are known to be used illegally

(2) Ineffective Investigation Activities

a. Present Situation   Yearly Sales at the Retail Outlets; $100,000,000
Yearly blackmarketed Amount; 50,000,000
Yearly Apprehensions; 500,000 (Equivalent to 1%)

b. Difficulties in Investigation Activities

1. Large Scale Theft Cases Disguised in Legality

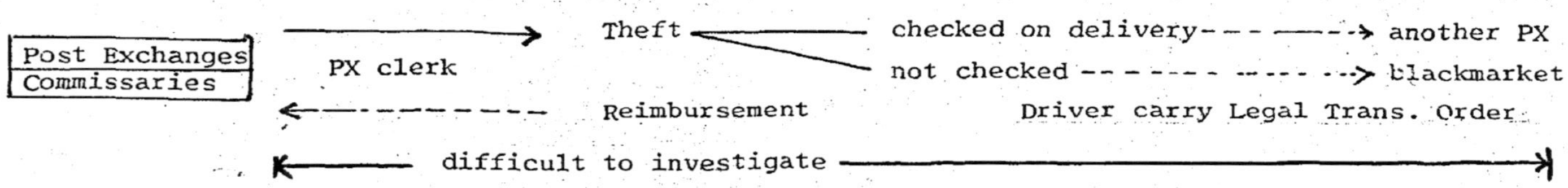

2. Concealed Transactions

e.g. inside of the apartment

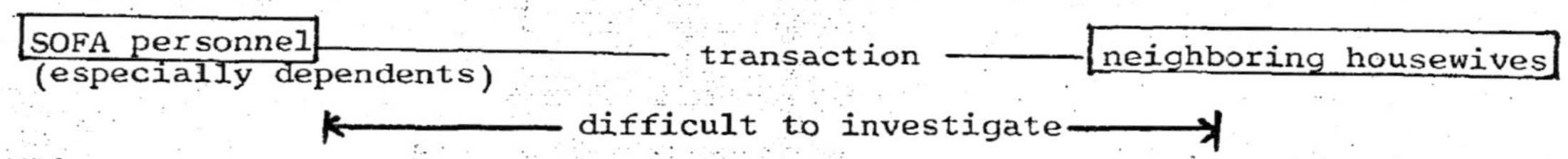

3. Inveterate blackmarketing activities

a. lucrative and prompt fund flowing
b. high demand
c. Professionalization of blackmarketing

4. Insufficient Investigation Capability

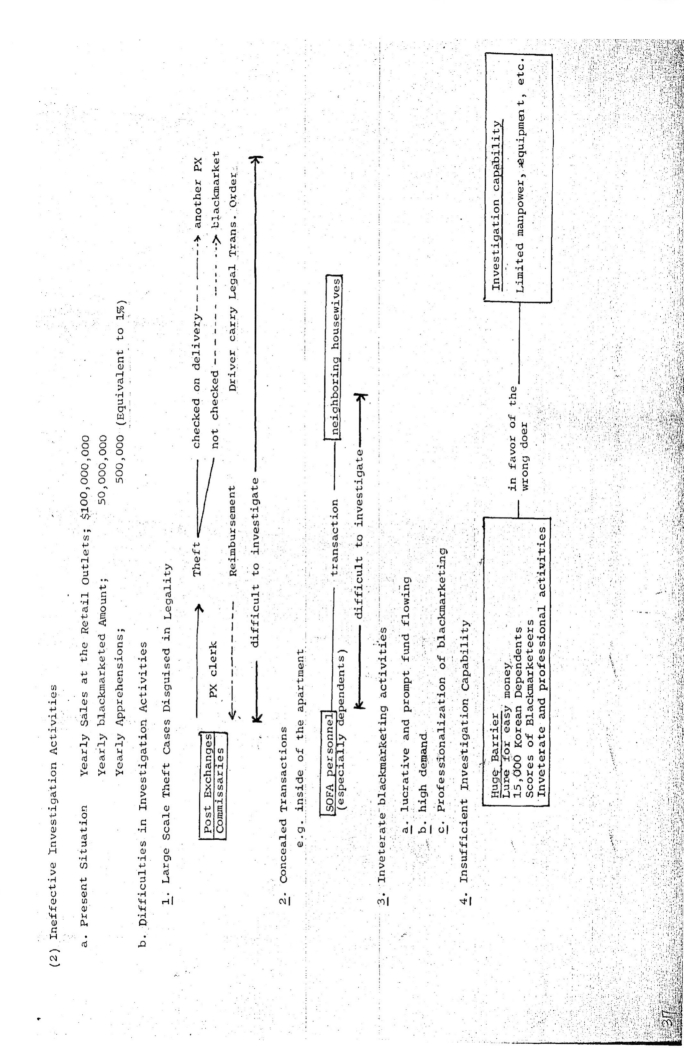

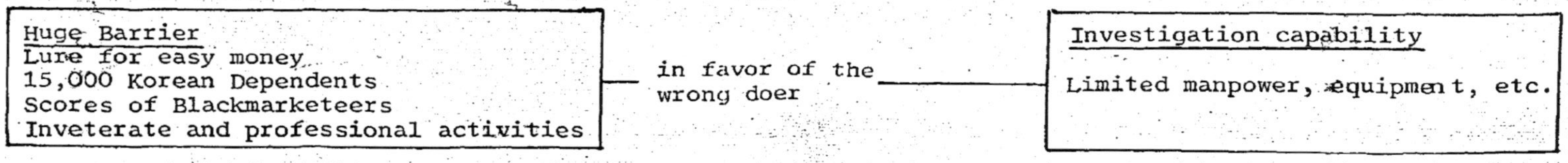

37

IV. Recommendation

QUANTITY LIMITATION ON IMPORTS OF CERTAIN ITEMS

A. Limitations: Eligible SOFA Patrons X Reasonable Per Capita Account = Import Limit

B. Recommended Items: Liquor, Beer, Coffee(instant/regular), Cigarettes and Cosmetics

C. Effects: (1) Effective control at the source

(2) Obedient SOFA personnel not induced to become involved in blackmarketing activities

(3) Comple elimination of blackmarketing due to the lack of supply

ITEM	PRESENT CONTROL	unit	SALES						ELIGIBLE PATRONS	MONTHLY REASONABLE & AVERAGE PER CAPITA ACCOUNT
			Average Monthly Sales			Per Capita Monthly Purchase				
			FY73	FY74	FY75	FY 73	FY 74	FY 75		
Liquor	06, GS-15 and above; no limitation 05, GS-14 and below; Accom. - 10 qt per month unacc. - 5 qt per month	btl	217,104	206,352	202,764	6.2	5.9	5.8	All SOFA personnel (Less dependents under 21 years age)	3
Beer	8 cases per month	case							All SOFA personnel (Less dependents under 18 years age)	3
Cigarettes		pack		2,195,240	3,237,560		44	65	All SOFA personnel	30
Coffee (instant/reg)	Instant coffee allowed only to A card holders	ounce		3,008,033	1,938,458		60	39	"	10
Cosmetics									All female SOFA pers over 16 years age	1/2 X (1 btl of any type)

*Note: Difficulties in distributing the items can be easily solved if patrons are required to use only one PX, commissary and Class IV store. Then, if only US retail outlets and patrons are furnished with the same brief record of how many items the patron purchased per month, there's no more needed action.

RECOMMENDATION TO PREVENT BLACKMARKETING ACTIVITIES INVOLVING EXPENSIVE AND DURABLE GOODS

I. Introduction

Present Situation	Imports Control	Blackmarketing Control	Problems	Recommendation	Effects
ENTRY Household goods, etc.	IAW SOFA Within 6 months; Customs exempted if reasonable After 6 months; Customs imposed		Free from Examination	Merchandise more than $25 in value put on record	Prevent SOFA personnel from becoming involved in blackmarketing, in advance and mentally
APO Mail	IAW SOFA should be reasonable in quantity		Free from Examination except 10%	"	"
PX Importation	IAW SOFA shall be limited to the extent reasonably required				
PX Purchase		LOA system	Ineffective	"	"
To Blackmarket		Investigation Activity	Ineffective & Insufficient		
EXIT (DEROS)			IAW SOFA Customs Examination exempted	Above items be checked on exit	1)Solve the blackmarke problems 2)Promote genuine frie ship and mutual unde standing

39

II. Present Situation

(1) Controlled Items, PX

Unreasonable Purchase Amount &
its increasing trend

Controlled Items (PX) Sales Amount

Year	Average Monthly Sales	Average Per Capita Purchase		Increasing Trend
		Monthly	Yearly	
1973	$563,832	$16.11	$193	100%
1974	724,933	20.71	249	129%
1975	867,376	24.78	297	154%

*Note: 1) Statistics from Jan to Apr
2) 35,000 were estimated as authorized patrons for controlled ites

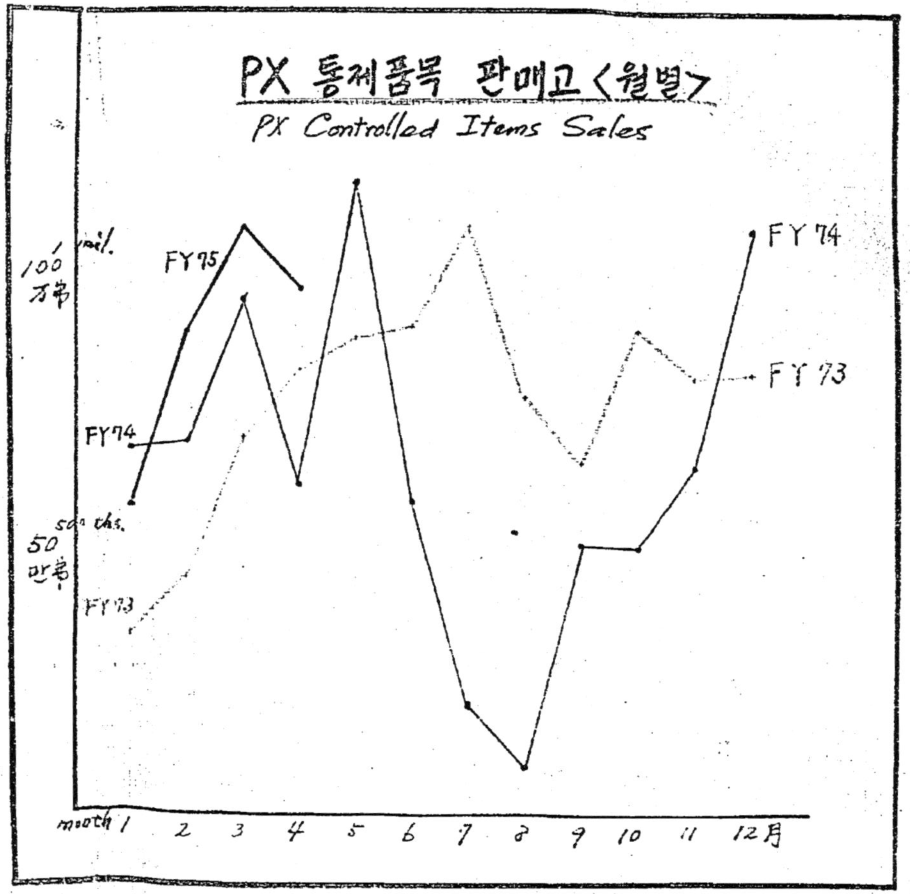

40

(2) How Much Blackmarketed?

Half of Controlled Items at PX Koreawide is assumed to be channeled to the domestic market

* Yearly importation of Controlled Items at PX; $10,000,000
  Yearly blackmarketed quantity; 5,000,000
  Yearly apprehensions; 50,000 (equivalent to 1%)

e.g. A. Firearm; Action Taken; FORCED CUSTODY ordered to civilian-possessed firearm by the Ministry of Domestic Affairs
Date issued; December 10, 1972
Effects;

	Average Monthly Sales at PX	Decreasing Trend
Before Action	307	100 %
After Action	16	5 %

B. Instant Coffee; Action Taken; Purchase not allowed except A card holders
Date effective; Decemer 1974
Effects;

	Average Monthly Sales at PX	Decreasing Trend
Before Action	2,462,128 oz	100 %
After Action	573,282 oz	23 %

*Consequently, 90% or more of firearms and 70% or more of instant coffee sold at military outlets were thought to be channeled to the domestic blackmarket before the actions were taken.

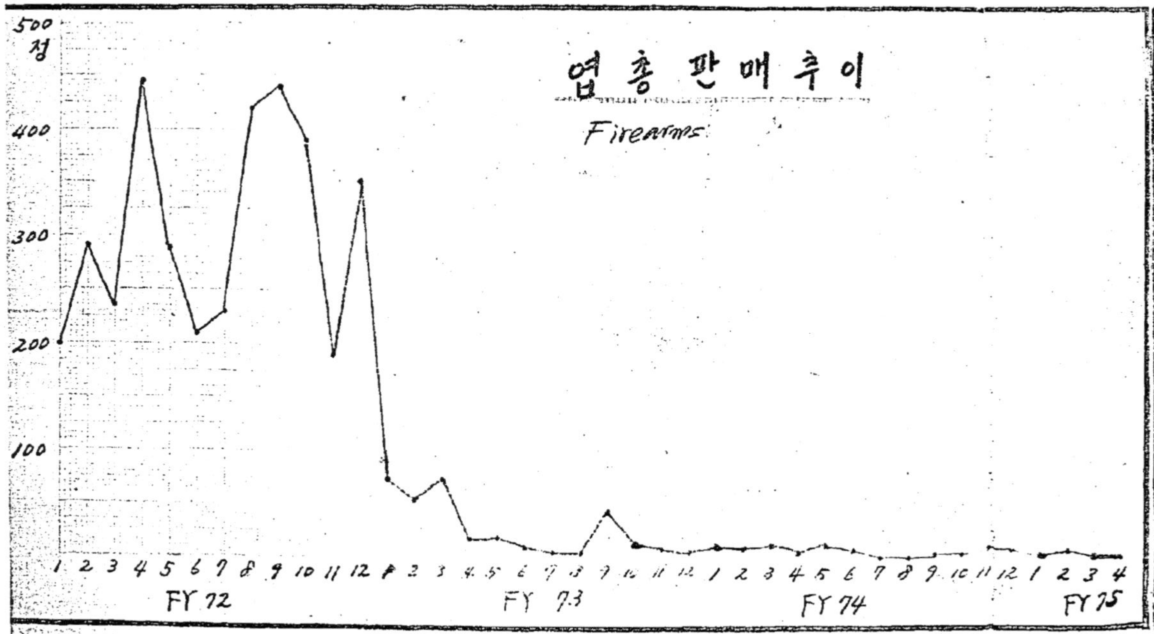

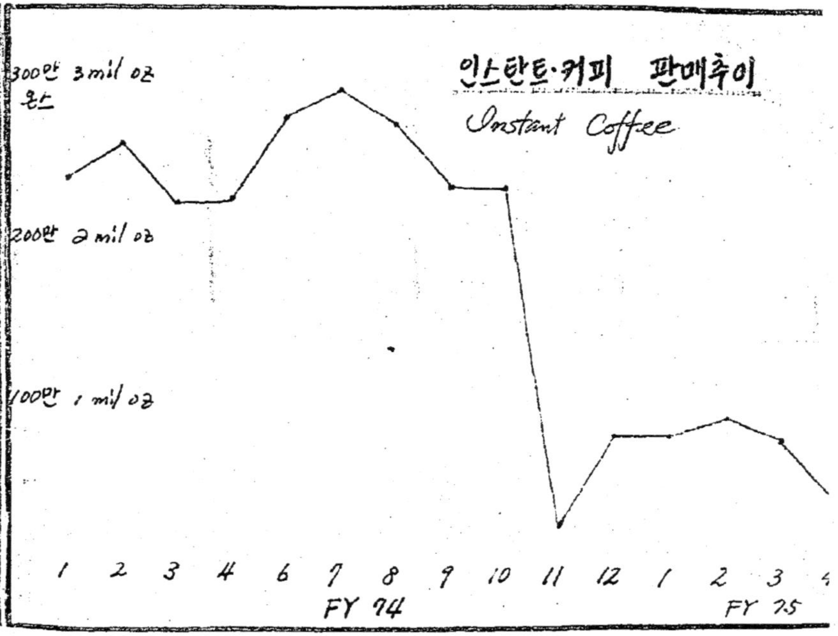

41

(3) Latest Tendency.

*Blackmarketing of Controlled Items on Increasing

Results gained by high level ROK-US joint investigative team (FY 75)

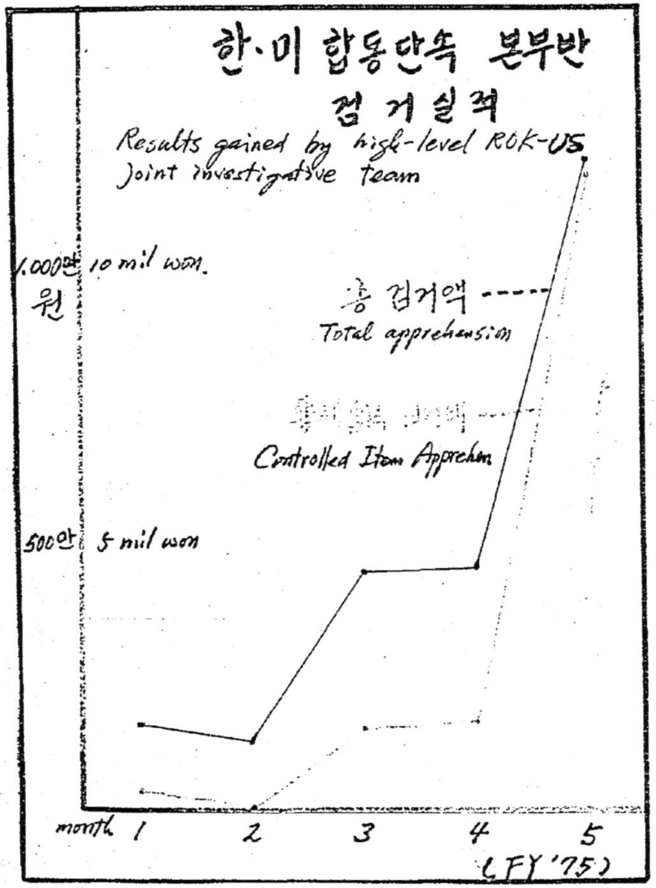

*How Much is Profited?

Item	PX Price	Market Price	Comparison
Refrigerator (24 Cu Ft)	$770	$2,400	312 %
Air-Conditioner (18,000 Btu)	$240	$1,000	417 %

42

III. Problems

A. Letter of Authorization (LOA) System

Very Ineffective after the scope of controlled items were expanded to 32 (June, 1974)

Right after the action: Quantity; 80% decreased
Value; 75% decreased

Present: Records climbed higher than before the action was taken

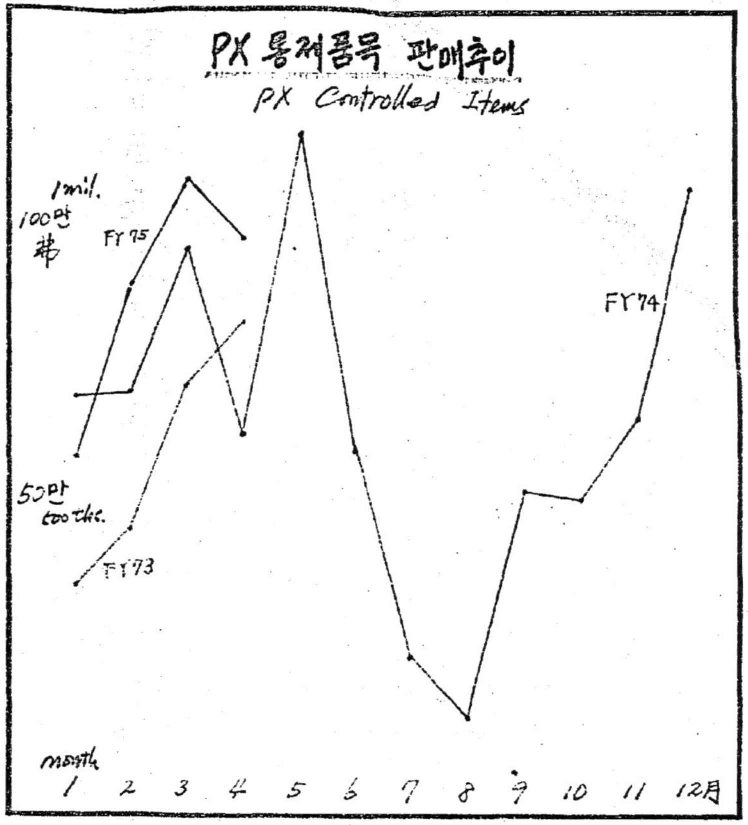

43

B. Household goods Shipments on Increasing

(1) Inbound

		E-5 & below	E-6 & above	Officers	Civilian Component	Total
1st quarter FY 74	Cases	9	69	73	42	193
	Weight	14,699 lb	147,394 lb	176,333 lb	149,027 lb	487,453 lb
	Average	1,633 lb	2,136 lb	2,416 lb	3,548 lb	2,526 lb
1st quarter FY 75	Cases	114	149	80	62	405
	Weight	185,375 lb	355,705 lb	177,040 lb	175,731 lb	893,851 lb
	Average	1,626 lb	2,387 lb	2,213 lb	2,834 lb	2,207 lb
Increasing Trend	Cases	1,267 %	216 %	110 %	148 %	210 %
	Weight	1,261 %	241 %	100 %	118 %	183 %

(2) Outbound

		E-5 & below	E-6 & above	Officers	Civilian Component	Total
1st quarter FY 74	Cases	132	163	283	63	641
	Weight	107,220 lb	177,725 lb	305,137 lb	181,271 lb	771,353 lb
	Average	812 lb	1,090 lb	1,078 lb	2,877 lb	1,203 lb
1st quarter FY 75	Cases	180	129	237	25	571
	Weight	182,234 lb	224,474 lb	321,116 lb	95,232 lb	823,056 lb
	Average	1,012 lb	1,740 lb	1,355 lb	3,809 lb	1,441 lb
Increasing Trend	Cases	136 %	79 %	84 %	40 %	89 %
	Weight	170 %	126 %	105 %	53 %	107 %

44

III. Recommendations

CHECKING THE POSSESSION OF INSPECTION ITEMS ON EXITING

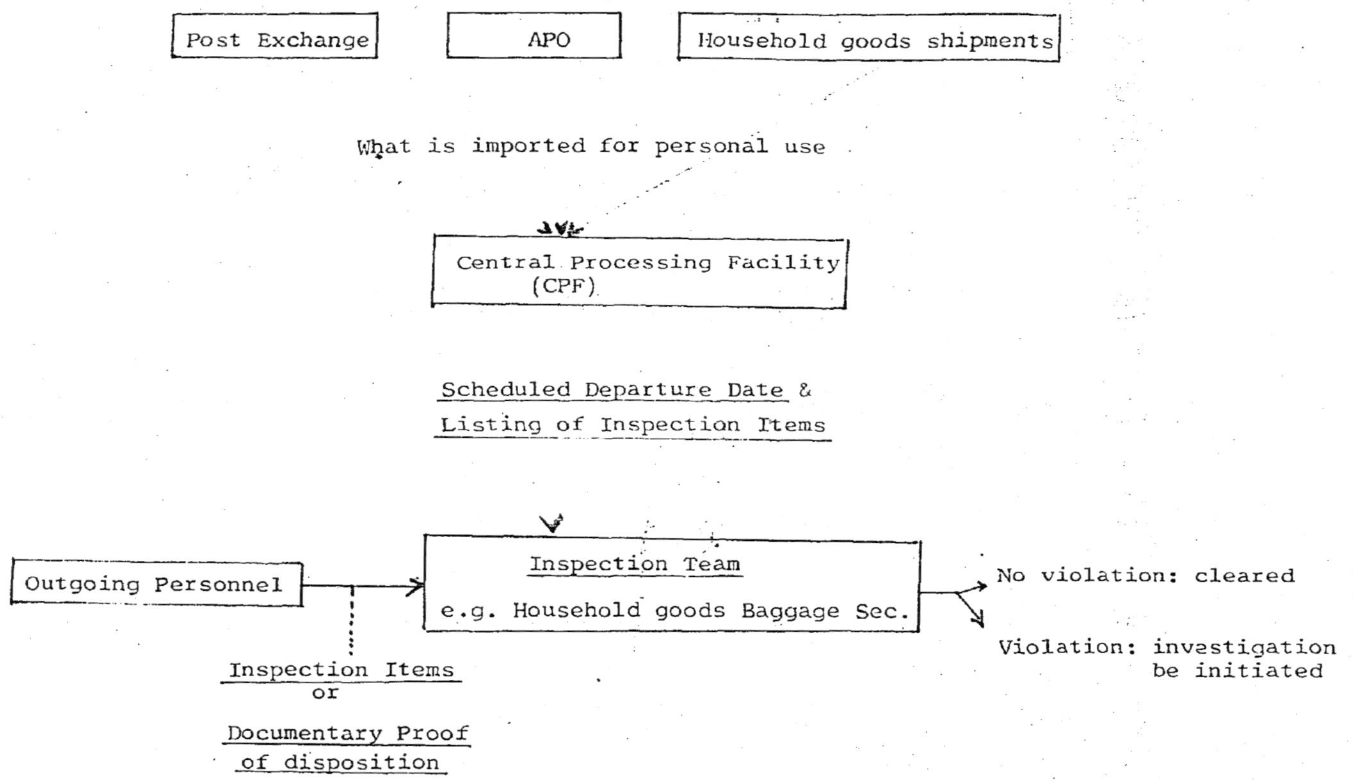

**** This recommendation will not need any new action by USFK. The PX purchased are already recorded individually by the Central Processing Facility (CPF). The need is only to record, in a same way, merchandise with a value of $25 or more, which will be in hands of SOFA personnel.

*** To check household goods, the recommendation requires only to have the ROK customs officials present at the time of pack out, where only US inspectors are presently used.

** If notified of the provisions of this agreement, no one be induced or involved in blackmarketing.

45

DEPARTMENT OF CUSTOMS ADMINISTRATION
REPUBLIC OF KOREA

FINAL DISPOSITION (Reference to High Level Team)

	Apprehension	Accused		Fined	
		confined	not-conf	persons	amount (won)
June					
Serviceman	8		7	1	15,816
Dependent	2			2	50,000
Others					
Korean	11	3	4	4	356,580
Total	21	3	11	7	422,416
July					
Serviceman	3		3		
Dependent	2		1	1	9,318
Others	2		1	1	18,600
Korean	19	3	11	5	256,337
Total	26	3	16	7	284,255
August					
Serviceman	2		1	1	165,252
Dependent	1		1		
Others					
Korean	33		1	32	1,778,539
Total	36		3	33	1,943,791
September					
Serviceman	13		13		
Dependent	2			2	19,567
Others	1	1			
Korean	13	7	2	4	265,302
Total	29	8	15	6	284,869

46

DEPARTMENT OF CUSTOMS ADMINISTRATION
REPUBLIC OF KOREA

*USFK Goods Confiscated by Customs on Domestic Markets

Month (FY 75)	Cases	Value(W 1,000)
1	535	20,535
2	425	21,363
3	727	29,459
4	515	24,298
5	475	38,030
6	1,017	70,958
7	656	21,862
8	888	49,304
Total	5,238	275,809

Note: (1) This data excludes the results made by ROK-US joint investigative teams.
(2) This statistic excludes the amount of smuggling through sea-routes or international airports, and covers USFK goods blackmarketing only.

*Reference

Period	Apprehension		Man-days utilized		
	Cases	Value(W1,000)	Customs	Police	Total
Jul 74 - Jun 75	8,899	429,884	29,342	4,504	33,846
July	656	21,862	1,479	82	1,561
August	888	49,304	2,251	297	2,548

47

DEPARTMENT OF CUSTOMS ADMINISTRATION
REPUBLIC OF KOREA

	Jul 74 - Jun 75	July	August
1. By item			
Clothing	61,363	3,608	6,914
Personal Ornaments	43,612	879	9,843
Food Stuffs & Beverages	86,297	6,346	11,951
Liquors	18,110	860	1,245
Cosmetics	36,045	3,537	2,152
Household Electric Appliances	65,938	3,705	5,369
School Supplies	11,301	10	224
Others	107,218	2,917	11,606
Total	429,884	21,862	49,304
2. By Customs House			
Seoul	(6,092) 231,248	(462)13,131	(573)30,542
Inchon	(289) 16,768	(11) 592	(60) 1,302
Pusan	(1,359) 70,834	(119) 3,190	(145) 5,340
Taegu	(529) 58,945	(20) 1,411	(67) 9,100
Taejon	(170) 14,399	(24) 1,034	(17) 1,070
Kunsan	(178) 11,198	(7) 256	(10) 1,230
Others	(282) 26,492	(13) 2,248	(16) 720
Total	(8,899) 429,884	(656)21,862	(888)49,304
3. By Location			
Department Store	(798) 22,666	(66) 869	(101) 3,169
Market	(3,602) 133,879	(256) 6,809	(335)15,721
Shop	(1,811) 99,002	(104) 4,285	(229)12,976
Street	(897) 24,231	(37) 957	(49) 1,520
Paddling	(470) 17,199	(34) 998	(32) 1,342
Bar	(33) 3,299	(6) 238	(1) 30
House	(338) 49,848	(112) 4,709	(50) 6,560
on Delivery	(51) 4,449	(1) 20	(5) 435
Others	(899) 75,311	(40) 2,977	(86) 7,551
Total	(8,899) 429,884	(656)21,862	(888)49,304

*Note; () ; Cases
 Price unit: W1,000

DEPARTMENT OF CUSTOMS ADMINISTRATION
REPUBLIC OF KOREA

APO Case

1. Date of Confiscation: September 30, 1975

2. Suspect: SFC Norris Ray Courts

3. List of Confiscated Items:

Item	Quantity
Mink Coat	8
Mink Shawl	66
Mink Tail	79

*Note: SFC Courts is allegedly involved in additional smuggling.

49

DEPARTMENT OF CUSTOMS ADMINISTRATION
REPUBLIC OF KOREA

APO Case

1. Date of Confiscation: September 30, 1975

2. Suspect: SFC Norris Ray Courts

3. List of Confiscated Items:

Item	Quantity
Mink Coat	8
Mink Shawl	66
Mink Tail	79

*Note: SFC Courts is allegedly involved in additional smuggling.

Statement attached hereto.

50

RIGHTS WARNING PROCEDURE/WAIVER CERTIFICATE

For use of this form, see AR 190-30; the proponent agency is the Office of the Provost Marshal General.

LOCATION	DATE	TIME	FILE NUMBER
APO SF 96301	30 Sep 75	0745	75-CIDC38-58325
LAST NAME, FIRST NAME, MIDDLE NAME: [redacted]	SOCIAL SECURITY NUMBER: [redacted]		GRADE/STATUS: SP5 E5
ORGANIZATION OR ADDRESS: 121st Med Det, APO SF 96301			

RIGHTS WAIVER CERTIFICATE

RIGHTS

The investigator whose name appears below told me that he is with the United States Army Criminal Investigation Command and wanted to question me about the following offense(s) of which I am suspected/accused: Smuggling, Mail Fraud and Evasion of Customs Duties

Before he asked me any questions about the offense(s), however, he made it clear to me that I have the following rights:

1. I do not have to answer any questions or say anything.
2. Anything I say or do can be used as evidence against me in a criminal trial.
3. *(For personnel subject to the UCMJ)* I have a right to talk to a lawyer before or after questioning or have a lawyer present with me during questioning. This lawyer can be a civilian lawyer of my own choice at my own expense or a military lawyer detailed for me at no expense to me. Also, I may ask for a military lawyer of my choice by name and he will be detailed for me if his superiors determine he is reasonably available.
3. *(For civilians not subject to the UCMJ)* I have a right to talk to a lawyer before or after questioning or have a lawyer present with me during questioning. If I cannot afford a lawyer and want one, arrangements will be made to obtain a lawyer for me.
4. If I am now willing to discuss the offense(s) under investigations, with or without a lawyer present, I have a right to stop answering questions at any time or speak to a lawyer before answering further, even if I sign the waiver below.

WAIVER

Understanding my rights as stated above, I am now willing to discuss the offense(s) under investigation without a lawyer being present.

WITNESSES *(If available)*:

[redacted]

Signature of interviewee

Signature of investigator

Organization or address and phone

DON M NEEDELS SA

Typed name of investigator

Korea Field Office, USACIDC
APO SF 96301

Organization or address and phone

Investigator's organization

NON-WAIVER

I do not want to give up my rights:

☐ I want a lawyer.

☐ I do not want to be questioned or say anything.

Signature of interviewee

ATTACH THIS WAIVER CERTIFICATE TO ANY SWORN STATEMENT (DA FORM 2823) SUBSEQUENTLY EXECUTED BY THE SUBJECT SUSPECT ACCUSED

DA FORM 3881 REPLACES DA FORM 2820, 1 OCT 67, WHICH IS OBSOLETE.

67

SWORN STATEMENT

For use of this form, see AR 190-30; the proponent agency is Office of the Provost Marshal General.

LOCATION	DATE	TIME	FILE NUMBER
APO SF 96301	30 Sep 75	0745 hrs	75-CID038-58325

LAST NAME, FIRST NAME, MIDDLE NAME	SOCIAL SECURITY NUMBER	GRADE/STATUS
[redacted]	[redacted]	SP5

ORGANIZATION OR ADDRESS

121st Med Det, APO SF 96301

I, [redacted], WANT TO MAKE THE FOLLOWING STATEMENT UNDER OATH

Q: Befor we discuss your involvement in this investigation, there are some things we must discuss. First, I understand that you have seen legal counsel and that the counsel instructed you to remain silent, however you have indicated to me that you want to tell your side of the incident, it that correct ?
A: Yes I want to tell youthe story.

Q: You understand that your legal rights still apply and that you do not have to discuss this matter if you don't wish too ?
A: Yes I understand, and I do want to discuss it.

Q: What is your involvementin this investigation ?
A: Sometime in Mar or early Apr 75 SFC COURTS approached me and wanted to know if I wanted to get in on some extra money by letting him use my name to receive some packages at the unit mail room. COURTS put it to me like, he knew I have a large family and that I could use some extra money. COURTS explained that he would order items from Sears and Wards in my name, that when the parcels came in, I would pick them up and deliver it to him and in return he would pay me twenty-five percent of the value of the package. I agreed to what he wanted and between that date and late May 75 I received about ten or fifteen packages for COURTS. The ten or fifteen parcels were all from Sears and or Wards out of California. Except for one package that was post marked New York they all came from California. The package from New York arrived sometime in May , this one was a small box, about one foot square, I don't recall just how much it weighted , however the weight wasn't significant. I would take each parcel home with me and shortly afterwards COURTS would visit my house and pick up the package, I never did have to tell him that a package was in, he always knew. Each time he came to my house he would pay me and take the package, he never opened any of them or said exactly what wasin the package. He always stated that the parcels contained clothes. There was one large package that contained Stereo Speakers, it was marked speakers when it arrived, when COURTS received that parcel he paid me one hundred dollars. I would guess that COURTS paid me about three or four hundred dollars during the period Mar to late May 75. I didn't ask COURTS what he was doing with the items and he didn't tell me. During the period Mar to May 75 several orders were returned from Sears and Wards along with the checks from each company for the amount of the orders, these checks were refunds due to the companies being out of stock on certain items that COURTS had ordered in my name. These refunds were for material, hats and dresses. When the checks came back I would cash the check and give him the money. My estimate would be about $200.00 in refunds between Mar and May 75. During Jun I didn't receive any packages and sometime in Jun around the 15th I believe COURTS approached me and said that I had beat him out of $400.00. COURTS said that he had ordered about $400.00 worth of items that he didn't receive and that I should have the refund checks. I told him that I hadn't beat him out of anything and that I didn't get the refund he was talking about. From that time until sometime

EXHIBIT	INITIALS OF PERSON MAKING STATEMENT	PAGE 1 OF ___ PAGES
	[redacted]	

ADDITIONAL PAGES MUST CONTAIN THE HEADING "STATEMENT OF___ TAKEN AT___ DATED___CONTINUED." THE BOTTOM OF EACH ADDITIONAL PAGE MUST BEAR THE INITIALS OF THE PERSON MAKING THE STATEMENT AND BE INITIALED AS "PAGE___ OF___ PAGES." WHEN ADDITIONAL PAGES ARE UTILIZED, THE BACK OF PAGE 1 WILL BE LINED OUT, AND THE STATEMENT WILL BE CONCLUDED ON THE REVERSE SIDE OF ANOTHER COPY OF THIS FORM.

DA FORM 1 JUL 72 2823 SUPERSEDES DA FORM 2823, 1 JAN 68, WHICH WILL BE USED. PPCH

52

STATEMENT OF SP5 [redacted], DATED 30 SEP 75, TAKEN AT APO SF 96301, CONTINUED.

In Jul 75 I didn't receive any other parcels. COURTS then approached me and said that I would be getting four packages from New York and that he would give me twenty-five percent of the value of each package. As far as I know the packages didn't come in, because he didn't pay me and I didn't pick up any packages for him or myself. In Aug nothing arrived and COURTS mentioned nothing to me, then in Sep 75 one package arrived during the first week of the month, this package was from Sears, after I received it I saw COURTS at the unit and gave it to him , COURTS gave me four dollars for that one. Shortly after that one I went TDY to Pusan with the Unit and while I was there I received notification that I had received a parcel in the mail room, I wasn't expecting one so I assumed that it was for COURTS. The following morning, which was Satruday I went to the mail room and the package was already gone. Later that day COURTS came to me and asked if he had any packages. I told him about the notice that I received and he told me that he picked it up already. COURTS then gave me twenty-five dollars. On about 23 Sep 75 COURTS told me that he had a package comming in and that when it arrived he was going to give me fifty dollars. To the best of my knowledge that package is the one that you confiscated with the furs in it. After I was busted Satruday I learned that SP4 HARBOUR was also letting SFC COURTS sent in packages using his name. I talked with HARBOUR on Monday 29 Sep 75 and he told me that he was also receiving parcels for COURTS in return for twenty or twenty -five dollars per package. Thats all I know about the incident.

Q: What was the size of the largest package ?
A: The speakers was the largest, it was about 18 inches x 12 inches x 12, the smallest one was about 12 inches x 4 inches x 6 inches. All of the parcels except the New York ones were from Sears and Wards.

Q: What were the return addresses on the New York packages ?
A: I don;t remember. The only one that ever had my name on it was the last one that listed Phyllis DALLIS on it. I tried to destroy the return address because I didn't want my name connected to it. There is no Phyllis DALLIS that I know of and I don't know where the package came from .

Q: Did COURTS ever discuss with you who sent any of the packages, other than the ones from Sears and Wards ?
A: No. I don't ask and he didn't say.

Q: Do you know how COURTS got some of the parcels from the mail room without you being present ?
A: No.

Q: Is there anything else that you want to add to this statement ?
A: No.
x x x x x x x x x x x x x x x END OF STATEMENT x x x x x x x x x x x x x x x

Page 2 of 3 pages

63

STATEMENT (Continued)

This side not used

AFFIDAVIT

I, [redacted] HAVE READ OR HAVE HAD READ TO ME THIS STATEMENT WHICH BEGINS ON PAGE 1 AND ENDS ON PAGE 3. I FULLY UNDERSTAND THE CONTENTS OF THE ENTIRE STATEMENT MADE BY ME. THE STATEMENT IS TRUE. I HAVE INITIALED ALL CORRECTIONS AND HAVE INITIALED THE BOTTOM OF EACH PAGE CONTAINING THE STATEMENT. I HAVE MADE THIS STATEMENT FREELY WITHOUT HOPE OF BENEFIT OR REWARD, WITHOUT THREAT OF PUNISHMENT, AND WITHOUT COERCION, UNLAWFUL INFLUENCE, OR UNLAWFUL INDUCEMENT.

[redacted]

(Signature of Person Making Statement)

WITNESSES:

Subscribed and sworn to before me, a person authorized by law to administer oaths, this 30 day of Sep, 1975 at APO SF 96301

ORGANIZATION OR ADDRESS

(Signature of Person Administering Oath)

DON M NEEDELS SA

(Typed Name of Person Administering Oath)

ORGANIZATION OR ADDRESS

Art 136 (b) (4) MCM 1969

(Authority To Administer Oaths)

INITIALS OF PERSON MAKING STATEMENT

PAGE 3 OF 3 PAGES

54

7

SWORN STATEMENT

(For use of th... orm, see AR 190-30; the proponent agency is Office o. the Provost Marshal General.

LOCATION	DATE	TIME	FILE NUMBER
OPM USAGY, MPI Section, APO SF 96301	28 Sep 75	1730	

LAST NAME, FIRST NAME, MIDDLE NAME	SOCIAL SECURITY NUMBER	GRADE/STATUS
[redacted]	[redacted]	E-2

ORGANIZATION OR ADDRESS

A Co, 122nd Sig Bn, APO SF 96224

I, [redacted], WANT TO MAKE THE FOLLOWING STATEMENT UNDER OATH

I arrived in Seoul at about 0900hrs, 28 Sep 75, and I was walking down the street in an unknown area, at which time I was approached by an unknown Korean National male who asked me if I know a USFK member by the name of "Orange", I then asked him if he was a PFC, and he replied that he was. He(the KN)then invited me to accompanied him to his place, we got into a Korean taxi and drove off. While in the taxi we just talked in general. We arrived at this bar, we went inside where he introduced me to this other KN which he told me was his brother. We stayed in the bar for about 15 to 20 minutes where I drank a coke, after this I was taken to an unknow location by the second KN where I had my picture taken and then he told that he was going to have a knew ID card and a ration control plate made for me so that I would not have to use mind. He never told me what his intentions were nor did I ask him any questions. We went back to the bar, while at the bar I was given a piece of paper which had some information pretaining to rod and reels. We then exited the bar and went outside where a PX taxi was already waiting for me, I got into the taxi and took me to the Rod and Gun club as instructed by MR LEE. I then went into the R&G club, where I bought a fishing reel val'd at about $35.00 dollar, I exited the R&G club and got into the same PX taxi who was waiting for me, we went back to the same bar where I waited for a short while. MR LEE then came back to the bar with an ID card and a ration control plate and told me that this([redacted], 19th APU)was going to be my new name and to forgette my own name. MR LEE had me pratice in writing the above name for about 30 minutes. I then told him that I would buy the whisky and the beer with my own ration control card and that I would not need his. He then gave me $60.00 dollars and told me to buy 8 case of cheap beer and as much whisky as I could, and he said to buy scotch. He then took me outside and put me in a PX taxi and told the driver where to take me. We then arrived at this one place where I bought 3 bottles of gin and 8 cases of beer. We then went back to (the same bar) where we took the stuff that I had just purchase and the beer and whisky taken to another location in the vicinity. I then waited at the bar again until MR LEE came back. Upon his return, he told me that he wanted me to make another purchase, I agreed to make the second purchase, I got into the PX taxi which was waiting , I still had $30.00 dollars left from the first purchase so he gave me another $30.00 dollars and told me to buy 5 qrts of scotch and 4 case of beer val'd at $4.00 dollars a case. The taxi driver then took me to this hotel where I bought the whisky and beer MR LEE had told me to buy. We returned back to the same location as the first time, and unloaded the beer and whisky where other KN'S unloaded the stuff. Again I was told to go to the bar and wait. A few minutes later I came out from the bar and went to the loaction where the PX taxi told me that he would be waiting for me. There I met another USFK member, we both got into the taxi and went to the store again, I was again given $ 60.00 dollars, There I bought 5 scotch and 8 cases of beer. While in the taxi, the unidentified USFK member told me that on the day before he had made a $600.00 dollars purchase for this very same KN'S, and making a $40.00

EXHIBIT	INITIALS OF PERSON MAKING STATEMENT	PAGE 1 OF ____ PAGES
	[redacted]	

ADDITIONAL PAGES MUST CONTAIN THE HEADING "STATEMENT OF___ TAKEN AT___ DATED___CONTINUED." THE BOTTOM OF EACH ADDITIONAL PAGE MUST BEAR THE INITIALS OF THE PERSON MAKING THE STATEMENT AND BE INITIALED AS "PAGE___OF___PAGES." WHEN ADDITIONAL PAGES ARE UTILIZED, THE BACK OF PAGE 1 WILL BE LINED OUT, AND THE STATEMENT WILL BE CONCLUDED ON THE REVERSE SIDE OF ANOTHER COPY OF THIS FORM

DA FORM 1 JUL 72 2823 SUPERSEDES DA FORM 2823, 1 JAN 68, WHICH WILL BE USED. PPC

55

for himself. At the Ic store that I went too, there I ught 5 bottles of scotch and 8 cases of beer. I then departed the store and was on my way back to the same bar where just as the taxi approached the gate, we were stopped by the MP'S, and I was taken to the MP station.

Q. How long have you been in Korea?

A. 2 months.

Q. Since you have been assigned to the Cp Casey area, how many times have you been to Yongsan and the Seoul area?

A. Today is the first time.

Q. How well do you know the Seoul area?

A. I don't know nothing about the Seoul area.

Q. Do you know the name and the location of the bar you were taken to by this unidentifi KN'S?

A. No, I know it if I saw it again.

Q. Do you know the names of the two KN'S you met and bought the whisky and beer for today?

A. One of the guys said he name was MR LEE, the other I don't know.

Q. How many purchases did you make for this KN'S today?

A. Five, I made four purchases at the class six stores, and one at the Rod and Gun Club.

Q. How many bottle of scotch and how many cases of beer did you buy for this KN'S today?

A. I bought 24 cases of beer, 3 bottles of gin, and 15 bottles of scotch.

Q. How much money were you paid for making this purchases?

A. I received nothing.

A. How much money were you suppose to get paid?

Q. 330.00 to 340.00 dollars.

Q. How many time did you use taxi # S-223, driven by MR PAK, SANG YONG?

A. I used it two times.

Q. Did you tell the taxi driver where to take you, or did he know where to go?

A. I did not tell the taxi driver nothing, he got his instructions from MR LEE.

Q. Do you know the locations of this stores where you made all this purchases today?

A. I don't know the locations, but I know them if I see them again.

Q. How many PX taxis were involved in transporting you today?

A. Two or three.

Q. Have you made any other purchases for unauthorized personnel other that those involve today?

A. No, this is my first time.

Q. Do you know that what you did today was illegal?

A. Yes, I did.

Q. If you knew it was illegal, why did you do it?

A. I made the first purchase without thinking, since I had already made the first purchase, I knew that I was already in trouble, and I decided to use my own RCP instead of using a false one which they had offered me.

Q. Do you have anything else you like to add or delete from this statement?

A. No.

x/x/x/x/x/x/x/x/x/x/x/x/x/x/x/x/x/x/x/x/END OF STATEMENT/x/x/x/x/x/x/x/x/x/x/x/x/x/x/x/x/x/x/x/

INITIALS [redacted] "PAGE____OF____PAGES"

56

STATEMENT (Continued)

AFFIDAVIT

I, [redacted] HAVE READ OR HAVE HAD READ TO ME THIS STATEMENT WHICH BEGINS ON PAGE 1 AND ENDS ON PAGE______. I FULLY UNDERSTAND THE CONTENTS OF THE ENTIRE STATEMENT MADE BY ME. THE STATEMENT IS TRUE. I HAVE INITIALED ALL CORRECTIONS AND HAVE INITIALED THE BOTTOM OF EACH PAGE CONTAINING THE STATEMENT. I HAVE MADE THIS STATEMENT FREELY WITHOUT HOPE OF BENEFIT OR REWARD, WITHOUT THREAT OF PUNISHMENT, AND WITHOUT COERCION, UNLAWFUL INFLUENCE, OR UNLAWFUL INDUCEMENT.

[redacted]

(Signature of Person Making Statement)

WITNESSES:

Subscribed and sworn to before me, a person authorized by law to administer oaths, this 28 day of ______, 19 75 at OPM, USAGY, Yon Hil Resrv., APO SF 96301

(Signature of Person Administering Oath)

ORGANIZATION OR ADDRESS

BLAS M. GARCIA, SGT, ...

(Typed Name of Person Administering Oath)

ORGANIZATION OR ADDRESS

Art 136b(4)UCMJ, 1969 ...

(Authority To Administer Oaths)

INITIALS OF PERSON MAKING STATEMENT

PAGE OF PAGES

67

DEPARTMENT OF CUSTOMS ADMINISTRATION
REPUBLIC OF KOREA

*APO Cases

I. a. Date of Apprehension: Dec 28, 1974
b. Suspect: [redacted]
c. List of Confiscated Items:

	Item	Quantity	Remarks
1.	Amplifier	1	Marantz 2270
2.	Color TV	2	Sanyo 15"
3.	B&W TV	1	RCA 19"
4.	Amplifier	4	Marantz 2270
5.	Amplifier	7	Marantz 2270
6.	Amplifier	1	Marantz 2275

II. a. Date of Apprehension: Jul 24, 1975
b. Suspect: [redacted]
c. List of Confiscated Items:

	Item	Quantity	Remarks
1.	Oriental Medicine A	498 bottles	Japanese Product
2.	Oriental Medicine B	293 bottles	Japanese Product
3.	Trousers & etc.	21	

*Medicines were concealed inside of the trousers & etc.

III. a. Date of Apprehension: Sep 22, 1975
b. Suspect: [redacted]
c. List of Confiscated Items:

	Item	Quantity	Remarks
1.	Rice Cooker	6	Sanyo
2.	Carsette Radio	2	Sanyo
3.	Color TV	2	Sony
4.	Music System	2	Sanyo
5.	Blender	4	
6.	Iron	5	
7.	Coffee Pot	2	
8.	Toaster	1	
9.	Polaroid Film	6	
10.	Vacuum Bottle	1	

58

DEPARTMENT OF CUSTOMS ADMINISTRATION
REPUBLIC OF KOREA

*Household Goods Shipment Case

a. Date of Apprehension: Aug 23, 1975
b. Suspect: [redacted]
c. List of Confiscated Items: attached herewith

59

LIST OF CONFISCATED ITEMS

	ITEM	QUANTITY	REMARK
1.	Mink Coat	10	Black
2.	Mink Coat	5	Brown
3.	Mink Coat	1	
4.	Mink Coat	3	Brown
5.	Coat(synthetic wool)	1	Black
6.	Women pajamas	26	
7.	Women trouser	2	
8.	Women Coat	2	
9.	Towel	12	
10.	Child trouser	3	
11.	Diaper	4	
12	Men T-shirt	4	
13	Men Pandy	2	
14	Men trouser	13	
15	Men Coat	4	
16	Men Shirts	15	
17	Men Best	2	
18	Men Under wool	4	
19	Men Pajamas	1	
20	Women trouser	14	
21	Women coat	26	
22	Women dress(1 piece)	5	
23	Women best	3	
24	Under shirts	2	
25	Under skirt	5	
26	Women Pajamas	18	
27	Women under wool	8	
28	Women panty	5	
29	Women T-shirt	2	
30	Child trouser	8	
31	Child coat	48	
32	Child dress(1 piece)	8	
33	Child pajamas	3	
34	Child skirt	4	
35	Women under wool	1	
36	Women panty	6	
37	Neck-tie	5	
38	Headoover(swimming)	7	
39	Bedcover	6	
40	Table cover	9	
41	Neckcloth	2	
42	Blanket	5	
43	Brassiere	5	
44	Diaper	2	
45	Cap	1	
46	Curtain	4	

60

47	Pillow cover	10
48	Seat cover	1
49	Cup	40
50	Cup	18
51	Oven trays	2
52	Coffee pot	2
53	Ceramic pot(USA)	1
54	"	1
55	"	1
56	Cup(porcelain)	6
57	Water pot(glass)	1
58	Dish	5
59	"	11
60	Candle	6
61	Glass pot	1
62	Spoon	15
63	Fork	13
64	Knife	6
65	Oven trays	2
66	Tray	8
67	Vessel	11
68	Vessel xx	2 set
69	Glass pot	16
70	Achtrayray	10
71	Ceramic(Italian)	3
72	Vessel(Italian)	9
73	"	7
74	Glass pot	3
75	Pot(USA)	6
76	"	5
77	Flower Vase	2
78	Oven	3
79	Mirror(USA)	6
80	Lamp	1
81	Ashtray	2
82	Cup(glass)	8
83	Clearsing	25
84	Du Cleam	10
85	Clearsing	7
86	Clearsing	8
87	"	5
88	Cold cleam	2
89	"	30
90	"	1
91	Du Lotion	2
92	Silk foundation	71
93	Du Foundation	6
94	Foundation	14
95	Tub Foundation	3

61

96	Compact	6	
97	Vitamin	3	
98	Louge	2	
99	Manicure	2	
100	Coffee pot	3	
101	Vessel	1	
102	Plastic box	2	
103	Electric frypan	10	
104	Scale	1	
105	Pan	5	
106	Toilet cover	2	
107	Vessel	3	
108	Baby Wagon	1	
109	Ceramic(Italian)	1	
110	Mattress	4	
111		1	
112	Mattress	2	
113	Sofa chair	2	
114	"	1	
115	"	1	
116	Trunk	2	
117	Plastic box	1	
118	"	1	
119	Icebox	1	
120	Chair	1	
121	Lug	4	
122	Cabinet(wooden)	1	set
123	Toy autho	6	
124	"	7	
125	Doll	8	
126	Toy(animal)	4	
127	Toy	2	
128	Toy	1	
129	"	1	
130	"	3	
131	"	1	
132	"	2	
133	"	1	
134	"	3	
135	"	1	
136	"	1	
137	Staple	1	
138	Toy	4	
139	Sport ball	1	
140	Western painting	1	
141	Bed frame	2	boxes

62

142	Shelf	1 set
143	Refrégerator	1
144	Iron	37
145	Blender(USA)	1
146	"	1
147	Vacumm	2
148	Water cooler	4
149	Electric frypan	23
150	" "	30
151	Coffee pot	1
152	Hot compress	1
153	Headphone	1
154	Color TV	2
155	Gas Range	1
156	Electric Vacuum	1
157	Coffee pot	1
158	Dress Material	514m
159	Material	83m

63

DEPARTMENT OF CUSTOMS ADMINISTRATION
REPUBLIC OF KOREA

*Post Exchange Case

a. Date of Apprehension: Jun 23, 1975
b. Suspect: PX clerks
c. List of Confiscated Items: attached herewith

64

LIST OF ITEMS CONFISCATED

1. Ten Sanyo Fans, Model #EF-8RV, 16 in, valued at $33.50 each.

2. Eighth Casserole Skillets, Model 520, valued at a total of $23.50.

3. Eighth Proctor Silex Toasters (Two Slice), valued at $8.15 each.

4. 144, nine ounce bottles of ZBT powder, valued at $.90 each.

5. Three, FM/AM Radio recorders, Brand GE, Model M8525C, valued at $51.00 each.

6. Seventy-two, 11 oz jars of Jeris Talc powder, valued at $.90 each.

7. Fifty, 7 in reel to reel blank tapes, brand name Capitol, valued at $1.90 each.

8. Forty-seven, 9 oz bottles of ZBT powder valued at $.90 each.

9. Eighteen, 9 cup automatic percolators, valued at $16.50 each.

10. Two Eskimo fans, 12 inch with three speed capabilities, valued at $16.00 each.

11. One QX 949 Pioneer 4/channel receiver, valued at $295.00.

12. Fifty-four small mug like cups, valued at $.31 each.

13. Twelve sugar pots, valued at $.80 each.

14. Twenty-four, 15 oz jars of Silkin Saltin Lotion, valued at $1.15 each.

15. Twenty-four, 18 oz jars of Tang, valued at $1.20 each.

16. Four cases of Pyrex ware, thirty-two oz containers, valued at $12.85 a case.

17. Sixth, 10 Oz bottles of Jergens lotion, valued at $1.00 a bottle.

18. One hundred and twenty, one pint jars of Mayonnaise, valued at $.80 a jar.

19. Two hundred and forty, 2 Oz jars of Maxwell House Instant Coffee, valued at $.55 a jar.

20. One hundred and twenty, 1 lb cans of Maxwell House Ground Coffee, valued at $1.30 a can.

65

21. Eight hundred and forty, 1 lb cans of Maxwell Regular Grind Coffee, valued at $1.30 a can.

22. Twenty-four, 6 oz jars of coffeemate creamer, valued at $.55 each.

23. Ninty-six, 10 Oz bottles of Silkin Saltin Lotion, valued at $1.15 a bottle.

24. Two-hundred and sixteen bars of Camay Soap, valued at $.20 each.

25. Thirty, 64 Oz bottles of Egg Shampoo, valued at $1.50.

26. Sixth, 32 Oz bottles of Deluxe Shampoo plus egg, valued at $.80.

27. Twenty-four cans of Cherry Blend Pipe Tobacco, valued at $1.30 a can.

28. One-hundred and forty-four, 3 Oz bottles of Tabu perfume, valued at $3.55 a bottle.

29. Four Reff, nine cup coffee pots, valued at $16.50 each.

30. Twenty-four, one lb cans of Maxwell House Coffee, valued at $1.30 each.

31. Thirty-six large colored bath towels, valued at $1.30 each.

32. One Samsonite Brief Case, valued at $32.00.

33. Twelve cotton panties, valued at $.70 each.

34. Four, 9 Oz bottles of Baby Magic Lotion, valued at $1.55 each.

35. Four Spaulding Tennis Rackets, valued at $36.50 each.

36. Seven Regent Tennis Rackets, valued at $5.00 each.

37. One wooden Spaulding Tennis Racket, valued at $22.50.

38. Girard, Three piece turntable, Model D2, valued at $129.00.

66

AGENDA ITEM ROK PRESENTATION

(1. FOR YOUR INFORMATION: The US Representative should invite the ROK Representative to present a recommendation received from the Ad Hoc Subcommittee on Illegal Transactions in Duty-Free Goods. That Subcommittee notes Korean statistics, which indicate that the volume of household goods imported by USFK personnel considerably exceeds the volume of such goods exported upon their departure from Korea. This raises the prospect that a major portion of goods accounting for this difference in volume of imports and exports may have been introduced into the Korean economy, either legally or otherwise. Based upon these findings and indications, the Subcommittee recommends that the Joint Committee task its Finance (Personnel Affairs) Subcommittee with the study of a ROK proposal for mutual action to deter, and possibly eliminate illegal disposal of duty-free goods at the last moment before departure of personnel from Korea. This proposal would become part of an existing task before the Finance (Personnel Affairs) Subcommittee on the subject of customs examination of household goods and unaccompanied baggage of USFK personnel subject to the SOFA. That Subcommittee, acting under Joint Committee direction, has a broad responsibility in the recommendation of measures related to the implementation of SOFA Article IX on customs and duties.)

2. Thank you, Mr. LEE. The United States Representative is pleased to concur in the approval of the recommendation of the Ad Hoc Subcommittee on Illegal Transactions in Duty-Free Goods which you have just presented. Please turn to the next agenda item.

67

AGREEMENT TO EMPLOY AND UTILIZE ROK-US JOINT INSPECTION TEAM TO PREVENT ILLEGAL TRANSACTIONS INVOLVING EXPENSIVE AND DURABLE GOODS

1. Purpose:

a. The purpose of this agreement is to prevent blackmarketing activities involving expensive and durable goods by employing appropriate controls to insure compliance with USFK directives and SOFA.

b. To prevent illegal transactions as a matter before the fact through the means of official inspection by appropriate joint enforcement authorities.

c. Every enforcement activities provided for in this agreement shall not be interpreted as the customs examination by the authorities of the Republic of Korea.

2. Definition:

a. "Inspection Item" - any item having a value of $25 or more.

b. "Outgoing Personnel" - All SOFA personnel deaprting the Republic of Korea on Permanent Change of Station orders or overseas employment orders.

c. "Inspection Team" - A joint team composed of ROK customs officials and appropriate US military officials.

3. Provision of Information:

a. USFK shall provide a listing of SOFA personnel scheduled to depart the ROK to the Inspection Team. The list shall contain the following information;

(1) Scheduled departure date

(2) Scheduled packout date (household goods and unaccompanied baggage)

b. Listing of Inspection Items which the individual has

68

imported, purchased or obtained through transfer since his/her arrival in the ROK. The foregoing includes furniture, household goods, personal effects and all inspection items obtained through the APO channel or Post Exchanges.

4. Procedures (Imports):

a. All personal items imported through the APO, MSTS, MAC, US GBL or Commercial should be opened and inspected by US officials in the presence of ROK officials at the time and place of importation.

b. Import shipments which appear to contain unreasonable quantities of inspection items, per se, will be held under the control of Customs House until mutual agreement as to their disposition is determined. Determination as to what constitutes reasonable/unreasonable quantities of any given item rests with US authorities based upon the addressee's mission, family requirements, stated purpose for importation and other consideration deemed appropriate by the US authority. A recommended guide for reasonable quantities of specific items is attached as Inclosure I.

5. Procedures (Exports):

a. Inspection Team will be located at designated stations available to inspect scheduled pack outs of departing SOFA personnel. The inspection will include to monitor the packing and loading activities of inspection items.

b. Outgoing personnel will be informed to provide to the inspection team documentary proof of disposition of all inspection items disposed of while in the ROK. These documents include import permits, bill of sale, certificate of loss, etc., all of which must be acceptable to the satisfaction of the Inspection Team.

c. Finding no violation, both the ROK and US inspectors will seal the outgoing shipment for onward movement.

d. Finding violation, and upon mutual agreement pack out of the individual will be suspended until disposition of the items in question is resolved to the satisfaction of the Inspection Team. If the latter cannot be effected then upon mutual agreement

69

an investigation will be initiated and the pack out for the individual rescheduled upon conclusion of the investigation.

6. Transfer:

a. The transfer between the SOFA personnel may be granted only to those personnel with an estimated date of departure from the Republic of Korea of 130 days or less. The SOFA personnel cannot transfer the inspection items to the other SOFA personnel who is supposed to leave Republic of Korea prior to his departure, and cannot transfer the inspection items without being confirmed by the inspection team.

b. The transfer should be promptly recorded to the individual listing by the USFK authority as soon as it is confirmed by the inspection team.

c. If inspection items were lost, the SOFA personnel should promptly report to and be confirmed by the inspection team.

7. Support:

a. ROK and US authorities shall provide adequate numbers of personnel to perform the required inspections described in this agreement. Base of operations for the inspection teams will be by mutual agreement.

b. USFK shall notify SOFA personnel of the provisions of this agreement to assure maximum understanding and cooperation in this endeavor.

c. Scheduled pack out will not be delayed because of non-availability of inspection teams and inconvenience to outgoing personnel will be held to an absolute minimum.

d. In the event of emergency, evacuation of non combatants necessitated by emergent military operations this agreement become null and void. Emergencies requiring pack out of personnel while absent may be accomplished in the presence of the inspection team and such shipments will not be delayed.

8. Supplements:

Any changes to this agreement will be coordinated through

170

appropriate ROK and US channels and presented to the SOFA Joint Committee for approval.

8. Effective date:

This agreement and any changes there to will become effective 30 days after approval by the ROK-US SOFA Joint Committee.

*Inclosure I

REASONABLE QUANTITIES OF SPECIFIED ITEMS FOR AN INDIVIDUAL

*Note: If an individual is authorized to live off-post, he will be considered as a "family" for the purposes of this list.

	per individual	per family
1. Air Conditioner	1	2
2. Dryer		1
3. Electric Fan	1	
4. Freezer		1
5. Water Heater		1
6. Movie Camera	1	
7. Gramophone	1	
8. Turntable	1	
9. Radio	1	
10. Gas Range		1
11. Regrigerator		1
12. Speaker System	1	
13. Camera (Still)	1	
14. Tape Deck	1	
15. Tape Recorder	1	
16. Television	1	
17. Amplifier	1	
18. Typewriter	1	
19. Washing Machine		1
20. Binoculars	1	
21. Stereo Music System	1	
22. Mixer		1
23. Rice Cooker		1
24. Toaster		1
25. Coffee Maker	1	
26. Cleaner (Vacuum)		1
27. Golf Set	1	
28. Car Cooler		1 (per car)
29. Car Radio		1 (per car)
30. Receiver	1	
31. Mink (coat, shawl, collar)	1	
32. Handbag (aligator)	not authorized	
33. Noble metals, Diamond	not exceed $100 totally	
34. Watch	1	
35. Textiles	maximum of 25 yards per shipmer to include no more than 5 yard: same color/design	

172

REPUBLIC OF KOREA - UNITED STATES
AD HOC SUBCOMMITTEE ON ILLEGAL TRANSACTIONS
IN DUTY-FREE GOODS

MEMORANDUM FOR: THE JOINT COMMITTEE

SUBJECT: Agreement Pertaining to the Listing of Durable Goods which are Imported or Purchased Duty-Free by USFK Personnel

1. Subcommittee members:

2. The Ad Hoc Subcommittee on Illegal Transactions in Duty-Free Goods, newly established by the Joint Committee on 6 May 1974, has been charged with the responsibility to study and analyze problems involving the blackmarketing of goods brought into the ROK by the US armed forces and US SOFA personnel and to make recommendations for necessary actions, both preventive and corrective, designed to eliminate blackmarketing and to promote Korean-American understanding and friendship.

3. The subcommittee, having reviewed available statistics on import of USFK goods as opposed to export, have concluded that the amount of exported household goods shipments by SOFA personnel upon PCS are only equivalent to that of imported household goods shipments. It can be safely assumed that such amounts of the durable goods as were imported through non-appropriated fund organizations or APO channels have found their way to the local economy, either through legal procedures or otherwise. The subcommittee also concluded from the sales statistics that 70% or more of the PX controlled items are illegally outflown to the local economy.

4. After comprehensive study and careful analysis of these kinds of problems, this subcommittee concluded that it is due to the lack of system to guarantee that the items which were imported or purchased for personal use are also re-exported by the individual upon PCS. At this time, there is no organizational procedure whereby imports and exports are monitored to insure that the duty-free goods which were imported or purchased by SOFA personnel are also exported by the same personnel at the end of an individual's tour in Korea. This deficiency in checks and balances inadvertently provides an avenue for last minute disposal of duty-free goods through other than legally accepted procedures, and results in an almost unlimited supply of many items having a high resale value on the blackmarket. A ready supply of these items coupled with a ready market inadvertently induce personnel to become involved in highly lucrative blackmarketing activities. In other words, if not checked at the time of illegal disposition, everyone feels relieved because no authority keeps the records of what were imported through household goods shipments and APO channels; no authority can check who disposed the items of illegally at the time of leaving Korea.

173

5. After careful deliberation, this subcommittee has mutually agreed that tne listing of durable goods which contained in the import shipments of household goods or purchased at PX for verification at the time of leaving Korea would be in the best interest of all concerned and agreeable to both component, both from a procedural and cost point of view.

6. Though the Finane(Personnel Affairs) Subcommittee has been assigned similar task on 1968, the subcommittee has not reached any resolution for eight years while the blackmarketing activities are on the increasing trend. On the other hand, this ad hod subcommittee, which were specially established to make recommendations for necessary actions designed to eliminate blackmarketing activities, has ever recommended such action as "Denial to direct access to USFK PX, commissary and etc."

7. It is proposed that the attached recommendation be approved by the Joint Committee to become effective immediately upon such approval.

LOUIS E. HERRICK, COL, USAF
CHAIRMAN, UNITED STATES COMPONENT
AD HOC SUBCOMMITTEE ON ILLEGAL
TRANSACTIONS IN DUTY-FREE GOODS

KIM, JIN WOO
CHAIRMAN, REPUBLIC OF KOREA COMPONENT
AD HOC SUBCOMMITTEE ON ILLEGAL
TRANSACTIONS IN DUTY-FREE GOODS

074

REPUBLIC OF KOREA - UNITED STATES
FINANCE(PERSONNEL AFFAIRS) SUBCOMMITTEE

MEMORANDUM FOR: THE JOINT COMMITTEE

SUBJECT: Agreement Relating to the Customs Examination of Unaccompanied Baggage and Household Goods of USFK Personnel under Article IX of the US-ROK SOFA

1. Subcommittee members:

2. This subcommittee has been assigned task relating to the customs examination of unaccompanied baggage and household goods of USFK personnel under article IX of the US-ROK SOFA on 25 May 1967 at the eighth meeting of the Joint Committee.

3. A US component proposal to resolve the task was delivered to the ROK component on 9 April 1970 and on 18 August 1972. The US and ROK members have been actively engaged in attempting to reach an agreed position to resolve the household goods examination issue. The US side has repeatedly acknowledged the right of ROK customs inspectors to examine unaccompanied baggage and household goods, the problem being where such examination should be conducted.

4. After careful deliberation, ROK component agreed that the locations at which the examination should occur would be at the point of delivery. This subcommittee has mutually agreed that the listing of durable goods contained in the import shipments of household goods, as well as durable goods purchased at Post Exchanges, to verify at the time of leaving Korea would be in the best interest of all concerned and agreeable to both component, both from a procedural and cost point of view.

5. It is proposed that the attached recommendation be approved by the Joint Committee to become effective immediately upon such approval.

LOUIS E. HERRICK, COL, USAF
CHAIRMAN, UNITED STATES COMPONENT,
FINANCE(PERSONNEL AFFAIRS)
SUBCOMMITTEE

SONG, BYUNG SOON
CHAIRMAN, REPUBLIC OF KOREA COMPONENT
FINANCE(PERSONNEL AFFAIRS)
SUBCOMMITTEE

75

REPUBLIC OF KOREA - UNITED STATES
AD HOC SUBCOMMITTEE ON ILLEGAL TRANSACTIONS
IN DUTY-FREE GOODS

MEMORANDUM FOR: The Joint Committee

Subject: Actions Recommended to prevent the Abuse of Duty-Free Import Privileges and to promote Korean-American Friendship and Mutual Understanding

1. Subcommittee Members:

United States	Republic of Korea
COL L. E. Herrick, USAF Chairman	Mr. Kim Jin Woo, Chairman
CPT David G. Ramsey, USN	Mr. Lee Seung Kon
COL William A. Zeigler, USA	Mr. Jung Hae Chang
COL Kenneth Weinstein, USA	Mr. Lee Jin Moo
Mr. Paul Cleveland, Amb Emb	Mr. Suh Jung Wook
LTC Thomas L. Waters, USA	Mr. Park Jong Yup
COR Raymond P. LeClerc, USN Sec	Mr. Choe Kun Suk
	Mr. Park Joon Hwa, Sec
	Mr. Lee Jae Byung, Alt Sec

2. The Ad-hoc Subcommittee on Illegal Transactions in Duty-Free Goods, has concluded that efforts to repress the abuse of duty-free import privileges is a matter after the fact attempt to control violations. The present modus operendi of activities importing duty-free goods is to import goods to satisfy the demand without taking into account what is a reasonable amount to satisfy the legitimate needs of SOFA personnel. This results in an almost unlimited supply of many items having a high resale value on the blackmarket. A ready supply of these items coupled with a ready market inadvertently induce personnel to become involved in highly lucrative blackmarketing activities and it is this after the fact violation that is difficult to pin point and control. It is the opinion of this Subcommittee that effective control can only be effected at the source. Accordingly it is recommended that imports of certain items having a high resale value on the blackmarket be limited to quantities reasonably required for the legitimate use of SOFA personnel.

3. Reference is made to the provisions of paragraph 1 of the Agreed Minutes, Article IX of the Status of Forces Agreement which provides that: "The quantity of goods imported under paragraph 2 by non-appropriated fund organizations of the United States armed forces for the use of persons authorized by Article XIII and its Agreed Minutes shall be limited to the extent reasonably required for such use."

176

4. It is recommended that the following items of import be limited to a monthly quantity based on a reasonable per capita account multiplied by the total number of eligible SOFA personnel in Korea:

Item	Eligible Patrons	Reasonable monthly import limit
Liquor	All SOFA Personnel (Less dependents under 21 yrs age)	3 bottles x Elig Patrons = Monthly Import Limit
Beer	All SOFA Personnel (Less dependents under 18 yrs age)	3 cases x Elig Patrons = Monthly Import Limit
Coffee (instant/reg)	All SOFA Personnel	10 ounces x Elig Patrons = Monthly Import Limit
Cigarettes	All SOFA Personnel (Less dependents under 18 yrs age)	30 packs x Elig Patrons = Monthly Import Limit
Cosmetics	All Female SOFA Pers over 16 yrs age	1/2 x (1 bottle of any type x Elig Patrons) = Monthly Import Limit

5. Imports presently on order will not be changed however subsequent orders, after approval of this recommendation by the SOFA Joint Committee, will reflect the new limitations as set forth in the preceding paragraph. Stocks, after approval of this recommendation by the SOFA Joint Committee, cannot exceed mutually agreed quantity; or, imports for the following period, plus stocks remaining from previous period can not exceed mutually agreed quantity as set forth in the preceding paragraph.

6. The US component agrees to provide the ROK component information pertaining to the monthly import orders sent out on the five categories of items addressed herein. Information provided will include the calculations used to arrive at the monthly import requirements. This information is requested to be submitted no later than 10 days after compilation of the import orders.

7. After an appropriate trial period mutually agreed to, additions, deletions and changes to import limitations may be considered by the Subcommittee for submission to the Joint Committee for approval.

8. It is proposed that this recommendation be approved by the SOFA Joint Committee to become effective upon approval.

0717

LOUIS E. HERRICK, COL. USAF
Chairman, United States
Component
Ad Hoc Subcommittee on Illegal
Transactions in Duty-Free Goods

KIM JIN WOO
Chairman, Republic of Korea
Component
Ad Hoc Subcommittee on Illegal
Transactions in Duty-Free Goods

718

REPUBLIC OF KOREA - UNITED STATES
AD HOC SUBCOMMITTEE ON ILLEGAL TRANSACTIONS
IN DUTY-FREE GOODS

MEMORANDUM FOR: THE JOINT COMMITTEE

SUBJECT: Agreement Pertaining to the Joint Inspection of Incoming and Outgoing Household Goods Shipments

1. Subcommittee Members:

UNITED STATES	REPUBLIC OF KOREA
COL L.E. HERRICK, USAF, CHAIRMAN	MR. KIM JIN WOO, CHAIRMAN
CAPT DAVID G. RAMSEY, USN	MR. LEE SEUNG KON
COL ZANE E. FINKELSTEIN, USA	MR. JUNG HAE CHANG
COL KENNETH WEINSTEIN, USA	MR. LEE JIN MOO
MR. PAUL CLEVELAND, AMEMB	MR. SUH JUNG WOOK
LTC JAMES S. EMERY, USA	MR. CHOE KUN SUK
CDR RAYMOND P. LeCLERC, USN, SEC	MR. PARK JOON HWA, SEC
	MR. LEE JAE BYUNG, ALT SEC

2. The Ad Hoc Subcommittee, having reviewed available statistics on import shipment tonnages of household goods as opposed to export tonnages, have concluded that an average of 8 tons of imported household goods per month is never re-exported by SOFA personnel upon PCS. It can be safely assumed that the major portion of these possibly expensive durable goods have found their way to the local economy, either through legal procedures or otherwise. At this time, there is no organizational procedure whereby imports and exports are monitored to insure that duty-free household goods imported by SOFA personnel are also exported by the same personnel upon PCS. In other words, there is no system to indicate or insure that items imported for personal use are also exported at the end of an individual's tour in Korea.

179

3. This defინciency in checks and balances may inadvertently provide an avenue for last minute disposal of household goods through other than legally accepted procedures, thus adding to blackmarketing sources of supply. It is felt that possible illegal traffic in this area is of sufficient magnitude to warrant positive mutual action to deter, and possibly eliminate any last minute illegal disposal of duty-free goods. Resolution of the deficiency cited would also deter the possible importation of questionable inordinate quantities of high value durable goods.

4. After careful deliberation, this Subcommittee has mutually agreed that joint inspection of important and export shipments of household goods would be in the best interests of all concerned.

5. Accordingly, it is recommended that the SOFA Joint Committee task the Finance (Personnel Affairs) Subcommittee to review the attached proposed agreement for possible acceptance and resubmission to the Joint Committee for final approval.

? Lee C.

LOUIS E. HERRICK, COL, USAF	KIM JIN WOO
CHAIRMAN, UNITED STATES	CHAIRMAN, REPUBLIC OF KOREA
COMPONENT, AD HOC SUBCOMMITTEE	COMPONENT, AD HOC SUBCOMMITTEE
ON ILLEGAL TRANSACTIONS IN	ON ILLEGAL TRANSACTIONS IN
DUTY-FREE GOODS	DUTY-FREE GOODS

80

U.S. 8th Army To Revise Ration Control

'75.10.28 K.H

With the advent of the Command Unique Personnel Information Data System (CUPIDS) many changes are due in ration control procedures beginning Nov. 1, according to U.N. Command information officials yesterday.

The monthly exchange rational limitations are to be decreased for the family except for the unaccompanied individual.

The basic dollar limit for single individual is $100 with an increase of $20 for each additional person.

The amount of beverage consumption will increase for accompanied personnel in case of soda from eight cases per month to 12 cases and will be the same for the unaccompanied.

Golf clubs, fondue pots and cosmetic items have been added to the controlled items list. Purchases of controlled cosmetics will not exceed $30 per month per family.

The alcoholic beverage limit for accompanied personnel has dropped from 10 quarts and fifths to eight per month and from five to four for the unaccompanied patron.

The Ration Control Plate (RCP) and identification card at the entrance must be presented to the cashier at the time of sales transaction.

These new procedures will go into effect Nov. 1 even though the new RCPs, which are expected to be in the field after Dec. 1, have not been circulated.

81

외교문서 비밀해제: 주한미군지위협정(SOFA) 32
주한미군지위협정(SOFA) 재무 · 상무 · 교통 분과위원회 1

초판인쇄 2024년 03월 15일
초판발행 2024년 03월 15일

지은이 한국학술정보(주)
펴낸이 채종준
펴낸곳 한국학술정보(주)
주 소 경기도 파주시 회동길 230(문발동)
전 화 031-908-3181(대표)
팩 스 031-908-3189
홈페이지 http://ebook.kstudy.com
E-mail 출판사업부 publish@kstudy.com
등 록 제일산-115호(2000. 6. 19)

ISBN 979-11-7217-043-1 94340
979-11-7217-011-0 94340 (set)

책에 대한 더 나은 생각, 끊임없는 고민, 독자를 생각하는 마음으로 보다 좋은 책을 만들어갑니다.